Middle East and North Africa Investment Policy Perspectives

OECD
BETTER POLICIES FOR BETTER LIVES

Please cite this publication as:
OECD (2021), *Middle East and North Africa Investment Policy Perspectives*, OECD Publishing, Paris, *https://doi.org/10.1787/6d84ee94-en*.

ISBN 978-92-64-83359-3 (print)
ISBN 978-92-64-47304-1 (pdf)

Photo credits: Cover © Swillklitch/iStock.com.

Corrigenda to publications may be found on line at: *www.oecd.org/about/publishing/corrigenda.htm*.

Preface

As governments in the Middle East and North Africa (MENA) region – and across the globe – seek to address the profound health, economic and social effects of the COVID-19 pandemic, many have prioritised attracting and retaining investment as key to supporting the recovery. Indeed, improving the investment climate has long been a priority for the region's governments, recognising the developmental benefits that foreign direct investment (FDI) can bring – from job creation, to productivity, to green growth. To this end, many MENA governments have advanced meaningful reforms in the past decade, including easing entry of foreign business and streamlining regulations for investors. Despite these developments, MENA governments overall have been less successful than other emerging and developing economies at leveraging investment to advance sustainable development.

Attracting investment in the MENA region – and harnessing its benefits – is needed now more than ever with the COVID-19 pandemic exacerbating existing challenges and adding new ones. FDI flows have dropped significantly across the globe, and the decline in the MENA region has been particularly acute. Youth and overall unemployment – a key contributing factor to popular discontent – is higher today in many MENA countries than it was in 2010, while conflict and insecurity continue to have damaging effects on the wider region. In this context, any additional shocks can be devastating. While MENA governments have begun ambitious efforts to improve the investment climate and respond to the pandemic, further reforms are needed to make investment work for inclusion and sustainable development. This includes addressing longstanding structural challenges through bold reforms of the private sector, improving implementation of existing policies, and adopting new investment strategies to exploit opportunities arising from a possible reorganisation of global value chains.

Based on original data and comparative analysis, *Middle East and North Africa Investment Policy Perspectives* (MENA IPP) provides policymakers with a comprehensive picture of the investment climate in Algeria, Egypt, Jordan, Lebanon, Libya, Morocco, the Palestinian Authority and Tunisia. The report encourages MENA governments to consider further reforms with four overarching objectives in mind: (1) improve the clarity, consistency and transparency of investment rules and procedures; (2) advance reforms to boost competition and private sector development; (3) target investment policy and promotion to better serve sustainable development goals; and (4) strengthen good governance and co-ordination to deliver better investment policy.

MENA IPP also builds on the long-standing relationship of these economies and the OECD, notably through the adherence of four countries – Egypt, Jordan, Morocco, and Tunisia – to the OECD Investment Declaration; the support, expertise and exchanges developed under the *EU-OECD Programme on Promoting Investment in the Mediterranean*; as well as the wider and long-term partnership in the framework of the *MENA-OECD Competitiveness Programme*. Through these partnerships, MENA governments have demonstrated commitment to addressing investment climate challenges and sharing experiences on creative policy solutions.

As governments across the globe seek to recover from the unprecedented shocks of 2020, it is now imperative that we continue to build partnerships and expertise in order to support each other and to leverage investment for a resilient and inclusive recovery in the months and years ahead.

Angel Gurría
Secretary-General, OECD

Foreword

Middle East and North Africa Investment Policy Perspectives (MENA IPP) highlights the considerable progress in investment policy reforms made by governments in the region over the past decade. This reform momentum needs to be sustained and deepened so that the benefits of investment can be shared with society at large, particularly given the global health and economic upheaval provoked by the Covid-19 pandemic. The publication takes stock of investment policy trends and reforms in Algeria, Egypt, Jordan, Lebanon, Libya, Morocco, the Palestinian Authority, and Tunisia, drawing out common challenges and offering suggestions for reform priorities. It considers several dimensions of the policy framework that affect the investment climate, and places strong emphasis on how investment can help governments to improve the lives of their citizens. The report serves as a point of reference for policymakers as they continue their work to attract investment that advances inclusive and sustainable development.

MENA IPP draws on analytical work, regional dialogues and capacity-building seminars conducted under the *EU-OECD Programme on Promoting Investment in the Mediterranean*. The Programme, which began in 2016, has benefited from the active engagement of MENA governments and public institutions, private sector organisations and civil society. The publication supports efforts to boost the quality and quantity of investment in areas governments in the region have identified as a priority, using OECD instruments for assessing the investment climate such as the *Policy Framework for Investment*, the *Guidelines for Multinational Enterprises* and the *FDI Qualities Indicators*. It also builds on the wider long-term partnership between the OECD and the MENA region within the *MENA-OECD Competitiveness Programme*, which has promoted policy dialogue and advice on investment since 2005.

MENA IPP is a joint product of the OECD Directorate for Financial and Enterprise Affairs (DAF) and the Global Relations Secretariat (GRS). It was prepared by a team led by Fares Al-Hussami and Sarah Marion Dayan of the Investment Division (DAF) and Marie-Estelle Rey of the Middle East and Africa Division (GRS), under the strategic guidance of Ana Novik, Head of the Investment Division, and Carlos Conde, Head of the Middle East and Africa Division. The drafting team included Hélène François of the Investment Division, Alin Horj, Jorge Galvez-Mendez, Mattia Tomay and Iris Monderer of the Middle East and North Africa Division, Coralie Martin and Nicolas Hachez of the Responsible Business Conduct Centre (DAF), Diane Pallez of the Anti-Corruption Division (DAF), Cushla Thompson of the Development Co-operation Directorate, and Emilio Chiofalo, an external consultant.

The report benefited from valuable comments from members of the OECD Investment Committee, participants at the Advisory Board of the *EU-OECD Programme on Promoting Investment in the Mediterranean* and participants in the MENA-OECD Investment and Trade Working Group. Alexander Böhmer, Head of South Asia and Southeast Asia Division (GRS), and Stephen Thomsen, Head of Investment and Sustainable Development Unit (DAF), provided valuable comments and suggestions as lead reviewers. Comments and inputs were also received from Alexandre de Crombrugghe, Emilie Kothe, Fernando Mistura, Baxter Roberts, and Martin Wermelinger of the Investment Division, Alessandra Celani of the Centre for Tax Policy and Tihana Bule, Benjamin Michel and Frédéric Wehrle of the Responsible Business Conduct Centre. Nadia Kameleddine and Kany Ondzotto provided administrative assistance. Edward Smiley prepared the report for publication.

Table of contents

Tables

Figures

Boxes

Abbreviations and acronyms

AMDIE	Agence Marocaine de Développement de l'Investissement et des Exports (Morocco)
ANDI	Agence Nationale de Développement de l'Investissement (Algeria)
ASEAN	Association of Southeast Asian Nations
BHR	Business and human rights
BDS	Business development services
BIT	Bilateral Investment Treaty
CIT	Corporate income tax
CSR	Corporate social responsibility
FDI	Foreign direct investment
FIPA	Foreign Investment Promotion Agency (Tunisia)
GAFI	General Authority for Investment (Egypt)
GDP	Gross domestic product
GCC	Gulf Co-operation Council
GVC	Global value chain
ICT	Information and communications technology
IDAL	Investment Development Authority of Lebanon
IIA	International Investment Agreement
ILO	International Labour Organisation
IMF	International Monetary Fund
IPA	Investment promotion agency

ISDS	Investor-State Dispute Settlement
JIC	Jordan Investment Commission
LAC	Latin America and the Caribbean
LCR	Local content requirement
M&A	Merger and acquisition
MENA	Middle East and North Africa
MNE	Multinational enterprise
NCP	National Contact Point
OECD	Organisation for Economic Co-operation and Development
OSS	One-stop shop
PA	Palestinian Authority
PIB	Privatisation and Investment Board (Libya)
PIPA	Palestinian Investment Promotion Agency
PPP	Public-private partnership
RBC	Responsible Business Conduct
SEZ	Special Economic Zone
SME	Small- and medium-sized enterprise
SOE	State-owned enterprise
SSEI	Sustainable Stock Exchanges Initiative
TIA	Tunisian Investment Authority

Executive Summary

Harnessing the benefits of investment for sustainable development in the Middle East and North Africa (MENA) is more imperative than ever. The health and economic crises precipitated by the Covid-19 pandemic have added to already pressing socio-economic challenges in the region. Global foreign direct investment (FDI) flows fell by 50% in the first half of 2020 compared to the preceding six months, and the OECD predicts world economic output to contract by 4.2% in 2020. The effect on MENA economies could be even greater. FDI inflows to the region declined sharply in 2020, and forecasts suggest a significant economic contraction ahead, with sharp increases to already high unemployment and poverty, as well a rising risk of macro-economic, political and social instability.

While MENA governments have begun ambitious efforts to improve the investment climate and respond to the pandemic, bolder reforms are needed to make investment work for sustainable development. The MENA economies covered in this report are diverse: Algeria, Egypt, Jordan, Lebanon, Libya, Morocco, the Palestinian Authority, and Tunisia each face unique obstacles, opportunities and goals. Many of these countries nevertheless share common challenges. The report offers reform proposals, considering several policy dimensions that affect the investment climate, and places strong emphasis on how investment can help MENA governments improve the lives of their citizens.

A common challenge: making investment work for sustainable development

Recognising the positive role investment can play in supporting development goals – from economic diversification to creation of quality jobs – MENA governments have advanced meaningful reforms in the past decade to promote and facilitate FDI. Governments have revised investment legislation, eased market entry, streamlined regulations on business operations, strengthened investment promotion agencies (IPA), and adopted policies to direct investment to under-performing regions. While some economies have attracted sizable FDI inflows, MENA governments have been less successful than other emerging and developing economies at leveraging investment to advance sustainable development. Political instability, conflict, and social and economic shocks over the past decade have all negatively affected the investment climate. The benefits of FDI have also been hindered by structural challenges shared by the diverse economies, including barriers to competition, skills shortages, inadequate infrastructure, governance challenges, and weak regional integration.

In much of the MENA region, FDI has been concentrated in a few capital-intensive sectors, including extractive industries, real estate and construction, as well as light manufacturing. Many of these sectors have not sufficiently advanced job creation or economic diversification nor have they supported the growth of small and medium enterprises (SMEs), or economic activity outside of coastal and urban regions. In most MENA economies, there is a popular perception that investment has not benefited the average citizen. Despite notable reforms, many areas of the investment climate continue to pose challenges to investors and private sector growth more broadly, limiting the positive impact of investment.

Improve the investment climate and realise the benefits of FDI: four priorities

- **Improve the clarity, consistency and transparency of investment rules and procedures.** MENA economies have undertaken sustained efforts to improve legislation governing the investment climate. But in some cases, the fast-paced rhythm of recent reforms may have created legal overlaps and loopholes, whether perceived or real, which can create confusion for investors. Ensuring coherence and clarity across various investment-related laws is essential for an attractive investment climate, and reduces opportunities for inconsistent implementation or bureaucratic discretion. Authorities in most MENA economies have wide discretion to determine tax incentives, and in some cases, in deciding which investors can enter the market and receive permits and land. Greater specificity in laws and regulations, which reduces scope for interpretation, might contribute to limiting corruption, unfair competition risks and potential investor-state disputes.
- **Advance reforms to improve competition and private sector development**. On average, MENA economies impose more restrictions on foreign investors' entry and operations, particularly in service sectors, than peer countries. Limiting FDI in key services, such as transport, hinders competition and productivity in these sectors and the industries that rely on them, including manufacturing, in turn holding back potential productivity gains throughout the economy. FDI restrictions in services also limit participation in global value chains (GVC). Gains from GVCs, such as knowledge transfers, have been limited. More broadly, while several MENA governments have removed important *de jure* restrictions on market entry, other barriers to competition are often prevalent. These include institutional or informal barriers to investment (such as excessive bureaucracy or corruption), inconsistent enforcement of statutory rules, as well as distortions caused by state ownership of key sectors, and special treatment received by certain firms.
- **Target investment policy and promotion to better serve sustainable development goals**. MENA governments may have to re-think investment promotion strategies, both to respond to new challenges, including investor caution, and harness opportunities arising from a possible reorganisation of GVCs. Digitalisation of procedures should be expanded, along with a renewed focus on aftercare and retention. Strategies should be developed through wide consultations and should focus on clear targets. Policies to attract investment with high development impacts should include more targeted, cost-based incentives in line with government priorities, to foster spill-overs such as skills development, innovation, and linkages to local SMEs. In fragile contexts, governments could target investors that are more familiar with fragility and the national context and prioritise sectors that support post-conflict or disaster rebuilding efforts. In supporting investment that can best advance sustainable development, MENA governments could also do more to promote and enable responsible business conduct. This includes advancing human and labour rights, gender equality and environmental protection in business activities and their supply chains.
- **Strengthen good governance and co-ordination to deliver better investment policy**. MENA governments have undertaken numerous reforms of their institutional framework for investment, boosting the roles of IPAs with a breadth of mandates, including regulatory and supervisory roles often overseen by ministries in other countries. This can create confusion of roles and affect IPAs' credibility to voice private investors' concerns while they also regulate their operations. Governments should clarify responsibilities and strengthen co-ordination over investment policy, promotion and facilitation – as well as dispute management and prevention – to reduce institutional overlaps and conflicting objectives. Moreover, aligning investment with other policies that influence the investment climate, including trade, competition, innovation, infrastructure connectivity, and anti-corruption, would promote policy coherence, while sharing responsibilities between national and subnational bodies could improve policy delivery. Lastly, MENA governments could further solicit investors' and other stakeholders' views when developing policies; facilitating an environment of trust and accountability between the government and business community is especially important in uncertain times.

1 Overview and key policy messages

Middle East and North African governments have advanced notable reforms to improve the investment environment in the past decade. But further efforts are required to leverage investment to advance inclusive and sustainable development, and support recovery from the economic crisis provoked by the global pandemic. This chapter provides an overview of liberalisation reforms and investment climate constraints in the region, drawing out common challenges shared by the eight diverse economies. It offers an overarching reform agenda based on the main findings and policy considerations of *MENA Investment Policy Perspectives*.

Introduction

The Middle East and North Africa (MENA) has the regional market, resource and human capital potential to attract high levels of foreign direct investment (FDI). While some MENA economies have been fairly successful at attracting foreign business, FDI inflows in much of the region – including the eight economies covered in this report (MENA focus economies) – are below their potential. As are the potential benefits from greater integration within the region and with the European market. MENA governments have also been less successful than other emerging and developing economies at leveraging investment to advance sustainable development. Periods of political instability, conflict, and social and economic shocks over the past decade have negatively affected the investment climate and economic growth across the region. But the benefits of FDI have also long been constrained by structural challenges shared by the eight diverse economies, which have hindered the growth of a dynamic, competitive and rules-based private sector. The Covid-19 pandemic and the ongoing economic crisis have created further – and for some economies severe – challenges. Leveraging investment to support the economic recovery will require policymakers to address persistent challenges to competitive markets and advance policies to support more inclusive growth.

In much of the MENA region, economic activity, as well as FDI, has been concentrated in a few capital-intensive sectors, including extractive industries, real estate and construction, as well as light manufacturing. Many of these sectors not have sufficiently advanced job creation or productivity, nor have they supported the growth of small and medium-sized enterprises (SMEs), or economic activity outside of coastal and urban regions. In most MENA economies, there is a popular perception that FDI – and economic growth more broadly – has not benefited the average citizen (OECD, 2018[1]) (World Bank, 2018[2]). The eight economies covered in this report nonetheless differ widely. Some countries have had more success than others diversifying their economies and supporting job creation, while shocks, including conflict, insecurity and popular uprisings, have added substantial challenges in other economies.

MENA governments recognise that attracting more investment, with a greater developmental impact, will depend on further reforms, and all of the eight focus economies have made considerable efforts to improve the investment environment in the past decade. Some countries have already seen positive developments, including more investment in sectors that can advance job creation, exports and productivity, and more diversified sources of FDI. But further efforts are required. Structural challenges continue to constrain, to varying degrees, the investment climate in the MENA focus economies, from insufficient competition to skills shortages, inadequate infrastructure, political instability, poor governance, and weak regional integration.

Several more immediate challenges persist for investors. Investment-related regulations are not always clear or transparent, and many rules are enforced in an overly-discretionary or *ad hoc* manner. Co-ordination among government agencies in promoting and facilitating investment is often insufficient, limiting effectiveness in implementing strategies and impact on improving the business climate. MENA economies rank poorly on many measures related to business integrity and responsible business conduct. More targeted investment policies, including on tax incentives and linkages between SMEs and foreign companies, could better serve sustainable development objectives and countries' engagement in global value chains (GVCs).

Improving the investment climate will require that MENA governments make rules more transparent and less discretionary. Implementing clear, transparent and targeted strategies to attract FDI in more diversified sectors, and towards specific development aims, would help maximise the benefits of investment. Further reforms are also needed to address challenges to competition and dynamic private sector growth. These include reducing formal and informal barriers to competition, including privileges received by certain firms. This is particularly important in service sectors and infrastructure, crucial for strengthened participation in GVCs and greater regional integration.

MENA governments have demonstrated their commitment to addressing investment climate challenges, although implementing these reforms will not be quick or easy. But the stakes have never been higher. The Covid-19 pandemic and resulting economic and social shocks have added new challenges and exacerbated existing ones. Already, FDI inflows have declined sharply and projections suggest a significant economic contraction ahead in nearly all the focus economies. This will increase the risk of rising poverty, unemployment as well macro-economic and political instability across the region (UN, 2020[3]). This new reality makes it even more imperative to commit to bold reforms that will make investment work for sustainable development.

A diverse group with a common challenge: make investment work for sustainable development

Early economic reforms advanced aggregate growth

MENA governments have undergone numerous periods of economic reform. By the 1990s, most of the focus economies had advanced profound transitions from decades of predominately state-led development towards more open market economies. In Morocco, Tunisia, Jordan and Egypt, this process involved successive waves of reforms that drastically reduced state spending, privatised many state-owned enterprises and removed important barriers to trade and investment. Though less ambitious, reforms in Algeria and Libya also sought to partially open markets to foreign investors. In Lebanon, advancing private sector development, in part through open capital markets, was central to the post-civil war reconstruction strategy. Liberalisation reforms were also adopted by the Palestinian Authority after the Oslo Accords with Israel in 1993.

This process contributed to strong GDP growth in all of the focus economies, averaging between 4% and 5.4% between 1995-2007 (Figure 1, panel a). Growth was also aided by higher oil prices, which increased revenue for exporters (Algeria and Libya) and benefited energy importers through higher remittances and investment from neighbouring Gulf States. Exports also grew in many of the focus economies, and FDI reached record volumes in the years before the 2008 global financial crisis (Figure 1.1, panel c and d). On aggregate, there were initial labour productivity gains in several countries, as employment in agriculture and government services decreased (Figure 1.1, panel b).

The 2008 global financial crisis, followed by social unrest and political instability across the MENA region starting in 2010, halted many of the positive economic gains of the previous two decades. Average GDP growth across the eight economies dropped to 1.6% between 2009 and 2011. FDI plummeted, particularly in countries most affected by political upheavals (Egypt and Tunisia) or conflict (Libya). But across the whole MENA region, instability or uncertainty had a negative spill-over effect on trade and investment. In Jordan and Lebanon, conflicts in Iraq and Syria severely affected trade networks, and the influx of Syrian refugees has strained the two economies. Security concerns have affected tourism across the region. Several countries suffered from a sharp decline in exports and foreign reserves, pushing up macroeconomic risk.

Over the past decade, prior to the global health and economic crises of 2020, economic output and investment had been slowly recovering from the twin shocks of 2008 and 2011. Some countries, including Morocco and Egypt, saw noticeable increases in FDI in recent years. In the eight economies overall, FDI as a share of GDP has been comparable to other emerging and developing economies. But in many of the focus economies, inflows over the past decade have stagnated, decreased, or in the case of Libya, halted. This mirrors trends in global FDI inflows, which have been declining in the past few years, until their collapse after the Covid-19 pandemic and resulting economic crisis (OECD, 2020[4]). Investment has also remained relatively un-diversified. With some notable exceptions, the majority of FDI to the eight focus economies has consistently been concentrated in real estate, construction, mining and fuels.

Figure 1.1. Growth, productivity, exports and investment in MENA and comparator groups

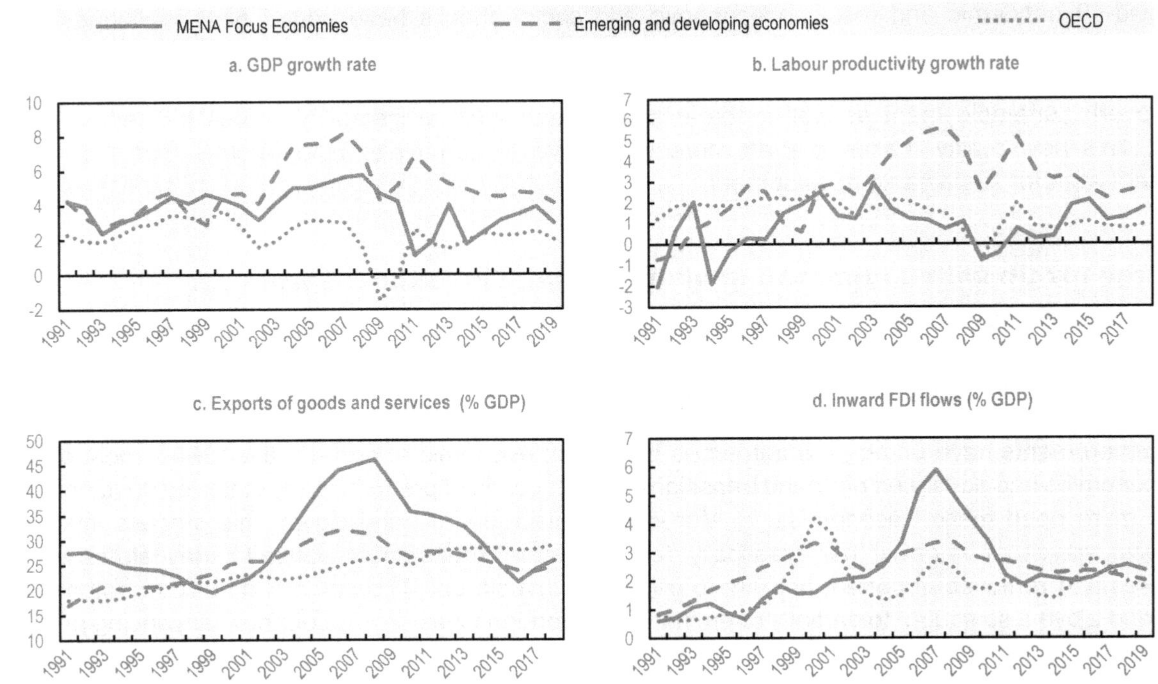

Note: Variables are expressed as two-year moving averages. OECD statistics on inward FDI for 1990 to 2004 relate to unrevised BMD3 data.
Source: OECD National Accounts, OECD FDI statistics database, The Conference Board Total Economy database, IMF World Economic Outlook, UNCTAD Statistics, and World Bank National Accounts.

Further reforms are required to support a dynamic, competitive and rules-based private sector…

Supporting a durable recovery from the pandemic will require deeper reforms to address the structural challenges that have continued to negatively affect sustainable growth in the region. Even after the substantial liberalisation reforms of the 1990s and early 2000s, strong GDP growth rates, and notable expansion of trade and investment, mass social movements in 2011 confirmed that these trends did not achieve inclusive economic growth. Crucially, reforms did not create enough opportunities for the majority of the population (OECD, 2016[5]) (World Bank, 2018[2]). Explanations for the failings of pre-2011 reforms are numerous, and depend on country specificities. Progress was affected by regional developments, including civil and regional conflicts, and the global context of rising competition from Asia and Eastern and Central Europe. But a common challenge is persistent across the region: reforms did not sufficiently support a dynamic, competitive, and rules-based private sector that can generate inclusive growth.

While successive reforms reduced public sector investment and related employment in several countries (most notably in Egypt, Jordan and Tunisia), the private sector did not, and still has not, filled this gap. In the two decades before 2011, Lebanon was the only focus economy to increase private investment to above 20% of GDP. Private investment has remained at around just 10% of GDP in Egypt since the late 1990s (OECD, 2020[6]). In particular, private sector reforms did not create enough jobs for the growing labour force, and well-educated youth in particular – jobs that were previously provided by the public sector (Assaad and Krafft, 2016[7]). While GDP growth was fairly strong in the 1990s and early 2000s, the growth of the labour force was stronger, and private sector jobs did not keep pace with labour supply. With some exceptions, unemployment in the focus economies has remained static at between 10 and 20% of the labour force in the decade before 2011 – and in the decade after. Youth unemployment has consistently averaged 30% (ILO Stat). Notwithstanding the limited ability of the private sector to generate jobs, boosting youth employment has also been constrained by considerable skills mismatches (OECD, 2016[5]).

Competitive markets have been hindered by various *de jure* and *de facto* barriers. This includes a wider legal and regulatory framework that has enabled conflicting interpretations and inconsistent application of rules. These various barriers have contributed to a dualistic private sector, dominated by a few large firms and a vast informal economy, with little room for SMEs to grow. There is also growing consensus that a key challenge to competitive markets in many MENA economies is linked to the outsized role of privileged firms in the economy. These include some state-owned enterprises (SOEs) as well as politically-connected private-sector firms.[1] Economic activity in many states has historically been concentrated in the hands of a few, and networks of patronage have benefited these firms to the detriment of growth of others.[2] Privileges granted to preferential firms can include special regulatory treatment (including selective enforcement of rules), trade protection (often through non-tariff barriers), beneficial access to credit and land, tax benefits, energy subsidies, and preference in public contracts (Atiyas, Diwan and Malik, 2019[8]).[3] In some cases, politically-connected firms have tilted regulations towards their favour and could be shielded from competition via restrictions on foreign investors.[4] Special advantages granted to certain firms has lowered aggregate productivity, employment and innovation, as well as the entry of new competitors.

Other cross-cutting factors have limited the potential for higher levels of growth and investment, and more inclusive development, in the MENA region. Good governance, including respect for the rule or law, underpins an attractive investment climate, and trust in government and public institutions – crucial for effective policy reform – is notably low in the region, particularly among youth (OECD, 2018[1]). Meanwhile, low quality infrastructure and poor logistics are limiting investment opportunities, as well as links to less-developed regions. Weak governance and low quality infrastructure, together with existing barriers to trade and investment, have also hindered regional integration – among MENA countries and with Mediterranean neighbours. Among the eight focus economies, the share of intra-regional trade in goods as a share of total trade was just 4% in 2017, a substantially lower share than for regional economic communities in West Africa (intra-regional trade among ECOWAS members is around 9%) and Southeast Asia (ASEAN intra-regional trade in goods is around 23%).[5] FDI flows between the MENA focus economies are also marginal, representing only 1% of total greenfield investment since 2003 (fDi Markets).

...and to increase the benefits of FDI to the economy and society

Harnessing the benefits of FDI requires, foremost, an enabling investment environment that allows firms to operate efficiently, and the aforementioned challenges to a competitive private sector have limited the potential of firm entry and growth. It also requires more targeted policies that can maximise the direct and indirect impacts FDI can have on sustainable development. Along with productivity improvements, FDI can create jobs, boost exports, spread knowledge, trigger innovation, improve living standards and, more generally, advance inclusive and sustainable development (OECD, 2019[9]). Yet, the realisation of this potential has been unequal across MENA focus economies: some have benefited more from FDI than others and, within economies, some segments of the population have been left behind.

Liberalisation reforms in the 1990s and 2000s sought to accelerate the structural transformation of MENA economies – the movement of labour and capital, including FDI, from low-productivity to high-productivity sectors.[6] While aggregate productivity initially increased, growth in higher-productivity sectors has been limited. Other developing countries, mostly in East Asia, had more success using foreign knowledge to accelerate innovation. In most MENA economies, an increase in employment and FDI in light manufacturing and some business services have generated modest productivity gains, although at varying degrees across the region – foreign manufacturers have recently contributed to the emergence of strong automotive and aeronautic sectors in Morocco. In oil exporters, FDI has remained concentrated in the energy sector, limiting economic diversification.

Growth in labour-intensive industries in Morocco and Tunisia have attracted FDI with the largest effects on job creation in the region in the last two decades, and comparable to other countries at similar stages of economic development (Figure 1.2).[7] FDI-related job creation has been weaker in other MENA focus economies. Sectors that receive the most foreign investment, including natural resources and real estate, have not created the most jobs, limiting the ability of the growing labour force to move to more productive, better-paid and higher-skilled employment.

In the past decade, some countries have made notable progress in attracting investment in a more diverse group of sectors. FDI in manufacturing has increased as a share of total greenfield investment in Algeria, Egypt, Morocco and Tunisia since 2013, compared to the years before the 2008 global financial crisis. Lebanon, Morocco and Tunisia have also seen service sectors attract a greater proportion of total FDI. But manufacturing still receives a relatively small amount of foreign investment in several of the focus economies, and the service sector even less.

Figure 1.2. FDI-related job creation and GDP per capita of MENA focus economies

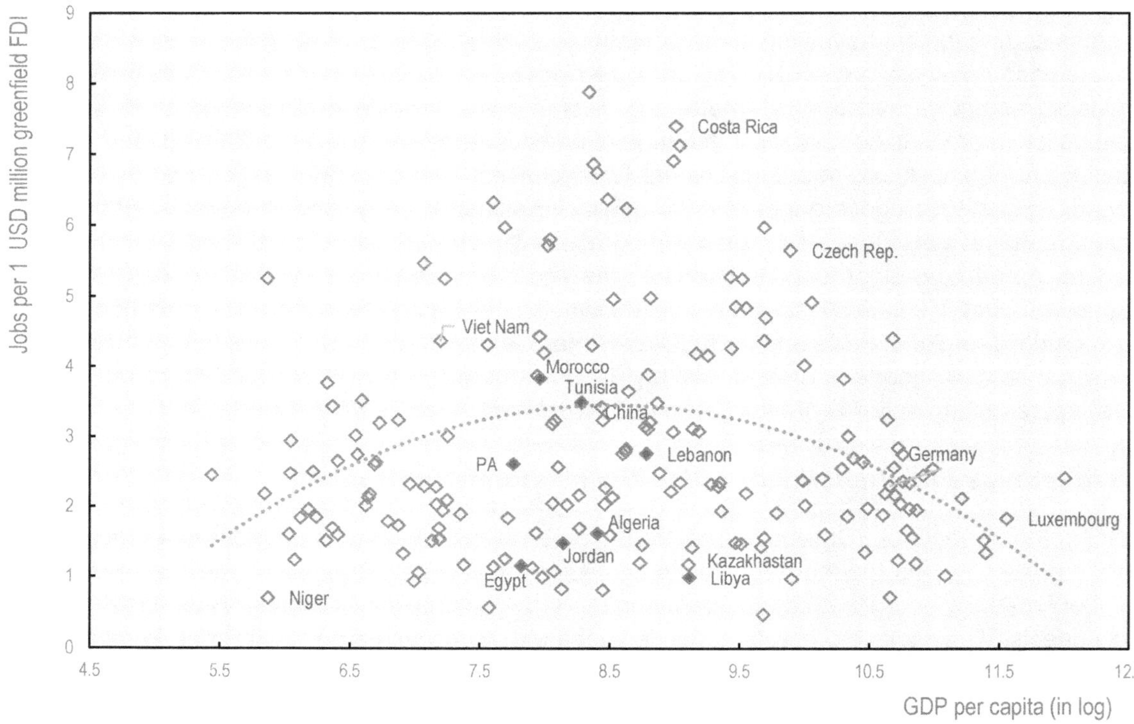

Note: Greenfield FDI is defined as announced capital expenditure (capex). Number of jobs and capex are partly based on estimates between January 2003 and December 2017. GDP per capita is calculated as an average between 2003 and 2017.
Source: OECD based on Financial Times' fDi Markets database and the World Development Indicators.

FDI in tradeable goods such as natural resources or light manufacturing has helped most MENA focus economies engage in GVCs. Algeria and Libya, for instance, boosted exports of commodities while other economies relied, to varying degrees, on foreign inputs to increase their exports of manufactured products. But gains in terms of export diversification, skills upgrading and technology diffusion have been insufficient. Weak private sector competitiveness has meant domestic SMEs primarily supply low-skilled goods and services to foreign firms. In addition, linkages between foreign and domestic firms are largely confined to the developed coastal areas and urban centres of the MENA focus economies. This has helped these areas connect with global economic networks, but linkages have been weak outside these centres, which tend to have inadequately skilled labour force and poor infrastructure, limiting the possibility for enhanced labour mobility. While regional disparities are not specific to the MENA region, they have nonetheless reinforced within-country inequality, a key factor in popular discontent in several countries.

Harnessing the benefits of investment will be key to the post-pandemic recovery

In the past decade, many MENA governments have put new or renewed emphasis on advancing reforms to foster economic diversification, productivity gains and job creation. Recognising the positive role investment can play in supporting these aims, all of the focus economies have adopted important measures to promote and facilitate investment. These reforms are explored in detail in thematic chapters of this report, and summarised below.

The imperative to advance inclusive development has perhaps never been greater. The Covid-19 pandemic, resulting supply disruptions, demand contractions and the pessimistic outlook of economic actors has precipitated an economic and social shock unprecedented in modern times. Global FDI flows fell by 50% in the first half of 2020 compared to the preceding six months, and the OECD projects world economic output to fall by 4.2% in 2020 (OECD, 2020[4]) (OECD, 2020[10]) (OECD, 2020[11]). The effect on the MENA focus economies could be even greater, as low oil prices put additional fiscal constraints on exporters, and reduce remittances, investment and direct aid from Gulf States to importers.[8] Several sectors particularly affected by the crisis, including tourism, energy and manufacturing, are critical to MENA economies. Estimates suggest economic output in 2020 contracted by -5.3%, on average, in focus economies excluding Libya and Lebanon, which face drastic recessions due to other political and security shocks. Most economies are likely to recover GDP growth by 2021 or 2022, though forecasts are subject to high degrees of uncertainty (World Bank, 2019[12]).

Investment to the eight focus economies has already been significantly affected by the pandemic. The total value of greenfield investments in the first half of 2020 was 80% less than in the first six months of 2019 (Figure 1.3). This is twice the reduction in greenfield investment in emerging and developing economies as a whole (42%), and a significantly sharper decline than experienced by OECD countries (17%) (fDi Markets by the FT). At the time of writing, recent contractions in FDI appear largely due to projects being put on hold, rather than divestments or cancellations of projects (OECD, 2020[13]).

The economic contraction has added new risks and exacerbated existing ones. Before the current crisis, in all of the eight focus economies, both overall unemployment and youth unemployment were higher in 2019 than in 2010 (ILO Stat). Government crisis response measures to the pandemic, combined with a sharp decline in revenue streams, has put strong pressure on already high deficit and debt levels. The pandemic has also exposed acute vulnerabilities in food supply in some countries. In this context, any additional shocks – including the explosion at Beirut's port in August – can be devastating.

MENA governments have put in place numerous measures to respond to the health, economic and social impacts of the crisis.[9] These include fiscal packages to support hard-hit sectors and SMEs, including through cash and in-kind transfers, deferred tax and loan payments, and reduced utility bills. Several governments have taken notable measures to target groups that usually fall outside of social safety nets, including informal and seasonal workers (OECD, 2020[14]). To respond to investors' concerns, most IPAs in the region have refocused their services on aftercare to support and retain existing investors. Governments are also considering revising incentives policy to attract investment in sectors vulnerable to supply chain disruptions, including agriculture (OECD, 2020[13]).

These measures have been crucial to respond to the immediate effects of the pandemic. But in the medium- to long-term, many MENA governments may have to re-think investment promotion strategies, both to respond to new challenges and to harness potential opportunities. MENA economies could attract new multinational firms considering diversifying – if not shortening – their supply chains. Harnessing the positive benefits of investment will be key to the post-pandemic recovery.

Figure 1.3. Effect of Covid-19 on greenfield FDI

Announced capital expenditure, USD millions

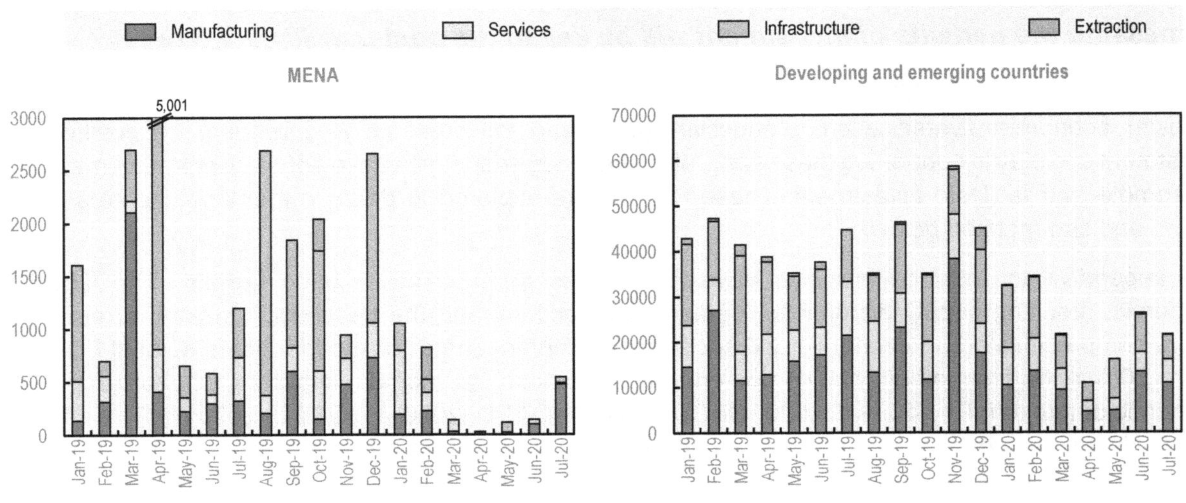

Source: OECD based on Financial Times fDi Markets, as of 10 September 2020.

Investment policy priorities for the MENA region

Many of the MENA focus economies have accelerated reforms in recent years in an effort to attract more investment, with a higher development impact. Governments have adopted new investment legislation, eased market entry, streamlined regulations on business operations, strengthened investment promotion agencies (IPAs) mandates, and adopted policies to direct investment to under-performing regions. Some countries have already seen positive returns to reforms, including more investment in sectors that can advance job creation, exports and productivity, and more diversified sources of FDI (Chapter 2).

But many areas of the investment climate continue to pose challenges to private sector growth, limiting FDI inflows and the positive impact of investment on sustainable economic development. The eight economies are diverse; each face their own unique challenges. Several policy priorities apply to the whole region, however. The following section presents several cross-cutting themes of the report, highlighting where reforms have been made and where further progress is needed to improve the overall investment climate and realise the positive benefits of FDI.

Priority 1: Improve the clarity, consistency and transparency of investment-related rules and procedures

MENA governments have adopted numerous reforms to improve investment-related legislation

The eight MENA focus economies have adopted numerous reforms to improve investment-related legislation (Chapter 3). In particular, MENA governments have expended considerable resources and political capital to revise their investment laws. Since 2010, Algeria, Egypt, Jordan, Libya, the Palestinian Authority and Tunisia have all adopted new investment laws. These laws set conditions for market access for foreign firms, property protection guarantees, as well as other provisions relevant for investors, such as conditions for tax incentives and authority of IPAs. Though these provisions and guarantees can be secured in other laws, the investment law is often the first point of reference for a potential investor, and can be used as a signalling devise to promote the country as an investment destination. Recent revisions to investment laws in the MENA focus economies removed some restrictions on foreign investors (Chapter 4), streamlined business registration, and reinforced and expanded IPA mandates (Chapter 6).

MENA governments have also recently revised or are in the process of amending other legislation pertinent to investors, including: commercial codes (Morocco and Lebanon), companies acts (Egypt), Public-Private Partnership laws (Jordan, Morocco and Tunisia), public procurement regulations (Algeria), as well as legislation on bankruptcy (Egypt and Morocco), competition (Egypt and Tunisia) and SMEs (Libya and PA). Establishing clear rules on market entry, business operations and contract enforcement, through investment-related legislation, are essential to attract investors.

Revisions of investment legislation can, but do not always, improve legal clarity

In some cases, however, the fast-paced rhythm of regulatory amendments may have created superfluous legislation, leading to overlaps and inconsistency. New iterations of investment laws are not always an improvement over the earlier version. Some highly publicised amendments may have been adopted to signal a new political direction, following frequent governmental reshuffles, rather than to address a clear legal gap. Frequent amendments can also hinder implementation of regulations.

In some cases, adopting new laws can add layers of complexity to the overall regulatory environment for investment, which encompasses a variety of sectoral and thematic legislation, as well as international investment treaties (Chapter 5). In many MENA countries, regulations are scattered across a wide range of laws and decrees; when designed in silos, this can create legal overlaps or loopholes, of the perception thereof, which can have a deterrent effect on investors, particularly in jurisdictions where non-commercial risks are higher than the average. For example, restrictions on foreign investors' entry and operations can involve lengthy and frequently updated positive lists (of sectors open to foreign investors), making it difficult for investors to understand prevalent rules (Chapter 4). All the focus economies grant fiscal and financial incentives through multiple pieces of legislation, decrees and executive orders, in addition to one-off agreements with firms, limiting transparency over incentives offered (Chapter 7). Similarly, regulation around procurement for infrastructure projects sometimes overlaps with older sector-specific or project-specific laws (Chapter 9).

Such overlaps and loopholes can deter investors by creating confusion but they can also create incentives for investors to exploit uncertainty, preventing countries from reaping the potential benefits of investment. Ensuring coherence and clarity across various investment-related laws is essential. Some countries have taken steps in this direction. In Jordan, sectors restricted to foreign investors are clearly outlined in a negative list (Chapter 4), while Morocco has consolidated most of its tax incentives in its tax code, in line with international best practice (Chapter 7).

To the extent possible, international investment treaty (IIA) provisions should also be consistent with domestic laws. The MENA focus economies have entered into a significant number of IIAs, which creates an additional layer of legal obligations pertaining to the treatment of investment. Inconsistencies between IIAs and domestic laws can create room for disputes between the State and foreign investors that benefit from such treaties (Chapter 5).

MENA governments should avoid short-term fixes and ensure that no unnecessary additional layers of regulation are created when endeavouring to modernise legislative frameworks. Reducing the time gap between the adoption of new laws and their implementing regulations, and streamlining and empowering relevant institutions in charge of enforcing investment rules, are key to increase legislative efficiency. Revision of the investment treaty policy and practice should also be considered, as well as reforms that would limit exposure to investment arbitration claims.

Clarifying the regulatory framework for investment would reduce opportunities for discretionary decisions

Several MENA countries have made notable improvements to streamline regulations for investors, or ease procedures by centralising administrative steps in one-stop shops (OSS) (Chapter 6). However, the regulatory framework for investment is often not predictable or transparent. In addition to potential legal gaps and loopholes outlined above, the lack of clarity of investment-related regulations opens the door for discretionary decisions – which may be applied in discriminatory manner – or inconsistent implementation. Government authorities in most of the MENA focus economies have wide discretion to determine tax benefits investors can receive, and in some cases, which investors can enter the market, receive licences, permits and land. Specificity in laws and regulations, rather than wording that allows open interpretation by officials, helps reduce opportunities for corruption and aggressive tax planning by firms. Moreover, rules that are applied in an *ad hoc* manner across taxpayers creates unfair competition, and can deter investors.

MENA governments widely use tax and financial incentives to attract private investment and direct it into certain sectors, activities and locations (Chapter 7). Many investment incentives offered in the region are open to interpretation and discretion of implementing authorities. Often the law does not specify the length or ceiling of tax exemptions or reductions, and often conditions for receiving incentives are vague, such as broadly-defined sectors or activities "in the national interest". Some MENA IPAs have wide discretion in determining which investors receive incentives and the generosity of the benefit. Other incentives are given to firms on an *ad hoc*, contract-based manner. Investment contracts can indeed be problematic, as they can be inconsistent with the national and international legal framework and give leeway to discretionary powers (Chapter 5).

Notably, some governments in the region have reduced discretionary decisions around market entry (Chapter 4). Tunisia notably removed in 2016 a requirement that foreign investors receive approval for equity stakes exceeding 50% of a firm's capital. Libya is the only focus economy to apply economy-wide screening measures to regulate the entry of foreign investors. However, legislation in some MENA economies still imposes discriminatory approvals or criteria for admitting foreign investment in certain sectors. Screening requirements can dissuade foreign investors, as they create unpredictable and costly barriers to entry, particularly when approval criteria are poorly defined or not transparent. Approval mechanisms also impose administrative costs to governments and businesses. Ensuring effective and clear implementation of regulations governing the entry and operations of foreign investors, including by limiting excessive discretion of authorities, and implementing monitoring mechanisms, would reduce undesirable practices and help foster a more dynamic private sector.

MENA governments could enhance efforts to curb corruption across the investment process

Reducing discretionary application of rules and procedures for investors, such as those described above, would help reduce the incidence of corruption across the investment process. An investor may resort to corruption in order to enter a foreign market; obtain or retain a government contract, licence or clearance of customs procedures; get access to raw materials or foreign currency; or to receive specific incentives or tax benefits. Clear and unambiguous market entry rules and requirements are a prerequisite to reduce to a minimum opportunities for officials' discretion over the provision of licences, permits or public contracts.

Though some MENA governments have recently adopted new strategies to enhance business integrity, further reforms are required to lower the incidence of corruption in the public and private sectors (Chapter 11). The MENA focus economies rank among the bottom 50% on international indices measuring perceptions of corruption. Governments could greatly improve their image as investment destinations by showing their willingness to converge towards international standards. MENA economies can benefit from the proper implementation of the anti-corruption instruments they have adhered to, as this represents a strong signal of convergence to international standards vis-à-vis the international community and foreign investors. Moreover, other international instruments to which MENA economies have not yet adhered can provide guidance to inspire domestic efforts to promote integrity in business transactions.

Priority 2: Advance reforms to improve competition and private sector development

MENA economies have recently undertaken meaningful liberalisation reforms

Within the wider legislative framework for investment described above, a critical issue for foreign investors is the rules governing their entry and operations. All governments impose some legal or regulatory restrictions on FDI, often in an effort to protect domestic industries or safeguard national security interests (Chapter 4). But FDI restrictions involve economic costs, which can lead to lower competition, forgone government revenue, and reduced opportunities for knowledge spillovers.

The eight MENA focus economies are on average more restrictive than OECD and many non-OECD countries covered in the OECD *FDI Regulatory Restrictiveness Index*, though there is considerable variation in the region (Chapter 4). Based on statutory FDI restrictions (those explicit in regulations or laws) as of year-end 2019, Egypt and Morocco are as liberal as OECD countries, while Libya, the Palestinian Authority and Algeria are significantly more restrictive than OECD and non-OECD peers (Figure 1.4.). Jordan, Lebanon and Tunisia impose restrictions close to the average non-OECD economy. The high scores of the most restrictive MENA economies are largely driven by horizontal restrictions applied across various sectors to all or most foreign investors. Aside from these measures, sector-specific limits on foreign equity ownership are the most prevalent forms of discrimination against foreign investors.

Figure 1.4. OECD FDI Regulatory Restrictiveness Index (MENA 2019)

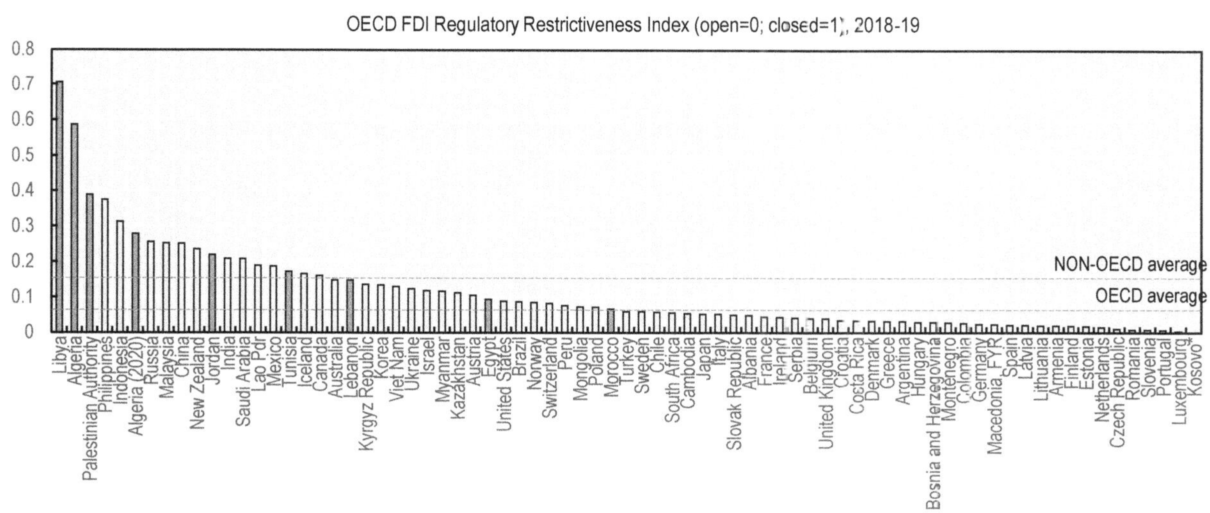

Note: The OECD FDI Regulatory Restrictiveness Index only covers statutory measures discriminating against foreign investors. The implementation of regulations, restrictions related to national security, state monopolies, preferential treatment for export-oriented investors and special economic zone regimes are not considered. Data reflect regulatory restrictions as of December 2019 for the MENA8 countries and 2018 for all others.

Source: OECD FDI Regulatory Restrictiveness Index (database), www.oecd.org/investment/fdiindex.htm.

Conscious of the negative impact of some of these restrictions, several MENA governments have recently adopted significant liberalisation reforms. Jordan revoked a minimum capital requirement for foreign investors, expanded sectors open to full foreign ownership, and eased restrictions in some service sectors. Tunisia removed a screening requirement for foreign majority-owned projects. Algeria in 2020 took a major step, ending its most substantial restriction, a cap on foreign equity of 49% in all non-strategic sectors.

Reducing FDI restrictions in services could support productivity gains from competition

Remaining statutory restrictions in MENA focus economies may nonetheless be inhibiting greater volumes of FDI as well as productivity gains from competition. Like most countries, the MENA focus economies impose more restrictions in service sectors than in manufacturing (Chapter 4). These sectoral restrictions are more severe and widespread than in peer emerging and developing countries, however. Several MENA countries restrict foreign ownership in business, financial, distribution and transport services, all of which are key inputs for other sectors. Restrictions in infrastructure sectors, including maritime and air transport and construction, also tend to be high (Chapter 9). Limiting FDI in such backbone services hinders competition and productivity in these sectors and the industries that rely on them, including manufacturing, in turn holding back potential productivity gains throughout the economy.

FDI restrictions in services particularly impede the deployment of foreign investment projects that are crucial for GVC participation and strengthened business linkages (Chapter 8). Gains from GVCs in MENA focus economies have been relatively limited in terms of knowledge and technology transfers to local firms as well as engagement in higher value added activities. Further openness could help raise efficiency (and reduce input costs) in sectors dominated by large state monopolies and improve the quality and availability of services. Openness in services can be important for the competitiveness and productivity of small manufacturers throughout the MENA region. SMEs often rely more on high quality backbone services and other services provided by upstream, external providers.

Governments should consider reassessing FDI restrictions against their public policy objectives (e.g. objectives of economic diversification or participation in GVCs) and, where relevant, streamline or remove them. Where such policies are deemed necessary, ensure that they are not more restrictive than needed to address identified risks and concerns.

Wider pro-competition reforms would encourage investors' entry and growth

Several MENA governments have removed important *de jure* restrictions on market entry. But other barriers to competition may be prevalent. These include institutional or informal barriers to investment (such as excessive bureaucracy or corruption), inconsistent enforcement of statutory rules, as well as distortions caused by state ownership of key sectors, and special regulatory treatment received by certain firms.

While privatisation programmes in most of the focus economies substantially reduced the economic role of the state, state-owned enterprises (SOEs) continue to play a fundamental role in MENA economies, and are dominant in many sectors. State ownership gives rise to unique governance and regulatory risks that can prevent SOEs from creating optimal value for the economy and society. When SOEs operate inefficiently and are subject to weak governance arrangements, they can crowd out more productive private sector activity, and in the worst case, be used as tools for political patronage or for self-enrichment at the expense of society at large (OECD, 2019[15]). Many MENA SOEs benefit from special regulatory treatment, from preference in public procurement to exemption from certain laws (World Bank, 2018[16]). The OECD *Guidelines on Corporate Governance of State-Owned Enterprises* outline good practice standards on how SOEs can manage more effectively their responsibilities, thus helping to make them more competitive, efficient and transparent.

Fair competition is also hindered when private firms with influential political (and in some cases military) connections benefit from formal or informal preferential treatment. In several MENA countries, some firms have been protected from competition through non-tariff import barriers, preferential access to land or government contracts, favourable tax treatment, and non-uniform application of doing business procedures (World Bank, 2015[17]) (Atiyas, Diwan and Malik, 2019[8]) (Diwan, Keefer and Schiffbauer, 2020[18]) (El-Haddad, 2020[19]). Such crony behaviour by firms makes it more difficult for other firms to compete. All MENA governments could do more to promote competition and address the externalities associated with the prevalence of a few dominant firms, one of the main impediments to more dynamic job and firm growth in the region.

Priority 3: Target investment policy to better serve sustainable development objectives

Investment promotion activities target investment with high development impacts

Countries attract higher levels of FDI when they choose to prioritise certain types of sectors, investors or countries – through prioritisation, IPAs can better focus their resources and tailor their services. Most MENA agencies prioritise investment in certain sectors, including industries that have the potential to diversify the economy, promote regional development and reinforce their competitive position vis-à-vis other countries. This reflects an effort to find the right balance between diversifying the economy and tapping into strong domestic capabilities, an approach that is similar to OECD IPAs. The majority of MENA agencies also prioritise certain investment projects, notably those that will have a positive impact on domestic firms' production capabilities, the country's image, regional development, jobs and innovation.

MENA IPAs' have priorities that are often in line with their national development goals, although investment promotion strategies, and related objectives, are not always publicly available. The decision to prioritise often comes from the highest levels of government, but some agencies have more autonomy in selecting priority sectors that will help achieve the government's wider development goals, similar to OECD countries. Prioritising investment promotion efforts should be conducted according to a set of criteria in line with wider development objectives. The decision to prioritise should be based on carefully crafted economic rationales and transparent consultations with public agencies and with the private sector, and not only serving political agendas.

The Covid-19 pandemic and its consequences on the global economy may propel MENA agencies to revise their investment promotion strategies to support the recovery. Indeed, in response to the outbreak, MENA IPAs have re-oriented their priorities to focus on existing investors and have expanded their aftercare services. The health crisis also pushed them to innovate and develop new digital tools and services that they could consider operating permanently. Policy advocacy may become even more relevant in a context where governments are rethinking their wider economic strategies and related business climate reforms. As FDI declines, sound business environments will become even more salient for investors. IPAs are well-placed to advocate for open, transparent and well-regulated markets. Particularly relevant are the policy reflections taking place to assess the disruption of value chains and the future positioning of the MENA region within global investment networks (OECD, 2020[13]).

Investment incentives should focus on achieving specific spillovers

As mentioned above, MENA governments widely use tax and financial incentives (Chapter 7). But the costs of incentives, particularly tax incentives, can outweigh the benefits. Tax incentives may subsidise firms that would have invested without favourable treatment and can constitute a significant cost for governments in terms of revenue forgone. However, carefully designed and targeted incentives may help correct market failures and advance certain development goals, such as supporting renewable energy or skills and technology upgrades, enhancing the positive impact of investment.

Incentives in the MENA region tend to be given to a wide range of investors. The eight MENA governments grant fiscal and financial incentives primarily to investors in agricultural, tourism and industrial sectors (broadly defined), export-oriented activities, and under-developed regions. Also common are incentives to investors that advance environmental protection, as are fiscal benefits to hydrocarbon industries. Several of the focus economies give tax breaks or grants to firms that create jobs or enhance skills. Fewer give incentives to firms that use new technologies or support technology transfer and R&D activities, unlike OECD countries.

Benefits to eligible investors are often generous. All of the eight MENA focus economies offer tax holidays – total exemptions from corporate income tax (CIT) – to investors in certain sectors and locations. Several governments have taken steps to reduce the length of tax holidays and number of firms eligible for them. But profit-based incentives (tax holidays and CIT rate reductions) remain widespread and are often easy for firms to receive, with broad eligibility requirements. Profit-based incentives, by benefiting firms that are already profitable, are more likely to be redundant than cost-based incentives.

MENA governments should consider how widely to offer tax and financial benefits, if these incentives are necessary to attract investment, and if their costs – in terms of revenue forgone and economic distortions – outweigh their benefits. Cost-benefit analysis and monitoring would help governments assess the effectiveness and efficiency of incentives. Simple tax incentive reports, identifying and describing all available incentives, their policy goal, and legal reference, is an important first step to create accountability and transparency. Replacing permanent incentives with temporary benefits would also encourage evaluation.

MENA governments should also consider moving gradually from broad-based tax holidays to more targeted, cost-based incentives in line with government priorities. The more targeted the incentive – for example to foster positive spill-overs such as skills training, innovation, and linkages to local firms – the more likely it is to reach its stated goal. Some MENA governments have begun to implement such targeted incentives, but these make up a small minority of incentives offered to investors.

Many governments in the region have added or revised incentives, or plan to do so, to respond to the economic and social costs of the Covid-19 pandemic. As governments seek swift measures to advance their economic recovery, assessments on the effectiveness and efficiency of incentives will be key to support already strained state budgets, and to ensure incentive design matches its goals.

Targeted policies and programmes can enhance SME-MNE linkages in GVCs

Leveraging FDI to integrate SMEs in global production networks can be an opportunity for the MENA region to achieve more inclusive and sustainable growth, especially in the post-Covid-19 recovery (Chapter 8). SMEs can plug into GVCs through the provision of inputs of goods and services to multinational enterprises established in their countries. This enables them to create jobs, develop skills, upgrade products and services to meet global standards, or adopt more sustainable production processes.

Foreign manufacturers in MENA countries including Egypt and Morocco are a key source of revenue for domestic suppliers. But business relationships are often limited to the sourcing of low-skilled inputs, rather than contractual arrangements for R&D or other upstream activities. Relatively low levels of SME productivity in MENA economies reduce the propensity to forge linkages with foreign firms in higher value-added segments of the supply chain. They also reduce the possibility of transfers of technology and managerial and technical expertise.

MENA governments should opt for targeted policy actions to enhance SME-MNE linkages. They could further develop business development services (BDS). This includes supplier development programmes such as those helping SMEs to form consortia (e.g. to respond to large orders from clients), improving quality, and strengthening managerial and technical skills. Other programmes could facilitate SMEs access to resources such as finance and technology. Governments can also support business linkages through the provision of matchmaking services and the development of high-quality supplier databases. All MENA IPAs offer such services but these are often implemented on an *ad hoc* basis, and are not part of a specific, more explicit, linkages programme. IPAs could also help maintain, through intensified and digitalised aftercare services, close contact with foreign firms with established relationships with local suppliers to address temporary challenges related to disruption in GVCs resulting from Covid-19.

Strengthening responsible business conduct would help advance sustainable development goals

In an effort to attract quality investment, MENA governments could do more to promote and enable responsible business conduct (RBC) (Chapter 10). While nearly all MENA governments have adopted measures to support sustainable development, more could be done to create an environment that fosters the positive contribution of the private sector to development objectives. This includes advancing human and labour rights, reducing opportunities for corruption, and improving environmental protection in business activities and their supply chains. Governments are also encouraged to implement RBC standards in their own economic activities, through state-owned enterprises and in public procurement processes.

The notion that businesses should contribute to society is prevalent throughout the MENA region. In line with global trends, awareness and understanding of RBC in the region is growing and increasingly moving from approaches based on philanthropy and social investments towards a more comprehensive approach that looks at how core business operations affect society. Promising initiatives driven by businesses and other stakeholders could be leveraged to communicate clear expectations on RBC and support a common understanding of RBC among businesses of all sizes and types.

The impetus to promote RBC among MENA businesses is not only a social matter but also an economic one. As demands for RBC are growing, companies that participate in global supply chains must be aware of international expectations of RBC. Some of the key trading partners of the eight MENA focus economies, such as the EU, have integrated RBC principles and standards in their policies and legislations. This makes promoting RBC particularly important for MENA countries to ensure integration in supply chain networks.

Businesses that implement RBC principles and standards are also better equipped to sustain supply chain and operational shocks, and ultimately build resilience and long-term value. This is also relevant in the context of the Covid-19 pandemic and its impact on supply chains as well as occupational safety at work.

Important commitments towards RBC have been made, although approaches differ across countries. Four MENA governments – Egypt, Jordan, Morocco, and Tunisia – have adhered to the OECD Declaration on International Investment and Multinational Enterprises, thus committing to promote the OECD Guidelines for Multinational Enterprises and to establish a National Contact Point (NCP) to further their effectiveness. NCPs are agencies established by governments to promote the Guidelines, and to handle cases as a non-judicial grievance mechanism. In Morocco, the NCP has taken an active role in the promotion of RBC. In most cases though, this mechanism has been under-utilised and should be strengthened to fulfil its mandate and support the sound design and implementation of RBC policies in the region.

Governments could also leverage existing collaborative initiatives to actively promote and disseminate RBC due diligence instruments among businesses in key industries. In particular, supporting collaborative initiatives, facilitating dialogue and supporting application of the OECD Due Diligence Guidance for Responsible Supply Chains in the Garment and Footwear Sector could improve industrial relations and enhance competitiveness of the garment sector in MENA economies.

Priority 4: Strengthen good governance and co-ordination to deliver better investment policy

MENA countries have undertaken numerous reforms of their institutional framework for investment…

An effective investment policy and transparent environment for investors are grounded in good public governance and strong institutions. Notably, the regional wave of investment law reforms in the past decade has significantly revamped the institutional framework governing investment policy in the MENA focus economies. Reforms have bolstered the roles of IPAs as key bodies responsible for investment issues. Most agencies have been given organisational autonomy and regulatory power to improve the business climate, a task that is often handed to ministries in other countries (Chapter 6). Depending on the agency, this includes screening of foreign investment projects, granting fiscal incentives or delivering business licences. Morocco and, to a lower extent, Algeria and Lebanon, separate more than other focus economies investment policymaking, a mandate fulfilled by ministries, from investment promotion and facilitation.

…but clarifying responsibilities and strengthening co-ordination over investment policies continue to be priorities

Combining investment promotion and facilitation with policymaking responsibilities has given some IPAs the ability to administer regulatory procedures themselves so that they can help investors better navigate them. But investment policy is an issue requiring policy responses that do not fit neatly within any single governmental department or agency. The breadth of MENA IPAs' mandates, which has frequently evolved, means their responsibilities overlap with those of other government bodies, more than in other countries. This can generate confusion of roles and affect IPAs' credibility to voice private investors' concerns while they also regulate their operations. Such wide mandates also weigh on agencies' ability to properly achieve their mission of promoting and facilitating investment.

One priority for MENA governments is to clarify responsibilities and strengthen co-ordination over investment policy, promotion and facilitation to reduce institutional overlaps and conflicting objectives. This is particularly important in institutional settings where the IPA has numerous mandates and holds regulatory functions, which may negatively affect their ability to carry out their core investment promotion functions. Investment-related responsibilities across different government bodies and agencies need to be balanced, sufficiently funded, explicit, and mutually understood by all actors. In this endeavour, clear and targeted institutional reforms should be preferred to hastily executed reorganisations as these could create uncertainty for investors.

Inter-agency collaboration would deliver better investment policies and services

Good governance where administrations work in a collaborative manner is crucial for delivering clear and transparent investment-related strategies. In particular, crafting an investment promotion strategy requires a whole-of-government approach as investment priorities need to be aligned with other major strategies – including trade, innovation, skills, and infrastructure (Chapter 9). Such strategies are not systematically developed in a collegial manner and not always publicly available in MENA focus economies, although they help raise countries' positive image within the international business community and inform it about investment opportunities.

Whole-of-government approaches to investment policy also involve crafting strategies and programmes that improve FDI sustainability outcomes and enhance business services delivery. In most of the MENA focus economies, initiatives to help SMEs establish business linkages with MNEs lack an overarching government strategy and tend to be scattered across different institutions (Chapter 8). But effective delivery of linkages programmes require close collaboration between IPAs, SME agencies and the private sector, among others. This co-operation is also essential to establish mechanisms to facilitate the flow of information on supply chain opportunities for both local suppliers and foreign investors. This will help address temporary challenges related to disruption in GVCs resulting from the Covid-19 pandemic.

Governments of the region so far have addressed their integrity and investment agendas independently, but inter-agency co-ordination is also essential to improve business integrity (Chapter 11). Several of the eight MENA focus economies have enacted in recent years laws and strategies to strengthen the anti-corruption framework and promote business integrity, and have established specialised anti-corruption bodies. But the links between integrity and investment call for better integrating both the policy and the institutional framework. Investment and anti-corruption agencies and policy-makers need to coordinate more closely to advance their respective agendas in a mutually reinforcing manner.

Co-ordination between various governmental bodies is also essential to manage investment disputes and set up prevention mechanisms. Investors' claims often arise from measures taken at the sub-national level or by a sectoral ministry, not always prepared and competent to deal with the issue. Dispute prevention policies also require institutional links with a leading body having a co-ordinating role (Chapter 5).

Sharing responsibilities between national and subnational bodies could improve investment promotion and facilitation outcomes

MENA governments have been seeking to attract FDI to less developed regions, but policies sometimes have failed to account that each region is unique in the way it competes in global investment networks. The majority of MENA countries have a centralised approach to investment promotion and facilitation. Around a third of MENA IPAs never contact subnational agencies and only a few consult them to integrate local development plans into their national attraction strategy. IPAs work with their own local branches, when these exist, rather than with separate regional entities. Branches provide facilitation and aftercare services and sometimes run OSS services. The Moroccan agency is the only IPA with no subnational branches. The IPA cooperates with regional investment centres, which operate under the authority of governorates and the Ministry of Interior.

Investment promotion and facilitation should strike a balance between centralised strategic decision-making and sufficient leeway for subnational agencies to exercise their power. Whether there is a network of national IPAs with local branches or a system of independent subnational IPAs, MENA governments could give subnational bodies more room to conduct investment promotion and facilitation tasks, in co-operation with the national IPA. Regional institutions often have more knowledge on local assets and challenges, and could help develop investment promotion strategies that are better suited to the local context. In Morocco, for instance, a recent reform granted regional investment centres financial autonomy and the mission to provide single window services, conduct economic intelligence, promote the regions, and offer dispute settlement services. Implementation of the reform is ongoing.

Investment facilitation entails a whole-of-government approach and digitised services

Investment facilitation is one business service that requires close co-operation between government agencies, including at the subnational level. All MENA focus economies provide a wide range of investment facilitation services, although they tend to focus on pre-establishment services and less on aftercare and retention activities. Despite considerable efforts, business registration services in the region are often defined by administrative structures working in silos.

Digitalisation can support a whole-of-government approach to investment facilitation. It lowers corruption risks throughout the business establishment process and speeds-up procedures. In addition, as shown during the Covid-19 crisis, there is a benefit to having paperless procedures to obtain relevant information, licences or permits. Yet, progress on investment facilitation as well as digitisation of procedures lies far beyond the responsibility of IPAs. It takes a concerted government effort to implement the necessary regulatory adjustments to make public services available online. Digitisation of pre-establishment procedures will also help MENA IPAs to focus on aftercare services, which are crucial to retain investors that may be considering relocating their operations during economic recovery from the pandemic.

Dialogue with the private sector on future reforms contributes to policy legitimacy

MENA focus economies could further include the private sector in government consultations over priority reforms and next strategies. Soliciting investor views, along with those of other stakeholders, when developing or revising policies contributes to policy legitimacy and effectiveness. It also instigates an environment of trust between the government and the business community, particularly in uncertain times. MENA governments could review IPAs' board membership to ensure a more balanced representation between governmental and non-governmental stakeholders (Chapter 6). They could also establish, or reinforce when they already exist, whole-of-government public-private dialogue platforms to consult systematically with the private sector. To avoid regulatory capture by a small group of large and influential companies, private sector participation in such consultation mechanisms must be based on transparent selection criteria.

Good governance of investment policy entails transparency in the monitoring of government actions

Pressure on MENA governments to demonstrate impact of reforms has been growing in the past few years, because of tighter budgets, popular demands, and overall governmental accountability. This trend is likely to accelerate following the Covid-19 outbreak as governments are more pressed than ever to attract FDI that can make the greatest contribution to sustainable development.

To ensure accountability, governments should set up proper monitoring and evaluation mechanisms of the reforms they plan and implement to improve the business and investment climate and communicate adequately. They also need to have accurate information about their IPAs' activities and impact. For instance, MENA focus economies could better spell out their objectives and targets on investment, and equip investment promotion strategies with key performance indicators (KPIs) to raise transparency about objectives and improve monitoring and evaluation of agencies' actions.

References

ASEAN (2018), *ASEAN Statistical Highlights 2018*, https://www.aseanstats.org/wp-content/uploads/2018/10/ASEAN-Statistical-Highlights-2018.pdf. [23]

Assaad, R. and C. Krafft (2016), "Labor market dynamics and youth unemployment in the Middle East and North Africa: Evidence from Egypt, Jordan, and Tunisia", *Working Paper Series*, No. 993, Economic Research Forum, https://erf.org.eg/publications/labor-market-dynamics-and-youth-unemployment-in-the-middle-east-and-north-africa-evidence-from-egypt-jordan-and-tunisia/. [7]

Atiyas, I., I. Diwan and A. Malik (2019), "Introduction: Crony Capitalism in the Middle East: What Do We Know and Why Does it Matter?", in *Crony Capitalism in the Middle East*, Oxford University Press, http://dx.doi.org/10.1093/oso/9780198799870.003.0001. [8]

Cammett, M. et al. (2015), *A Political Economy of the Middle East*. Routledge, London. [21]

Diwan, I., P. Keefer and M. Schiffbauer (2020), "Pyramid capitalism: Cronyism, regulation, and firm productivity in Egypt", *Review of International Organizations*, Vol. 15/1, pp. 211-246, http://dx.doi.org/10.1007/s11558-018-9327-2. [18]

El-Haddad, A. (2020), "Redefining the social contract in the wake of the Arab Spring: The experiences of Egypt, Morocco and Tunisia", *World Development*, Vol. 127, p. 104774, http://dx.doi.org/10.1016/j.worlddev.2019.104774. [19]

Malik, A. and B. Awadallah (2013), "The Economics of the Arab Spring", *World Development*, Vol. 45, pp. 296-313, http://dx.doi.org/10.1016/j.worlddev.2012.12.015. [20]

Morsy, H. (2017), "Growth without change: MENA needs structural transformation", *Economic Research Forum*, https://theforum.erf.org.eg/2017/11/07/growth-without-change-mena-needs-structural-transformation/ (accessed on 29 September 2020). [25]

Morsy, H. and A. Levy (2020), "Growing without changing: A tale of Egypt's weak productivity growth", *African Development Review*, Vol. 32/3, pp. 271-287, http://dx.doi.org/10.1111/1467-8268.12438. [24]

OCDE (2017), *Examen multidimensionnel du Maroc: Volume 1. Évaluation initiale*, Les voies de développement, Éditions OCDE, Paris, https://dx.doi.org/10.1787/9789264274945-fr. [27]

OECD (2020), *COVID-19 crisis response in MENA countries*, OECD Policy Responses to Coronavirus (COVID-19), https://www.oecd.org/coronavirus/policy-responses/covid-19-crisis-response-in-mena-countries-4b366396/ (accessed on 11 February 2021). [14]

OECD (2020), *FDI in Figures: October 2020*, OECD, http://www.oecd.org/investment/investment-policy/FDI-in-Figures-October-2020.pdf (accessed on 8 December 2020). [4]

OECD (2020), *Foreign direct investment flows in the time of COVID-19*, OECD Policy Responses to Coronavirus (COVID-19), https://www.oecd.org/coronavirus/policy-responses/foreign-direct-investment-flows-in-the-time-of-covid-19-a2fa20c4/ (accessed on 9 July 2020). [10]

OECD (2020), *Investment in the MENA region in the time of COVID-19*, OECD Policy Responses to Coronavirus (COVID-19), http://www.oecd.org/coronavirus/policy-responses/investment-in-the-mena-region-in-the-time-of-covid-19-da23e4c9/ (accessed on 11 February 2021). [13]

OECD (2020), *OECD Economic Outlook, Volume 2020 Issue 2*, OECD Publishing, Paris, https://dx.doi.org/10.1787/39a88ab1-en. [11]

OECD (2020), *OECD Investment Policy Reviews: Egypt 2020*, OECD Investment Policy Reviews, OECD Publishing, Paris, https://dx.doi.org/10.1787/9f9c589a-en. [6]

OECD (2019), *Corporate governance in MENA: Building a Framework for Competitiveness and Growth*, OECD Publishing, https://doi.org/10.1787/20776535. [15]

OECD (2019), *FDI Qualities Indicators: Measuring the sustainable development impacts of investmnet*, OECD, Paris, http://www.oecd.org/fr/investissement/fdi-qualities-indicators.htm. [9]

OECD (2018), *OECD Economic Surveys: Tunisia 2018: Economic Assessment*, OECD Publishing, Paris, https://dx.doi.org/10.1787/eco_surveys-tun-2018-en. [28]

OECD (2018), *Youth Engagement and Empowerment in Jordan, Morocco and Tunisia*, MENA-OECD Governance Programme, https://www.oecd.org/mena/governance/youth-engagement-and-empowerment-report.pdf. [1]

OECD (2016), *SMEs in Libya's Reconstruction: Preparing for a Post-Conflict Economy*, The Development Dimension, OECD Publishing, Paris, https://dx.doi.org/10.1787/9789264264205-en. [26]

OECD (2016), *Strengthening governance and competitiveness in the MENA region for stronger and more inclusive growth*, Better Policies, OECD Publishing, Paris, https://dx.doi.org/10.1787/9789264265677-en. [5]

Rijkers, B., C. Freund and A. Nucifora (2017), "All in the family: State capture in Tunisia", *2017*, Vol. 124, pp. 41-59. [22]

UN (2020), *The Impact of COVID-19 on the Arab Region: An Opportunity to Build Back Better*, UN, https://unsdg.un.org/resources/policy-brief-impact-covid-19-arab-region-opportunity-build-back-better (accessed on 25 September 2020). [3]

World Bank (2019), *MENA Economic Update: Trading Together, Reviving Middle East and North Africa Regional Integration in the Post-COVID Era*, World Bank, Washington, DC, https://www.worldbank.org/en/region/mena/publication/mena-economic-update-trading-together-reviving-middle-east-and-north-africa-regional-integration-in-the-post-covid-era (accessed on 11 February 2021). [12]

World Bank (2018), *Eruptions of Popular Anger: The Economics of the Arab Spring and its Aftermath. MENA Development Report*, World Bank, Washington, DC. [2]

World Bank (2018), *Privilege-Resistant Policies in the Middle East and North Africa: Measurement and Operational Implications*, World Bank Group, Washington DC, http://dx.doi.org/10.1596/978-1-4648-1207-1. [16]

World Bank (2015), *Jobs or Privileges: Unleashing the Employment Potential of the Middle East and North Africa*, World Bank Group, Washington DC. [17]

Notes

[1] See, among others: (World Bank, 2015[17]) (Malik and Awadallah, 2013[20]) (Cammett et al., 2015[21]).

[2] Connections to the state can be formalised by current or former members of government on board, or involve more informal connections (such as family or other close personal relationships). For more details on privileged firms and their impact on economic growth see, (World Bank, 2015[17]) (Atiyas, Diwan and

Malik, 2019[8]) (compilation of analysis on the region, Egypt, Morocco, Lebanon, Tunisia and Jordan); (Diwan, Keefer and Schiffbauer, 2020[18]) (Egypt); (Rijkers, Freund and Nucifora, 2017[22]) (Tunisia).

[3] In some countries, privileged firms have been concentrated in a few sectors, while there are indications that in Egypt before 2011, politically-connected firms were present in half of all sub-sectors. Politically-connected firms appear to be more prevalent in natural resources and service sectors, including banking, real estate, tourism, media, distribution, and telecommunications. There is also evidence that privileged firms have benefited from special treatment in light manufacturing (Atiyas, Diwan and Malik, 2019[8]).

[4] In Tunisia, prior to 2011, 64% of politically connected firms operated in sectors subject to restrictions on FDI, relative to only 36% of non-connected firms (World Bank, 2015[17]).

[5] Data for 8 economies author's calculation based on COMTRADE for the year 2017 (last year available for most of the economies), except for Libya, for which 2016 data was used (last available). Total trade in goods is calculated as exports plus imports. Data for ECOWAS the average share for 2016-2018 (World Bank, 2019[12]), ASEAN data from 2017 (ASEAN, 2018[23]).

[6] For a discussion on productivity growth and structural transformation in selected MENA focus economies, see for instance (Morsy and Levy, 2020[24]) and (OECD, 2020[6]) for Egypt (Morsy, 2017[25]) for Jordan, (OECD, 2016[26]) for Libya, (OCDE, 2017[27]) for Morocco, and (OECD, 2018[28]) for Tunisia

[7] FDI can also have an indirect impact on job creation. In Jordan, for instance, FDI inflow had positive employment spillovers among domestic service providers, although it also led to a partial crowding-out of domestic firms operating in the same sector (World Bank, 2015[17]).

[8] Remittances play an important role in several of the focus economies. In 2019, remittances totalled between 10 and 16% of GDP in Jordan, Lebanon and the Palestinian Authority, and between 5 and 9% of GDP in Morocco and Egypt (World Bank Development Indicators).

[9] For details on the Covid-19 crisis response in MENA countries, see (OECD, 2020[13]) and (OECD, 2020[14]) for specific information on investment policy responses.

2 Foreign investment trends and sustainable development benefits

This chapter reviews trends in foreign investment in the eight MENA focus economies, including top investing partners and which countries and sectors attract the most greenfield investment. The chapter also explores the development benefits of FDI in the region, including the impact of investment on productivity, jobs, skills, gender equality and carbon footprint, based on the OECD FDI Qualities Indicators.

Summary

Middle Eastern and North African economies have the market, resource and human capital potential to attract high levels of foreign direct investment (FDI). Yet they have not been as successful as other emerging and developing economies at attracting FDI, or leveraging investment to advance socio-economic goals. Reliance on a few industries, periods of political instability, and macroeconomic and labour market challenges have, and continue to negatively affect economic and investment growth.[1] In the past several years however, most MENA governments have undertaken meaningful reforms to improve the investment climate. These important efforts are explored in the subsequent chapters of this report. Some countries have already seen positive returns to reforms, including more investment in sectors that can advance job creation, exports and productivity, and more diversified sources of FDI. An analysis of recent FDI trends in the region points to several challenges ahead however.

The coronavirus (Covid-19) health and economic crisis has significantly reduced FDI inflows across the globe. In the first half of 2020, global flows fell by 50% compared to the preceding six months (OECD, 2020[1]). Initial data shows an acute decline in investment in MENA region. In the first half of 2020, greenfield investments to the eight economies covered in this report (MENA focus economies) were 80% less, in total announced value, than in the first half of 2019, a substantially sharper decline than in emerging and developing economies as a whole and OECD countries (fDi Markets by the FT). The pandemic and related supply disruptions, demand contractions and pessimistic outlook of economic actors are likely to depress global FDI flows through the end of 2021 at least (OECD, 2020[1]). Low oil demand and prices will particularly affect energy exporters in the region. There may be opportunities for some MENA countries to take advantage of potential changes to global supply chains in the aftermath of the crisis; some governments have begun to market themselves to European MNEs as an alternative to Asian labour markets. But several countries remain reliant on a few source investors, making them even more vulnerable to external shocks. Worsening political and security dynamics in some MENA countries are also likely to negatively affect FDI inflows in the near to medium term.

The ongoing global and regional economic challenges make improving the positive impact of investment all the more important. The sectors that attract the most FDI in the MENA region – including real estate, construction, mining and fuels – do not contribute the most to productivity, employment or green growth. Nearly 50% of all jobs created by FDI in the eight focus economies have been in manufacturing, but despite some growth, the sector only accounts for 25% of total FDI, compared to 40% in most ASEAN economies (OECD, 2018[2]). In the MENA region, the benefits of FDI for productivity, labour market outcomes and the environment do not always materialise, and not as much as host governments expect. The extent of the benefits of FDI differ across MENA countries, highlighting that local economic factors and policy play key roles in shaping the impact of FDI on sustainable development.

Investment trends point to challenges ahead

FDI to the MENA economies remains below potential

Before the pandemic, investment in the eight focus economies had been stagnating. On average, the region did not recover from the 2008 global financial crisis and Arab Spring movements of 2010-11 (Figure 2.1). Inward FDI rose following weak inflows in 2011, and by 2014 FDI performance was fairly strong relative to the size of the regional economy. But inflows then plateaued and slightly declined, mirroring an overall decline in global FDI flows in recent years. In 2018, inflows to the eight MENA focus economies were only half the levels reached ten years prior. There are some positive outliers: investment in Morocco in 2019 surpassed 2008 levels, and Egypt achieved six years of steady increases in FDI until 2016. But in the years before the pandemic, FDI in most countries in the region had stagnated, decreased, or in the case of Libya, halted.

Figure 2.1. MENA inward FDI flows: trends and performance

MENA FDI inflows in USD millions (left axis); FDI inflows as a share of GDP (right axis)

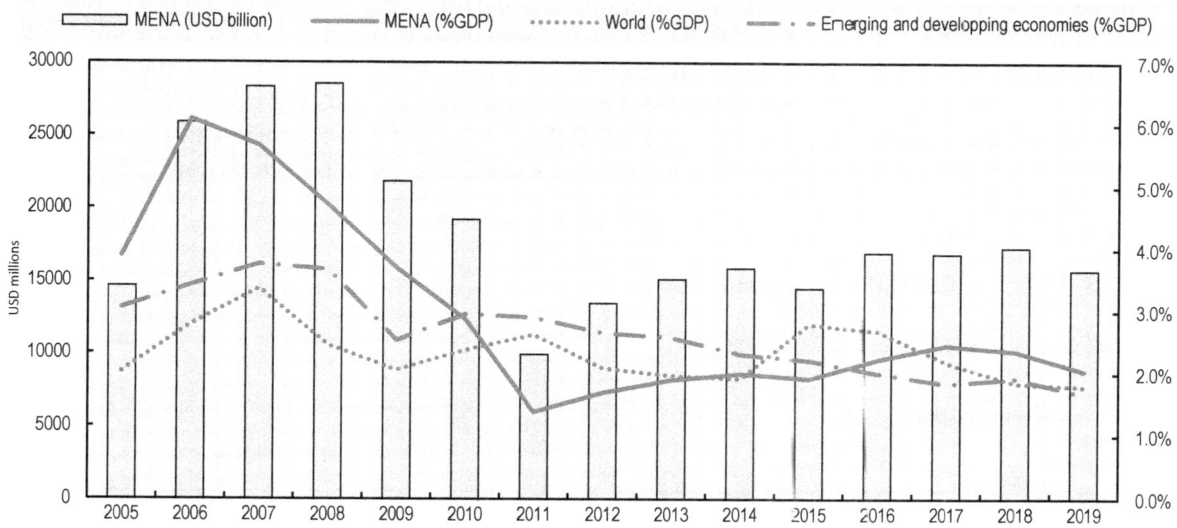

Note: Data for the eight economies covered by the report. MENA inflows as share of GDP exclude the Palestinian Authority.
Source: IMF Balance of Payments database, IMF World Economic Outlook database and OECD FDI statistics database.

Global competition for investment in the aftermath of the 2008 global financial crisis has been high, particularly among developing economies, and the MENA region has remained a minor destination for FDI (Figure 2.2). In 2019, FDI inflows to the eight focus economies accounted for less than 1% of global FDI inflows; comparatively, ASEAN countries and Latin American and Caribbean countries each received 11% of global inflows in 2018.[2] This was the highest share the MENA region received in almost a decade, however, and in recent years the focus economies have attracted a higher share of investment relative to their weight in the global economy.

Figure 2.2. MENA FDI attractiveness relative to the rest of the world

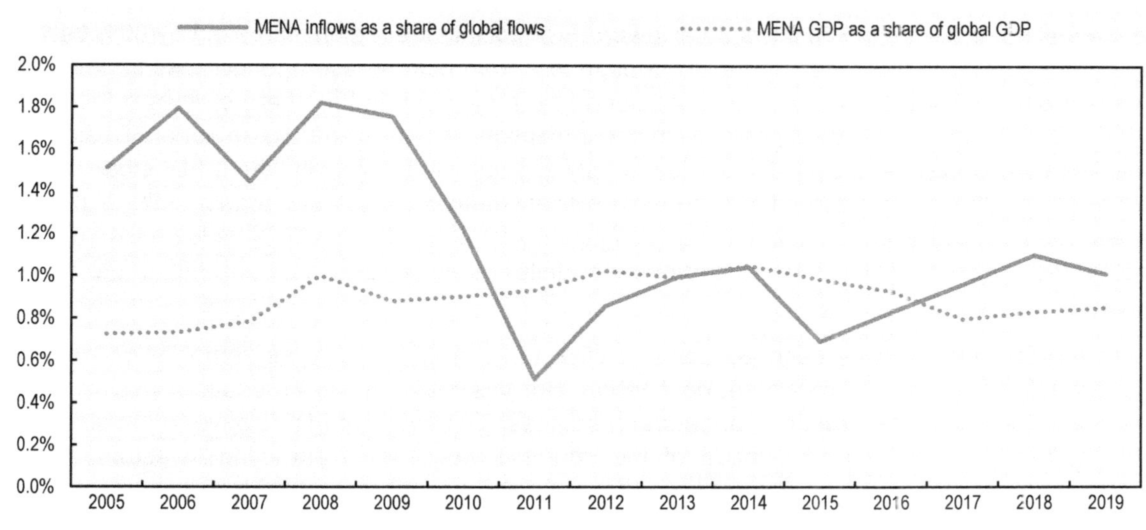

Note: MENA GDP as share of global GDP for the eight focus economies except the Palestinian Authority.
Source: IMF Balance of Payments database, IMF World Economic Outlook database (GDP) and OECD FDI statistics database.

FDI inflows to the MENA region, and to all countries, have declined sharply due to COVID-19 pandemic and resulting global supply disruptions, demand contractions, and pessimistic outlook of economic actors. In the first stages of the pandemic, the OECD projected a 40% decline in global FDI flows in 2020 under the most pessimistic scenario, but this percentage could drop even lower as new investment projects and earnings of MNEs remain depressed (OECD, 2020[1]). Greenfield investments – the dominant mode of entry of FDI in most of the MENA focus economies – have been significantly affected. Initial data shows that capital expenditures on announced greenfield projects declined by 80% in the eight focus economies in the first half of 2020 compared to the first half of 2019 (Figure 2.3). This is a significantly greater decrease than in emerging and developing economies as a whole and OECD countries, which saw declines of 42% and 17% respectively.

Figure 2.3. Effect of Covid-19 on greenfield FDI

Announced capital expenditure, USD millions

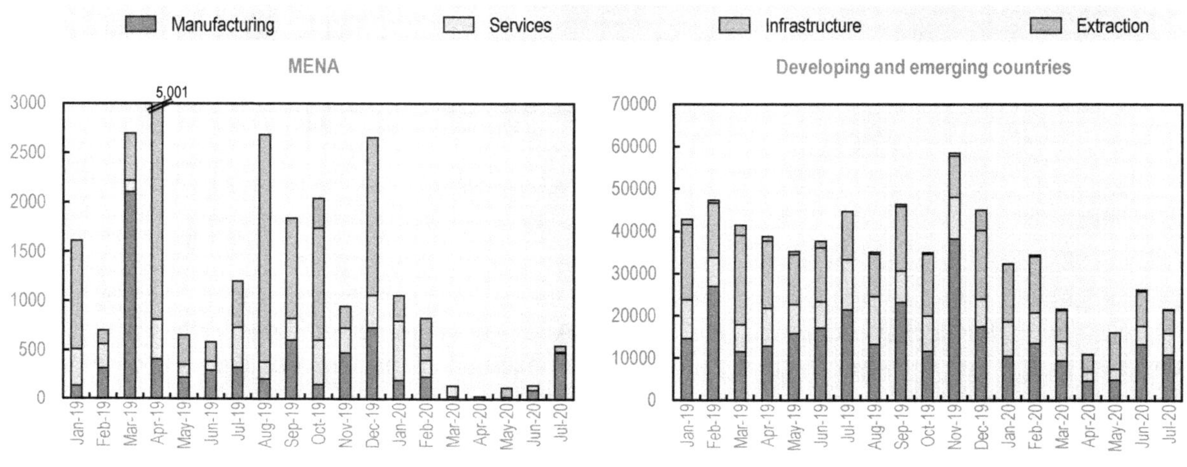

Source: OECD based on Financial Times fDi Markets, as of 10 September 2020.

Some MENA economies were more resilient to economic shocks than others

Despite stagnating or declining FDI flows, total inward FDI stock in the region increased by 80% between 2008 and 2019, similar to increases in the EU, though less than half the average increase in developing countries overall (UNCTAD, 2020[3]). There has been little movement in the share of inward FDI stocks obtained by each country since 2008 peaks, with one exception: Tunisia's share of regional FDI stock has substantially decreased (Figure 2.4). Tunisia is the only economy in the region where FDI stock declined following the Arab Spring protests and subsequent political changes. Egypt, the largest of the eight focus economies in terms of GDP and population, has consistently attracted the most FDI, holding a third of total FDI stock in the region in 2019. Morocco and Lebanon follow, holding just under one-fifth of the region's stock each.

The share of FDI stock held by each economy relative to its neighbours gives some indication of the country's attractiveness as an investment destination. But this may be due to location-specific factors, including market size and the presence of natural resources. The share of FDI relative to the size of the domestic market gives a better indication of the country's success in attracting investors and the importance of FDI to the economy. The average FDI-to-GDP ratio in the eight MENA economies is fairly high compared to other emerging economies, as well as the average for OECD and G20 countries (Figure 2.5) (OECD, 2020[4]). This is partly explained by Lebanon, where investment in real estate and the financial sector contributed to a stock level equal to 116% of GDP in 2019. Algeria, Egypt, Libya, Morocco and Tunisia have all seen increases in FDI relative to the size of their economy in the past decade; this ratio has decreased in Jordan, Lebanon, and the Palestinian Authority. In Libya however, the growth of FDI stocks as a share of GDP is largely due to a drop in GDP following the start of armed conflict in 2010, rather than an increase in FDI.

Figure 2.4. Changes in distribution of FDI stock within MENA focus economies

Share of total inward FDI stock to the 8 economies

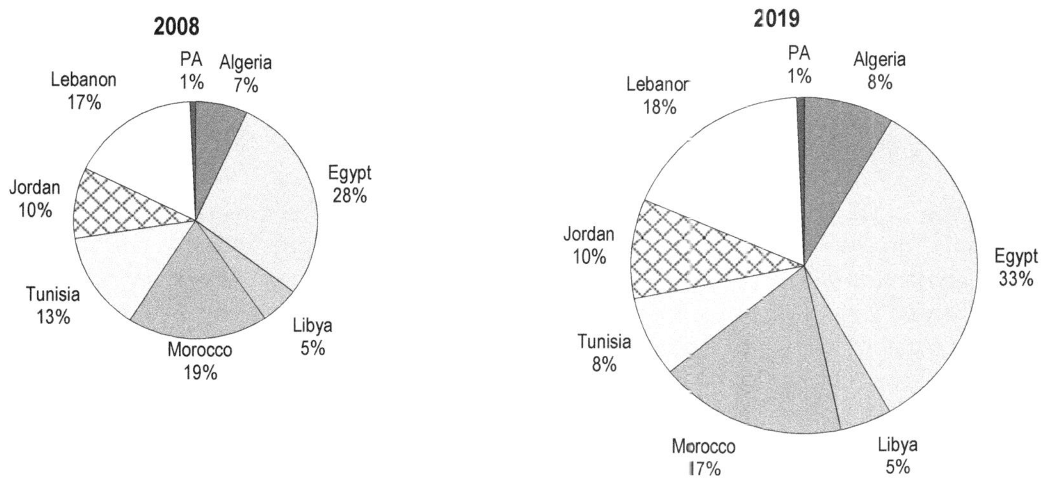

Note: Figure not to scale. Inward FDI stocks in 2019 were 1.8 times more than stocks in 2008. P.A. refers to Palestinian Authority.
Source: UNCTAD Statistics.

Figure 2.5. Importance of FDI to GDP in MENA and other economies

Inward FDI stocks as % of GDP

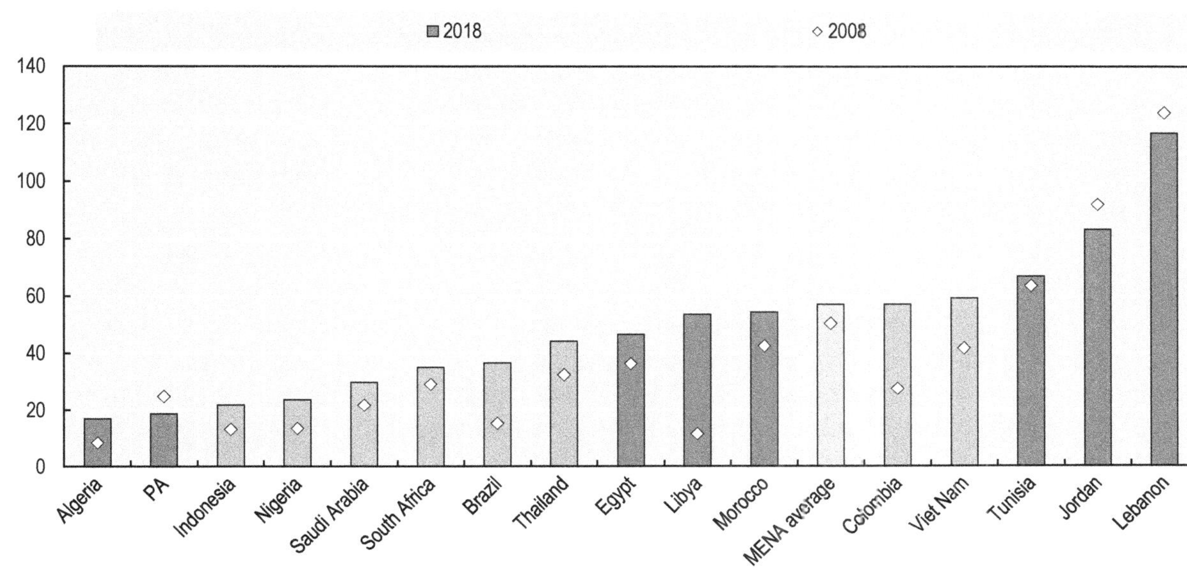

Source: UNCTAD Statistics.

MENA economies primarily attract FDI from Gulf countries and increasingly from Asia-Pacific

Not all MENA countries collect data on FDI inflows by partner country, and those that do can sometimes differ in their methodology and in their degree of compliance with international guidelines (Box 2.1). Discrepancies in the definition, coverage or estimation methods used to compile the statistics are common.[3] In absence of comprehensive and comparable official statistics on bilateral and sectoral FDI flows, data on announced greenfield investment projects can be helpful to support a comparative analysis for the eight focus economies.[4] Greenfield investment is the dominant mode of entry of FDI in most MENA countries, as in many developing economies (Burger, Ianchovichina and Rijkers, 2013[5]). Greenfield projects data also gives an indication of growth of a sector, as it captures new investments or expansions, as opposed to changes in ownership or mergers of existing activities.

Box 2.1. OECD's Benchmark Definition for FDI, 4th edition

FDI is one of the major types of investment included in the balance of payments (BOP) and international investment position (IIP) statistics. The IMF in its Balance of Payments and International Investment Position Manual, 6th edition (BPM6) and the OECD in its Benchmark Definition of Foreign Direct Investment, 4th edition (BMD4) set the international standards for compiling FDI statistics. BMD4 is completely consistent with the guidance in BPM6 but provides more detailed guidance on the compilation of FDI statistics; for example, BMD4 provides more detailed guidance for compiling FDI statistics by immediate partner country and by industry than BPM6. BMD4 also provides guidance on compiling inward FDI statistics that produce more meaningful measures of inward investment, such as an inward FDI statistics by ultimate investing country. This presentation provides information on the country of the investor who ultimately controls the investment. It also identifies the amount of inward investment that results from round-tripping, which is the channelling abroad of local funds and their subsequent return to the country in the form of direct investment.

The recommended measures of FDI statistics in BMD4 produce FDI statistics that are part of the larger System of National Accounts (SNA), on internationally agreed standard set of recommendations on how to compile measures of economic activity, such as GDP, gross national income, trade, and foreign borrowing and lending.

FDI statistics can be an important input for evaluating the impact of reforms to improve the investment climate in countries. To support informed policy-making, the OECD has undertaken reviews of four MENA countries' compilation of FDI statistics (Egypt, Jordan, Morocco and Tunisia). These reviews assess their implementation of the international guidelines for FDI statistics, including the OECD's BMD4, and make concrete recommendations for improvement. The reviews are available at: https://www.oecd.org/investment/foreign-direct-investment-statistics-review-series.htm.

Most greenfield investment to the eight focus economies comes from within the wider MENA region (Figure 2.6). Between 2003-2019, 37% of all greenfield investment to the eight economies came from Gulf Cooperation Council (GCC) countries. Europe (including the EU, EEA, the UK and Switzerland) was the second largest regional source of greenfield FDI over the same period, followed by Asia-Pacific and eastern Europe (notably Russia and Turkey). North America has been a much less prominent source of investment, though some US firms may invest through EU affiliates.

Countries in East and South Asia have become more important investors in the MENA region in the past five years (Figure 2.6, right panel). Firms based in Asia have supplied more FDI to the eight MENA economies since 2015 than any other region, although this high percentage is largely due to one Chinese megaproject in Egypt, an agreement in 2016 to invest 20 billion USD to build a new administrative capital.[5]

Figure 2.6. Greenfield FDI to MENA focus economies by source region

As a % of total announced greenfield FDI 2003-2019 (left) and 20015-2019 (right)

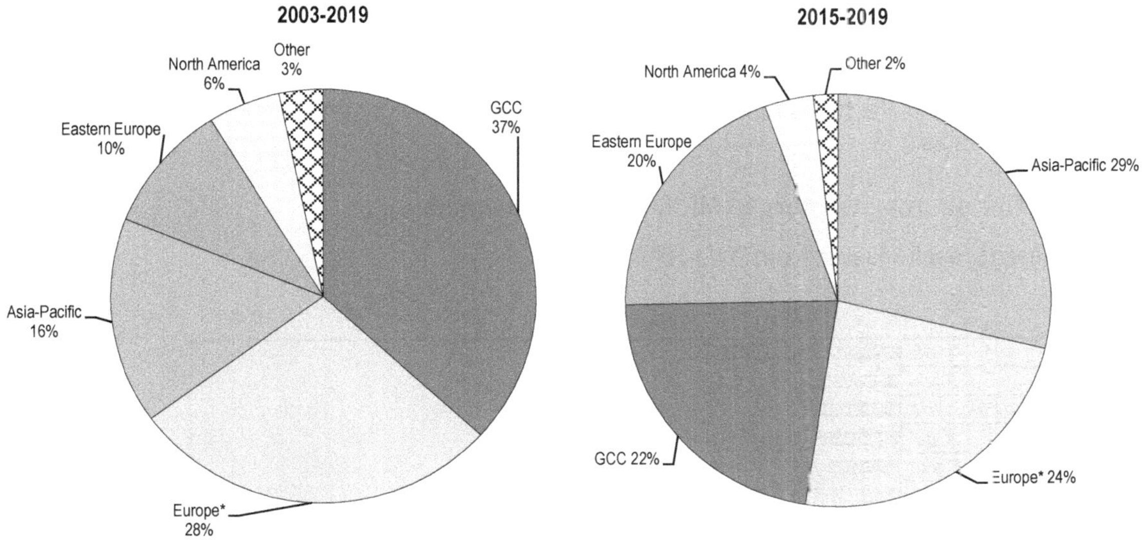

Note: Europe* refers to countries in the EU and EEA, as well the UK and Switzerland. Eastern Europe includes Russia, Turkey, Ukraine and Belarus. Other includes non-GCC MENA countries, Africa, Latin America and the Caribbean.
Source: fDi Markets by the FT.

High intra-MENA greenfield investment contrasts with overall low regional trade integration. Among the eight focus economies, the share of intra-regional trade in goods as a share of total trade was just 4% in 2017, a substantially lower share than for regional economic communities in West Africa (intra-regional trade among ECOWAS members is around 9%) and Southeast Asia (ASEAN intra-regional trade in goods is around 23%).[6]. Trade restrictions (including tariffs and non-tariff barriers), poor regional infrastructure, and geopolitical relations have all negatively affected trade integration (OECD, 2018[6]), (Kireyev et al., 2019[7]). While intra-regional investment is stronger, it is primarily in the non-tradeable sector and one-directional. Gulf countries are important sources of investment for other MENA countries, but FDI flows between non-GCC MENA economies are marginal, representing only 1% of total greenfield investment since 2003.

Within the GCC, the UAE has been the largest individual investor in the eight economies; more than half of all greenfield investment from MENA countries between 2003 and 2019 came from Emirati-based firms. Bahrain, Saudi Arabia and Qatar follow, each providing between 10 and 16% of greenfield investment from MENA countries over the 17 year period. Saudi Arabia has become a more important investor in focus economies in recent years, however; around a third of greenfield FDI from MENA countries in the past five years came from firms based in the Kingdom. This follows a push by the Kingdom to diversify the economy, including investments in its sovereign wealth portfolio, away from oil and gas.

Investors from the GCC have overwhelmingly favoured projects in real estate and construction. Just under two-thirds of GCC investment to the eight focus economies between 2003-19 has been in the sector. Moreover, 70% of all investment in real estate and construction has come from GCC firms. Investors from Eastern Europe have also primarily invested in one sector; nearly 80% of investment from the region over the 17 year period went to mining and fuel projects. Conversely, investments from Asia-Pacific and Europe have been slightly more diversified; both regions have primarily invested in manufacturing projects, followed closely by real estate (for Asia Pacific investors) and mining and fuels (for European investors).

Maghreb countries have generally attracted more investors from Europe than the other MENA economies covered in this report, corresponding to historical and linguistic ties, as well as trade networks, between Europe and North Africa. Of the eight economies, Tunisia is the most reliant on European investors, four out of the top five source countries (in terms of announced greenfield investment since 2003) are European (Figure 2.7). Other economies in the region are more dependent on one source country for FDI. In Lebanon, Libya and the Palestinian Authority, half or more of all announced greenfield investment since 2003 has come from one country (UAE, Bahrain and Qatar, respectively). High reliance on one or small group of economies leaves the host country vulnerable to changes in economic and geopolitical conditions in those source countries.

Figure 2.7. Top five source investors to MENA focus economies

% of total announced greenfield investment 2003-2019

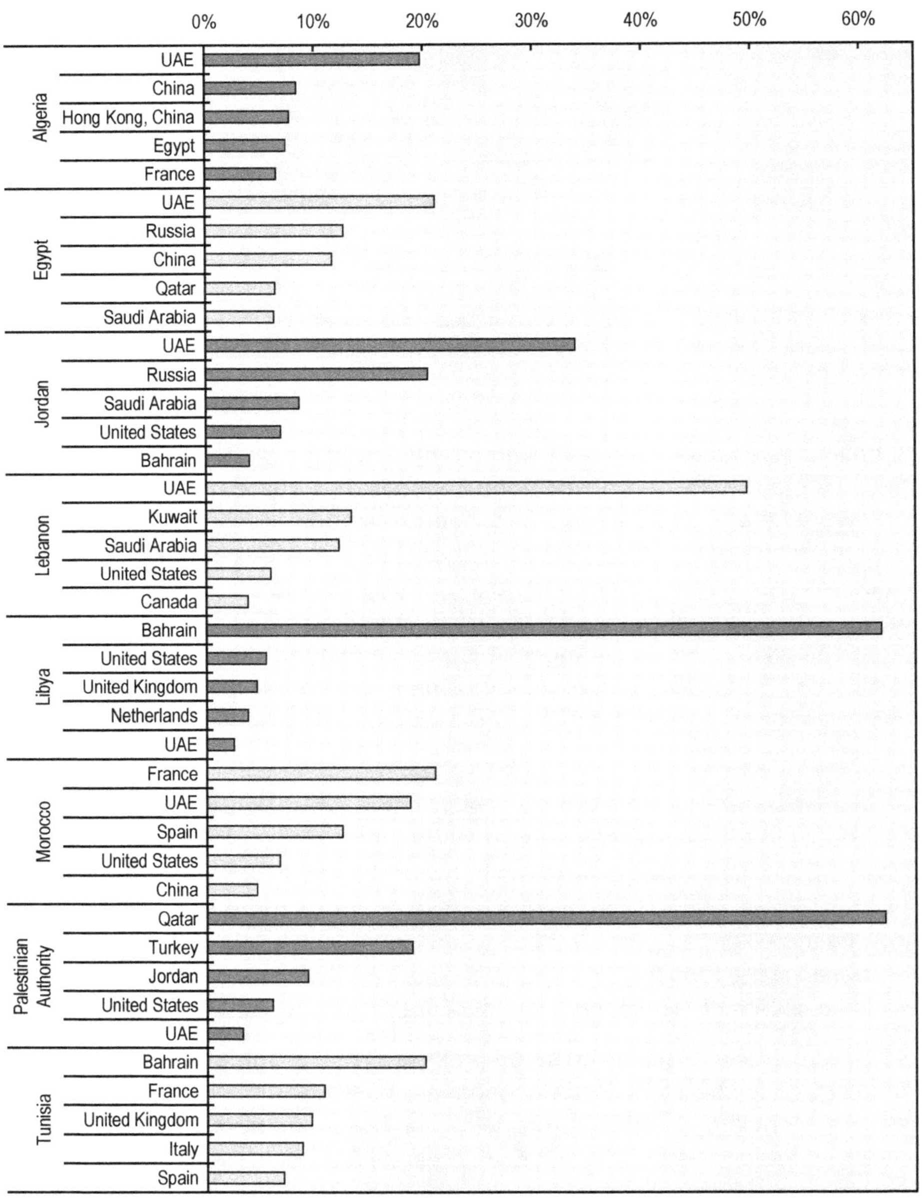

Note: Sources of greenfield investment can differ substantially from bilateral FDI positions as reported by central banks.
Source: fDi Markets by the FT.

Based on greenfield data, Algeria and Morocco have the most diversified sources of investment, their top five investors come from the MENA region, Asia-Pacific, Europe, and in the case of Morocco, North America. It is notable that sources of greenfield investment can differ substantially from bilateral FDI positions as reported by central banks, which take into account other types of FDI and historical inflows. These data, while not comparable across countries due to different methodologies used in collection, also reveal substantial reliance on investors from the EU and Gulf countries.

Mining and fuels have attracted the most greenfield investment in recent years, but manufacturing investment is growing

FDI to the MENA region has long been concentrated in a narrow group of sectors. Real estate and construction has attracted the most greenfield investment in the focus economies, receiving more than one-third of total announced greenfield FDI between 2003 and 2019. Mining and fuel projects follow with around one-fourth of FDI, while manufacturing industries attracted just under one-fourth during the same period. Service sectors, including transport and warehousing, business services and tourism received 15% of announced greenfield FDI. Comparatively, around 40% of greenfield FDI to ASEAN countries goes to manufacturing, and 40% to services (excluding Singapore and Malaysia) (OECD, 2018[2]).[7] A closer look at variations between years reveals a different ordering of sectors, suggesting some of the implications of the economic and political shocks that most affected the region from 2009 to 2012, and market developments since then (Figure 2.8). FDI inflows increased in most of the focus economies after 2012; it is therefore useful to consider how investment evolved in the period 2013-19, during which many MENA governments implemented important investment and economic reforms.

Figure 2.8. Greenfield FDI in MENA focus economies by sector

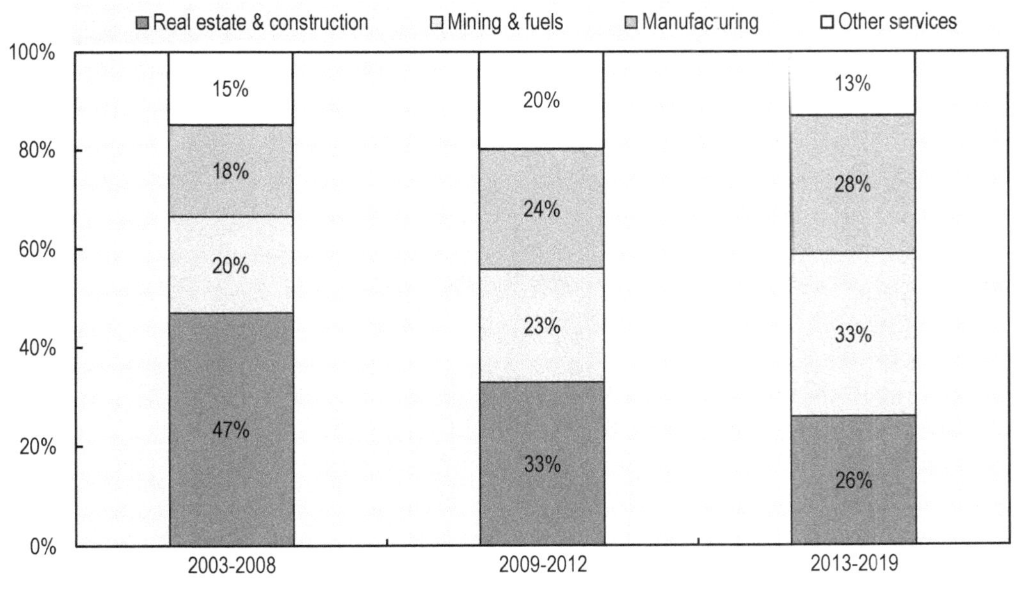

Note: Investment as percentage of total announced greenfield FDI in the eight economies during years indicated.
Source: fDi Markets by the FT.

The share of investment in mining and fuels increased substantially from 2013 to 2019 compared to the period before the last economic crisis (2003-2008), while the share of FDI in real estate and construction nearly halved (Figure 2.8). That minerals and fuels received a greater percentage of greenfield investment in the region, relative to other sectors, is in line with research that shows that FDI in natural resources is fairly insensitive to political instability (Burger, Ianchovichina and Rijkers, 2013[5]). The substantial increase in mineral and fuel investments was largely driven by a few mega-projects: Egypt attracted USD 20 billion to its off-shore gas fields in 2017, while Jordan reached a USD10 billion agreement in 2013 for the creation and operation of a nuclear power plant.[8] Egypt has consistently attracted the vast majority of investment in mining and fuels among the eight focus economies.

Notably, investment in manufacturing has also increased in recent years, though some countries have been more successful than others at growing this sector (Figure 2.9). FDI in manufacturing has considerably increased as a share of total greenfield FDI in Algeria, Morocco and Tunisia – more than half of greenfield investment to these economies in recent years has gone to manufacturing. Manufacturing investment has also increased in Egypt, which receives the most investment in the sector in terms of capital expenditure. Despite a relative increase in Algeria, in absolute value greenfield investment in manufacturing in the country has declined. FDI in manufacturing in Lebanon has also declined in absolute value and as a share of total greenfield investment. Jordan and Libya have not seen an increase in manufacturing FDI relative to other sectors or in absolute value.

Figure 2.9. Greenfield FDI in manufacturing has increased in recent years

A. Manufacturing as % greenfield FDI

B. Manufacturing FDI by sub-sector, 2003-2019

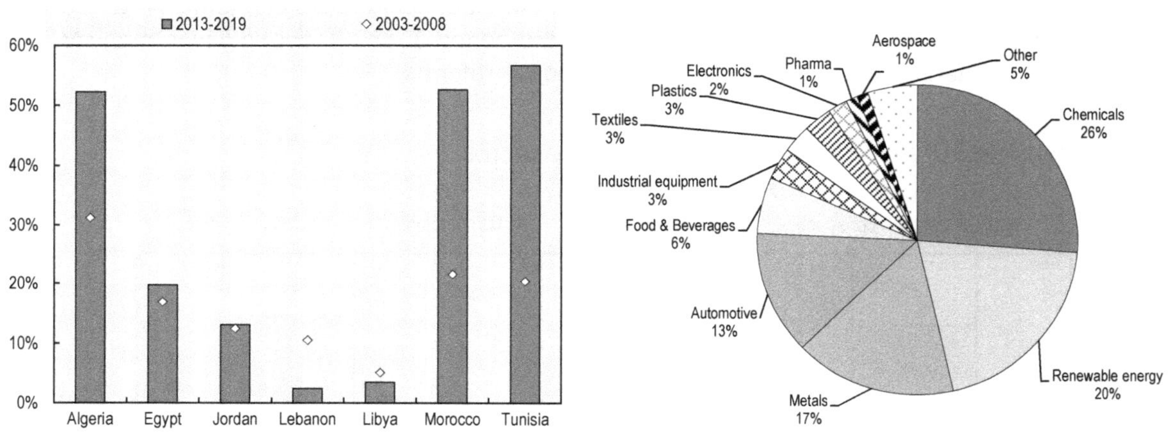

Note: A. Palestinian Authority omitted due to absence of data. B. Percentage of greenfield manufacturing FDI received by each sub-sector.
Source: fDi Markets by the FT.

Within manufacturing, the sectors that have received the most investment in the region since 2003 are chemicals, renewable energy, metals, and automotive components (Figure 2.9, panel B). Renewable energy has become a more important manufacturing sector in the region in recent years, receiving around one-third of all manufacturing greenfield FDI since 2013, more than any other manufacturing sector.

Service sectors have consistently attracted the least greenfield investment in region; services other than transport and warehousing received only 7% of total greenfield FDI between 2013 and 2019. There are nonetheless a few examples of increased investments in services in recent years, notably in Lebanon, Morocco and Tunisia. In Lebanon, one-quarter of FDI in recent years has gone to services, including communications, transport and warehousing, and financial services, compared to only 5% before the 2008 economic crisis.

The growth of FDI in manufacturing in recent years is notable, but manufacturing still attracts a relatively small amount overall investment in most of the focus economies, and the service sector even less (Figure 2.10). The vast majority of FDI to MENA region has been, and continues to be, in capital-intensive sectors. These sectors have contributed little to productivity and job creation, key to sustainable economic growth.

This report argues that further diversifying investment will require adapting policies and addressing challenges across the investment policy framework. Subsequent chapters provide analysis and policy recommendations to this end, in order to boost investment that will support development aims. MENA policymakers could consider, for example, reassessing remaining statutory restrictions on foreign investors, particularly in service sectors (Chapter 4), as well assess whether investment promotion strategies and tools, including investment incentives, are clear, targeted and well aligned with national development strategies (Chapters 6 and 7). Supporting investment in infrastructure and greater linkages between multinational and local firms can help promote FDI in more diverse locations and sectors, and advance participation in global value chains (Chapters 8 and 9). As the rest of this chapter will explore, there is substantial opportunity to harness FDI for sustainable development.

Figure 2.10. Greenfield FDI by sector per MENA economy

% of announced greenfield FDI 2003-2019

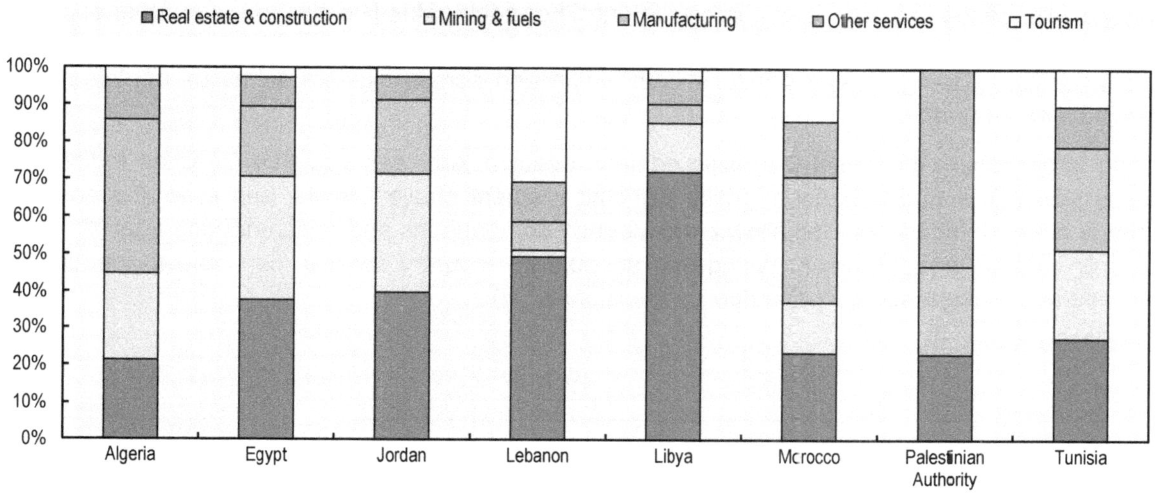

Source: fDi Markets by the FT.

Harnessing FDI for sustainable development

FDI can play a crucial role in advancing the Sustainable Development Goals (SDGs) in MENA countries, as well as in supporting their recovery from the Covid-19 pandemic and subsequent economic crisis. FDI can create quality jobs, enhance productivity growth and innovation, develop human capital, and raise living standards and environmental sustainability. By linking domestic firms to multinational enterprises (MNEs), FDI also serves as a conduit to access international markets and integrate in global value chains (GVCs) (see chapter 8).

However, realising the positive contribution of FDI to sustainable development is not a given. Maximising benefits and minimising potential risks associated with FDI may not be a primary concern for profit-seeking investors, and may not receive sufficient attention by policymakers seeking to attract investment. While in principal FDI has the potential to advance sustainable development, private sector incentives and both home and host country policies require careful consideration as they play a critical role in realising this potential.

This section reviews how FDI relates to sustainable development outcomes in the MENA region. It draws on the findings of the OECD FDI Qualities Indicators (Box 2.2), which measure the relationship between

FDI and five sustainable development goals: productivity and innovation, employment and job quality, skills, gender equality, and carbon footprint.

Box 2.2. The OECD FDI Qualities Indicators

FDI Qualities Indicators describe how FDI relates to specific aspects of sustainable development in host countries. They are structured around economic, social and environmental sustainability. An in-depth assessment of all 17 SDGs, and their corresponding targets, was undertaken to identify the full spectrum of FDI Qualities – that is, areas where FDI may contribute to achieving the SDGs. This assessment further considers the extent to which FDI potential for advancing the SDGs is reflected in the OECD Policy Framework of Investment, including related frameworks and guidelines, such as the OECD Guidelines on Multinational Enterprises and the OECD Policy Guidance for Investment in Clean Energy Infrastructure.

The FDI Qualities Indicators focus on five clusters: productivity and innovation, employment and job quality, skills, gender equality, and carbon footprint. For each of the five clusters, a number of different outcomes are identified and used to produce indicators that relate them to FDI or activity of foreign multinationals, allowing for comparisons both within and across clusters so as to identify potential sustainability trade-offs.

Taking into account the country-specific context, policymakers can use FDI Qualities Indicators to assess how FDI supports national policy objectives, where challenges lie, and in what areas policy action is needed. Indicators also allow cross-country comparisons and benchmarking against regional peers or income groups, which, taking into account the country context, can help to identify good practices and make evidence-based policy decisions.

Source: (OECD, 2019[8]).

The sectors that receive the most investment in the MENA region do not create the most jobs

MENA governments devote large resources to attract foreign investment in the hope that it will create jobs. Unemployment in the region has worsened since 2011; the average unemployment rate before the Covid-19 crisis was 14.6%, and twice as high among youth (ILOSTAT, 2020[9]). The extent to which FDI creates jobs varies depending on the host country's economic structure and level of development. FDI in capital intensive sectors, including natural resources and real estate, generate fewer jobs per dollar invested than those in labour-intensive industries or services (OECD, 2019[8]).

In the MENA region, as described above, periods of political instability in many countries has skewed the sectoral composition of FDI towards the natural resources sector, thus limiting the creation of new job opportunities. Overall, countries with stronger industrial sectors, such as Morocco and Tunisia, see larger effects of greenfield FDI on employment than countries where natural resources or other capital-intensive sectors dominate, including Algeria, Egypt, Jordan and Libya (Figure 2.11, panel A). FDI projects hosted by the relatively small Lebanese and Palestinian economies created more jobs than in the average host country.

Across the eight MENA focus economies, half of all jobs created by greenfield projects are in the manufacturing sector, which only receives one-fourth of the region's FDI (Figure 2.11, panel B). Within manufacturing, automotive components have created the most FDI-related jobs, followed by textiles, food and beverage, and metals. These results are only a partial picture of the impact of FDI on jobs however, as they reflect greenfield projects and not foreign takeovers (M&A). They also do not take into account indirect job creation or destruction through FDI spillovers to other firms. For instance, FDI in Jordan led to a partial crowding-out of old and small domestic firms operating in the same sector, but had positive employment spillovers among service providers and young firms (World Bank, 2015[10]).

Figure 2.11. FDI is not concentrated in sectors with greatest job-creating potential

Total announced greenfield FDI 2003-2019, aggregate for the eight MENA focus economies (left)

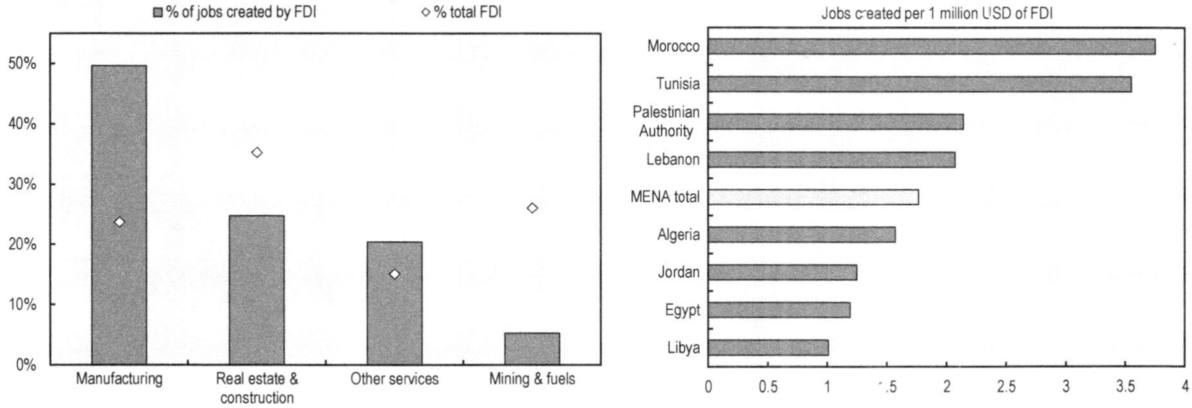

Note: Based on total (announced) Greenfield FDI in the eight countries between 2003 and 2019. Panel A. (left) compares which sectors receive the most FDI in the region and which sectors generate the most jobs (based on the total number of jobs created by FDI investments). Panel B. (right) shows the estimated number of jobs created per 1 million USD of FDI per country.
Source: fDi Markets by the FT.

FDI has the potential to improve working conditions, but benefits are often not realised in MENA

While job creation is crucial, job quality is equally important to advance inclusive development. Wage is one aspect of job quality. On average across OECD and many non-OECD countries, foreign affiliates pay higher wages than domestic firms (Figure 2.12, panel A). This is because foreign firms are often more productive, larger and have more skilled worker than their domestic peers (see next sub-section). However, except in Egypt, there is no significant difference in wages between foreign and domestic firms in observed MENA focus economies. This is consistent with the findings that foreign firms in these economies tend not to be more productive or employ more skilled workers than domestic firms (see next sub-sections).

Morocco is an interesting exception; MNEs in Morocco are on average more productive, but do not pay higher wages. This could be because foreign firms may be concentrated in sectors with competitive labour costs. It could also be that MNEs are active in highly-concentrated markets with little competition – which in turn can generate rents. In most countries, higher productivity of foreign firms does not fully translate to wage benefits for workers. On average across OECD and non-OECD countries, foreign firms are twice as productive as domestic firms, but they pay only 50% higher wages (OECD, 2019[8]).

FDI also has the potential to foster skills development in host countries Foreign firms are often more technologically advanced, and tend to hire more skilled workers than domestic firms operating in the same sector. Across sectors, the average foreign firm in the MENA region do not employ more skilled workers than its domestic peer, an outcome also observed in OECD and non-OECD countries (Figure 2.12, panel B). As outlined in this chapter, greenfield FDI in the eight focus economies is largely concentrated in sectors with lower shares of skilled workers, including construction, mining and light manufacturing (such as textiles). In general, countries with a large labour force and relatively low labour costs tend to attract more FDI in labour-intensive and low-skilled manufacturing activities. This can also result from a shortage or inadequate supply of skills needed for foreign investors' activities.

Figure 2.12. Wage and non-wage working conditions of foreign and domestic manufacturers

Are foreign firms more performant than their domestic peers? (yes if score > 0)

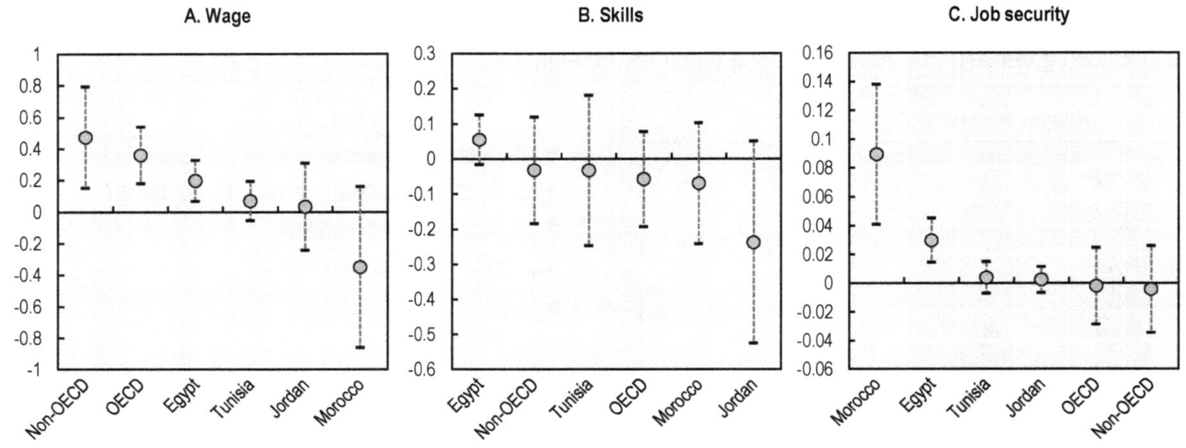

Note: The figure includes confidence intervals that indicate statistical significance at the 95% level. If the confidence interval crosses the zero line, the difference between foreign and domestic firms is statistically insignificant. Job security is measured as the share of workers with permanent contracts. For further details, see OECD (2019a).
Source: Based on OECD (2019a) and World Bank Enterprise Surveys of Egypt (2020), Jordan (2019), Morocco (2019), and Tunisia (2020). Jordan's indicator on wage is based on the 2013 Survey.

Attracting FDI in low-skilled activities is not necessarily a negative outcome if foreign firms can expand and upgrade workers' skills in these sectors. On-the-job training is one avenue by which companies can contribute to skills development, and some MENA governments provide fiscal or financial incentives to firms that provide skills training (see Chapter 7 on investment incentives). Across countries in the region with available data, foreign affiliates in Egypt, Jordan and Tunisia do not offer significantly more job training than domestic peers, an outcome observed in other developing countries too (OECD, 2019[8]).

Also important to job quality are non-wage aspects such as job security or occupational health – the latter has become even more relevant since the outbreak of the Covid-19 pandemic. Across countries, foreign firms tend to rely more on temporary workers than domestic firms (Figure 2.12, panel C). But this less the case in some MENA economies, particularly in Morocco and Egypt, since foreign firms offer more permanent contracts than domestic peers. In general, a higher reliance on temporary work could reflect MNEs concentration in sectors with more exposure to global trade fluctuations, or in special regulatory regimes with more flexible labour rules, such as special economic zones.

FDI can enhance productivity, but foreign firms in MENA are not always more productive

Foreign firms are on average more productive and innovative than domestic ones (Figure 2.13). This is not surprising, as affiliates of foreign firms are often larger, and bring advanced technology and managerial knowhow. This positive outcome of FDI can be observed in Egypt and Morocco, as labour productivity is significantly higher among foreign firms compared to domestic peers. They also engage more in R&D activities (Panel B) and rely more on foreign technology in their production (Panel C). Foreign firms in Jordan and Tunisia are not significantly more productive or innovative than their peers, however.

In some cases, the absence of a productivity premium among foreign businesses may be because they are concentrated in low-productivity sectors. In other cases, some domestic firms (such as state-owned or linked- enterprises) may have significant advantages, market protection and rents in some sectors (OECD,

2020[11]). For instance, in Tunisia prior to 2011, 64% of politically connected firms operated in sectors subject to restrictions on FDI, relative to only 36% of non-connected firms (World Bank, 2015[10]).

While the existence of a productivity premium among foreign firms is a positive outcome for host countries, excessive performance gaps between foreign and domestic firms could also impede MNEs from forging linkages with, or passing knowledge to, domestic firms (see chapter 8 on SME linkages with foreign firms). This may be the case in Morocco, where global leaders in the automotive and aeronautic sector have only partially connected with local SMEs. Large productivity gaps could also lead to crowding out of domestic competitors.

Figure 2.13. Productivity and innovation outcomes of foreign and domestic manufacturers

Are foreign firms more performant than their domestic peers? (yes if score > 0)

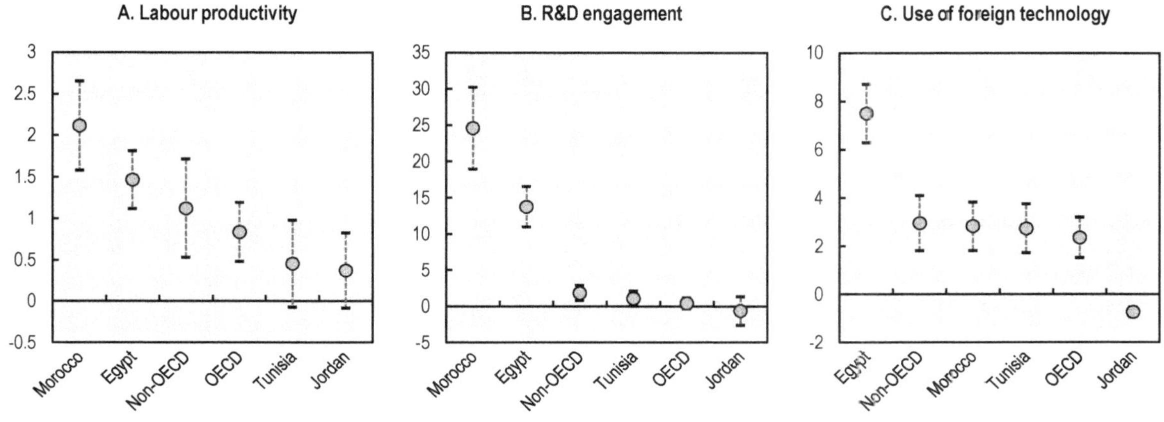

Note: The figure includes confidence intervals that indicate statistical significance at the 95% level. If the confidence interval crosses the zero line, the difference between foreign and domestic firms is statistically insignificant. For further details, see OECD (2019a).
Source: Based on OECD (2019a) and World Bank Enterprise Surveys of Egypt (2020), Jordan (2019), Morocco (2019), and Tunisia (2013). Jordan's indicator on productivity is based on the 2013 Survey.

Foreign firms tend to perform better than domestic firms on measures of gender equality in MENA

Women face particular challenges when it comes to labour market participation and access to decent job opportunities in the region. In the average MENA focus economy, the female unemployment rate is 12 percentage points higher than the overall unemployment rate, and the unemployment gender gap is nine percentage points wider than the world average (ILOSTAT, 2020[9]).

FDI could affect gender equality in host countries by altering the relative demand for female labour. However, across most economies, FDI is concentrated in sectors with lower female employment and high gender pay gaps, such as construction, finance and transport. Within the manufacturing sector however, FDI is in some cases positively related to female employment, notably in countries with large textile and food sectors, which tend to employ more female workers. This is the case in Egypt and Tunisia, where foreign firms have significantly higher shares of female workers than domestic businesses (Figure 2.14, panel A). While working in labour-intensive, low-value added sectors has allowed more women to participate in the labour force, it has also increased the risk of locking them in low-paid, low-skilled positions, perpetuating gender segregation in the labour market.

Figure 2.14. Gender outcomes of foreign and domestic manufacturers

Are foreign firms more performant than their domestic peers? (yes if score > 0)

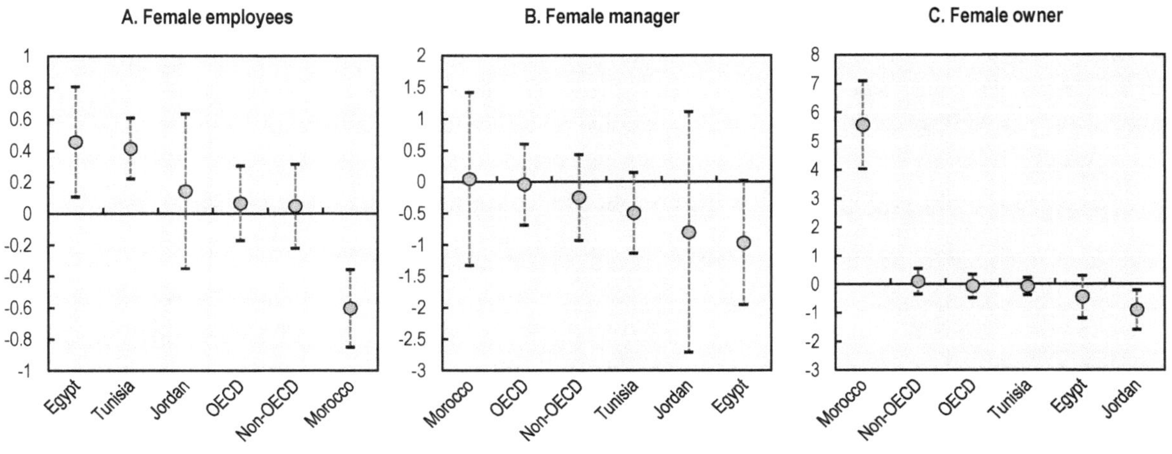

Note: The figure includes confidence intervals that indicate statistical significance at the 95% level. If the confidence interval crosses the zero line, the difference between foreign and domestic firms is statistically insignificant. Job security is measured as the share of workers with permanent contracts. For further details, see OECD (2019a).
Source: Based on OECD (2019a) and World Bank Enterprise Surveys of Egypt (2020), Jordan (2019), Morocco (2019), and Tunisia (2020).

Foreign investors may also affect career progression opportunities of women in host countries. Employment practices can depend on corporate culture and foreign firms from more gender-equal countries may incentivise domestic firms to adopt similar practices to attract and retain female talent. Evidence for MENA countries that foreign firms perform better than domestic peers on measures of female career progression is inconclusive, as it also for other countries (Figure 2.14, panel B and C). Only in Morocco significantly more foreign manufacturing firms are owned by women than domestic peers. These results might also reflect the labour market and cultural norms in the host country, and require more context to assess the role of FDI in improving (or discouraging) female labour outcomes (OECD, 2019[8]).

Foreign firms tend to be more energy efficient than domestic peers

FDI can affect host countries' carbon footprint by increasing the scale of economic activity, affecting the structure of economic activity, inducing the adoption of new energy-saving technologies, and influencing the uptake of clean energy sources. In most countries, FDI is concentrated in industries with lower CO_2 emissions (OECD, 2019[8]). This is the case in Morocco and Tunisia, for example. FDI also tends to be prevalent in sectors that are more energy efficient, as measured by electricity and heat consumption. However, these findings do not necessarily hold for countries where fossil fuels dominate the economy. Aside from fuels, the MENA region is home to abundant non-fuel minerals resources. For instance, Algeria, Morocco, Tunisia, and Jordan produce more than 60% of the world's phosphate.

There is also evidence that foreign firms can be more energy efficient than their domestic peers. This suggests that FDI could lead to improvements in energy efficiency, which may be amplified if energy-saving technologies are diffused to domestic firms. In the MENA region, foreign firms are significantly more energy efficient than domestic businesses in Egypt, Morocco and Tunisia but not in Jordan (Figure 2.15, panel A). Local economic factors, policy considerations or both could drive the observed difference between the two groups of countries (see Chapter 9 on infrastructure investment).

Despite these positive indicators, fossil fuels in the MENA region attract more FDI relative to renewables, and in proportions that are higher than in the OECD area (Figure 2.15, panel B). The region also receives the lowest investment in renewables, as a share of total investment, than other regions. This is not surprising in light of the importance of fossil fuels in several MENA economies. The share of investment in renewables is higher in countries that are not fossil-fuel exporters however, such as Morocco and Tunisia.

Figure 2.15. Foreign and domestic firms' energy efficiency and FDI in renewable energy

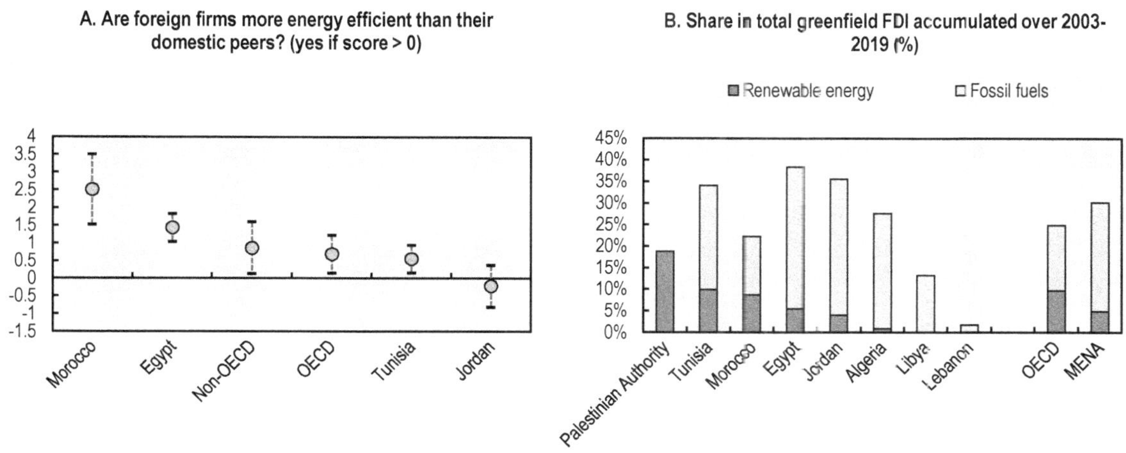

Note: Figure A includes confidence intervals that indicate statistical significance at the 95% level. If the confidence interval crosses the zero line, the difference between foreign and domestic firms is statistically insignificant. For further details, see OECD (2019a).
Source: Based on OECD (2019a) and World Bank Enterprise Surveys of Egypt (2020), Jordan (2013), Morocco (2019), and Tunisia (2020).

References

Burger, M., E. Ianchovichina and B. Rijkers (2013), "Risky Business Political Instability and Greenfield Foreign Direct Investment in the Arab World", *Policy Research working paper*, No. WPS 6716, World Bank Group, Washington DC, http://documents.worldbank.org/curated/en/450971468110956873/Risky-business-political-instability-and-greenfield-foreign-direct-investment-in-the-Arab-world (accessed on 13 March 2020). [5]

Cammett, M. et al. (2013), *A Political Economy of the Middle East* Routledge, London, https://www.routledge.com/A-Political-Economy-of-the-Middle-East-4th-Edition/Cammett-Diwan-Richards-Waterbury/p/book/9780813349381 (accessed on 13 December 2018). [12]

ILOSTAT (2020), *International Labour Statistics*, https://ilostat.ilo.org/. [9]

Kireyev, A. et al. (2019), *Economic Integration in the Maghreb: An Untapped Source of Growth*, Middle East and North Africa Departmental Paper No.19/01, https://www.imf.org/en/Publications/Departmental-Papers-Policy-Papers/Issues/2019/02/08/Economic-Integration-in-the-Maghreb-An-Untapped-Source-of-Growth-46273 (accessed on 13 August 2020). [7]

OECD (2020), *FDI in Figures: October 2020*, OECD, http://www.oecd.org/investment/investment-policy/FDI-in-Figures-October-2020.pdf (accessed on 8 December 2020). [1]

OECD (2020), *OECD Investment Policy Reviews: Egypt 2020*, OECD Investment Policy Reviews, OECD Publishing, Paris, https://dx.doi.org/10.1787/9f9c589a-en. [11]

OECD (2020), *OECD Review of Foreign Direct Investment Statistics: Egypt*, http://www.oecd.org/investment/OECD-Review-of-Foreign-Direct-Investment-Statistics-Egypt.pdf. [15]

OECD (2020), *OECD Review of Foreign Direct Investment Statistics: Jordan*, http://www.oecd.org/investment/OECD-Review-of-Foreign-Direct-Investment-Statistics-Jordan.pdf. [13]

OECD (2020), *OECD Review of Foreign Direct Investment Statistics: Tunisia*, OECD, Paris, http://www.oecd.org/investment/OECD-Review-of-Foreign-Direct-Investment-Statistics-Tunisia.pdf. [4]

OECD (2020), *OECD Review of Foreign Direct Investment Statistics: Tunisia*, http://www.oecd.org/investment/OECD-Review-of-Foreign-Direct-Investment-Statistics-Tunisia.pdf. [14]

OECD (2019), *FDI Qualities Indicators: Measuring the sustainable development impacts of investmnet*, OECD, Paris, http://www.oecd.org/fr/investissement/fdi-qualities-indicators.htm. [8]

OECD (2018), *Examen des statistiques d'investissements directs internationaux au Maroc*, http://www.oecd.org/investment/Report-on-FDI-statistics-of-Morocco-FR.pdf. [16]

OECD (2018), *OECD Investment Policy Reviews: Southeast Asia*, https://www.oecd.org/investment/oecd-investment-policy-review-southeast-asia.htm. [2]

OECD (2018), *Trends in trade and investment policies in the MENA region*, OECD, http://www.oecd.org/mena/competitiveness/WGTI2018-Trends-Trade-Investment-Policies-MENA-Nasser-Saidi.pdf (accessed on 13 August 2020). [6]

UNCTAD (2020), *World Investment Report 2020: International Production Beyond the Pandemic*, United Nations Publications, New York. [3]

World Bank (2015), *Jobs or Privileges: Unleashing the Employment Potential of the Middle East and North Africa*, World Bank, Washington DC. [10]

Notes

[1] See, among others, (OECD, 2020[11]), (Cammett et al., 2013[12]), (Burger, Ianchovichina and Rijkers, 2013[5]).

[2] Data from the IMF Balance of Payments Database and the OECD International Direct Investment Statistics Database.

[3] See OECD Review of FDI Statistics of Jordan, Tunisia, Morocco and Egypt for an in-depth assessment of statistical methods employed in these countries (OECD, 2020[13]) (OECD, 2020[14]) (OECD, 2020[15]) (OECD, 2018[16]).

[4] Greenfield data cited in this chapter is from the Financial Times' fDi Markets database The fDi dataset includes details on the source country of each investment project, based on the location of parent company headquarters. Data from FT FDI Markets differ from greenfield FDI as reported in BMD4.

[5] Absent the Chinese megaproject in Egypt, and a Russian 30 billion USD investment in Egypt's gas sector in 2017 (the only two projects in the last five years that have exceeded 10 billion USD), Europe ties the MENA region as the most prominent source of greenfield investment in the eight economies in recent years.

[6] Data for 8 economies author's calculation based on COMTRADE for the year 2017 (last year available for most of the economies), except for Libya, for which 2016 data was used (last available). Total trade in goods is calculated as exports plus imports. Data for ECOWAS the average share for 2016-2018 (World Bank (2020), ASEAN data from 2017 (ASEAN, 2018).

[7] Based on announced greenfield FDI between 2000-2016, as recorded in fDi Markets by FT database.

[7] The FDI Qualities Indicators provide an average of the productivity premium across different sectors, and thus there could be a premium in industries where market distortions are lower.

[8] Nuclear power project captured under coal, oil and natural gas.

3 Towards modernised legislative frameworks for investment

Regulatory predictability and certainty are essential to create sound and enabling investment environments. In a significant effort to mitigate their reputational risks as investment host states, MENA countries have embarked on a major drive to modernise and strengthen the regulatory corpus framing investment and business activities, and investment legislation has gained central importance in their regulatory reform agendas. This chapter gives an overview of the recent wave of legal amendments and looks at the commonalities and variations in the content and structure of MENA domestic legislative frameworks. It identifies patterns in their reform processes and provides policy considerations to further advance on the regulatory modernisation path.

Summary and policy considerations

Providing strong, clear and predictable guarantees of legal protection for investors is fundamental to reinforce investors' confidence and to mitigate perceived reputational risks as investment host states. Enforcing regulatory reforms to set the conditions for a healthy and sound investment climate is a key priority for the eight MENA economies covered in this report (MENA focus economies), where the business climate has, to varying degrees, suffered from the economic and political turmoil of the past decade. In the aftermath of the Covid-19 global crisis, it will be an essential element of governments' reform agendas for recovery.

Nearly all of the MENA focus economies have, in recent years, undertaken sustained legislative reforms to improve the frameworks governing the protection and facilitation of investment. Investment regulatory reforms that have been initiated or achieved have often been accompanied by a revamping of institutions governing investment, the adoption of aggressive incentives measures, steps to lighten administrative procedures, and a range of other legal amendments affecting the wider business climate. These different aspects are examined here and in subsequent chapters of the report. To achieve more enabling investment frameworks, MENA authorities need to sustain momentum and step up their reform efforts in areas where they are at a standstill.

A longstanding legalistic tradition prevails in the majority of the MENA focus economies, which accordingly have robust legislative foundations. This is reflected in the overall comprehensiveness and high protection standards contained in MENA de jure domestic regimes for investment. Meanwhile, other provisions directly affect the operations of investors, such as the bankruptcy regime, the protection on intellectual property rights, FDI restrictions, the incentives regime, as well as, among others, the Special Economic Zones regime, which matter as much as the core investment legislation itself. The quality of the investment regulatory regime should be considered as a whole and not only by the content of each relevant law.

Revising investment laws has helped countries to build more robust investment regulatory frameworks and signal a pro-investment stance, but it is only one way to create strong and consistent domestic regulatory frameworks. The appetite for reform and the willingness to create business-friendly environments have prompted governments to embark on a fast-paced rhythm of regulatory amendments. In some cases, this may have resulted in legislative hypertrophy. Adopting new laws can also add unnecessary layers of complexity to the overall regulatory environment for investment, which encompasses a wide range of sectoral and thematic laws, decrees, along with international investment treaties.

Ensuring clarity across related pieces of legislation, reducing the time gap between the adoption of new laws and of their implementing regulations, and streamlining and empowering relevant institutions in charge of enforcing investment rules are key to create an enabling business environment and to increase legislative efficiency. While modernising their respective legal frameworks, governments will also ultimately need to fill gaps between the treatment granted to domestic and foreign investors that are not justified by national development strategies, as well as review their restrictions to foreign investment that are not consistent with their stated development objectives.

The challenge is two-fold: MENA governments' policy goal is now to provide the highest standards of protection to investors, and balance the potentially conflicting interests of investors and host states. MENA governments should ensure that private businesses are protected against arbitrary decisions or changes of policies, while at the same time preserving sufficient regulatory space to adopt relevant public policy.

Policy considerations

- Limit the time lapse between the adoption of new legislation and the introduction of implementing regulations. Legislative reform efforts can only reach their full potential if promptly followed by the adoption of executive regulations and adequately implemented by relevant authorities, at all government levels. The institutional ecosystem in charge of implementing investment rules should also be further streamlined and adequately empowered to translate regulatory reforms into concrete improvements to the business climate.
- Avoid short-term fixes and ensure that no unnecessary additional layers of regulation are created when endeavouring to modernise legislative frameworks.
- Improve the overall clarity and intelligibility of national legislative architecture. In most of the eight MENA focus economies, regulatory regimes tend to be scattered over many pieces of legislation. This can create legal overlaps and loopholes, or the perception thereof, which can have a deterrent effect on investors and prevent countries from reaping the potential benefits of investments. Consistency of the various legal instruments applying to investment is a prerequisite to creating a more transparent regulatory framework. Meanwhile, legislation plays a strong role as a signalling device, especially in jurisdictions where non-commercial risks are higher than the average. When perceived by business operators as overly complex, a regulatory environment may therefore also have a significant deterrent effect on the investment environment.
- Address investment legislation reform as part of a wider development policy equation. While legal guarantees need to provide high standards to protect investors' rights, the investment regime's ultimate goal is to nurture a healthy investment climate that supports sustainable and inclusive development processes. High investment protection standards and other public policy measures should be implemented in a balanced manner, and governments should preserve sufficient policy space to introduce such measures while committing to high standards of property right protection.

Investment-law making is at the core of countries' business regulatory environment

An investment law is not essential and many advanced economies do not have one, but over 100 developing and emerging economies have adopted this approach as part of their overall legal framework for investment (OECD, 2015[1]). Many have used an investment law, the scope of which varies from one country to another, partly as a signalling device for investors and to promote transparency. An investment law can also be a way for host governments to signal expectations concerning responsible conduct by imposing certain investor obligations. For these reasons, the investment law is often the first point of reference for a potential investor, and MENA governments have expended considerable resources and political capital to periodically revise and update their investment laws.

Investment laws typically contain a set of core, substantive guarantees for the protection of investors' property rights, and detail the mandate of investment agencies, be it merely promotional or also regulatory (Chapter 6). Often, investment laws and their executive regulations also establish the degree of openness to investment and the rules for market entry, include a list of sectors where investors face restrictions (Chapter 4) and set the conditions for receiving fiscal or non-fiscal investment incentives (Chapter 7). More recent investment laws commonly have a chapter dedicated to the settlement of investment-state disputes (Chapter 5).

The scope and purpose of investment laws remains variable, which shows that there is no single formula for building an enabling domestic regulatory environment. Some countries have multiple investment-related laws, while others have adopted a single, comprehensive investment law. MENA economies have largely subscribed to the latter approach and have chosen to have a dedicated investment law, of which they have progressively reinforced the provisions pertaining to the protection of investors' rights.

Jordan and Libya's latest investment law reforms, in 2014 and 2010 respectively, aimed to bring the regimes for domestic and foreign investors under the same umbrella of a unified legislation, thus providing the legal foundations for a non-discriminatory treatment for all established investments, regardless of their nationality. A common feature across MENA jurisdictions is the prominence of unified investment legislation, also called "omnibus investment laws", framing both foreign and domestic investment under the same core provisions, underlined by a general principle of non-discrimination.

In Lebanon and Morocco, the Investment Law does not stipulate the core standards of protection, which feature across a wider range of laws. Lebanon's Investment Promotion law focuses on the mandate and powers of the Investment Promotion Agencies (IPAs) and on the regime for investment incentives, while Morocco's Investment Charter mostly provides for the incentives and tax advantages regime. The more recent Egyptian (2017), Palestinian Authority (2014) and Tunisian (2016) investment laws have a wider scope, more in line with modern global practice. They contain substantive rights, including access to dispute resolution, the institutional mandate of the IPA and the incentives regime. Meanwhile, Libya has adopted a hybrid approach, providing core investment guarantees while focusing on the regime for incentives and advantages given to investors. Lastly, the regime for Economic Zones, which play a prominent role in MENA economies' investment strategies, is governed by the investment legislation in Algeria, Jordan and Lebanon. In Egypt, the regime for economic zones is scattered over several laws, including the investment law (OECD, 2020[2]).

Regardless of its material scope, clear investment legislation is used as a signalling device and can hence help to promote the country as an investment destination. Most MENA governments have faced serious reputational challenges due to the persistent political instability of the past decade. In response, they have engaged in comprehensive investment climate reforms by streamlining their institutional infrastructures (e.g., the revamping of the institutional framework for investment promotion and facilitation in Egypt, Jordan, Morocco, and Tunisia), revising not only the investment legislation *stricto sensu* but also other key legislations such as bankruptcy laws, SME laws and PPP laws (Box 3.1). Most MENA countries have tended to adopt aggressive investment incentives schemes, a trend that is likely to continue in the aftermath of the Covid-19 crisis. Some countries have progressively lifted restrictions to foreign direct investment (FDI) that may not be in line with their stated economic development objectives (e.g. objective of economic diversification) as, for example, was recently done in Algeria.

There is no presumption that one legislative approach is better than others for all economies at all levels of development. Advanced and liberal economies worldwide, like Singapore, or most OECD economies, often do not have a dedicated investment law, and instead regulate investment through a broad legislative framework. For many other jurisdictions however, particularly those where business operations are perceived as overly complex, an investment law can add to transparency and predictability, provided that the content and scope of the investment law is in line with other relevant legislation. In the MENA region, while most economies have a dedicated investment law, some of them, including Lebanon and Morocco, provide investment protection guarantees and regulations in a range of laws.

Box 3.1. The overall legislative framework for investment in MENA economies

As reflected in the *Policy Framework for Investment*, the investment environment is the sum of many different policies, as well as the interaction among them. It cannot be reduced to one specific variable, whether the World Bank's *Doing Business* indicator or the OECD's *FDI Regulatory Restrictiveness Index*. By the same token, the overall legislative framework for investment will depend on a panoply of legislation, often combined in idiosyncratic ways that differ widely across countries. One of the most important laws in many emerging and developing economies is the investment law. It can cover domestic and foreign investors in one law or in separate laws and set the conditions for market access for foreign firms, and offer national treatment for established investors. It can also include the provision of incentives and offer guarantees of protection of the investor's assets. These conditions could be provided in other rules and regulations, but an investment law is nevertheless often used as a signalling device to investors, particularly foreigners, that the economy is open and accommodating to foreign investment. For this reason, an investment law is often the first point of reference for a potential investor.

Incentives may be included in the investment law (e.g. in Lebanon, Egypt) or they may appear in the general tax law, as is considered good practice. Similarly, the rules governing special economic zones are either included in the investment law or in separate decrees or legislation (e.g. Egypt's SEZ Law). The negative list of sectors restricted to foreign investors might be embedded in the investment law itself or may appear in a separate decree, as in Jordan. Market access commitments for a specific set of investors may also be established in international agreements signed by the government.

Other relevant laws for investors include, inter alia, Public-Private Partnership laws, commercial codes, companies acts, which establishes among other things the procedures for registering a business and the rules covering corporate governance, together with securities and accounting laws. Independently of any legislation, corporate practices can also shape entry conditions for both domestic and foreign investors, together with the presence of "golden shares" or residency or nationality requirements for the board of directors. Competition law, or the lack thereof, also determines the potential contestability of markets. Other relevant regulations for potential investors may be contained in sectoral legislation, particularly in financial or natural resource sectors.

The protection of investors' property rights is often included in the investment law, if it exists, but also, and more commonly in the constitution itself. An arbitration law can set out the procedures for settling disputes. In some countries, large investors in important sectors such as mining or infrastructure might sign individual contracts with the state which set out investor rights. To complement and strengthen this protective structure, governments have signed international investment agreements or broader agreements that confer rights on investors from partner countries. Some of them, especially Egypt, have concluded a very high number of IIAs, through which they provided an additional layer of protection and guarantees to a wide range of foreign investors (Chapter 5).

Going beyond this legislative and treaty structure, investors are also concerned about the issue of public governance: how these laws are actually implemented in practice and the general quality of the rule of law and the institutions in the host country. This wider legislative corpus sets out the process for law-making, including public consultations and regulatory impact assessments.

Source: Based on *Policy Framework for Investment* (OECD, 2015[1]).

The overall regulatory environment matters as much as the investment legislation itself

The degree of openness encountered by investors when establishing in a host country, and the conditions they face in their ongoing operations, is only one part of the broader investment environment. The protection of property, contractual rights and other legal guarantees provided to investors, combined with effective enforcement mechanisms and guarantees of access to efficient dispute settlement mechanisms (Chapter 5) are key building blocks of an enabling investment climate, at the core of which is often the investment law. When procedures for establishing investments, operating businesses and enforcing contracts are perceived as cumbersome and lack predictability, investors may restrict their activities or refrain from engaging in the country. Countries with high standards of legislation are hence better armed to position themselves as safe investment destinations and to minimise the adverse reputational effect that can be prompted by political instability.

MENA countries' legal corpus governing investment typically involve several layers of rules and regulations covering many different areas (Box 3.1). The quality of investment laws should not be looked at in isolation from the broader regulatory framework. What matters most is the coherence of the wider legal environment, the application of the rule of law, and the clarity of the wide range of legal instruments that apply in a given jurisdiction.

Unnecessary regulatory obstacles can deter investment and the sectoral diversification of the economy. In some jurisdictions, including Lebanon and the Palestinian Authority, a series of outdated laws and regulations, and the absence of key pieces of legislation, such as competition and intellectual property (IP) laws, also negatively affect the investment climate. Across the region, integrity and anti-corruption legislation are often either missing or incomplete (Chapter 11).

The regulatory framework is indispensable yet not sufficient to create the right conditions for an enabling business climate. Shortages in institutional capacities, as often encountered at the sub-national level in some of the MENA focus economies, also have a deterrent effect on the implementation of the regulatory framework.

Regional wave of investment law reforms

All eight MENA focus economies have, as shown in Table 3.1, recently accelerated the pace of reform of their domestic legislation toward more enabling frameworks for investment and private sector development. In the virtual absence of regulatory regional integration, unlike in other regional blocks such as in Southeast Asia, each MENA economy has reformed its regulatory framework at its own pace and based on its national policy priorities. There are no legislative standards adopted or agreed upon at the regional level, and achieving greater legal harmonisation across the region is not a priority in the reform agenda of the MENA focus economies. By way of comparison, Southeast Asian countries have progressively brought their domestic legislation in line with common protection standards, drawing on the provisions of ASEAN Comprehensive Investment Agreement (ACIA), so as to maximise the benefits of building a regional entity as an attractive and dynamic investment destination. Attempts to adopt a similar supra-national approach have met little success in the MENA focus economies.

Algeria adopted a new Investment Law in 2016, which repealed most of the provisions of the Ordinance No. 01-03 on the development of investment. Overall, the law brought more legal certainty and marked a significant improvement of the investment regulatory framework, through the removal of a number of regulatory constraints, while maintaining fundamental guarantees for foreign investors and bringing the investment incentives regime under the responsibility of the Ministry of Finance. In June 2020, in a context of the Covid-19 health crisis and falling oil prices, Algeria adopted its Finance Law for 2020. The law enshrines Algeria's reopening to FDI by defining the strategic sectors, restricted to foreign investors, in a relatively limited manner and by repealing the State's right of pre-emption and right of repurchase (see Chapter 3 for further details on liberalisation reforms in the region).

In the past four years, the government of **Egypt** has put strong emphasis on adopting more modern investment legislation and regulations for investment. The 2017 Investment Law, promptly followed by a modernised Companies Law, marked an important milestone in efforts to provide a safer and more consistent regulatory environment for foreign and domestic investment (OECD, 2020). Recent reforms have focused on streamlining business registration processes and GAFI departments in charge of investment entry, incentives and facilitation.

Libya, meanwhile, lifted many FDI restrictions and introduced a number of investors' guarantees through the adoption of its 2010 investment law, which accompanied the creation of a new investment promotion institution, the Privatisation and Investment Board (PIB), in 2009. Along with the adoption of the 2010 Investment Law, a number of business-related laws were introduced, including the 2010 Commercial Code (which was subsequently revised in 2012), and the Registration Law. No major legal reform has been undertaking since then.

The **Palestinian Authority** achieved a major improvement with the adoption in **2014** of an investment legislation which content is closely aligned with global standards It has, since then, focused its reform agenda on other key business regulations, with various degrees of success. The efficiency of its overall regulatory framework remains largely impeded by the persistence of long outdated laws.

Morocco and **Lebanon** have, since the adoption of Morocco's 1995 Investment Charter, and Lebanon's 2001 Investment Promotion Law, focused their respective reform agendas less on the investment legislation *stricto sensu*, which remains less comprehensive than most commonly encountered in the region. They have however been pro-active reformers of the overall business regulatory environment. Morocco, in particular, has revised its Commercial Code, with the introduction of a new regime for private limited companies. The competition regime was also modernised, along with the introduction of revised PPP provisions, and an ongoing plan to revise the bankruptcy legislation.

Last, **Tunisia** has undertaken a comprehensive revamping of its investment legal framework, starting with the 2016 Investment Law, which was adopted after extensive consultations with public and private stakeholders. The reform process complied with transparency and accountability requirements that remain, to this day, unprecedented across MENA countries. It has since then continuously pursued legislative reforms, with successive amendments intended to progressively strengthen investor rights, create a more investor-friendly environment and narrow the policy gap between foreign and domestic investors. The strong impetus for reform might have displayed excessive zeal in the revamping of the institutional framework for investment promotion and facilitation, which is now composed of several bodies which mandates are, in some areas, partly overlapping (see Chapter 5).

MENA countries have generally been active legislative reformers in the past years, with many regulatory revisions still ongoing. Each iteration of investment laws has been designed to address weaknesses in the existing one, although each new version is not always in all areas an improvement over the earlier version. Some highly publicised amendments might have been undertaken to mark a political footprint, in a context of frequent governmental reshuffles, rather than for legal improvement purposes.

Frequent changes also have the disadvantage of creating temporary uncertainty for investors prior to the issuance of implementing regulations. This happened in Egypt in the immediate aftermath of the enactment of the 2015 investment law, for which implementing regulations were adopted with a delay, temporarily leaving businesses in a "wait-and-see" position (OECD, 2020[2]). If not done in a comprehensive and coherent manner, engaging major legal revisions can have short-term counterproductive effects. In Jordan, for example, the successive legal amendments and repeals of previous regulations in the early 2000s created major regulatory loopholes that lasted until the adoption of the unified 2014 Investment Law (OECD, 2018[3]).

In a region where inter-governmental regulatory coordination efforts are nearly absent and in the virtual absence of a regional regulatory integration process, as mentioned above, the pro-active reform agenda of individual countries also reveals the growing regulatory competition among them. While the race towards competitiveness may yield positive results in term of legal quality, it also has a potential for counter-productive regulatory inflation. It may also lead to an unsustainable regulatory race to the bottom, particularly if governments use aggressive incentive strategies as part of their reform agenda. This effect might be reinforced in a post Covid-19 context, in which some countries, such as Egypt, have already responded by expanding tax incentives and holiday schemes (see Chapter 7 on investment incentives). Such regional competitive tension also carries a potential risk of lowering norms on labour rights and environmental standards, especially in Free Zones and Special Economic Zones which often operate in derogation from general laws (see Chapter 10 on Responsible Business Conduct).

Table 3.1. Investment-related legislation in MENA economies

Economy	Recent amendments to the investment legislation	Recent investment-related reforms
Algeria	• 2016 Investment Law on the promotion of investment (*Loi n°2016-09 du 3 juillet 2016 relative à la promotion de l'Investissement*) • 2017 Implementing Decrees of 5 March • 2020 Finance Law revising the negative list of restricted sectors	• 2015 public procurement regulation (*Décret présidentiel n° 15-247 du 16 septembre 2015 portant réglementation des marchés publics et des délégations de service public*)
Egypt	• 1997 Investment Law • 2015 Investment Law and its Executive Regulations • 2017 Investment Law • 2019 Amendment to the 2017 Investment Law	• 2015 Collateral Registry Law and 2016 Executive regulations of the movable collateral law • 2016 Value-added tax (VAT) Law • 2017 Law on Streamlining Industrial Establishments Licensing • 2018 Companies Law • 2018 Bankruptcy Law
Jordan	• Investment Law No. 30 of October 2014 • Regulation on Non-Jordanian Investments No 77 of 2016	• 2018 Revision of the Arbitration Law • 2014 Public-Private Partnership Law
Lebanon	• 2001 Investment Development Law No.360 of 16 August 2001 • Decrees 9311 and 9326 of 21 December 2002	• 2018 PPP law • 2019 Revision of the Commercial Code • 2020 Private Equity Law
Libya	• 2010 Law on the Encouragement of National and Foreign Investment • Executive decrees of 2012 and 2013 on foreign direct investments (Decree 22 of 2013, Decree 207 of 2012, Decree 103 of 2012, Decree 186 of 2012)	• Draft SME Law
Morocco	• 1995 Investment Charter (*Charte de l'Investissement – Loi-cadre No.18-95 de 1995*) → Suspended reform of the 1995 Investment Charter	• 2014 Adoption of Competition Laws • 2017 Reform of the Stock Exchange Law (*Loi 19-14 relative à la Bourse des valeurs de Casablanca, aux sociétés de Bourse ainsi qu'aux conseillers en investissement financier du 25 août 2016 publiée le 31 mars 2017*) • 2016 reform of the Commercial Code - Law on limited liability companies (*Loi n°78-12 modifiant et complétant la loi n°17-95 relative aux sociétés anonymes au Maroc*) • 2014 Law on Public- Private Partnerships • Ongoing reform of foreign exchanges regime, since 2018 • Ongoing reform of the bankruptcy regime

Economy	Recent amendments to the investment legislation	Recent investment-related reforms
Palestinian Authority	• 2014 Amendments to the Law on the Encouragement of Investment of 1998 (*Law No.1 of 1998, amended by Presidential Decree n°2 of 2011 and Presidential Decree n°7 of 2014*)	• Draft SME Law under preparation
Tunisia	• 2016 Investment Law (*Loi n° 2016-71 portant loi de l'Investissement*), *Décret gouvernemental n°2017-388 relatif à (i) La fixation de la composition du Conseil Supérieur d'Investissement et les modalités de son organisation* ; et (ii) *L'organisation administrative et financière de l'Instance Tunisienne de l'Investissement et du Fonds Tunisien de l'Investissement* • *Décret gouvernemental n°2017-389 relatif aux Incitations financières au profit des investissements réalisés dans le cadre de la loi de l'investissement* • *Décret gouvernemental n°2017-390 relatif à la création d'une unité de gestion par objectif* • 2018 Executive Regulation on investment authorisations and screening (*Décret gouvernemental n° 2018-417 du 11 mai 2018 relatif à la publication de la liste exclusive des activités économiques soumises à autorisation et de la liste des autorisations administratives requises pour la réalisation de projets*)	• 2016 Banking Law (*Loi relative aux banques et aux institutions bancaires N°2016-48 of 15 July 2016*) • 2015 PPP Law (*Loi 2015-49 sur les partenariats publics-privés (PPP) du 27 novembre 2015*), 2016 PPP Decrees • 2015 Competition Law (*Loi n° 2015-36 du 15 septembre 2015, relative à la réorganisation de la concurrence et des prix*) • 2017 Law on fiscal incentives (*Loi n° 2017-8 du 14 février 2017, portant refonte du dispositif des avantages fiscaux*) • 2019 Law on improving the Investment Climate, amending sections of the 2015 PPP Law (*loi n°2019-47 du 29 mai 2019 sur l'amélioration du climat des investissements*)

While a comprehensive reform of existing legislation can provide an opportunity to revisit certain longstanding policy approaches, such as on incentives or concerning discrimination against foreign investors, the age of legislation is not necessarily a sufficient justification for reform. Morocco's 1995 Investment Charter is the oldest investment law in force in the region. After more than a decade of amendment plans, the government recently decided to leave it unchanged and to focus its reform agenda on sectoral laws, which have as much of an impact on the business climate in their respective fields.

Despite variations in policy approaches, dominant patterns of legal reforms can be identified across the region, and are commonly found in national legislations of economies at similar level of development, such as in Southeast Asia. Recent reforms of investment-related regulations have mostly focused on facilitating investment: streamlining business registration, reinforcing and expanding IPA mandates (e.g. Egypt's 2017 Investment Law, Tunisia's 2016 Investment Law), and on amending the investment incentives regime (Tunisia's 2016 Investment Law, Jordan's 2017 set of Executive Regulations) – although incentives continue to be widespread and are often easy for firms to receive, with broad eligibility requirements (Chapter 7). As for the core standards of protection, which are the historical backbone of investment legislation, they were not substantially changed by the recent wave of legal changes. Core *de jure* property rights were already legally enshrined, either in previous investment regulations, in other legislations or in the Constitution.

Protection of investors' rights in domestic legislation of MENA economies

Investors' treatment in MENA countries is governed by a set of core protection standards that feature both in the investment legislation and in other relevant regulatory instruments. The notion of protection of investors' rights embraces not only the guarantee against unlawful expropriation but also secure land rights, high standards of intellectual property rights, free repatriation of foreign investment, and the enforcement of contractual rights, including through a guarantee of access to dispute settlement mechanisms (Chapter 5).

With a few exceptions, MENA investment legislations provide strong *de jure* standards of protection, generally consistent with internationally recognised practices. Although reiterating standards of protection in the investment law may be a reassuring signal, there is no best approach as to where these core guarantees should be provided. Core protection guarantees are no better addressed in investment laws than in other laws of general application. For example, expropriation provisions can appropriately be addressed in other laws of more general application or even in the Constitution itself.

Lebanon's investment legislation does not contain core standards of protection of investors' rights, which feature in other pieces of legislation. Specifically, the Lebanese legislation does not enshrine guarantees of post-establishment non-discrimination or national treatment, nor of the transfer of funds, expropriation or dispute settlement. These core protection standards also feature in international investment treaties, which provide an additional layer of protection to foreign investors covered by such treaties.

In the absence of protection guarantees in the investment law, the protection against expropriation is provided in the Constitution as well as in international investment agreements. The Lebanese Constitution, along with the Expropriation Law (1991, amended in 2006) govern the regime for expropriation, which can only occur for public interest purposes, and provides for prior market-value compensation. Although there is no explicit mention of non-discrimination, the Law does not refer to the nationality of the owner.

Likewise, Morocco's Investment Charter contains only a few protection provisions, which by no means indicate a lesser degree of protection against unlawful expropriations, which is governed in distinct pieces of legislation. It does however contain a guarantee of free transfer of funds and gives foreign investors the freedom to transfer profits and capital.

Egypt's domestic legal framework grants *de jure* property rights protections to investors that are consistent with high, modern standards of protection. The protection of investors' rights is recognised at the constitutional and legislative levels, and, notwithstanding the application of bilateral investment treaty provisions, the same legal protections and available incentives are granted to foreign and domestic investors.

The Egyptian Investment Law provides the full spectrum of investment guarantees and protection standards that are required to provide a safe *de jure* regime for investors. It contains a provision granting fair and equitable treatment to both foreign and Egyptian investors, and a guarantee that the invested capital cannot be subject to any coercive or discriminatory measures. It also provides protections against nationalisation and expropriation and guarantees against sequestration and seizures, as well as the confiscation and freezing of property, except under court order. The state can only expropriate property for "public utility", with fair compensation and in a prompt manner. The law stipulates this value "shall equal the fair economic value of the expropriated property on the day preceding the expropriation decision date". These provisions are completed by the 1990 law on expropriation of real estate for public interest, amended in 2018, which specifies the compensation rules. "Public utility" is not defined in the Investment Law or in the Law on expropriation of real estate for public interest.

Meanwhile, Algeria's investment law provides guarantees of fair and equitable compensation for expropriation; fair and equitable treatment to foreign investments and of free transfers of funds. It contains a provision on the intangibility of law, stating that future revisions to the investment legislation will not apply to projects undertaken in the framework of the legislation in force at the time of the investment, unless the investor expressly requests it. The expropriation provision is succinct: while it grants fair and equitable compensation, it does not specify the criteria for expropriation, nor the procedures of compensation. This matter is left to international treaties when applicable, thus providing a more protective treatment to foreign investors covered by such treaties. As for the settlement of investment disputes, the 2016 law gives competence to domestic courts, notwithstanding the applicability of international investment treaties or agreements with an arbitration clause.

Jordan's investment law provides for investors' guarantees of protection, with no detailed provisions on the procedural guarantees. The law provides for a standard of national treatment, a principle of equal treatment, guarantees against expropriation, transfer of capital and profits rights, including currency convertibility and profit repatriation rights. An important provision introduced by the Law relates to dispute settlement. While the interim Investment Law of 2003 did not contain dispute settlement provisions per se and only referred to international conventions, the new Law gives foreign investors access to arbitration in the event of a conflict between a foreign capital investor and the Jordanian governmental authorities.

The 2014 Palestinian Investment law provides a comprehensive set of protection standards. It grants a principle of non-discrimination of investors, except in exceptional cases for a public purpose with due process of law, and fair compensation. It also contains a guarantee that investments cannot be nationalised, confiscated or expropriated except for public purposes in which case a compensation of the fair market value must be paid, as well as a general principle of free transfer of funds.

Likewise, Tunisia's core investment legislation provides a comprehensive set of standards of protection, in line with what is commonly seen as best practice. It provides a guarantee of fair and equitable compensation for expropriation, free transfer of funds abroad, and of non-discrimination.

Annex 3.A compares the provisions of each country's core investment legislation and looks at whether countries have adopted a positive or a negative list approach to the entry of foreign investment. The availability of arbitration, as well as adherence to international investment treaties, are also included.

While this chapter focuses on the domestic legal framework, the interplay between domestic legislation and international investment treaties, which play a major role in protecting foreign investments, should not be overlooked (Chapter 5). Their purpose and scope vary in many regards, and the content of some increasingly controversial treaty provisions, such as fair and equitable treatment (FET) and most-favoured nation treatment (MFN), is not meant to be replicated at legislative level. Moreover, while the main goal of investment treaties is to provide a high level of protection guarantees to foreign investors, the scope of investment laws is much wider.

More room for reform through the gradual incorporation of investor obligations

The incorporation of legal investor obligations to preserve the environment and other public policy objectives is a growing trend in global investment-law making. While the increasing awareness of the need to promote and implement responsible business conduct is mirrored in national strategies that go well beyond the legislative framework (Chapter 10), investment laws have a strong potential role to play in introducing obligations binding upon investors. This evolution in rule-making is reflected in the domestic laws of some developing and advanced economies, which increasingly contain provisions to ensure that investors bind themselves to responsible business conduct. This practice aims to strike a better balance between guarantees offered to investors and obligations that investors must respect in order to be eligible for these guarantees and for incentives. With a few exceptions, MENA economies have not yet clearly embarked on this path (Table 3.2). Their investment legislation generally does not contain obligations binding upon investors, except through the required conditions to benefit from incentives and advantages. Measures taken by MENA governments to guarantee minimum standards for domestic workers and to promote gender diversity are most often reflected in other types of regulations, such as Codes of Corporate Governance and Labour Laws, as in the case of many OECD countries. Jordan and Morocco, for example, have adopted corporate governance codes that mention gender diversity on boards (OECD/ILO/CAWTAR, 2020[4]).

Investment laws could however be used as a channel to encourage women's access and participation on corporate boards and in senior management positions. There is a strong case for promoting gender equality through investment regulatory reforms: FDI has the potential to improve gender balance in corporate leadership. In general, the share of foreign firms with female top managers, and the share of women in managerial positions in foreign firms, are significantly higher than in domestic firms, including in some MENA countries (see Chapter 2 on FDI trends and development benefits). These practices of foreign firms may be imitated by domestic firms (OECD, 2019[5]).

Egypt has started instilling provisions aiming at striking a balance between investors' rights and obligations. The 2017 Investment Law introduced provisions on corporate social responsibility (CSR), stated in very broad terms, with no specific requirements binding on investors. In its article 2, the Law prohibits discrimination in investment, including on the basis of gender, and encourages small investors. GAFI, Egypt's IPA, has also opened a special window at the Investors Services Centre where women investors can obtain all necessary information and complete all necessary paperwork at a one-stop-shop. Meanwhile, Morocco has set up a fully operational body to implement investors' CSR obligations (Chapter 9). Compared to other regions, MENA countries' attempts to impose development-related obligations upon investors remain incipient.

The incorporation of such provisions into the core investment legislation could be envisaged as a way to strike a better balance between investors' rights and obligations, and bring their legislation closer to international standards for responsible business conduct, such as those contained in the OECD *Guidelines for Multinational Enterprises.* As further developed in Chapter 10, the Guidelines are the most-widely recognised global policy instrument for promoting and enabling RBC. They are part of the OECD Declaration on International Investment and Multinational Enterprises (the Declaration), a policy commitment to provide an open and transparent investment environment and to encourage the positive contribution businesses can make to economic and social progress. Among the eight MENA focus countries, Egypt, Jordan, Morocco and Tunisia have adhered to these policy instruments.

References

OECD (2020), *OECD Investment Policy Reviews: Egypt 2020*, OECD Investment Policy Reviews, OECD Publishing, Paris, https://dx.doi.org/10.1787/9f9c589a-en. [2]

OECD (2019), *FDI Qualities Indicators: Measuring the sustainable development impacts of investmnet*, OECD, Paris, http://www.oecd.org/fr/investissement/fdi-qualities-indicators.htm. [5]

OECD (2018), *Enhancing the legal framework for sustainable investment: Lessons from Jordan*, Jordan Competitiveness and Investment Project, OECD, https://www.oecd.org/mena/competitiveness/Enhancing-the-Legal-Framework-for-Sustainable-Investment-Lessons-from-Jordan.pdf (accessed on 26 May 2020). [3]

OECD (2015), *Policy Framework for Investment, 2015 Edition*, OECD Publishing, Paris, https://dx.doi.org/10.1787/9789264208667-en. [1]

OECD/ILO/CAWTAR (2020), *Changing Laws and Breaking Barriers for Women's Economic Empowerment in Egypt, Jordan, Morocco and Tunisia*, OECD Publishing, Paris, https://dx.doi.org/10.1787/ac780735-en. [4]

Annex 3.A. MENA economies' investment frameworks

Annex Table 3.A.1. Comparative table of MENA economies' investment frameworks

	Investment law covering domestic and foreign investments	Recent amendments of the investment legislation	Provisions on distributional effects of investment : environmental impact, sustainable development, gender, etc.	Non-discrimination at post-establishment stage enshrined in domestic legislation	Negative list approach of FDI restrictions	Protection against expropriation	Guarantee of free transfer of funds provided by law	Possible recourse to investment arbitration provided by law	Adherence to international conventions on arbitration (ICSID Convention, & New York Convention)	International Investment treaties
Algeria	✓	✓	No	✓	Unclear – under revision				Yes	✓
Egypt	✓	✓	Yes, general considerations	✓		Yes	✓	✓	Yes	✓
Jordan	✓	✓	No	✓	✓	Yes	✓	✓	Yes	✓
Lebanon	✓		No	✓		Yes, not specific to investors		✓	Yes	✓
Libya	✓		No	✓		Yes			Not a member State of ICSID; has not adhered to the NY Convention	✓
Morocco	✓		Not in the Investment Charter, but active NCP	✓		Yes, not specific to investors	✓	✓	Yes	✓
Palestinian Authority	✓		Yes, through the criteria for granting incentives	✓		Yes	✓		Not a member of ICSID; Adhered to NY Convention in 2015	✓
Tunisia	✓	✓	✓	✓	*Unclear*	Yes	✓	Yes	Yes	✓

Source: Authors' compilation

Notes: National Contact Points (NCP) are government agencies in charge of promoting the OECD Guidelines for Multinational Enterprises and related due diligence guidance, and of handling cases (referred to as "specific instances") as a non-judicial grievance mechanism. Adhering governments have an obligation to establish an NCP to further the effectiveness of the Guidelines (Chapter 9).

4 Openness to foreign investment and recent liberalisation reforms

This chapter provides an overview of the main regulatory restrictions to foreign investment in the MENA focus economies, drawing on the OECD FDI Regulatory Restrictiveness Index (the Index). The Index gauges the level of restrictiveness of an economy's statutory measures on FDI in over 70 countries worldwide and in 22 sectors. Despite important reforms, MENA economies are on average more restrictive than other regions, potentially limiting FDI inflows and economy-wide productivity gains. This can have implications for MENA economies' stated objectives of economic diversification and participation in global value chains.

Summary and policy considerations

The attractiveness of MENA economies to foreign investors depend on myriad factors, including market size, geography, and crucially, the policies and institutions that support a coherent and predictable investment environment. As other chapters of this report explore in detail, the legal framework for investment (Chapter 3), the quality of infrastructure (Chapter 9), and policies to promote FDI (Chapter 6) and link foreign and domestic investors (Chapter 8) are all areas governments can influence not only to attract more FDI, but to enhance its positive benefits to society. For foreign investors, another important policy area concerns the rules governing their entry and operations in the host country. All governments impose some legal or regulatory restrictions on FDI, often in an effort to protect domestic industries or safeguard national security interests. But FDI restrictions involve economic costs, which can in turn lead to lower competition, forgone government revenues, and reduced opportunities for productivity spillovers.

The MENA economies covered in this report (MENA focus economies) vary substantially in their level of openness to foreign investors. Based on statutory FDI restrictions (those explicit in regulations or laws) as of year-end 2019, Egypt and Morocco are as liberal as OECD countries, while Libya and the Palestinian Authority impose wide-ranging *de jure* restrictions. On average, the eight MENA focus economies tend to be more restrictive than OECD and many non-OECD countries. However, several MENA governments have undertaken significant liberalisation reforms recently, recognising the role of FDI in creating jobs, enabling economic diversification and supporting participation in global value chains. For example, Jordan in 2016 revoked a minimum capital requirement imposed on foreign investors, expanded the sectors open to full foreign ownership and, in 2019, further eased restrictions in some service sectors. Tunisia in 2016 removed a requirement that foreign investors receive approval for equity stakes exceeding 50% of a firm's capital. In 2020, Algeria ended its most substantial restriction, a cap on foreign equity of 49% in all sectors.

Remaining statutory restrictions may nonetheless inhibit greater volumes of FDI as well as productivity gains from competition – crucial for a resilient recovery from the Covid-19 crisis. Like most countries, the MENA focus economies impose more restrictions in service sectors than in manufacturing. These sectoral restrictions are more severe and widespread than in peer countries, however, including in Southeast Asia and Latin America. Several MENA countries restrict foreign ownership in business, financial, distribution and transport services, all of which are key inputs for other sectors. Limiting foreign investment in such backbone services hinders competition and productivity in these sectors and the industries that rely on them, including manufacturing, in turn holding back potential productivity gains throughout the economy.

Even in instances where MENA governments have removed statutory limits on FDI, *de facto* restrictions may be prevalent. While not covered in this chapter, these include informal or institutional barriers to investment (such as excessive bureaucracy or corruption), state ownership, or inconsistent enforcement of statutory rules. In some MENA countries these *de facto* barriers have disproportionately benefited a small number of politically-connected firms (Diwan, Keefer and Schiffbauer, 2015[11]). When restrictions are used as a tool for crony practices, they inhibit competition between foreign and domestic investors, as well as among domestic firms. A more competition-friendly environment would allow for a better allocation of resources towards higher-productivity firms and enable new entrants to bring in new ideas and innovate.

Policy considerations

- Consider reassessing remaining regulatory restrictions to foreign investment, notably horizontal restrictions and those in service sectors, against their public policy objectives and, where relevant, streamline or remove them. Restrictions should also be reviewed against MENA governments' national development objectives (e.g. objectives of economic diversification or participation in global value chains). Where such policies are deemed necessary, ensure that they are not more restrictive than needed to address identified risks and concerns.
- Consider improving the legibility and transparency of the legal framework for foreign investors. Often details on discriminatory measures are not available in English or involve lengthy and frequently updated lists of open sectors, making it difficult for investors to understand prevalent rules. A negative list approach, where restricted sectors are clearly outlined (as in Jordan), could improve clarity.
- Ensure effective and clear implementation of the regulations governing the entry and operations of foreign investors. Fewer discretionary regulations on foreign firms' market entry, both *de jure* and *de facto*, would reduce undesirable practices, such as corruption and cronyism, and foster a more dynamic private sector.

FDI restrictions can inhibit investment and its economic benefits

An open and non-discriminatory international investment environment has long-term benefits. Investment is critical to spur economic growth and sustainable development. It expands the productive capacity of an economy and drives job creation and income growth. International investment can provide further advantages. Beyond bringing additional capital to a host economy, FDI can help improve resource allocation, production capabilities, and access to international markets. It can also act as a conduit for local diffusion of technological and managerial expertise (see Chapter 2 on FDI trends and benefits in the MENA region for empirical evidence on the how FDI contributes to sustainable development outcomes).

The potential benefits of FDI are mostly accepted across governments, and attracting FDI has become an important policy tool to finance development in many countries. Nonetheless, nearly all governments impose some legal or regulatory limits on foreign investors' entry and operations, often to shield domestic investors from foreign competition for purely economic reasons. FDI restrictions are also commonly motivated by concerns over the loss of national sovereignty to protect essential security interests. Governments often justify FDI restrictions to secure the proper functioning of the economy against threats of denial or disruption of the supply of critical goods and services to the economy (Moran, 2009[2]). National security is a legitimate concern, but should not be a cover for protectionist policies (see Box 4.1 for an overview of OECD guidelines regarding restrictions based on national security) (OECD, 2008[3]) (OECD, 2020[4]).

FDI restrictions should be used narrowly, and only as a measure of last resort, if other non-discriminatory measures cannot adequately mitigate the identified risks or concerns. Moreover, as described below, discriminatory policies may not always be optimal for tackling identified risks or concerns. Restrictions on foreign investment involve economic costs that can in turn lead to lower competition and productivity, forgone government revenues, and reduced opportunities for spillovers.

The FDI restrictions analysed in this chapter are discriminatory measures explicit in regulations or laws. There are, however, other *de facto* restrictions on foreign investors. These include institutional or informal barriers to investment (such as excessive bureaucracy or corruption), inconsistent enforcement of statutory rules, as well as distortions caused by state ownership of key sectors, and special regulatory treatment received by certain firms. In the MENA region, state-owned enterprises (SOEs) (either civil or military) dominate many sectors, and often receive preferential regulatory treatment, which if abused, can crowd out private sector activity (World Bank, 2018[5]) (OECD, 2019[6]).

Fair competition is also hindered when private firms with influential political connections benefit from formal or informal preferential treatment, creating barriers to foreign and domestic firm entry.[1] For example, there is evidence that politically-connected firms in Egypt were protected from competition through non-tariff import barriers, such as exclusive license requirements, prior to 2011 (Diwan, Keefer and Schiffbauer, 2015[1]). Other benefits received by politically-connected firms in several countries in the region include preferential access to land or government contracts, favourable tax treatment, or non-uniform application of doing business procedures (World Bank, 2015[7]) (Atiyas, Diwan and Malik, 2019[8]). Though not covered in this chapter, these other restrictions, and crucially the enforcement of statutory restrictions, play a key role in the overall investment climate (Kalinova, Palerm and Thomsen, 2010[9]).

Box 4.1. OECD Investment Policy Principles and Guidelines for Recipient Country Investment Policies Relating to National Security

The OECD Investment Committee has been a forum for intergovernmental dialogue on how governments can reconcile the need to preserve and expand an open international investment environment with their duty to safeguard the essential security interests of their people. As the custodian of key international investment instruments – the *Code of Liberalisation of Capital Movements* and the *Declaration on International Investment and Multinational Enterprises* – the Organisation has overseen progress in liberalisation for more than 40 years.

Three principles underpin these instruments: transparency, liberalisation and non-discrimination. The non-discrimination principle sets out that all investors in like circumstances are treated equally, irrespective of their ownership. **National treatment** requires that a government treat foreign-owned or -controlled enterprises no less favourably than domestic enterprises in like situations.

OECD members and other participating governments have developed additional guidance for the one exception to non-discriminatory investment policies provided for in these instruments – that governments may take measures they "consider necessary to protect essential security interests" and to maintain "public order or the protection of public health, morals and safety". Investment policy measures addressing essential security interest should follow three principals:

1. Transparency and predictability: Information on restrictions on foreign investment should be comprehensive and accessible to everyone. While it is in investors' and governments' interests to maintain confidentiality of sensitive information, regulatory objectives and practices should be made as transparent as possible so as to increase the predictability of outcomes.
2. Proportionality: Restrictions on investment, or conditions on transaction, should not be greater than needed to protect national security and they should be avoided when other existing measures are adequate and appropriate to address a national security concern.
3. Accountability: Procedures for parliamentary oversight, judicial review, periodic regulatory impact assessments, and requirements that decisions to block an investment should be taken at high government levels should be considered to ensure accountability of the implementing authorities.

Source: (OECD, 2008[3])

Common statutory FDI restrictions and their economic costs

In most countries foreign equity limits, usually in specific sectors, are the most prevalent form of FDI restriction. This is the case among the MENA focus economies, with the exception of a few countries that apply wider restrictions across all or most sectors (Algeria, Libya and the Palestinian Authority, detailed below). The rational for equity limits, beyond national security concerns, is usually to protect domestic investors from foreign competition, or to push domestic investors to upgrade by forcing linkages between foreign investors and the host economy. The benefits of FDI to host economies are indeed partly associated with their spillovers to domestic firms, particularly knowledge transfers. Governments expect foreign equity limitations or joint venture requirements to facilitate such spillovers by strengthening interactions between domestic and foreign firms (see chapter 8 for other policies to promote linkages).

Such foreign equity conditions may not necessarily achieve their intended purpose. The exercise of control over foreign operations is one key underlying characteristics of foreign investment by multinational firms. Ownership restrictions limit investors' ability to exercise this control, possibly affecting their decision to invest in the first place. Foreign equity restrictions can also limit the potential financial and economic gains of a project. Foreign investors may be reluctant to enter into a joint venture with local investors, including because it may be difficult to find suitable local partners with the required capacity and skills. Investors might not want to share new technology and production techniques with these local partners, thereby limiting spillovers (Moran, Graham and Blomström, 2005[10]).

Screening and approval mechanisms are another common means to regulate the entry and behaviour of foreign investors, though their use has declined substantially in the past three decades (Mistura and Thomsen, 2017[11]). Discriminatory screening involves approval requirements for foreign investors beyond licensing or permit rules for domestic investors. Some countries screen FDI projects horizontally across all sectors, such as Tunisia before reforms in 2016; others screen only specific strategic sectors, or large projects (above a certain investment threshold). Governments that impose screening measures argue that they help to keep out potentially harmful projects to consumers or the environment, and ensure that projects generate the maximum potential benefit for the local economy, in terms of employment, R&D, or technology or managerial spillovers. What distinguishes screening from other licensing and authorisation processes is its discriminatory nature against foreign-owned investments. For this reason, screening based on economic criteria is listed as an exception to national treatment in international agreements and under the OECD Declaration and Decisions on International Investment and Multinational Enterprises, as well as a reservation under the OECD Code of Liberalisation of Capital Movements. Screening which is exclusively for considerations of national security is listed for transparency purposes under the Declaration (Box 4.1).

Screening requirements can dissuade foreign investors, however, as they create unpredictable and costly barriers to entry. Criteria for approving investors, such as national interest, are often vague or left undefined. Conditions imposed can be arbitrary, inconsistent and non-transparent, creating restrictions that are discretionary and sometimes fairly stringent, such as limitations on foreign shareholding, forced technology transfer and asset divestment. Approval mechanisms also impose administrative costs to the government and investors.

Other barriers to FDI, including restrictions on employment of foreign key personnel, land acquisition by foreigners, or limits on the repatriation of profit and capital, also affect the profitability or structure of the business activity. As such, even when governments justify these restrictions by policy concerns, they raise transaction costs for foreign-owned firms relative to competing locations, and may negatively influence firms' investment decisions (Mistura and Roulet, 2019[12]). Alternative policy instruments may be better suited to achieve certain goals.

By potentially dissuading foreign investors, FDI restrictions also reduce competition, thereby inhibiting sectoral and even economy-wide productivity gains. In the MENA region, weak private sector competition, marked by the prevalence of a few dominant firms, is one the main impediments to more dynamic job and firm growth.[2] FDI restrictions can limit domestic as well as foreign firm entry and further entrench market power of select businesses. Under the pre-2011 government in Tunisia for example, firms connected to the government were more prevalent in sectors restricted to foreign investors under the previous 1993 Investment Code. There is evidence that these firms performed better than peers, in terms of market share and profit, largely because of these entry regulations, effectively crowding out competitors (Rijkers, Freund and Nucifora, 2017[13]).

Beyond the types of restrictions in place, the legibility and transparency of laws and regulations on FDI also affect investors' entry (See chapter 3 for more details on the importance of a coherent investment policy framework). In the MENA region, details on discriminatory measures often involve lengthy and frequently updated lists of un-restricted sectors, making it difficult for investors, particularly smaller firms with fewer resources, to understand prevalent rules. A more transparent and predictable approach involves a "negative list", whereby all foreign investment projects are authorised without any discriminatory conditions, except specific sectors or sub-sectors clearly outlined in the negative list. Among the MENA focus economies, Jordan has a negative list, and Tunisia and Algeria are in the process of adopting this approach. When a negative list is used, however, it is important that the list is publically available, with sufficient detail on the sectors involved, and easy to understand. A long delay between the publication of legislation authorising a negative list and the details of the list, as occurred in Tunisia, can confuse and hold up investors, adding an additional hurdle on top of the restriction itself.

MENA economies tend to be more restrictive than their peers

Despite the economic costs of these measures, nearly all governments impose some restrictions on foreign investors. The OECD *FDI Regulatory Restrictiveness Index* allows for a comparative assessment of statutory FDI restrictions in over 70 countries across four main types of FDI restrictions (Box 4.2). In the MENA region, Egypt, Jordan, Morocco and Tunisia are adherents to the OECD *Declaration on International Investment and Multinational Enterprises*. As such, they commit to accord national treatment – to treat foreign-owned or -controlled enterprises operating on their territory no less favourably than domestic enterprises – subject to a list of exceptions. These countries' scores on the *Index* reflect their reported list of exceptions to national treatment under the OECD National Treatment Instrument, updated yearly.[3] Scores for Algeria, Lebanon, Libya and the Palestinian Authority reflect the results of a questionnaire completed by relevant authorities, supplemented by a comprehensive legal review of the relevant legislations of each economy by the OECD secretariat.

FDI restrictiveness varies greatly across countries and regions (Figure 4.1). OECD economies are among the least restrictive, while large countries, resource-rich economies and countries in the Asia-Pacific region tend to be more restrictive. The eight MENA focus economies are on average more restrictive than most countries covered by the *Index*, but there is considerable variation among them. Morocco and Egypt impose foreign investment restrictions that are close to the average level of restrictions in OECD countries. Algeria, Libya and the Palestinian Authority, however, have the highest levels of restrictions of all economies covered by the *Index*. Jordan also imposes restrictions that are on the upper end of the spectrum, while Tunisia and Lebanon's restrictions are close to the average for non-OECD economies covered by the *Index*.

The high scores of the most restrictive MENA economies are largely driven by horizontal restrictions applied across various sectors to all or most foreign investors. Among the most stringent measures is Palestinian Authority's prohibition of majority foreign ownership across sectors with few exceptions (e.g. manufacturing, banking, hotels and restaurants). Until recently, Algeria restricted foreign ownership to less than 50% of the firm's equity in all sectors, but the government lifted this restriction in 2020. Libya prohibits foreign investment in a relatively long list of sectors. It also restricts entry by requiring foreign investors to carry out business through joint-ventures with minority foreign shareholding or wholly-owned greenfield specific investment vehicles, subject to government approval and discriminatory minimum capital requirements. Except for Libya, none of the MENA focus economies apply economy-wide screening measures to regulate the entry of foreign investors, though some governments impose discriminatory approvals or criteria for admitting foreign investment in certain sectors, or in some cases both.

Box 4.2. The OECD FDI Regulatory Restrictiveness Index

The OECD *FDI Regulatory Restrictiveness Index* gauges the restrictiveness of an economy's FDI rules. The FDI *Index* is currently available for more than 70 economies, including all OECD and G20 members, allowing comparison of FDI policies and identification of potential areas for reform. It is commonly used on a stand-alone basis to assess the restrictiveness of FDI policies when reviewing candidates for OECD accession and in OECD Investment Policy Reviews, including reviews of new adherent countries to the OECD *Declaration on International Investment and Multinational Enterprises*.

The *Index* does not provide a full measure of an economy's investment climate as it does not score the actual implementation of formal restrictions and does not take into account other aspects of the investment regulatory framework, such as the extent of state ownership and other institutional and informal restrictions that may also affect the FDI climate. Nonetheless, FDI rules are a critical determinant of an economy's attractiveness to foreign investors; the index, used in combination with other indicators measuring the various aspects of the FDI climate, may help to explain variations among economies in attracting FDI.

The FDI Index covers 22 sectors, including agriculture, mining, electricity, manufacturing and main services (transports, construction, distribution, communications, real estate, financial and professional services). For each sector, the scoring is based on the following elements:

- the level of foreign equity ownership permitted
- the screening and approval procedures applied to inward foreign direct investment
- restrictions on key foreign personnel (e.g. CEO, technical expert)
- other operational restrictions (e.g. land ownership, branching, profit repatriation).

Restrictions are evaluated on a 0 (open) to 1 (closed) scale. The overall restrictiveness index is the average of the 22 individual sectoral scores. The discriminatory nature of measures, i.e. when they only apply to foreign investors, is the central criterion for scoring a measure. State ownership and state monopolies, to the extent they are not discriminatory towards foreigners, are not scored. For OECD and non-OECD country adherents to the OECD *Declaration on International Investment and Multinational Enterprises*, the measures taken into account by the Index are limited to statutory regulatory restrictions on FDI, as reflected in their list of exceptions to national treatment and measures notified for transparency under OECD instruments, without assessing their actual enforcement.

For non-OECD economies, information is collected through Investment Policy Reviews or, when not in the review process, through a dedicated questionnaire. Regulatory information is updated on a yearly basis following the monitoring of investment measures carried in the context of OECD Freedom of Investment Forum for participating economies, and on the basis of ad hoc monitoring for the remaining ones.

Source: (Kalinova, Palerm and Thomsen, 2010[9])

Figure 4.1. OECD FDI Regulatory Restrictiveness Index (MENA 2019)

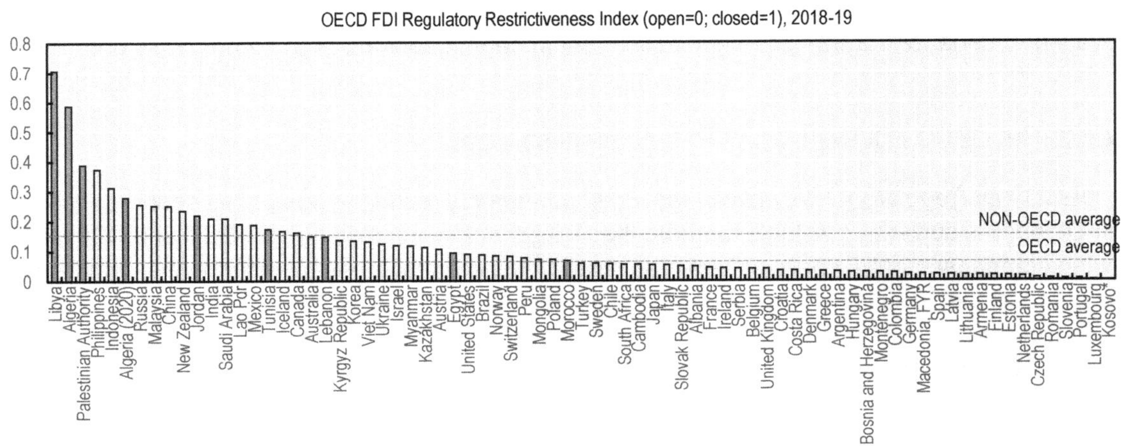

Note: The OECD FDI Regulatory Restrictiveness Index only covers statutory measures discriminating against foreign investors. The implementation of regulations, restrictions related to national security, state monopolies, preferential treatment for export-oriented investors and special economic zone regimes are not considered. Data reflect regulatory restrictions as of December 2019 for the MENA8 countries and 2018 for all others.
Source: OECD FDI Regulatory Restrictiveness Index (database), www.oecd.org/investment/fdiindex.htm.

Other horizontal restrictions among the MENA focus economies include limits on foreign land ownership – Lebanon and Jordan require approvals for land purchases for business use by foreigners – and preference to domestic firms in government procurement – applied in Algeria, Jordan and the Palestinian Authority. Algeria also maintains conditions for the repatriation of profits by foreigner investors, guaranteeing free transfer of capital only to those investments above a minimum threshold.

Aside from these horizontal restrictions, sector-specific limits on foreign equity ownership are the most prevalent forms of discrimination against foreign investors among the MENA focus economies (Figure **4**.2). This is also the most common restriction in most countries covered by the *Index*. Also like most countries, the MENA focus economies impose more restrictions in service sectors than in manufacturing, which is for the most part open to foreign investors (except when horizontal restrictions are in place). Sectoral restrictions are more severe and widespread than in peer countries, however, including in Southeast Asia and Latin America. Limiting foreign access to certain sectors holds back potential economy-wide productivity gains.

By hindering competition in service sectors, for instance, restrictions consequently raise costs of service inputs, such as financing and logistics, for other economic sectors. Empirical studies demonstrate the negative relationship between manufacturing productivity levels and barriers to competition or foreign participation in services sectors (OECD, 2015[14]) (OECD, 2018[15]). Market access reform allow for more competition in service sectors, and consequently, higher productivity. This in turn allows downstream manufacturers to benefit from higher quality or low cost services inputs, key to moving manufacturing up the value chain (see Chapter 8 on enabling SME linkages with foreign firms in global value chains). Among the MENA focus economies, restrictions on business, financial, distribution and transport services – all key inputs for all other sectors – are common. These sectors tend to be mostly open to foreign investors in OECD and many Latin American countries, with the exception of some limited restrictions in transport. The restrictions on foreign investment in these services in the MENA region are also higher than in other emerging markets, including ASEAN countries, particularly in distribution and business services, though there is wide variation in restrictions among ASEAN members (OECD, 2020[16]).

Figure 4.2. OECD FDI Regulatory Restrictiveness Index by sector (MENA 2019)

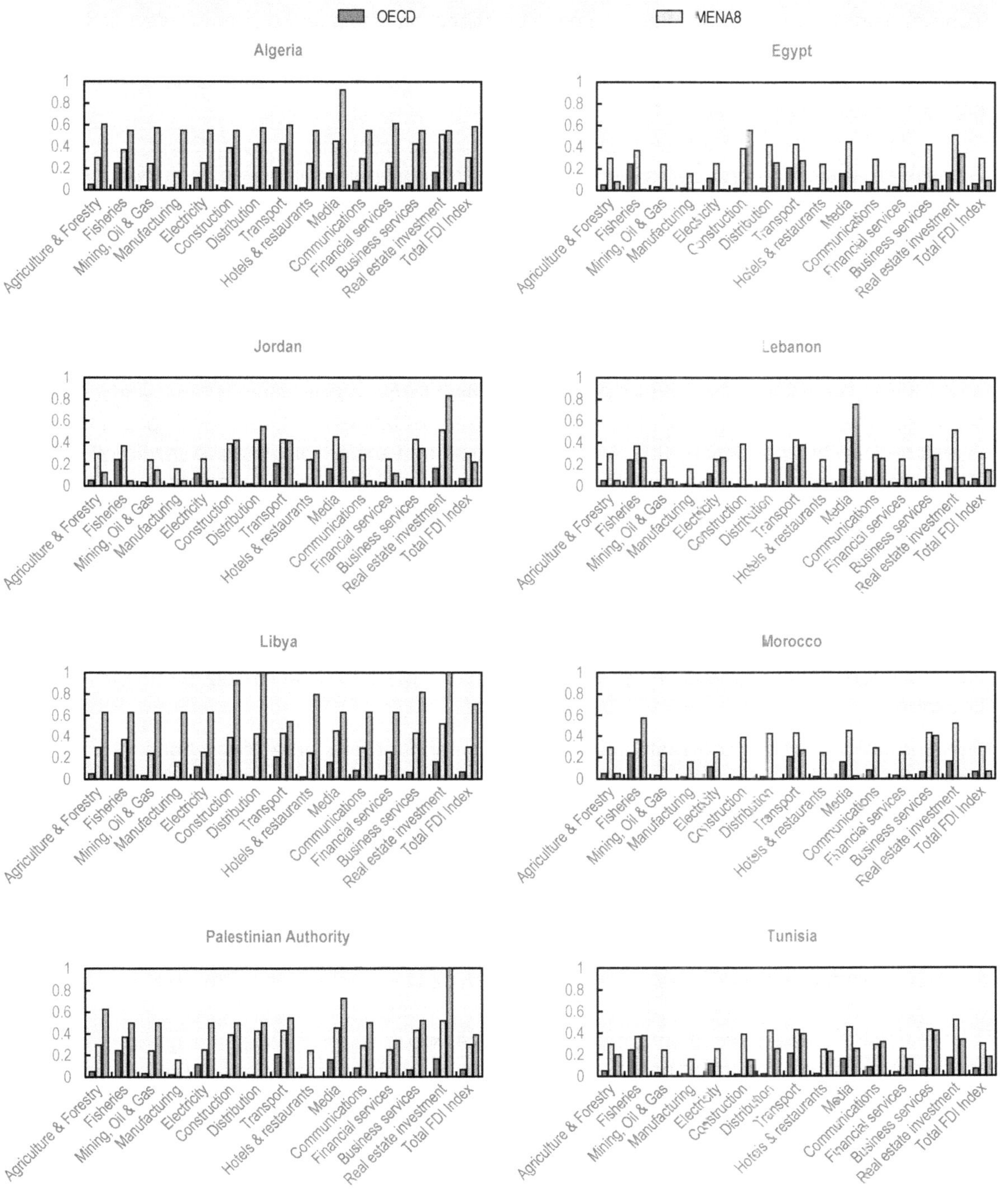

Note: see Figure 4.1 note.
Source: OECD FDI Regulatory Restrictiveness Index (database), www.oecd.org/investment/fdiindex.htm.

Sectoral foreign equity restrictions among the MENA economies include:

- Business & financial services: Foreign ownership in legal services is restricted in Lebanon and Tunisia. Tunisia and Jordan place some restrictions on engineering, and Jordan limits foreign control of scientific and technical consulting firms. Foreign ownership in architectural, accounting and auditing services is limited in Morocco. Algeria, Lebanon, Jordan and Tunisia restrict foreign equity in some financial services.
- Distribution: Wholesale trade and retail is open only to domestic firms in Egypt, Libya and the Palestinian Authority. Jordan and Lebanon restrict foreign equity ownership in distribution services to under 50%. Majority ownership by foreigners in distribution enterprises in Tunisia is subject to prior government authorisation
- Transport: Algeria, Egypt, Jordan, Lebanon, Morocco and Tunisia place limits on foreign ownership in air and maritime transport. Jordan also restricts foreign equity control to less than 50% in rail and road transport, and Lebanon limits foreign ownership in land cargo transport. Libya prohibits foreign investment in road transport and auxiliary transport services in ports.
- Agriculture: Algeria and Palestinian Authority prohibit foreign ownership of most agricultural land (although the Palestinian Authority allows long-term leases). Algeria also prohibits foreign investment in the production, use, transport, import and export of certain agricultural products. While Morocco allows foreign investors to lease agricultural land, outright ownership is prohibited, though a proposed law may revise this restriction.
- Real estate: real estate investments by foreigners are in many cases prohibited in Jordan, Libya and the Palestinian Authority.
- Construction: foreign equity in construction is limited to under 50% in Egypt and Jordan. In Tunisia, foreign majority investments are subject to prior government authorisation.
- Fisheries: foreign investments in fisheries prohibited in Morocco and limited to minority interest in Lebanon.

Some MENA countries also place restrictions on key personnel and other operations. For example, Lebanon requires that nationals make up the majority of boards of directors of joint-stock companies, and joint-stock companies are mandatory in several service sectors, including insurance, banking and finance. Business services, including auditing, accounting and insurance, are subject to personnel requirements or reciprocity agreements in several MENA economics, including in Algeria, Tunisia and the Palestinian Authority.

Several MENA governments have removed important FDI restrictions

While FDI restrictions remain prevalent across the MENA focus economies, some governments have implemented important reforms in the past several years to ease discriminatory measures against foreign investment. As mentioned above, Algeria recently took steps to remove its most significant restriction, the cap on foreign ownership to 49% of a firm's equity in all sectors. The 2020 Finance Law provides that foreign equity restrictions apply only in sectors of national strategic interest and for distribution services. Strategic sectors listed in the law include: minerals, energy, military industries, airports, railroads, ports, and pharmaceuticals (Government of Algeria, 2020[17]).

Jordan has also eased some of its horizontal restrictions on FDI. In 2016 it removed the minimum capital requirement for foreign investors (Regulation No.77). The measure placed foreign investors at a disadvantage to Jordanian competitors in low-capital industries, such as knowledge-based sectors, and likely diminished Jordan's competitiveness compared to other countries where capital requirements are mostly non-existent or much less burdensome. The previous capital requirement was substantially greater than non-discriminatory capital requirements (applied to both domestic and foreign investors) in OECD countries and large emerging countries including China, Indonesia, India and Russia (OECD, 2018[18]). The 2016 reform also expanded the sectors open to full ownership by non-Jordanians. In 2019, Jordan further eased restrictions placed on foreign investors in certain services activities including construction, distribution, transport and media (Regulation No. 80 of 2019).

Tunisia also removed a significant FDI restriction in its 2016 Investment Law. Previously, foreign investment required prior approval if foreign equity exceeded 50% of a firm's capital, except in the case of fully export-oriented activities, which were exempt from such requirement (OECD, 2012[19]). The 2016 law removed this requirement, guaranteeing national treatment for foreign investors with few exceptions, notably in sectors where foreign equity conditions apply and those subject to obtaining a foreign merchant card (Government of Tunisia, 2018[20]). Other recent reforms in the region include a 2019 amendment to Lebanon's Code of Commerce partly easing the restriction on foreign personnel on boards of directors of Lebanese Joint Stock Companies (Law No.126 of 29/03/2019).

These reforms are important steps towards a more open and predictable investment framework for foreign companies (see Chapter 3 on Legal Reforms for more examples of investment-related legislative reforms in the MENA region). Jordan and Tunisia's liberalisation measures have changed their positions on the *Index,* and are now closer to the non-OECD average. Algeria's position is likely to change in next year's *Index* (2020) as per simulated results below (Figure 4.3). However, barriers to FDI in the three continue to be greater than in the average OECD and non-OECD country. Algeria and Jordan remain among the most restrictive of the MENA focus economies. Even for MENA countries more open to foreign investment, the effects of remaining restrictions on both inward investment and economic development can be sizable.

Figure 4.3. Tracking FDI reforms in Algeria, Jordan, Lebanon and Tunisia

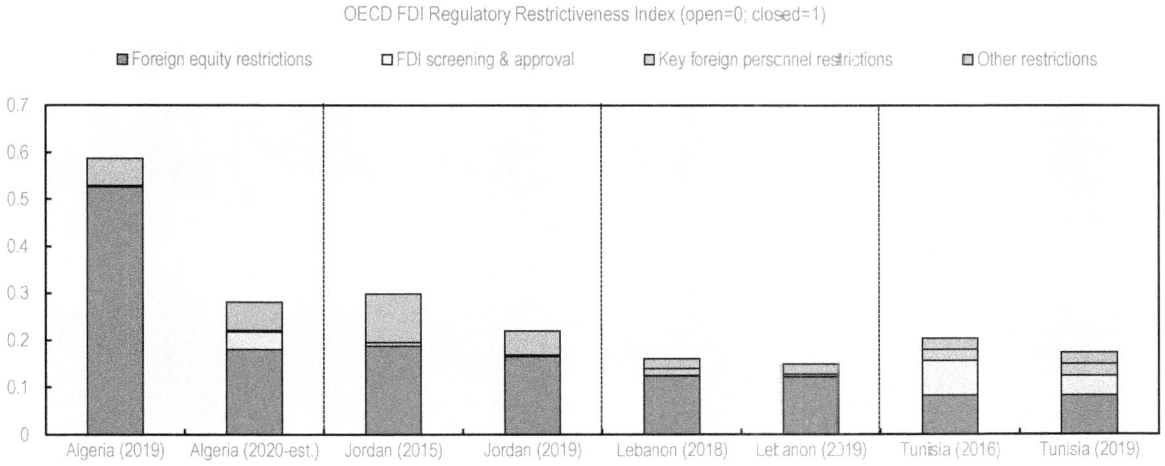

Note: The above results reflect regulatory changes introduced by mainly: (1) Algeria: Finance Law No. 20-07 of 2020; (2) Jordan: Regulation No. 77 of 2016 on non-Jordanian investors, and its revision by Regulation No. 80 of 2019; (3) Lebanon: Law No. 126 of 2019 modifying certain provisions of the Lebanese Code of Commerce (No. 304 of 1942); (4) Tunisia: Investment Law No. 2016-71 of 2016 and Government Decree No. 2018-407 of 2018 related to the issuance of the exclusive list of economic activities subject to licensing and the list of administrative licenses to complete a project and to control and simplify the relevant provisions and simplify them.
Source: OECD FDI Regulatory Restrictiveness Index (database), www.oecd.org/investment/fdiindex.htm.

Egypt's own experience seems to confirm that foreign investors respond favourably to regulatory reforms that level the playing field for all investors. Liberalisation reforms in the early 2000s corresponded with a significant rise in inward FDI, though global FDI flows also rose during this period (Figure 4.4).

Even partial restrictions to FDI can inhibit investment. Recent OECD research shows that liberalisation reforms can have a sizable and significant effect on FDI (Mistura and Roulet, 2019[12]). Reducing the level of FDI restrictiveness, as measured by the *Index*, by 10% could lead to 2.1% increase in bilateral FDI inward stocks on average, all else held equal. If this average effect were to apply equally across all countries, the more restrictive economies could expect FDI stocks to be between 7 and 95% higher if they were to ease FDI restrictions to the OECD average level. Egypt, for example, could expect its FDI stocks to be up to 37% higher (OECD, 2020[21]). The magnitude of the impact of liberalisation reforms on FDI would in practice vary between countries, but the estimation gives a sense of how restrictions act as barriers to investment. Foreign equity limitations appear to have the greatest effect on FDI, followed by screening policies (Mistura and Roulet, 2019[12]). The persistence of both forms of restrictions across the MENA focus economies suggests that there is substantial room for FDI growth if governments continue to advance liberalisation reforms.

Figure 4.4. Co-movement of liberalisation reforms and FDI stocks in Egypt

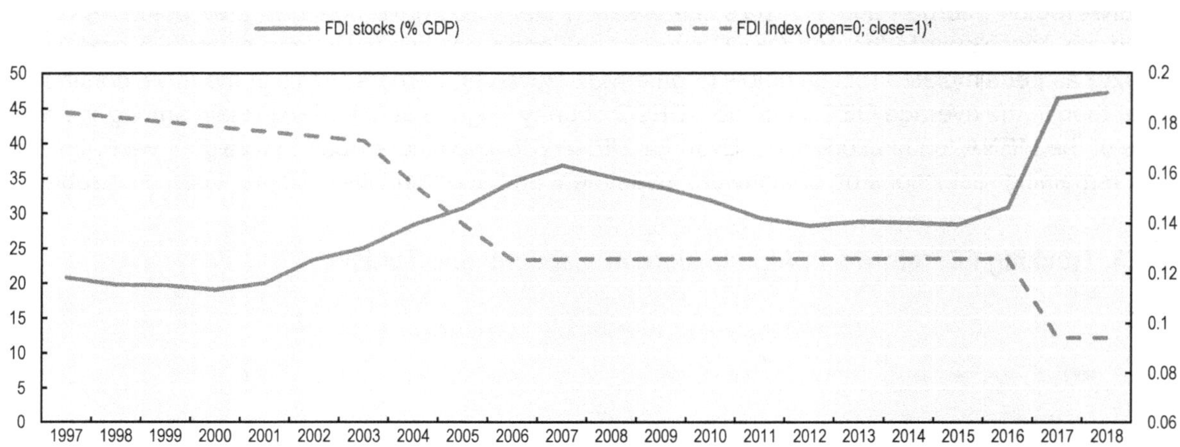

Note: Index scores linearly interpolated over missing periods
Source: (OECD, 2020[22])

References

Atiyas, I., I. Diwan and A. Malik (2019), "Introduction", in *Crony Capitalism in the Middle East*, Oxford University Press, http://dx.doi.org/10.1093/oso/9780198799870.003.0001. [8]

Diwan, I., P. Keefer and M. Schiffbauer (2015), "Pyramid Capitalism: Cronyism, Regulation, and Firm Productivity in Egypt", *Center for International Development Working Paper*, No. 291, Harvard University, Cambridge. [1]

Government of Algeria (2020), "Loi n. 20-07 du Chaoual 1441 correspondant au 4 juin 2020 portant loi de finances complentaire pour 2020", *Journal Officiel de la Republique Algerienne* 33, https://www.douane.gov.dz/IMG/pdf/loi_no20-07_du_04_juin_2020_portant_loi_de_finances_complementaire_pour_2020.pdf (accessed on 14 August 2020). [17]

Government of Tunisia (2018), *Décret gouvernemental n° 2018-417 du 11 mai 2018 relatif à la publication de la liste exclusive des activités économiques soumises à autorisation et de la liste des autorisations administratives requises pour la réalisation de projets*, http://www.legislation.tn/fr/detailtexte/D%C3%A9cret%20Gouvernemental-num-2018-417-du-11-05-2018-jort-2018-038__20180380041732 (accessed on 27 May 2020). [20]

Kalinova, B., A. Palerm and S. Thomsen (2010), "OECD's FDI Restrictiveness Index: 2010 Update", *OECD Working Papers on International Investment*, No. 2010/3, OECD Publishing, Paris, https://dx.doi.org/10.1787/5km91p02zj7g-en. [9]

Malik, A. and B. Awadallah (2013), "The Economics of the Arab Spring", *World Development*, Vol. 45, pp. 296-313, http://dx.doi.org/10.1016/j.worlddev.2012.12.015. [23]

Mistura, F. and C. Roulet (2019), "The determinants of Foreign Direct Investment: Do statutory restrictions matter?", *OECD Working Papers on International Investment*, No. 2019/01, OECD Publishing, Paris, https://dx.doi.org/10.1787/641507ce-en. [12]

Mistura, F. and S. Thomsen (2017), *Is investment protectionism on the rise? Evidence from the OECD FDI Regulatory Restrictiveness Index*, OECD, https://www.oecd.org/investment/globalforum/2017-GFII-Background-Note-Is-investment-protectionism-on-the-rise.pdf (accessed on 28 May 2020). [11]

Moran, T. (2009), *Foreign acquisitions and national security: what are genuine threats? What are implausible worries?*, http://www.oecd.org/investment/globalforum/44231367.pdf. [2]

Moran, T., E. Graham and M. Blomström (2005), "Conclusions and Implications for FDI Policy in Developing Countries, New Methods of Research, and a Future Research Agenda", in Moran, G. and Magnus Blomström (eds.), *Does Foreign Direct Investment Promote Development?*, Institute for International Economics, Washington, D.C. [10]

OECD (2020), *Acquisition- and ownership-related policies to safeguard essential security interests: current and emerging trends, observed designs, and policy practice in 62 economies*, OECD, Paris, http://www.oecd.org/investment/OECD-Acquisition-ownership-policies-security-May2020.pdf (accessed on 28 May 2020). [4]

OECD (2020), *OECD Investment Policy Reviews: Egypt*, OECD, Paris. [22]

OECD (2020), *OECD Investment Policy Reviews: Egypt 2020*, OECD Investment Policy Reviews, OECD Publishing, Paris, https://dx.doi.org/10.1787/9f9c589a-en. [21]

OECD (2020), *OECD Investment Policy Reviews: Indonesia 2020*, OECD Investment Policy Reviews, OECD Publishing, Paris, https://dx.doi.org/10.1787/b56512da-en. [16]

OECD (2019), *Corporate governance in MENA: Building a Framework for Competitiveness and Growth*, OECD Publishing, https://doi.org/10.1787/20776535. [6]

OECD (2018), *Enhancing the legal framework for sustainable investment: Lessons from Jordan*, Jordan Competitiveness and Investment Project, OECD, https://www.oecd.org/mena/competitiveness/Enhancing-the-Legal-Framework-for-Sustainable-Investment-Lessons-from-Jordan.pdf (accessed on 26 May 2020). [18]

OECD (2018), *OECD Investment Policy Reviews: Southeast Asia*, https://www.oecd.org/investment/oecd-investment-policy-review-southeast-asia.htm. [15]

OECD (2015), *The Future of Productivity*, http://www.oecd.org/economy/growth/OECD-2015-The-future-of-productivity-book.pdf. [14]

OECD (2012), *OECD Investment Policy Reviews: Tunisia 2012*, OECD Investment Policy Reviews, OECD Publishing, Paris, https://dx.doi.org/10.1787/9789264179172-en. [19]

OECD (2008), "Freedom of investment, national security and 'strategic' industries", *Progress report published following the 7th Roundtable on Freedom of Investment, National Security and 'Strategic' Industries*, OECD, Paris, http://www.oecd.org/daf/investment/foi. (accessed on 28 May 2020). [3]

Rijkers, B., C. Freund and A. Nucifora (2017), "All in the family: State capture in Tunisia", *2017*, Vol. 124, pp. 41-59. [13]

World Bank (2018), *Privilege-Resistant Policies in the Middle East and North Africa: Measurement and Operational Implications*, World Bank, Washington DC, http://dx.doi.org/10.1596/978-1-4648-1207-1. [5]

World Bank (2015), *Jobs or Privileges: Unleashing the Employment Potential of the Middle East and North Africa*, World Bank, Washington DC. [7]

Notes

[1] Connections to the state can be formalised by current or former members of government on board, or involve more informal connections (such as family or other close personal relationships). For more details on privileged firms and their impact on economic growth see, (World Bank, 2015[7]), (Atiyas, Diwan and Malik, 2019[8]) (compilation of analysis on the region, Egypt, Morocco, Lebanon, Tunisia and Jordan); (Diwan, Keefer and Schiffbauer, 2015[1]) (Egypt); (Rijkers, Freund and Nucifora, 2017[13]) (Tunisia).

[2] See, among others: (OECD, 2020[21]), (World Bank, 2018[5]), (World Bank, 2015[7]), (Malik and Awadallah, 2013[23]).

[3] The National Treatment obliges adhering countries to notify their exceptions to National Treatment and establishes follow-up procedures to deal with such exceptions in the OECD.

5 Investment treaty policy and dispute settlement

The eight MENA economies covered in this report have entered into a significant number of international investment agreements and experienced a rise in investor-state investment dispute cases in the last decade. This chapter takes stock of these developments. It highlights the need to consider and engage in reforms with a focus on the revision of investment treaty policy, clarifications of legal provisions and implementation of dispute avoidance measures and mechanisms.

Summary and policy considerations

The eight MENA economies covered in this report (MENA focus economies) have concluded a significant number of international investment agreements (IIAs). Based on publicly-available information, these economies have concluded at least 420 bilateral investment treaties (BITs), out of which 309 are understood to have entered into force (which represents around 13 % of the total BITs that are understood to have entered into force worldwide), two main regional investment agreements (the Arab Investment Agreement between members of the Arab League and the Investment Agreement of the Organization of Islamic Cooperation), as well as several trade and investment agreements and other international investment-related agreements. Many of these agreements show features of the so-called first-generation treaties and include relatively vague substantive provisions, with lack of clarity that could be broadly interpreted by arbitral tribunals. A global trend towards revision of investment treaty policy and practice is reflected in the approaches of some of the MENA focus economies, but reforms need to be further encouraged to ensure an appropriate balance between investment protection and the state's right to regulate.

The number of investor-State dispute settlement (ISDS) cases in the region rose sharply in the last decade. The total number of known treaty-based ISDS cases against MENA focus economies reached 84 (8.2 % of the world total) and the majority were initiated in the last decade. ISDS mechanisms protect states and investors against misbehaviours, but raise concerns at the global level given the rise in cases, their impact, costs, complexity, transparency and legitimacy. These developments have triggered reforms at the international and national levels in many countries. MENA focus economies are encouraged to engage continually with international policy debates regarding the outcomes of ISDS cases and reflect on measures to limit their exposure to and avoid investment disputes.

The social and political upheavals in many MENA countries beginning in 2011 indicate some correlation between political and economic crises and the increased use of ISDS mechanisms by investors in some of the MENA focus economies. While it may be too soon to identify a similar link between investment disputes and the Covid-19 crisis, MENA governments need to remain vigilant, build awareness and understanding, and take proactive approaches to dispute prevention and management. There are already relevant dispute prevention mechanisms in place in some of the focus economies and the crisis units established in some investment promotion agencies (IPAs) as a response to the Covid-19 pandemic also play a preventive role. This trend should be further encouraged based on existing good practices to accelerate effective implementation.

Policy considerations

- Revise investment treaty policy and practice: evaluate the treaty network, assess the costs and benefits of key provisions and their potential impact, and where appropriate, consider ways to update key provisions to bring them in line with current priorities add further clarifications and ensure a better balance between investor protection and the government's right to regulate. Depending on the context and treaty language, it may be possible to achieve these goals through joint interpretations agreed with treaty partners. In other cases, treaty amendments may be required. Replacement of older investment treaties by consent may also be appropriate in some cases.
- Participate in multilateral and regional discussions on investment agreements and dispute mechanisms to build awareness on the issues at stake, avoid inconsistencies with the bilateral treaty network, ensure coherence (including with investment laws and contracts), and develop reforms that respond to governments' intent while continuing to protect investors. To that end, engage with treaty partners and relevant regional organisations' secretariats, follow-up on on-

going discussions in international fora (OECD, UNCITRAL and ICSID) and engage actively in shaping the design of future treaties under negotiation, such as the Investment Protocol of the African Continental Free Trade Area.

- Consider reforms that would limit exposure to investment arbitration claims, in particular in times of crisis, with clarified legal provisions to improve consistency in interpretations by arbitral tribunals, but also through dispute prevention and management mechanisms. To that end, build on the measures taken by MENA IPAs in response to the Covid-19 crisis to enhance communication with investors and identify potential issues, and reinforce governmental co-ordination and mechanisms to prevent and manage potential disputes.

MENA economies have concluded a significant number of international investment agreements

Content and purpose of investment agreements

Like many countries around the world, the MENA focus economies have taken on international obligations to grant foreign investors specific treatment in a significant number of international investment agreements (referred to as investment treaties or IIAs). These obligations in bilateral investment treaties (BITs), regional investment agreements or investment chapters of trade and investment agreements grant certain protections to covered investors in addition to and independently from protections afforded by domestic law. Domestic investors are generally not covered by these treaties.

Investment treaties typically contain substantive protections for covered investments against expropriation or discrimination. Provisions requiring "fair and equitable treatment" (FET) are also common and have given rise to widely varying interpretations. While there are some significant recent exceptions, investment treaties also generally give covered investors access to investor-state dispute settlement (ISDS) mechanisms that allow them access to international arbitration to seek monetary compensation in cases where they claim that the host country has infringed on these provisions. While domestic law does not typically provide compensation beyond narrowly-defined situations, such as cases of expropriation, compensation has been a common remedy for investors in ISDS cases.

Investment protection provided under investment treaties can play an important role in fostering a healthy regulatory climate for investment. Expropriation or discrimination by governments does occur. Government acceptance of legitimate constraints on policies can provide investors with greater certainty and predictability, lowering unwarranted risk and the cost of capital. Domestic judicial and administrative systems provide investors with one option for protecting themselves. Access to international arbitration under investment treaties gives substantial additional leverage to covered foreign investors in their dealings with host governments.

Investment treaties are frequently promoted as a method of attracting FDI and this is a goal for many governments. Despite many studies, however, it remains difficult to establish strong evidence of impact in this regard (Pohl, 2018[1]). Some studies suggest that treaties or instruments that reduce barriers and restrictions to foreign investment have more impact on FDI flows than BITs focused only on post-establishment protection (Mistura and Roulet, 2019[2]). These assumptions continue to be investigated by a growing strand of empirical literature on the purposes of investment treaties and how well they are being achieved.

Bilateral Investment Treaties (BITs)

MENA governments have been active signatories of bilateral investment treaties (BITs). Based on publicly-available information, the MENA focus economies have concluded 420 BITs as of September 2020, out of which 309 are understood to have entered into force (Figure 5.1).[1] This represents 13.1 % of the total BITs entered into force worldwide (2,340). It is noteworthy that a third of these MENA BITs (over 100 treaties in total) have not entered into force, i.e. they have only been signed but not ratified and hence do not have legal value. Some BITs were also terminated, while others were renegotiated.

Worldwide, Egypt is the fifth most active signatory of BITs, after Germany (129), China (125), Switzerland (112), Turkey (109) and equally with the United Kingdom (100). While Egypt has not signed BITs since 2014, Morocco continues to be active, having signed its 72nd BITs with Japan in January 2020.

The number of BITs concluded by the MENA focus economies has increased in 1990s and subsequently slowed down. The slowing and recent reversal in the number of existing investment treaty relationships in force is a broad phenomenon reflecting the policies of many governments. As for other governments, this may reflect experiences in the MENA focus economies as respondents in ISDS claims. These economies mostly signed BITs with OECD countries and the rest of the world, proportionally more than with the other countries of the MENA region. The signature of the Abraham Accords in September 2020 might open the way to BITs negotiations with Israel, which agreed to sign the first Arab-Israeli BIT with UAE.

Figure 5.1. BITs concluded by MENA focus economies, including intra-MENA BITs (as of July 2020)

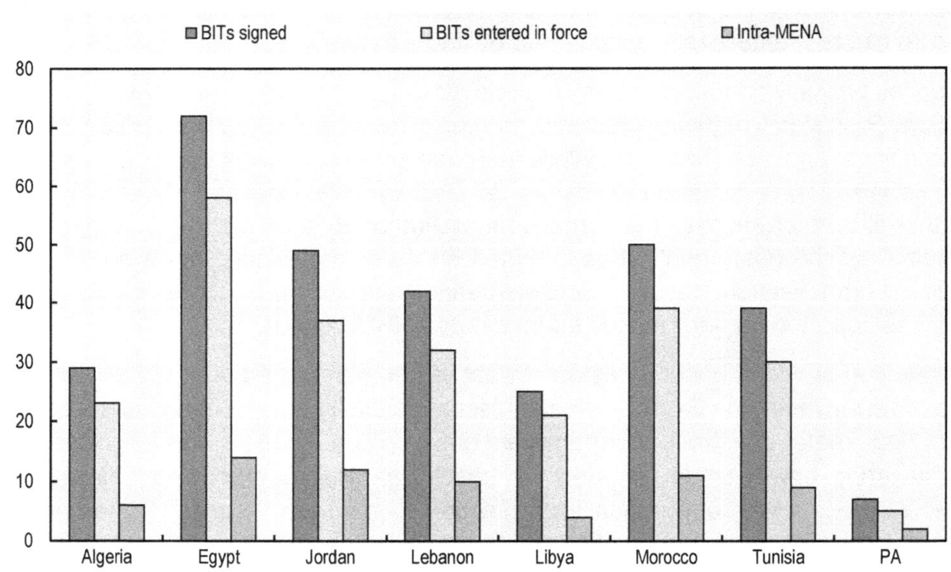

Source: UNCTAD Investment Policy Hub / MENA-OECD Competitiveness Programme, 2020.

MENA focus economies also entered into **bilateral economic agreements** which contain investment-related provisions, usually focusing on investment promotion and/or trade in services, but not the full set of investment protection provisions that are commonly found BITs:

- All MENA focus economies (except Libya and PA) have entered into **Association Agreements with the European Union**, which do not include specific investment provisions. Following the 2011 events in the region, and with a view to support the associated democratic and economic transitions, the European Commission has established a mandate to negotiate agreements establishing a Deep and Comprehensive Free Trade Area (DCFTA) with Morocco and Tunisia.

Expected to promote a progressive economic integration of these countries with the EU, these agreements should cover a full range of regulatory areas of mutual interest and, for the first time in EU agreements, investment market access. However, negotiations have stalled for the last few years, only a few rounds took place without concrete developments. Beside political and technical hurdles, there is an overall resistance from civil society and the business sector, as well as a lack of political backing.

- Several **free trade agreements** (FTAs) were signed by MENA governments, but only the FTA between Morocco and the United States contains a dedicated chapter on investment with core protection provisions. Egypt, Jordan, Lebanon, Morocco and Tunisia concluded FTAs with the European Free Trade Association (EFTA: Switzerland, Norway, Iceland and Liechtenstein). Turkey signed FTAs with Egypt, Morocco and Tunisia – the FTA with Jordan was terminated. Jordan also entered into FTAs with Singapore and the US.
- The United States signed **Trade and Investment Framework Agreements** (TIFA) with countries with which they do not have a FTA (Algeria, Egypt, Lebanon and Libya). However, they have not entered into force and only aim at promoting investment.
- Following Brexit and the Withdrawal Agreement with the EU, the United Kingdom concluded **continuity agreements** to maintain trade relationships – though without investment protection provisions – after 31 December 2020. Jordan, Morocco, PA and Tunisia entered into these agreements as of February 2020, the agreement with Egypt will come into effect on 31 December 2020 and Algeria engaged into negotiations (UNCTAD, 2020[3]).

Regional investment agreements

The MENA focus economies have also entered into regional investment agreements.

In 1980, the Unified Agreement for the Investment of Arab Capital in the Arab States (**Arab Investment Agreement** – AIA) was signed by the members of the League of Arab States. It entered into force in 1981 and was amended in 2013 – though the amendment was ratified by only a small number of countries.

In 1981, the member states of the Organization of Islamic Cooperation adopted the Agreement on Promotion and Protection and Guarantee of Investments (the **OIC Investment Agreement**). Effective since 1988, it has been ratified by 29 out of 36 member states to date.

Both of these agreements contain similar features to many older investment treaties. They include several investment protection provisions such as the prohibition of unlawful direct and indirect expropriation, protection and security, and most favoured nation (MFN) treatment, which requires governments to treat covered foreign investors not less favourably than investors from other countries. However, contrary to many investment treaties, these agreements do not contain provisions on fair and equitable treatment or provisions stating that foreign investors shall be treated no less favourably than domestic investors. They contain investor-state dispute settlement provisions which, until relatively recently, have not been frequently used. When interpreted by arbitral tribunal, some provisions of these agreements may prove to be problematic. Both have been the subject of reform discussions among their members. Reform efforts under the AIA were not consensual as many countries have not ratified the 2013 amendments. A draft investment protocol for the OIC Investment Dispute Settlement Organ is currently under discussion (see below).

Other regional economic integration initiatives, not involving all of the MENA focus economies, address some investment matters but do not contain core investment protections or ISDS. Libya and Egypt are members of the Common Market for Eastern and Southern Africa and entered into the COMESA Common Investment Area in 2007. The COMESA Regional Investment Agency is hosted by the General Authority for Investment of Egypt (GAFI). Algeria, Libya, Morocco and Tunisia signed the Arab Maghreb Union Investment Agreement in 1990, which did not enter into force mainly for political reasons.

Jordan, together with Yemen, are the only countries from the entire MENA region which have ratified the **Energy Charter Treaty (ECT)**. The ECT is a multilateral and sectoral trade and investment agreement under which 53 member states provide certain guarantees for investors in the energy sector. The ECT members are currently negotiating potential amendments to the ECT aimed at "modernising" the existing treaty. These discussions are potentially very significant for Jordan and Yemen.

Another ambitious initiative is the **African Continental Free Trade Area** (AfCFTA). While the agreement primarily concerns trade matters, the negotiation of an investment protocol is planned. Algeria, Egypt, Libya, Morocco and Tunisia have signed the AfCFTA, but only Egypt and Morocco have ratified it. The agreement, which entered into force in May 2019, could be an opportunity for the MENA region to promote more trade and investment with the rest of Africa. However, its implementation is likely to experience delays due to the Covid-19 crisis (FAO, 2020[4]). Trading rules in goods and services, originally scheduled for July 2020, are currently postponed (Signé and van der Ven, 2020[5]). Negotiations on the protocols on investment, competition and intellectual property rights, originally expected to be completed in December 2020, may also suffer delays. The investment protocol aims at promoting, protecting and facilitating sustainable investment and ultimately building regional value chains that will boost intra-African investment.

Other international investment-related agreements

The MENA focus economies are part of international investment-related agreements, which deal with investment dispute settlement, investment insurance and trade.

All of the economies, except Libya, are parties to the International Centre for Settlement of Investment Disputes (**ICSID**) Convention. Morocco and Tunisia were among the first signatories in 1965. ICSID provides facilities for conciliation and arbitration of international investment disputes and has administered a vast majority of known international investment cases. The MENA focus economies, excluding Libya, also ratified the 1958 **New York Convention** on the Recognition and Enforcement of Foreign Arbitral Awards, which is one of the key instruments in international arbitration.[2]

The MENA focus economies are members of the Multilateral Investment Guarantee Agency (**MIGA**), which promote cross-border investment by providing guarantees (political risk insurance and credit enhancement) to investors and lenders.

Egypt, Jordan, Morocco and Tunisia are members of the World Trade Organization (**WTO**) and therefore have to abide by some investment-related obligations. Algeria, Lebanon and Libya are only observers.[3] The WTO agreement includes provisions pertaining to investment. The General Agreement on Trade in Services (GATS) recognises that foreign investment is a mode of trade through the supply of services by a foreign company setting up operations in a host country. The agreement on Trade-Related Aspects of Intellectual Property Rights (TRIPs) extends to foreign services companies protection for patents, copyrights and trademarks. The agreement on Trade-Related Investment Measures (TRIMs) aims to facilitate foreign investment by prohibiting trade-related investment measures, such as local content requirements. The WTO is also holding Structured Discussions with the aim of developing a multilateral framework on investment facilitation.

It is noteworthy that four MENA countries have adhered to the **OECD Declaration on international investment and multinational enterprises**, i.e., Egypt (2007), Morocco (2009), Tunisia (2012) and Jordan (2013) (see Chapters 4 and 10 for more on the Declaration).

Towards investment treaty reforms

The majority of investment treaties concluded by the MENA focus economies show features associated with the so-called first-generation treaties concluded in great number in the 1990s and early 2000s. They generally include relatively vague substantive provisions, with lack of clarity that could be broadly interpreted by arbitral tribunals, as well as with limited guidance for arbitration proceedings. Many countries, including the focus economies (in particular Morocco), are revising their investment treaty policy and practice. Besides more precise definitions and scope of protection standards and obligations, recent BITs tend to reflect closer government scrutiny of the balance between investor protection and the government's right to regulate.

In this context, the MENA focus economies are encouraged to evaluate, individually and collectively, and where appropriate update their BIT model and existing investment treaties to bring them in line with current priorities. Policy makers should assess the costs and benefits of the design of key provisions in older investment treaties and their potential impact on foreign and domestic investors, together with legitimate regulatory interests and potential exposure to ISDS claims and damages. This may be particularly relevant in the context of the Covid-19 crisis (see below) and an opportunity to address investor responsibilities (see Chapter 10 for more on responsible business conduct). Depending on the context and treaty language, it may be possible to clarify the meaning of older investment treaties through joint interpretations agreed with treaty partners. In other cases, treaty amendments may be required. Replacement of older investment treaties by consent in the context of new treaty negotiations with the same partners may also be appropriate in some cases (Box 5.1).

Box 5.1. Recent developments in investment treaty policies and ISDS

Many governments have substantially revised their investment treaty policy in recent years.

- The European Union's rejection of investor-state arbitration has transformed EU investment policy, which continues to evolve under increasing public and academic questioning, and growing constraints imposed by EU law. EU member states concluded an agreement in May 2020 to terminate all intra-EU BITs (over 150 treaties in total); the agreement came into force for some member states in August 2020.
- Long-standing supporters of investment treaties like the United States have recently expressed fundamental doubts about treaty-based investor protection and have exited or sharply narrowed the substantive provisions and scope of ISDS, notably in the United States-Mexico-Canada Agreement (USMCA) with Canada and Mexico that entered into force in July 2020.
- Chinese investment treaty policy is still in flux, with pressures to strengthen covered investor protection in the context of growing outward investment accompanied by concerns about the reputation of Chinese business abroad and the possible exposure to claims which have remained minor to date.
- The Comprehensive and Progressive Agreement for Trans-Pacific Partnership (CPTPP) reflects the expansion of an updated North America Free Trade Agreement (NAFTA)-inspired investment treaty model to a broader range of eleven countries including relations between advanced economies. As of September 2020, the CPTPP is in force between Australia, Canada, Japan, Mexico, New Zealand, Singapore and Viet Nam.
- Major G20 capital importers like India, Indonesia and South Africa, as well as other countries like Bolivia, Ecuador, Namibia, Tanzania and Venezuela, have all rejected and exited first generation investment treaties with some exiting the system more broadly. Bolivia, Ecuador and Venezuela have withdrawn from the ICSID Convention, a key part of the institutional framework for many ISDS disputes. Brazil has developed a new model for investment treaties focused on investment facilitation and using state-to-state dispute settlement without ISDS.
- Multilateral reform of ISDS is now underway. Following inter-governmental debate, the UNCITRAL Commission entrusted its Working Group III in July 2017 with a broad mandate to work on possible reforms for ISDS. The 60 government members of UNCITRAL as well as many

government observers have found by consensus that reforms should be developed to address concerns raised with eleven different issues relating to ISDS.

- Parties to the Energy Charter Treaty (ECT), a multilateral trade and investment agreement between more than 50 governments addressing the energy sector, are negotiating possible amendments aimed at "modernising" the existing treaty. These negotiations are potentially very significant as the ECT is the most frequently-invoked investment treaty in ISDS cases: investors have filed more than 130 known ISDS cases under the ECT since the first such claim was filed in 2001. Formal negotiations in the ECT modernisation process began in November 2019. An approved list of topics for discussion includes all core investment protections and ISDS provisions. The Energy Charter Secretariat published a set of policy options identified by the ECT members on the various topics in October 2019; the EU published a detailed set of proposals separately in May 2020.

ISDS cases in the region raised in the last decade

Bilateral and regional investment agreements usually contain investor-state dispute settlement (ISDS) provisions allowing a covered foreign investor to bring a claim against a host country and seek monetary compensation for breaches of the agreement's provisions, in addition or as an alternative to domestic remedies.

ISDS mechanisms are included in the majority of investment treaties signed by the MENA focus economies. Investor-state arbitration involves arbitration tribunals selected on a case-by-case basis to adjudicate disputes in an approach derived from international commercial arbitration. Like many other first generation treaties, most the focus economies' treaties regulate ISDS very lightly leaving substantial decisional power to arbitrators, or to claimants and their counsel. For example, they usually do not contain clear scope and time limits for covered investor claims (so-called cooling-off periods allowing for amicable settlement); are not all consistent in terms of alternative dispute resolution, recourse to local tribunals and international arbitration; may not express references to the governing law in ISDS cases; give claimants and their counsel substantial power over key procedural issues, including the identity of the appointing authority; and do not address transparency in ISDS.

The main standards that are evoked in treaty claims relate to non-discrimination: fair and equitable treatment (FET) and indirect expropriation – most used legal grounds used – but also full protection and security for investors and their investment, and national treatment. However, these are subject to various approaches in treaties and interpretation by arbitral tribunals. Imprecise and inconsistent provisions, as seen as in many treaties, have impact on governments' legal responsibilities and defence in investor treaty-based claims.

While substantive reforms of IIAs and ISDS mechanisms are discussed in international fora, some states are beginning to circumscribe the limits of ISDS mechanisms, while others propose to reject ISDS mechanisms in favour of alternative approaches.

Analysis of cases

The increase of international investment agreements has occurred parallel to a rise in investor-state dispute settlement cases based on these treaties, raising a number of concerns. MENA economies, active IIA signatories, has been involved in numerous cases, in particular over the last decade (Figure 5.2). Egypt is the fifth most frequent respondent state for known ISDS claims worldwide with 37 cases. The total number of known treaty-based ISDS cases initiated against the MENA focus economies reached 84 as of

1st January 2020, 8.2% of the total number worldwide (1,023 cases).[4] The majority (60 cases) were initiated in the last decade.

Figure 5.2. Number of known cases involving MENA focus countries as respondent to the dispute or as home state of investor

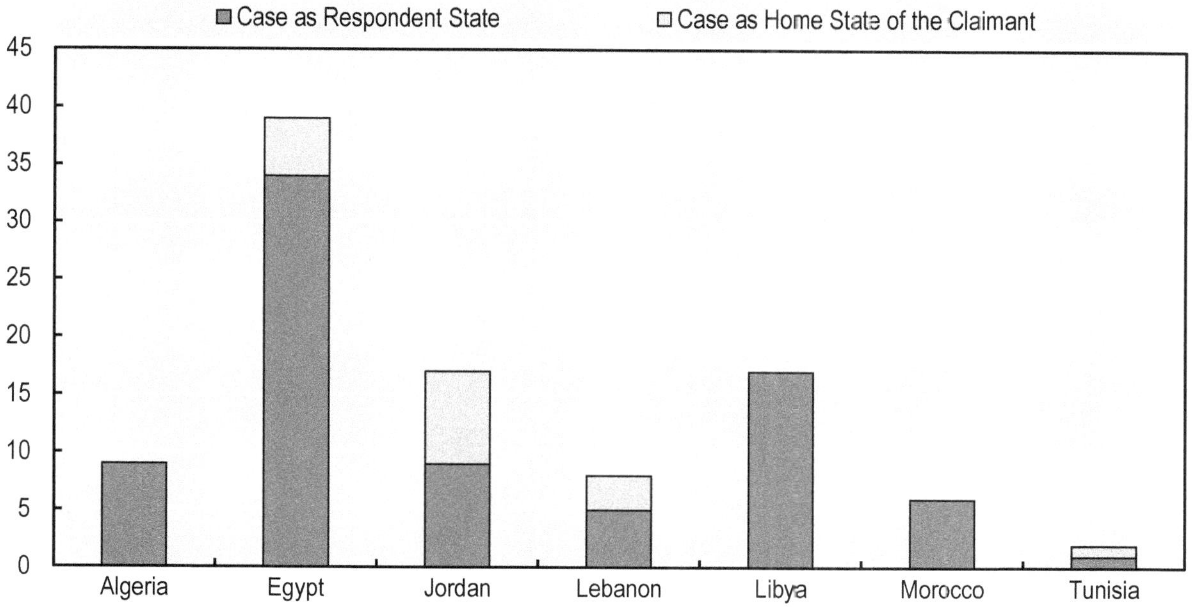

Source: UNCTAD Investment Policy Hub (2020).

In terms of **outcomes of the proceedings**, the region follows global trends in which most cases are rendered in favour of the state: 37% of all concluded cases were decided in favour of the state, 29% were decided in favour of the investor with monetary compensation awarded, and 21% were settled before arbitration proceedings (Figure 5.3).[5] Among the recent cases brought by investors against MENA countries, some have been dismissed on jurisdictional grounds (e.g. *National Gas v. Egypt*[6]), or resulted in liability decisions in favour of the state (e.g. *Veolia v. Egypt*[7]).

In terms of arbitration **fora**, various fora have been used including under the OIC Agreement and the Arab Investment Court. Since the first case initiated under the OIC investment agreement in 2011 (Saudi investor Al-Warraq against Indonesia[8]), more than ten other arbitrations were initiated under this Agreement (Hamida, 2013[6]).[9] Similarly, the Arab Investment Court (AIC), established under the Arab League Investment Agreement, have jurisdiction to settle investment disputes, though it has not been operational for almost 20 years. Since the first AIC case (*Tanmiah v. Tunisia*, decision rendered in 2004), there have been six cases at least in which the Arab Investment Court (AIC) or a tribunal appointed under the Arab Investment Agreement has rendered a decision (Hamida, 2006[7]) (Blanke, 2018[8]). It is noteworthy that publicly available information on these cases and arbitration fora is limited.

Figure 5.3. Status of the known cases involving MENA focus countries

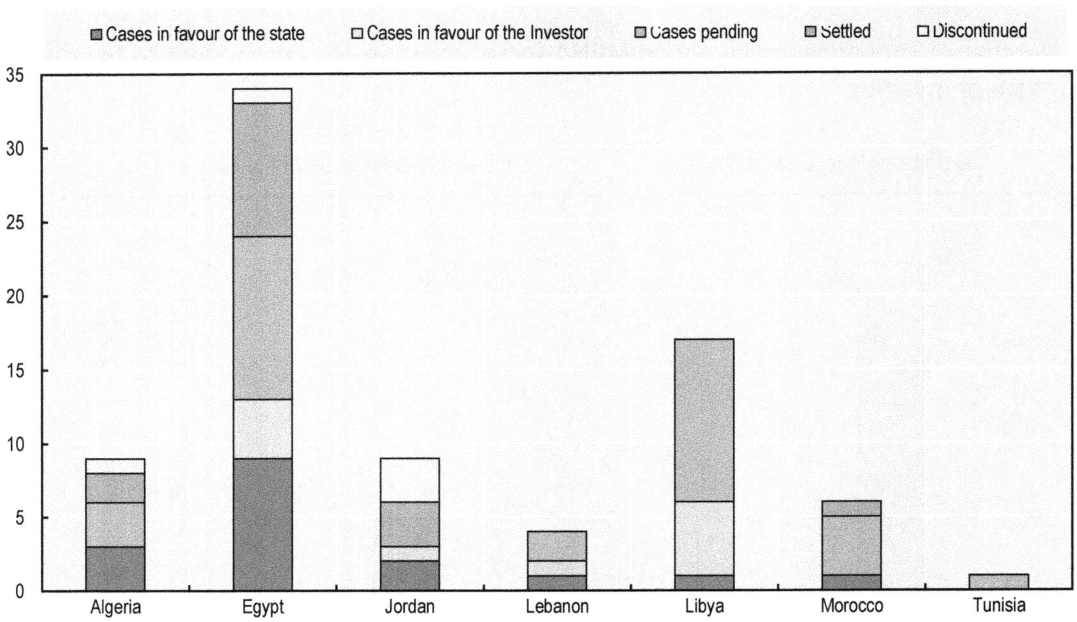

Source: UNCTAD Investment Policy Hub (2020).

In term of **distribution of the cases by economic sectors** to which the investment at issue belongs, half of the known MENA cases concerns, not surprisingly, infrastructure and construction, and oil and gas (Figure 5.4).

Figure 5.4. ISDS cases in the MENA focus countries by economic sectors

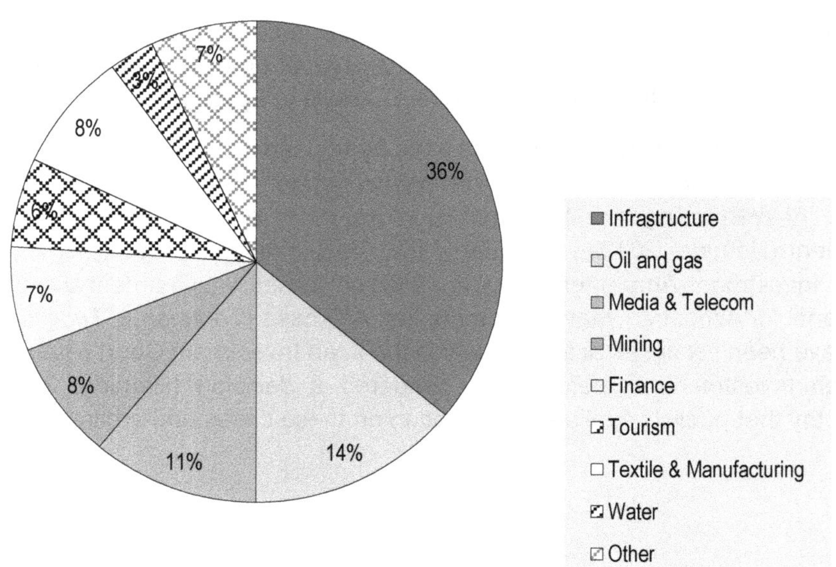

Source: UNCTAD Investment Policy Hub (2020).

ISDS raises concerns and triggers reforms, including in the region

ISDS mechanisms are giving rise to concerns due to:

- The increasing use of investor-State arbitration (more than 1,000 known cases, though the growth has been slowing since 2015) and the growing public attention on cases and related impact of investment treaties (Gaukrodger and Gordon, 2012[9]);
- Consequently, the potential impact on a country's reputation as an investment location and the challenge for states to protect investment on the one hand and to respect the legitimate right of governments to regulate for the public interest (Gaukrodger, 2017[10]);
- The financial costs involved in some arbitration awards (e.g. the amount awarded in the *Unión Fenosa v. Egypt* case reached more than USD 2 billion in favour of the investor, and in the *Olin v. Libya*, 18 million). See Boxes 5.3 and 5.4, below, for more information;
- The high costs involved in conducting procedures comprising legal counsel and tribunal costs (evaluated on an average per-case basis at USD 10 million in 2014) (Pohl, 2018[1]);
- The legitimacy, consistency and transparency of the system (e.g. impartiality of arbitrators, lack of appeal mechanism, third-party funding, secrecy of disputes and the proceedings, access to documents, public hearings, counterclaims, enforcement and execution of ISDS awards);
- The increasing technical complexity of ISDS and the capability of developing countries to prepare their defence and manage investment disputes;
- The interactions between international investment agreements, domestic investment laws and investment contracts (Box 5.2).

Box 5.2. Interactions between investment treaties, domestic law and contracts

An additional complexity of ISDS mechanisms in investment treaties is the existence of dispute settlement provisions in the national investment laws and investment contracts signed between a foreign investor and the host state. Most of these laws in the MENA focus economies refer to international investment agreements. Interactions between laws and IIAs should be taken into consideration when considering the scope of possible reforms. Policy-makers should seek to ensure coherence between these mechanisms and avoid inconsistencies.

Below is a succinct presentation of the dispute resolutions provisions in the **investment laws** of the MENA focus economies (Chapter 3).

- In their investment-related laws, **Algeria** and **Libya** settle dispute through the competent domestic courts with the exception of the matters regulated under international agreements (or contractual obligation in the case of Algeria). The reform that took place in Algeria in June 2020 does not tackle ISDS, but the repeal of the 51/49 rule for non-strategic sectors.
- The Lebanese investment law only refers to disputes between the Investment Development Authority of **Lebanon** (IDAL) and the investor resulting from the "incentive package deal contract" and provides for amicable settlement and arbitration.
- The 1995 Investment Charter of **Morocco** only mentions dispute settlement in the context of contracts for particularly large or important investment projects. The on-going revision of the Charter, actually in force for only tem years, may provide for extended and more detailed provisions.
- The investment law of **Tunisia** recommends the settlement of disputes through conciliation offering arbitration to foreign investors based on investment agreements.

- The 2014 **Jordan** Investment Law gives national and foreign investors' access to arbitration in accordance with its arbitration law, and opens the possibility for foreign investors to bring investment disputes before international arbitration by mutual agreement with the state.
- **Egypt** has detailed ISDS provisions following the revisions of the 1997 Investment Law in 2015 and 2017. In response to Egypt's increasing exposure to investor-state arbitration, a new dedicated chapter established three out-of-court committees to favour the amicable settlement of disputes between private investors and public institutions. However, "despite the creation of new dispute settlement bodies, the current institutional setting for the resolution of investor-state disputes appears overly complex and might therefore not serve its purpose in the most efficient way" (OECD, 2020[11]).

Investors can sometimes also recourse to investor-state arbitration through **investment contracts** rather than through an investment law or agreement. Investment contracts are not generally regulated in the investment laws of the MENA countries, except in the context of granting incentives in the case of Lebanon, Jordan and Morocco. These contracts can be particularly problematic as they are not generally available to the public; their content is unknown; and they can be inconsistent with bilateral investment treaties. Furthermore, they are often negotiated under pressure in the midst of obtaining a particularly large-scale investment project, and/or those investments done in sectors of the economy that are of certain interest to the host state.

The interlinkages between international agreements, laws and contracts related to foreign investment needs to be cautiously monitored by MENA focus economies and dealt with in a coherent and inter-institutional manner. The umbrella provisions in many treaties and the treaty-shopping practice of investors create risks for states to properly manage investment disputes and defend their rights in arbitration.

The international community, and in particular international organisations (UNCITRAL, ICSID, OECD, UNCTAD, EU), engaged into discussions on reforms of the ISDS mechanism and subsequently the IIAs system. The aim is to increase transparency, promote judicial economy, foster sound and consistent results, and create predictability for states involved (Box 5.1).

Some governments in the MENA region are engaging in ISDS reforms. Two examples can be cited.

Morocco reviewed its model BIT (published in December 2019). The new model BIT contains some reform elements that reflect trends in other IIAs.[10] Regarding ISDS provisions, the model limits the scope of the disputes, provides time limit to submit a claim, allows state counterclaims in case the investor has not complied with its obligations (e.g. related to corruption) and requires the exhaustion of local remedies before initiating an arbitration. The BIT with Nigeria ratified in 2017 introduces dispute prevention provisions (see below), while the BIT with Brazil, signed in 2019, does not contain ISDS provisions in line with the Brazilian policy. Similarly, many countries, including Egypt, are starting to exclude or significantly limit the scope of ISDS.

The OIC drafted a protocol for the establishment of a permanent **OIC Investment Dispute Organ** to be adopted by members, as revealed by non-governmental sources end 2019. The 1981 OIC Investment Agreement provided for *ad hoc* investor-state arbitration (Article 17) until the creation of such an organ. As mentioned above, several investors initiated arbitration under this Agreement. However, in some cases, respondent states refused to appoint arbitrators and the OIC Secretary General refrained from constituting the arbitral tribunal "because of the lack of time limits for appointment and supposed political pressure from some OIC member states, which claimed that they had not consented to arbitration under the treaty."[11] The proposal to set up a permanent body, echoing certain developments in other regions such as the EU, will facilitate proceedings (Box 5.1). Member governments are also considering a proposal to affiliate the Organ to the Islamic Development Bank, akin to the relationship between the World Bank and ICISD. The envisaged mechanism will restrict access to OIC investment arbitration, as it requires several preliminary steps – exhaustion of local remedies in domestic courts, denial of justice claim, state-state amicable settlement process – before commencing investor-state proceedings. An appellate Committee is also foreseen. These preconditions are likely to limit the number of ISDS arbitration brought under the OIC. The rationale of the reform hence is to limit arbitration claims and to allow the OIC to exercise more control over the judicial process with a negotiation stage and a dispute resolution body with an appellate mechanism.

Possible further developments under OIC will show the extent of its members' willingness and engagement for reforms. The amendment of the Arab League Investment Agreement in 2013, together with the Statutes of the Arab Investment Court, have gone unheeded, very few members having ratified these revisions.

Box 5.3. Case study: The Al-Kharafi v. Libya case

This case study gives an example of a dispute, its context, the amounts awarded and its outcomes through annulment procedures.

In 2006, the Libyan Ministry of Tourism concluded a 90-year leasing agreement with a Kuwaiti investor for the construction and operation of a tourism complex. Without any start of the project, the Libyan Ministry of Economy cancelled the project in 2010 and terminated the agreement. The investor initiated an arbitration case in 2011 under the Arab Investment Agreement (AIA). The arbitral tribunal was constituted and Cairo was chosen as the seat of the arbitration. In its decision, the arbitral tribunal issued a final award and ordered Libya to pay the following:

- USD 5 million for losses and expenses;
- USD 30 million for moral damages;
- USD 900 million for lost future profits for 83 years, representing the length of the agreement;
- USD 1,94 million for arbitration costs;
- 4% interest on all amounts from the date of the award until full settlement.

Following the arbitral award, Libya lodged an annulment action before the Cairo Court of Appeal which dismissed Libya's claim. Subsequently the judgment was challenged before the Court of Cassation which ruled that although the AIA prohibits challenging an arbitral tribunal through domestic courts, it does not impede a party to ask for an annulment action. After a second overturn of the Court of Cassation, the case went back to the Court of Appeal to be judged on the merit.

On a new judgement in June 2020, the Court annulled the arbitration award on the basis of serious mistake of law leading to a failure in observing the rules of public policy and the notions of equity and justice. Besides and importantly, the Court disagreed with the method of calculating the damages. The Court asserted the USD 900 million compensation to be "excessively unjust" and "abusive", the arbitral tribunal having ordered to pay it for "loss profits resulting from real and certain loss opportunities" while the investor had only invested USD 5 million.

The Court held that its ability to review an arbitral award remains very limited although it may review it when the award violates the main principles of international public policy rules such as the proportionality of damages, and when the arbitrators exceed their powers with an award that is "irrational" and is a "manifest disregard of the law".

Source: https://www.italaw.com/cases/2185; Kluwer Arbitration Blog, 19 July 2020, http://arbitrationblog.kluwerarbitration.com/2020/07/19/egypt-court-annuls-award-against-libya-on-the-substantive-ground-of-fundamental-error-of-law/?doing_wp_cron=1595496916.5686450004577636718750

Periods of crisis may increase ISDS risks

Government measures taken during economic and political crises, even non-discriminatory ones in the public interest, may increase the risk of investor-state disputes. The impact on disputes of the social and political upheavals in many MENA countries starting in 2011 exemplifies this potential linkage. Some are starting to consider the possible impact of government measures taken during the Covid-19 crisis on investment treaty policy in a similar vein. While the longer term consequences of the Covid-19 crisis for investment treaty policy remain unclear, this context could incentivise governments to reflect on the balance between investor protection and governments' right to regulate, including in times of crisis, in their national and international investment framework as a means to promote consistency in interpretations of key provisions and ultimately to avoid future disputes.

Link between periods of crisis and investment disputes in the MENA region

The MENA region experienced a relatively large number of investment disputes, which increased during the past decade in countries that went through political and economic crises. Egypt was involved in 37 known cases against foreign investors, with 24 that arose after the 2011 uprisings (6 cases in 2013) (Box 5.4). Libya saw a substantial rise with 17 known cases, all except one after 2011.[12] Noteworthy is the number of confidential cases that are not publicly known, hence not recorded. Other countries have not experienced such an increase. However, in Algeria, three claims were filed in 2017-18 among a total of nine and the situation may remain uncertain in a context of social disturbances. In Lebanon, the collapse of the financial system and the inability for investors to transfer or convert funds could represent grounds for future claims.[13]

Political instability and social unrest in many MENA countries beginning in 2011 was invoked in some recent arbitration cases (Box 5.5), though not all details are known and a third of the cases that arose since 2011 are still pending. Investors have been successful in some cases in invoking the political and subsequent economic turmoil, while respondent states have also prevailed on jurisdictional and liability claims. While some investors may have brought legitimate claims linked to the 2011 political events, it appears that others may have meritless claims or attempted to use such events as a strategy to influence the possibility of settlement.[14]

Box 5.4. Overview of Egypt's ISDS cases

Since 2011, 22 ICSID arbitration cases have been lodged against Egypt. This represents 65% of the total cases against Egypt since it joined the Convention.

The Egyptian Investment Law previously offered a unilateral consent to ICSID jurisdiction. The number of BITs referring the ICSID Convention (Egypt signed 100 BITs) may also explain why the country faced such an amount of cases as respondent state.

The treaty most frequently invoked was the Egypt-US BIT with 6 cases, followed by the Egypt-UK BIT with five cases. The majority of the disputes involved Western European countries with 17 cases, Middle East countries with nine cases, and North America with seven cases. Most Egyptian BITs were negotiated and concluded without anticipating future implications. The most recent BITs concluded require referring disputes to domestic administrative procedures before going to arbitration. Most of the cases were based on direct or indirect expropriation (78%), a common treaty standard in Egyptian BITs. Most of the cases involved the oil and gas sector, followed by the mining and tourism sectors.

The total amount of claims registered against Egypt amounted to approximately USD 22.760 billion. The majority of the awards were rendered in favour of Egypt and some cases were settled.

Figure 5.5. Number of ICSID cases filed against Egypt since 1972

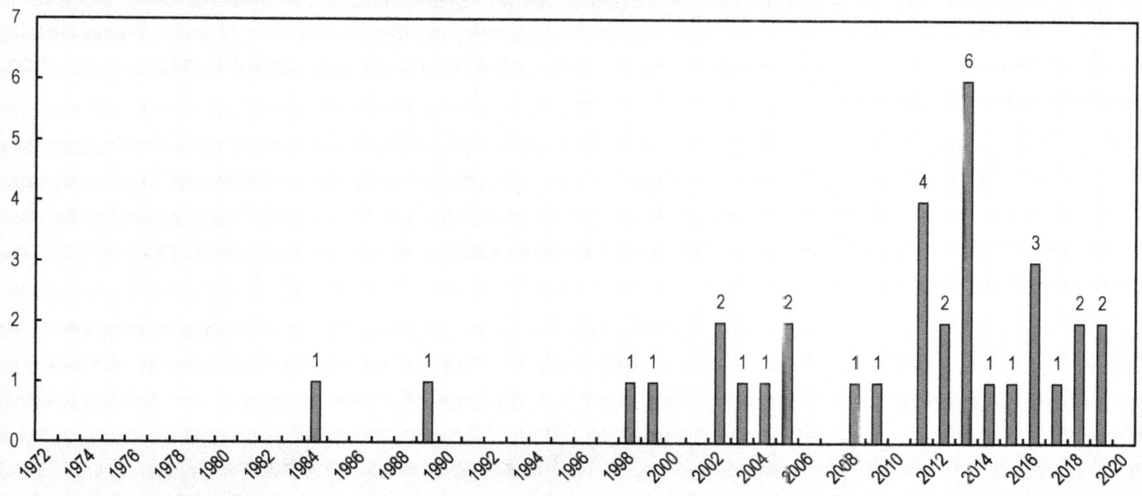

Source: OECD and Kluwer Arbitration Blog, 15 March 2020, http://arbitrationblog.kluwerarbitration.com/2020/03/15/after-48-years-at-icsid-1972-2020-an-overview-of-the-status-of-egypt-in-icsid-arbitrations/?doing_wp_cron=1593525394.4075820446014404296875

The 2011 protests, as well as the Argentinian crisis,[15] tend to show that economic and political crises can put states at risk of ISDS claims under older investment treaties – even where government measures are non-discriminatory and taken in the public interest. Investors might, in some cases, have considered ISDS as an opportunity to claim for losses, not only through arbitration, but also as means of pressure on the states to proceed to settlement, instead of engaging into costly and lengthy proceedings.

Box 5.5. Case studies on the impact of political and social instability after 2011 on international investment arbitration

The two case studies below show how respondents (in these cases, the State) use the facts of political instability and the linked events as the basis for treaty claims.

The **Unión Fenosa Gas v. Egypt** ICSID case concerns claims arising out of the alleged suspension of gas supplies by an Egyptian State-owned enterprise to a Spanish investor (liquefied natural gas plant in Damietta) in contravention of the gas purchase agreement. Egypt claimed that its prioritisation of supplying natural gas to feed domestic electricity in Egypt rather than export it as agreed with the investor, was an act of necessity aimed at maintaining Egypt's security, public order, and stability, safeguarding its essential interests, and sustaining basic services in the face of "grave and imminent peril". According to Egypt, the historic levels of violence, riots, and clashes constituted a threat to "the basic functioning of society and the maintenance of internal stability". It claimed that these events caused a "dramatic drop in the supply of natural gas both internally and for exportation" which led to repeated blackouts and more widespread violence and unrest.

However, in its 2018 award, the tribunal found missing elements to legitimise Egypt's necessity defence. The revolution began in 2011, however it was only in 2013 that Egypt evoked force majeure. In addition, the tribunal found that the events could not be the cause of curtailing gas supplies to the plant because such curtailment occurred both prior to and following the revolution. The tribunal also found that the act of the government was not the "only way" to maintain national security situation and that there was a disproportionality in the reduction of gas delivered by other users. The tribunal therefore held that the Egypt failed to prove the defence of necessity under customary international law. The case was decided in favour of the investor and the tribunal award amounted to more than USD 2 billion. Annulment proceedings are still pending.

In the **Olin Holdings Ltd. v. Libya** case administered by the International Chamber of Commerce (ICC), a Cyprus investor sought compensation for Libya's alleged expropriation of the land in which it had invested to build a dairy and juice factory. Libya argued that the harm the investor may have suffered after February 2011 was the result of the chaos arising out of the revolution and not from acts attributable to the state.

However, the tribunal was unconvinced by the Libyan state arguments. It recognised that while the events of the Libyan Revolution and civil war may have had an impact on the investment climate post-2011 and contributed to the underperformance of the investor, the events would not be sufficient to address the investor's underperformance prior to 2011. The proportionality argument was used as another competitor was able to make large profits in the same period, despite the events. The tribunal concluded that the events of the Libyan crisis "cannot be considered as an event that breaks the causal link between Libya's breaches of the BIT and Olin's underperformance after 2011". The amount of compensation for the investor as per the 2018 award, reached USD 18.2 billion (for an initial claimed amount from the investor of USD 105 million).

Source: Unión Fenosa Gas v. Egypt, https://www.italaw.com/cases/2456, Olin Holdings Ltd. v. Libya, https://www.italaw.com/cases/6667, Kluwer Arbitration Blog, 26 July 2019, http://arbitrationblog.kluwerarbitration.com/2019/07/26/impact-of-the-arab-spring-on-the-international-arbitration-landscape/

Uncertain links between the Covid-19 crisis and ISDS

The Covid-19 crisis and its economic aftermath are creating a new context with uncertain ramifications for investment treaty policies. Early suggestions by some that a wave of claims would arise from the crisis have not been borne out to date, but the longer term consequences of the crisis remain unclear.

The spread of the virus around the world is having a significant impact on foreign investors. A halt in activities, shift in production lines, confinement of employees, new export restrictions and border closures are all measures that have altered or discontinued activities of MNEs (OECD, 2020 a and b). Since the beginning of the crisis, some investors have notified governments of potential investment disputes linked to crisis measures.[16] However, no claims have yet been registered, but some claims remain confidential and mandatory notice periods in many investment treaties may not yet have elapsed, even if triggered by investors at the earliest possible occasion. Noteworthy are the calls from academia and civil society to suspend investment arbitration claims with a view to not hinder countries' recovery efforts.[17]

The Covid-19 crisis is very different from other crises. The pandemic was not caused by governments and requires emergency government policy measures that affect investors. In these extraordinary times, on one hand, investors are likely to be reluctant to bring claims in the context of a health crisis, not caused by the state, which may lead arbitrators to exercise a significant degree of deference to government measures. Public opinion is likely to be unforgiving on investors that are seen to be trying to profit from the crisis. On the other hand, the challenge for government could be the management of the crisis. The assessments of the nature and proportionality of measures taken during the crisis may constitute an uphill set of arguments for investors.

Therefore, while it is too soon to ascertain the ultimate effects of the crisis on ISDS, the possibility of litigation exists and this calls for vigilance from the MENA focus economies. Policymakers are encouraged to build awareness and understanding of the issues at stake at all level of government (ministries, agencies and local or sub-national government), follow up with foreign investors to maintain communication and identify potential issues – as most MENA IPAs are already doing – and ensure an efficient governmental co-ordination to prevent and manage potential disputes. The crisis may also represent an opportunity to test, assess and engage with the possible merits of reforms for investment treaties and the ISDS system, following the global discussions and recent countries' practices. Reform discussions may focus even more on governments' regulatory and policy space and the protection of public health, while maintaining effective investment protection provisions and minimising the risks of investor-state disputes (Gaukrodger, 2017[12]) (Gaukrodger, 2017[10]). Pursuing a regional response and making regional agreements more effective could also be further explored to ensure increasingly consistent levels of protection, rights and obligations throughout the MENA region, as done in other regions, in particular in Asia. In addition, reinforcing dispute prevention and management mechanisms should remain on the governments' agenda.

Proactive approaches to dispute prevention and management should be pursued

Alternative dispute resolution (ADR), dispute prevention policies and management mechanisms are useful means to avoid potential costly and lengthy disputes. The MENA focus economies are therefore encouraged to further develop mechanisms to prevent and achieve early settlement of investment-related disputes, as well as ensure efficient management of ISDS cases, learning from the experiences of other governments that have been frequent respondents in ISDS cases.

Dispute prevention policies

Dispute prevention policies are governmental policies and measures aimed at avoiding disputes between the foreign investor and the host state. The purpose is to address the issues encountered by the investor at an early stage, ensure compliance with clear procedures in order to retain the investment within the state and prevent any litigation. It also protects the reputation of the host state as being a safe and attractive destination to invest.

Depending on the objectives, needs and experiences of the state, dispute prevention measures generally include:

- Early detection systems to anticipate issues and communication with investors to discuss before a claim (Box 5.6);
- Training for public servants working in bodies involved in investment projects to build awareness on international obligations and potential repercussions of their actions;
- Institutional co-ordination and communication between relevant bodies;
- The creation of a dedicated institution in charge of implementing the measures and monitoring the disputes.

Many countries have implemented dispute prevention policies, including in the MENA region. Good practices should inspired the implementation of these policies. Some countries, such as Colombia and Peru, have adopted comprehensive legislative and regulatory frameworks to encourage the early detection and resolution of investment disputes (OECD, 2019[14]) (Joubin-Bret, 2015[15]). Other countries, such as Chile, have opted for an informal prevention system where sectoral agencies directly manage disputes with investors. Some governments established inter-ministerial committees to advise line agencies on investor grievances and supervise the government's defence of ISDS cases. Brazil does not include ISDS in its investment treaties but instead establishes with each treaty partner a focal point or ombudsman within each government to address investor grievances, with a Joint Committee of government representatives to oversee the administration of the agreement. This is the case of the BIT between Brazil and Morocco signed in 2019, but not yet entered into force.[18] Korea has also had a successful track-record of early dispute resolution with its Foreign Investment Ombudsman since it was established in 1999 (Nicolas, Thomsen and Bang, 2015[16]). Ukraine also set up a Business Ombudsman Council through which companies can register a complaint.

Box 5.6. Best practice measures of the World Bank Group's Systemic Investor Response Mechanism (SIRM) Protocol

- Lead agency: an administrative body responsible for co-ordinating information and leading responses to investor grievance should be established.
- Information sharing: it enables the lead agency to co-ordinate the diffusion to the relevant bodies of relevant information likely to generate political risks related conflicts, including information on the obligations provided by international investment agreements.
- Early alert mechanism: it enables the lead agency to learn about the existence of a grievance as early as possible.
- Problem solving methods: they allow the parties to seek for an invest-based solution to the conflict.
- Political decision making: a solution should receive the approval from the competent political authority, in order to guarantee that the solution would be effectively implemented.
- Enforcement of a decision: it ensures that the consensual solution agreed by the political authorities and the investor is respected by all the agencies and bodies.

Source: (World Bank, 2019[13])

Some states that have been frequent respondents in ISDS cases (e.g. Argentina, Spain, the United States, Canada and Mexico) have also developed dedicated teams of government lawyers who now exclusively handle all ISDS cases brought against their government with no reliance on external legal counsel. Despite the associated costs and co-ordination it entails, the MENA focus economies affected by a high number of disputes may consider learning from these experiences and follow the same path.

The United Nations Convention on International Settlement Agreements Resulting from Mediation (Singapore Convention), which entered into force in September 2020 and to which only Jordan is signatory to date, could also have a pivotal role in mediated settlement of investment claims.

Dispute prevention mechanisms in the region

The MENA focus economies implemented diverse prevention mechanisms and policies and the impact of the Covid-19 crisis on investors' operations seems to have accelerated the process. Indeed, several MENA Investment Promotion Agencies (IPAs) have established crisis units in response to the pandemic and the necessary emergency measures taken by states (see Chapter 6 for more on IPAs in the region). These units provide information to investors, answer queries, collect information on foreign investors' operations, co-ordinate responses to issues face by investors, and support the implementation of solutions.[19] These units should also interact with already existing dispute resolution and prevention entities set up in some countries to anticipate potential claims.

In the wake of the political turmoil and the surge of investment disputes, **Egypt** has been proactive and has the most advanced mechanism in the region, having increasingly made available alternative dispute resolution mechanisms for resolving commercial and investment disputes. The 2015 amendment of the

Investment Law established three different committees: the Grievances Committee, the Ministerial Committee for Resolving Investment Disputes, and the Ministerial Committee for the Settlement of Investment Contracts Disputes. The 2017 Investment Law brought further clarification and emphasis on the importance of investors' access to ADR mechanisms. GAFI plays an important role in preventing disputes at an early stage, as recognised by the business community. However, the respective roles, functioning and affiliation of each body could be further clarified and communicated, as these different institutional layers could create additional complexities for investors (OECD, 2020c). Noteworthy is also the role of Egyptian State Lawsuits Authority (ESLA), which established a Foreign Disputes Department to manage the Egyptian ISDS cases, following the trend mentioned above to have a dedicated team dealing with investment disputes.

In **Algeria**, the National Agency for Investment Development (ANDI) is in charge of strategies and priorities for investments and clarifies the role of the entities intervening in the investment process. It is also in charge of the establishment of interdepartmental committee of appeal in charge of receiving and giving ruling to the investors complaints.

The **Jordan** Investment Commission (JIC) recently launched an ambitious initiative through the establishment of the Grievance Committee (Grievance Hearing Instructions No. 1 of 2020).[20] Any investor may submit a grievance application in line with the periods of amicable dispute settlement in the related investment treaty or contract. The Committee, within two days, shall determine if the application is urgent or not (for example if the grievance greatly affects the operation or productivity of the economic activity or causes the interruption of business). The Committee can dismiss or accept the grievance application. If so, it will analyse the case, hold meetings with the investor, prepare its recommendations and notify them to concerned government entity for action and the applicant. It shall also submit to the Prime Minister the grievance applications, which may be presented to the Council of Ministers. The Committee should also implement a Computerized Grievance System to facilitate procedures. This new mechanism is very relevant, though it is too early to assess its implementation and monitor its efficiency.

Another interesting initiative developed by **Morocco** is the mechanism contained in the bilateral investment treaty with Nigeria signed in 2016. It sets out an innovative pre-arbitration procedure for preventing and resolving disputes, through the creation of a Joint Committee and disputes prevention provisions. The treaty stipulates that before initiating an eventual arbitration procedure, any dispute shall be assessed through consultations and negotiations by the Joint Committee, with the participation of both the investor and host state. If the dispute cannot be resolved within six months, the investor may, after exhaustion of domestic remedies, resort to international arbitration. While joint committees exist in other agreements (e.g. in the Comprehensive Economic and Trade Agreement (CETA) signed between EU and Canada), its role in dispute prevention in the Morocco-Nigeria BIT is a novel element. It remains to be seen how the Committee will work in practice, as the treaty has not yet been ratified by Nigeria.[21]

References

Blanke, G. (2018), *Investment arbitration in the Middle East: basic trends and developments (Part 2)*, Thomson Reuters: Practical Law Arbitration Blog, http://arbitrationblog.practicallaw.com/investment-arbitration-in-the-middle-east-basic-trends-and-developments-part-2/ (accessed on 12 February 2021). [8]

FAO (2020), *Intra-African trade, the African Continental Free Trade Area (AfCFTA) and the COVID-19 pandemic*, Food and Agriculture Organziation of the Un ted States (FAO), http://www.fao.org/3/ca8633en/ca8633en.pdf. [4]

Gaukrodger, D. (2017), "Addressing the balance of interests in investment treaties: The limitation of fair and equitable treatment provisions to the minimum standard of treatment under customary international law", *OECD Working Papers on International Investment*, No. 2017/3, OECD Publishing, Paris, https://dx.doi.org/10.1787/0a62034b-en. [10]

Gaukrodger, D. (2017), "The balance between investor protection and the right to regulate in investment treaties: A scoping paper", *OECD Working Papers on International Investment*, No. 2017/2, OECD Publishing, Paris, https://dx.doi.org/10.1787/82786801-en. [12]

Gaukrodger, D. and K. Gordon (2012), "Investor-State Dispute Settlement: A Scoping Paper for the Investment Policy Community", *OECD Working Papers on International Investment*, No. 2012/3, OECD Publishing, Paris, https://dx.doi.org/10.1787/5k46b1r85j6f-en. [9]

Hamida, W. (2013), "A Fabulous Discovery: The Arbitration Offer under the Organization of Islamic Cooperation Agreement Related to Investment", *Journal of International Arbitration*, Vol. 30/6, pp. 637-663. [6]

Hamida, W. (2006), "The first Arab investment court decision", *Journal of World Investment and Trade*, Vol. 7/5, pp. 699-721, http://dx.doi.org/10.1163/221190006X00360. [7]

Joubin-Bret, A. (2015), "Establishing an International Advisory Centre on Investment Disputes?", *E15Initiative (E1) Working Paper*, the International Center for Trade and Sustainable Development and the World Economic Forum, http://e15initiative.org/publications/establishing-an-international-advisory-centre-on-investment-disputes/. [15]

Mistura, F. and C. Roulet (2019), "The determinants of Foreign Direct Investment: Do statutory restrictions matter?", *OECD Working Papers on International Investment*, No. 2019/01, OECD Publishing, Paris, https://dx.doi.org/10.1787/641507ce-en. [2]

Nicolas, F., S. Thomsen and M. Bang (2015), "Lessons from Investment Policy Reform in Korea", *OECD Working Papers on International Investment*, No. No. 2013/0, OECD Publishing, Paris, https://doi.org/10.1787/18151957. [16]

OECD (2020), *Investment in the MENA region in the time of COVID-19*, OECD Policy Responses to Coronavirus (COVID-19), http://www.oecd.org/coronavirus/policy-responses/investment-in-the-mena-region-in-the-time-of-covid-19-da23e4c9/ (accessed on 11 February 2021). [17]

OECD (2020), *OECD Investment Policy Reviews: Egypt 2020*, OECD Investment Policy Reviews, OECD Publishing, Paris, https://dx.doi.org/10.1787/9f9c589a-en. [11]

OECD (2019), *OECD Investment Policy Review of Southeast Asia*, https://www.oecd.org/investment/oecd-investment-policy-review-southeast-asia.htm. [14]

Pohl, J. (2018), "Societal benefits and costs of International Investment Agreements : A critical review of aspects and available empirical evidence", *OECD Working Papers on International Investment*, No. 2018/1, OECD Publishing, Paris, https://dx.doi.org/10.1787/e5f85c3d-en. [1]

Signé, L. and C. van der Ven (2020), *How the AfCFTA will improve access to 'essential products' and bolster Africa's resilience to respond to future pandemics*, Brookings: Africa in Focus, https://www.brookings.edu/blog/africa-in-focus/2020/04/30/how-the-afcfta-will-improve-access-to-essential-products-and-bolster-africas-resilience-to-respond-to-future-pandemics/ (accessed on 12 February 2021). [5]

UNCTAD (2020), *IIA Issues Note: The changing IIA landscape: New treaties and recent policy developments*, UNCTAD, https://unctad.org/en/PublicationsLibrary/diaepcbinf2020d4.pdf. [3]

World Bank (2019), *Retention and Expansion of Foreign Direct Investment: Political Risk and Policy Responses*, World Bank Group, Washington, DC, http://documents1.worldbank.org/curated/en/387801576142339003/pdf/Political-Risk-and-Policy-Responses.pdf. [13]

Notes

[1] It is difficult to be precise about the exact status of these investment treaties due to some inconsistencies in publicly available information and lack of governmental sources, especially entry into force dates. The figures shown in this chapter rely on the UNCTAD Investment Policy Hub, https://investmentpolicy.unctad.org/international-investment-agreements/by-economy

[2] In 2019, Jordan also signed the United Nations Convention on International Settlement Agreements Resulting from Mediation which applies to commercial dispute. None of the MENA focus countries signed the 2014 United Nations Convention on Transparency in Treaty-based Investor-State Arbitration (Mauritius Convention). Only Iraq and Syria did in the MENA region.

[3] Negotiations for accession of these three countries are stalled. The Working Party for Algeria was established in 1987 and held its 12th meeting in 2014. The Working Party for Libya, established in 2004, never met. The Working Party for Lebanon, established in 1999, met for the 7th time in 2009.

[4] UNCTAD Investment Dispute Settlement Navigator, https://investmentpolicy.unctad.org/investment-dispute-settlement

[5] Data from the UNCTAD Investment Dispute Settlement Navigator, based on information on publicly known IIA-based international investor-State arbitration proceedings (non-exhaustive as some proceedings remain confidential), It refers to the current status of the original arbitration proceedings:
- Decided in favour of State: the tribunal dismissed the case for lack of jurisdiction or found that the respondent State has not committed any breach of the applicable IIA.
- Decided in favour of investor: the tribunal found that the respondent State committed one or more breaches of the applicable IIA and awarded monetary compensation or non-pecuniary relief to the claimant investor.
- Settled: the disputing parties settled the case and the arbitral proceedings were discontinued for that reason.

[6] https://www.italaw.com/cases/2494

[7] https://www.italaw.com/cases/2101; Kluwer Arbitration Blog, 22 January 2020, http://arbitrationblog.kluwerarbitration.com/2020/01/22/2019-in-review-a-view-from-north-africa/

[8] Hesham T.M. Al Warraq v. Republic of Indonesia, https://www.italaw.com/cases/1527

[9] Investment Arbitration Reporter, 11 August 2020, https://www.iareporter.com/articles/oic-round-up-an-update-on-pending-arbitration-cases-lodged-under-the-oic-investment-agreement/

[10] International Institute for Sustainable Development, Investment Treaty News, 20 June 2020, https://www.iisd.org/itn/2020/06/20/moroccos-new-model-bit-innovative-features-and-policy-considerations-hamed-el-kady-yvan-rwananga/

[11] Kluwer Arbitration Blog, 29 December 2019, http://arbitrationblog.kluwerarbitration.com/2019/12/29/investment-dispute-settlement-body-of-the-organisation-of-islamic-cooperation-a-dead-end-for-claims-under-the-oic-investment-agreement/

[12] IAReporter, 11 August 2020, https://www.iareporter.com/articles/libya-round-up-new-tribunals-a-discontinuation-and-further-details-about-a-number-of-investment-arbitrations-against-the-state/

[13] Kluwer Arbitration Blog, 8 March 2020, http://arbitrationblog.kluwerarbitration.com/2020/03/08/the-ongoing-lebanese-financial-crisis-is-there-potential-for-investor-state-arbitration/

[14] Kluwer Arbitration Blog, 26 July 2019, http://arbitrationblog.kluwerarbitration.com/2019/07/26/impact-of-the-arab-spring-on-the-international-arbitration-landscape/

[15] The economic downturn in Argentina linked to emergency devaluation and privatisation measures resulted in a high increase of cases (62 known cases, most arising after the crisis).

[16] Kluwer Arbitration Blog, 30 March 2020, http://arbitrationblog.kluwerarbitration.com/2020/03/30/covid-19-and-investment-treaty-claims/?doing_wp_cron=1595244086.3971068859100341796875, 13 April 2020, http://arbitrationblog.kluwerarbitration.com/2020/04/13/pandemics-emergency-measures-and-isds/

[17] E.g. Columbia Center on Sustainable Investment, (2020), https://mailchi.mp/law/call-for-isds-moratorium-covid-19?e=17b57bf90f; IISD, 14 April 2020, https://www.iisd.org/articles/protecting-against-investor-state-claims-amidst-covid-19-call-action-governments

[18] BIT Brazil-Morocco, Articles 14-19, https://investmentpolicy.unctad.org/international-investment-agreements/treaty-files/5889/download

[19] See examples of Tunisia, Morocco, Jordan and Egypt in (OECD, 2020[17]).

[20] https://www.jic.gov.jo/en/investors-grievance-scope/

[21] Morocco-Nigeria BIT, article 26, https://investmentpolicy.unctad.org/international-investment-agreements/treaty-files/5409/download, Thomson Reuters, Arbitration Blog, 16 November 2017, http://arbitrationblog.practicallaw.com/the-morocco-nigeria-bit-a-new-breed-of-investment-treaty/

6 Investment promotion and facilitation strategies

This chapter provides an inventory of practices among Investment Promotion Agencies (IPAs) in eight MENA economies, allowing practitioners and policy makers to benchmark their institutions against those from other countries in and outside the region. The chapter addresses IPA's institutional environments, mandates, strategic priorities, and core investment promotion and facilitation activities. It also provides insights on investment promotion and facilitation practices at the sub-national level across the region.

Summary and policy considerations

Middle Eastern and North African (MENA) economies have the potential to leverage their strategic location, considerable market size and young workforce to attract FDI. Governments of the eight MENA economies covered in this report (MENA focus economies) have accelerated reforms over the last decade to improve the business climate and respond to increased competition for investment among emerging and developing economies. Some reforms have bolstered the roles of investment promotion agencies (IPAs) to raise awareness of existing investment opportunities, attract investors, and facilitate the establishment and expansion of businesses.

IPAs are often the focal points for investment promotion and facilitation but rarely concentrate solely on this core mandate. Recent reforms have broadened the mandates of most MENA IPAs, and more so than most agencies from other regions. Algeria, Egypt and Jordan have the largest organisations and their mandates go beyond investment promotion to cover a variety of objectives, including regulatory and supervisory goals such as free zones management or negotiating international agreements. The Lebanese, Libyan and Palestinian IPAs are substantially smaller, but also have a wide range of mandates. Morocco's IPA and one of Tunisia's agencies (FIPA) are more specialised and, in this sense, are similar to OECD agencies focusing primarily on foreign investment promotion activities, although the Tunisian institutional landscape includes other agencies (including the Tunisian Investment Authority).

Most MENA agencies have organisational autonomy and regulatory power to improve the business climate, a task that is often the responsibility of ministries in other countries. The breadth of their mandates, which has frequently evolved, may however affect MENA IPAs' ability to properly achieve their core mission of promoting and facilitating investment. Such wide mandates also mean that the responsibilities of IPAs often overlap with those of other government bodies, to a greater extent than in other countries. The fact that agencies have established boards to supervise their activities, advise their strategies or enhance inter-governmental co-ordination helps, but representation from non-governmental stakeholders is often limited.

MENA IPAs have priorities that are often in line with their national development goals, although investment promotion strategies, and related performance targets, are not always publicly available. Egypt, Lebanon, and Libya focus on building their image as attractive investment destinations, while Algeria and the Palestinian Authority devote a large share of the IPA resources to facilitate investors' establishment. The priority given to overcoming negative perceptions and reducing information gaps is prompted by challenging investment climates and the volatile political and security context in some economies. Except in Morocco and Tunisia, all IPAs run one-stop shops (OSS) but the extent to which procedures are centralised in practice varies across agencies. Jordan and Morocco devote large resources to generating investment (including by targeting specific sectors), with the objective of supporting the economy's participation in global value chains (GVCs).

In response to the Covid-19 outbreak, MENA IPAs have re-oriented their priorities to focus on existing investors and have expanded their aftercare services. The health crisis also pushed them to innovate and develop new digital tools and services that they could consider operating permanently. Policy advocacy may become even more relevant in a context where governments are rethinking their wider economic strategies and related business climate reforms. The pandemic and its consequences on the global economy is propelling many IPAs to revise their investment promotion strategies to support the recovery. Particularly relevant are the policy reflections taking place to assess the disruption of value chains and the future positioning of the MENA region within global investment networks.

Countries' institutional configurations influence the way they promote and facilitate investment at the subnational level. MENA governments have been seeking to attract FDI to less developed regions but these attempts have mostly involved strategies and tools designed at the national level such as tax incentives, sometimes not taking into account how each region is unique in the way it competes in global investment networks. The majority of MENA economies have a centralised approach to investment promotion and most IPAs work with their own local branches, when these exist, rather than with separate, decentralised entities. Even if the priority of local branches to facilitate investors' establishment is well justified in light of the burdensome procedures to start a business, developing tailored investment promotion tools could be equally relevant to attract businesses that support local development.

Policy considerations

- Clarify responsibilities and strengthen coordination over investment policy, promotion and facilitation to reduce institutional overlaps and conflicting objectives in settings where IPAs have numerous mandates and hold regulatory functions. Responsibilities should be balanced, sufficiently funded, explicit, and mutually understood by all actors. Clear and targeted reforms should be preferred to hastily executed institutional reorganisations as these hamper IPAs' daily operations and create uncertainty for investors.
- Spell out IPA mandates, activities and targets in a well-defined and publicly available investment promotion strategy, developed in consultation with other relevant government agencies and aligned with national development goals. Equip the strategy with key performance indicators (KPIs) to raise transparency about objectives and improve monitoring and evaluation of agencies' efforts.
- Examine whether the financial and human resources allocated across investment promotion and facilitation activities are well balanced. Digitisation of pre-establishment procedures can help agencies shift their efforts to aftercare services to support existing investors during the recovery from Covid-19 crisis. Envisage permanently operating relevant digital tools that were developed during the crisis.
- Review IPAs' board membership to have a more balanced representation between governmental and non-governmental stakeholders. The inclusion of private sector representatives and other stakeholders in boards is crucial to better reflect their priorities and keep abreast of their challenges. To avoid regulatory capture, membership needs to be based on transparent selection criteria and roles should be clearly defined.
- Give IPAs' subnational offices (or subnational IPAs in the case of Morocco) some latitude to conduct investment promotion and facilitation activities jointly, or in co-operation with, the national IPA, and include them in the elaboration of the national investment strategy and regional development plans.
- Nurture the skills of IPAs' staff by expanding capacity-building opportunities and promoting peer-learning and sharing of good practices with other agencies through participation in international fora (e.g. OECD IPA Network; EU-OECD Programme on Promoting Investment in the Mediterranean; ANIMA Investment Network; World Association of IPAs (WAIPA)).

Institutional choices and mandates

Large differences exist among IPAs in terms of institutional settings, governance policy, strategic priorities, and the tools at their disposal. The way governments around the world organise the institutional framework for investment promotion and facilitation reflects their policy objectives and the priority they give to investment. These choices can greatly influence success in attracting investment in the most efficient and effective manner.

The main institutions responsible for investment promotion and facilitation in the eight MENA focus economies are: the National Agency of Investment Development of Algeria (ANDI), the General Authority for Investment and Free Zones of Egypt (GAFI), the Jordan Investment Commission (JIC), the Investment Development Authority of Lebanon (IDAL), the Privatisation and Investment Board of Libya (PIB), the Agency for Investment and Exportation Development of Morocco (AMDIE), the Palestinian Investment Promotion Agency (PIPA), and the Foreign Investment Promotion Agency of Tunisia (FIPA). The Tunisia Investment Authority (TIA) was recently created as part of a government-wide reform of the legal and institutional landscape for investment.[1]

In the context of the EU-OECD Programme on Promoting Investment in the Mediterranean, the MENA agencies listed above participated in a 2018 survey of IPAs conducted by the OECD. The results serve as the basis of the comparative analysis presented in this chapter, which benchmarks the IPAs against agencies from other regions and expands on the findings of the report *Mapping of Investment Promotion Agencies: Middle East and North Africa* (Box 6.1).

Box 6.1. The Mapping of Investment Promotion Agencies: Middle East and North Africa

The report *Mapping of Investment Promotion Agencies: Middle East and North Africa* (OECD, 2019[1]) provides an inventory of existing practices among IPAs in the Middle East and North Africa region. It covers eight MENA economies: Algeria, Egypt, Jordan, Lebanon, Libya, Morocco, the Palestinian Authority, and Tunisia. The mapping exercise covers a wide range of areas pertaining to investment promotion and facilitation with a view to enhancing peer-learning among practitioners.

The objective of the mapping is to support heads of MENA IPAs and investment policymakers in understanding options for effective investment promotion and facilitation strategies, based on comparative analysis with other agencies, and statistics on their own organisational setting. It aims to help them improve their policy advocacy role, make evidence-based decisions and reflect on future strategic orientations with new insights and ideas.

The mapping is based on a comprehensive survey designed by the OECD and Inter-American Development Bank (IDB) to identify trends across IPAs and provide comparisons across regions. IPAs from more than 70 economies participated in the survey, including from the OECD (32 countries), Latin America and the Caribbean (LAC) (19), Middle East and North Africa (MENA) (8), Eastern Europe, the South Caucasus and Central Asia (Eurasia) (10), and Southeast Asia (2).

The survey is divided into nine parts, including: (1) Basic profile of IPAs; (2) Budget; (3) Personnel; (4) Offices (home and abroad); (5) Activities; (6) Prioritisation strategy; (7) Monitoring and evaluation; (8) Institutional interactions; and (9) IPA perceptions on FDI.

Governance of IPAs: the composition of boards could be more inclusive

MENA authorities have undertaken numerous reforms and organisational changes to IPAs since their creation to adapt to changing environments and new challenges. Reforms have often followed the adoption of new investment-related legislation (see Chapter 3 on the legal framework for investment). Some organisational reforms have given agencies greater political weight with the objective of improving the business climate. For instance, all MENA IPAs are autonomous public agencies, and their top strategic relationships are frequently with the president or prime minister. The majority report directly to the head of government, in contrast with OECD and LAC agencies, which mostly report to their line ministry (Volpe Martincus and Sztajerowska, 2019[2]) (OECD, 2018[3]).

The board is an important element of IPA governance; it allows an external and independent entity to supervise or advise the work of the agency. The decision-making power and composition of boards vary considerably from one agency to another (OECD, 2018[3]). In most cases, the legal framework that establishes MENA IPAs also clarifies the role and the composition of their boards. The board of most

MENA agencies has a similar size (around 10 members) and composition (mostly public and private sector representatives) as most OECD and LAC IPAs. Only a couple of MENA IPAs have representatives from civil society or academia on their boards (Egypt and Morocco), a limited representation that is also observed in agencies in other regions.

Private sector representation on boards generally is weaker among MENA IPAs compared to agencies in other regions. There are two exceptions; Lebanon's IPA board is made up entirely of private sector members, and half of the Moroccan IPA's board is from the private sector. Including private sector representatives on boards ensures that businesses views are considered in strategic directions. Their inclusion should be based on transparent criteria and their responsibilities clearly defined as they may lobby for tax privileges or resist the entry of new competitors, particularly if they represent large or politically connected firms. Beyond boards, IPAs should regularly run surveys to gauge challenges faced by the private sector (OECD, 2020[4]).

Most MENA IPAs combine investment promotion with regulatory functions

MENA IPAs have broader mandates than agencies of other regions (Figure 6.1). They are often in charge of a wide range of responsibilities that go beyond inward foreign investment promotion and facilitation. Depending on the IPA, these can include investment functions such as screening of foreign investment projects or granting fiscal incentives and wider mandates related to export promotion or free zone management. Even if in lower proportions than in MENA IPAs, many agencies around the world have multiple mandates and conduct activities that go beyond foreign investment promotion, such as promoting exports and innovation. For instance, more than half of OECD IPAs combine one of these two mandates with their mandate of promoting inward foreign investment (OECD, 2018[3]).

Figure 6.1. Number of mandates by agency

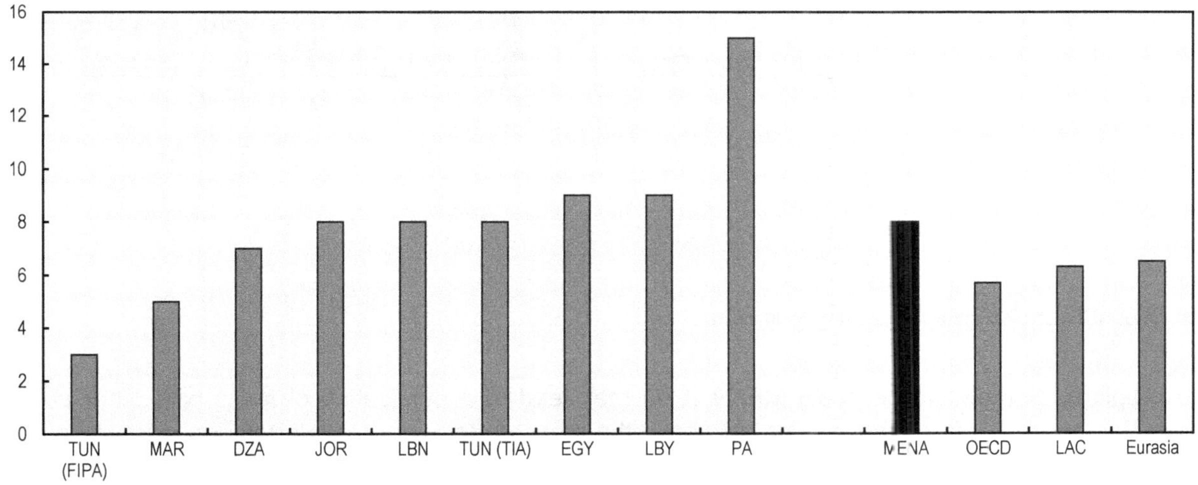

Source: OECD-IDB survey of investment promotion agencies

MENA agencies also differ from one another in terms of the scope of their mandates. Recent reforms have given some IPAs new mandates, such as operating one stop shops (Egypt), or expanded their responsibilities to include export promotion (Morocco) or zone management (Jordan). Only one recent reform involved removing a mandate – the mandate of granting tax incentives by the Algerian IPA was given to the Ministry of Finance in line with good practice. In Tunisia, FIPA only has three mandates, reflecting its role as a specialised agency focused on foreign investment promotion, but the recently created

TIA has wider mandates, including regulatory and investment facilitation functions. IPAs of smaller economies, such as the Palestinian Authority, often have more mandates than agencies in larger and wealthier economies, which tend to distribute mandates across other government bodies (OECD, 2018[3]).

Some MENA IPAs combine investment promotion with regulatory or supervisory responsibilities, such as screening foreign investment projects, issuing business permits, negotiating international agreements, granting tax incentives, or managing free zones (Figure 6.2, panel A). This may be prompted by a preference of IPAs to administer regulatory procedures themselves so that they can help investors better navigate them (World Bank, 2012[5]). IPAs in Southeast Asia, including Indonesia and Thailand, also perform regulatory roles, but this is rare among OECD IPAs (OECD, 2018[3]) (OECD, 2020[6]) (OECD, 2021[7]). Relatedly, MENA agencies often operate one-stop shops, aimed at centralising procedures to ease investors' entry. This is a key difference with OECD or LAC IPAs and is likely due to larger and complex institutional bureaucracies and business climates in some MENA economies. Furthermore, several MENA IPAs promote a variety of policy objectives that are adjacent to attracting foreign investment, such as supporting domestic investment, regional development or growth of export industries (Figure 6.2, panel B).

Figure 6.2. Beyond foreign investment promotion: other IPA mandates in MENA and OECD

In % of respondents

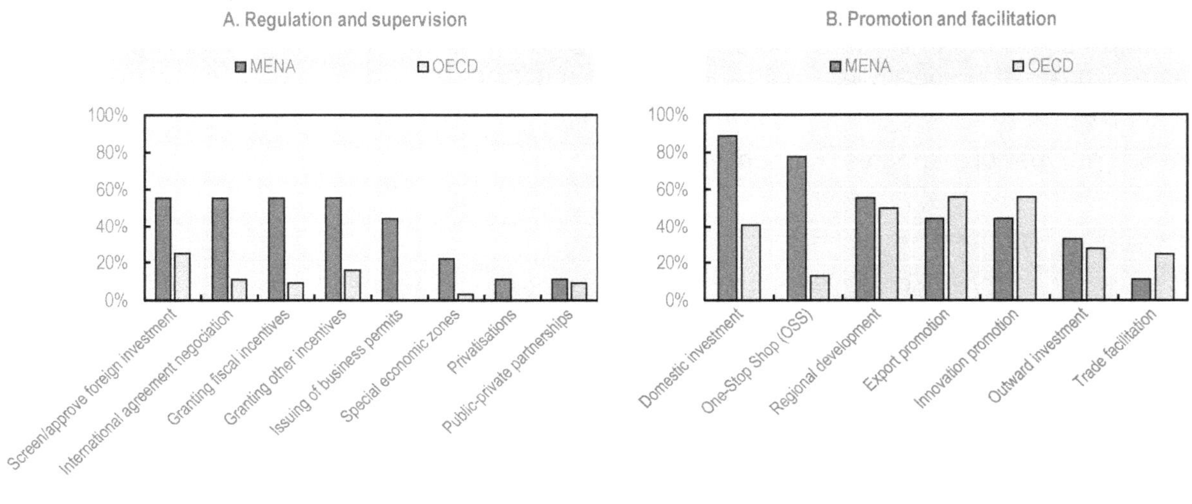

Source: OECD-IDB survey of investment promotion agencies

The multiplicity of mandates in most MENA IPAs may lead to a duplication of tasks with other public entities. For instance, often other bodies also have the mandate to negotiate international agreements or issue business permits, and notably, promote domestic investment. More specifically, the combination of investment promotion with regulatory or supervisory functions can generate confusion of roles and affect IPAs' credibility to properly voice private investors' concerns while they also regulate their establishment or monitor their operations. It also often leads to an organisational culture that serves regulatory functions well but is less suited to the marketing needs of promotion (World Bank, 2012[5]). On the other hand, as governments assess IPAs' performance based on their capacity to attract investors, agencies may opt for loose regulations to reach their objectives, including by having broad legal requirements and discretionary power to deliver permits or grant incentives. They may also have an incentive to negotiate international treaties that do not sufficiently take into account socio-economic priorities or environmental risks.

Strategic priorities and related resources

To promote countries as attractive investment destinations, IPAs can carry out a large variety of marketing and servicing activities. This mandate can be categorised into four core functions:

- *image building* consists of fostering the positive image of the host country and branding it as a profitable investment destination;
- *investment generation* deals with direct marketing techniques targeting specific sectors, markets, projects, activities and investors, in line with national priorities;
- *investment facilitation, retention and aftercare* is about providing support to investors to facilitate their establishment phase as well as retaining existing ones and encouraging reinvestments by responding to their needs and challenges; and
- *policy advocacy* includes identifying bottlenecks in the investment climate and providing recommendations to government in order to address them.

Image building and investment generation are meant to attract potential investors that have not yet selected an investment destination, whereas investment facilitation starts at the pre-establishment phase, when an investor shows interest in a location. The first two functions define what investment promotion stricto sensu is and are primarily the business of IPAs. Investment facilitation and policy advocacy are not limited to IPAs and involve a whole-of-government approach (Novik and De Crombrugghe, 2018[8]).

The way MENA IPAs allocate their resources is coherent with their priorities

IPAs require a wide range of skills and sufficient resources to fulfil their core investment functions. IPA budgets vary widely, reflecting the size of the economy and breadth of agencies' mandates. Many IPAs in the MENA region reported that their budgets did not change substantially between 2012 and 2017, though a few agencies experienced wide fluctuations in resources and substantial cuts. Only two IPAs saw their budget increase (IDAL in Lebanon and FIPA in Tunisia). Personnel decreased in half of the MENA agencies; Jordan and TIA in Tunisia were the only IPAs to increase their staff in six years.

Figure 6.3. IPA resource allocation across functions in MENA, OECD and LAC

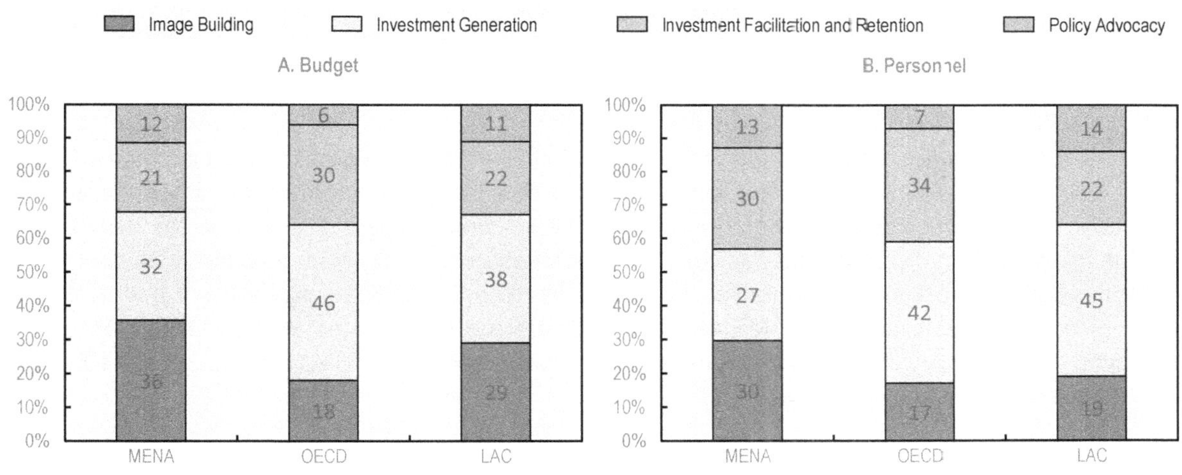

Source: OECD-IDB survey of investment promotion agencies.

Resource allocation reveals an IPA's strategic priorities relative to other agencies. Among the core investment functions, the average MENA IPA allocates the majority of its budget (Figure 6.3, panel A) and personnel (Figure 6.3, panel B) to investment promotion, i.e. the combination of image building and investment generation, and, to a lesser extent, to investment facilitation, retention and aftercare. Whether among MENA IPAs or worldwide, policy advocacy is the function with the smallest amount of dedicated resources, both in terms of budget and personnel.[2]

Although MENA IPAs allocate their resources in a broadly similar order of priorities to agencies of other regions, some notable differences exist. Relative to OECD and LAC IPAs, the average MENA agency dedicates more resources to image building and less to investment generation. OECD IPAs usually use fewer resources to work on branding or improving their country's image and dedicate most of their promotion efforts to more sophisticated and targeted attraction and generation activities. LAC IPAs also allocate the greatest proportion of their resources to investment generation activities, but dedicate more resources to image building than OECD agencies. IPAs in emerging markets may privilege improving the image of the country as an attractive investment destination due to high competition from labour-intensive, low-wage markets.

Differences in the allocation of budget and personnel across the four investment functions exists in all IPAs. In the MENA region, agencies have much larger gaps between the budget and personnel allocated to investment facilitation compared to other IPAs. One explanation for this could be that most MENA IPAs run one-stop shops (OSS) (a key activity under investment facilitation), which are labour intensive but do not require high-skilled workers. Another explanation for the discrepancy is that, in some agencies, the OSS hosts employees seconded and paid by their line ministries and agencies (e.g. Egypt). That image building and investment generation receive more financial than human resources is due to costly advertisement campaigns (image building) and reliance on high-skilled staff (investment generation), particularly if they work in overseas offices.

The Covid-19 outbreak is reorganising the way IPAs' do business

At the start of the Covid-19 outbreak, MENA IPAs and agencies around the world re-oriented their functions and took emergency action to support and retain existing investors (OECD, 2020[9]). They redesigned and reinforced their aftercare services to focus on existing clients, in particular in strategic and essential sectors. As some of their activities were cancelled (e.g. fairs) and functions put on hold (e.g. marketing and prospection), most of their resources were directed to emergency retention programmes. For example, aftercare represented 70% of FIPA's activities during the outbreak while the agency usually focuses on attracting new investors (OECD, 2020[10]). Some agencies also responded to the crisis by extending fiscal incentives, as GAFI did in Egypt.

The speed of the economic recovery, changes to global FDI flows, and government policies may influence the way MENA IPAs "do business" in the long-term, and how they allocate their resources across their core functions. Some trends apparent before the Covid-19 crisis may accelerate, such as the use of digital means for investment promotion and facilitation. The creation or extension of e-services and digital platforms to support investors were notable among MENA IPAs during the crisis, a trend that is likely to continue. Policy advocacy, a function MENA IPAs dedicate more resources to than OECD IPAs, may become even more relevant in a context where governments are rethinking their wider economic strategies and related investment climate reforms.

Investment promotion: strategies and implementing tools

Investment promotion requires a well-defined and transparent strategy

Strategies define what to promote (i.e. sectors, countries, projects, investors) and how to implement this promotion in practice. They also set targets and related performance indicators to monitor success. It is important that the investment promotion strategy and its main features are developed through a whole-of-government approach as investment priorities need to be aligned with other major policy strategies – including trade, innovation and skills. These strategies are not always publicly available in MENA economies although they could help raise countries' positive image within the international business community and inform about investment opportunities (OECD, 2020[4]).

Prioritising investment promotion efforts should be conducted according to a set of criteria in line with national development objectives. The decision to prioritise should follow an evaluation of the economy's strengths, weaknesses, opportunities and threats, to ensure that it is based on carefully crafted economic rationales rather than political agendas. In the MENA region, prioritisation decisions often come from the highest levels of government, but some MENA IPAs have more autonomy in electing priority sectors, in line with the government's wider development goals. For example, Tunisian law sets out certain priority sectors, but government agencies also seek to prioritise investment that will further certain development goals. The Algerian agency on the other hand primarily executes the directives set by the executive branch.

Virtually all IPAs target some investment over others, even without a clear investment promotion strategy in place. In the MENA region, most IPAs target investment from certain countries (90%), in selected sectors (90%), as well as specific investment projects (70%). Egypt is the only country to prioritise specific investors as well, although the IPA uses the same criteria used to prioritise sectors, including whether the project can support job creation, technology transfer and export potential. Eurasia IPAs mostly prioritise sectors and projects; only a few target specific countries or investors (OECD, 202[11]). Less than half of OECD IPAs prioritise based on country, sector, project and investor (OECD, 2018[3]).

Countries shape their strategies to attract investment that is expected to generate the greatest benefit for the economy. All MENA agencies seek projects that will have a positive impact on domestic firms' production capabilities, the country's image, regional development, jobs and innovation. All agencies that prioritise by sector target industries that have the potential to diversify the economy, and the majority target sectors that promote regional development and reinforce their competitive position vis-à-vis other countries. This reflects an effort to find the right balance between diversifying the economy and tapping into strong domestic capabilities, an approach that is similar to OECD IPAs (OECD, 2018[3]).

MENA IPAs primarily favour partners in international investment and free trade agreements when they prioritise some countries or regions as sources of investment over others. This is similar to LAC agencies, but such agreements are a less important factor for OECD IPAs in their targeting strategy. This difference is probably due to higher barriers to trade and investment in MENA economies compared to OECD countries.

The Covid-19 pandemic and its consequences for the global economy may propel MENA agencies to revise their investment promotion strategies and related prioritisation choices. Particularly relevant are the policy reflections taking place to assess the disruption of value chains and the future positioning of the MENA region within global investment networks (OECD, 2020[10]). For instance, some MENA IPAs such as FIPA in Tunisia plan to adjust their strategies to focus on European companies relocating from China and, following the same logic, to attract Chinese firms to invest in their countries and export to the EU market.

Most economies focus on building their image as an investment destination

To implement a country's investment promotion strategy, an IPA dedicates resources to a variety of tools, including image building and investment generation activities. Most of the MENA agencies dedicate the greatest proportion of their budget to image building activities – between 40-50% – while proactive investor targeting and lead generation activities, i.e. investment generation, receive a higher proportion of budgets in Morocco, Jordan and the Palestinian Authority (Figure 6.4).

Figure 6.4. Investment promotion: image building and investment generation

In % total budget allocated to the core functions, 2017

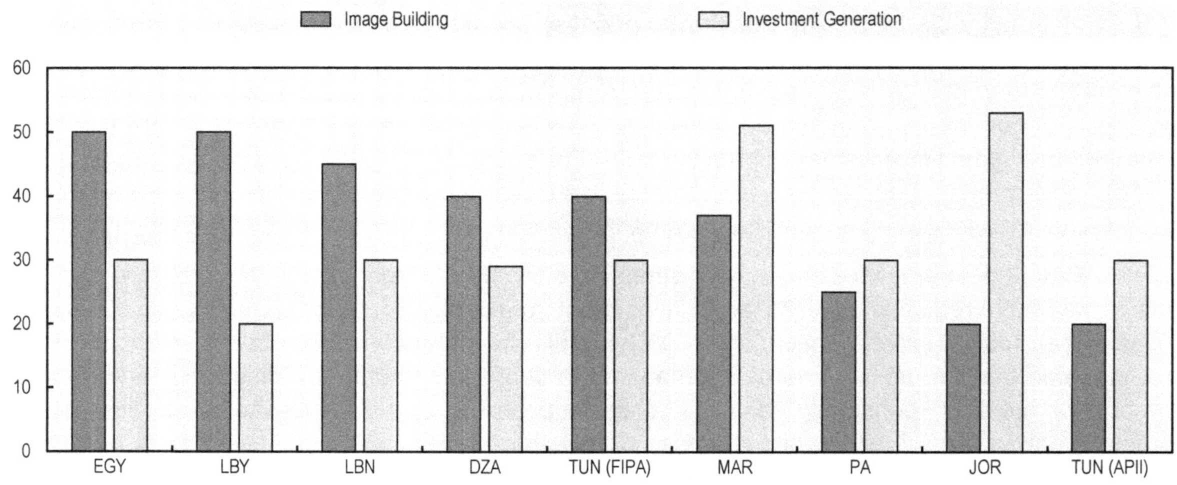

Note: The functions are image building, investment generation, investment facilitation, and policy advocacy
Source: OECD-IDB survey of investment promotion agencies.

Egypt and Libya, for instance, allocate half of their budgets to image building activities. These often comprise general marketing activities (website and web services, TV, print, and promotion materials such as brochures), and public relations events (road-shows and fora as well as general mission abroad and incoming missions). The priority given to branding the country as an attractive investment destination may be explained by the political and security context in some MENA economies and high competition from other markets with similar capabilities but lower labour costs.[3]

Investment generation is the most important function for three MENA agencies, two of which (Jordan and Morocco) allocate more than 50% of their budget to generation activities. Morocco's focus on investment generation is coherent with AMDIE's recent reorganisation into sector-specific departments and the decision to merge investment and export promotion to promote specific value chains. This structure is similar to OECD agencies such as Business France. Germany, Greece, Poland and Spain also merged investment and export promotion relatively recently (OECD, 2018[3]).

Investment generation can hardly be outsourced as it encompasses sophisticated activities such as intelligence gathering (raw data analyses and market studies), sector and investor-specific events (such as road-shows and missions abroad and incoming missions) and direct targeting of investors (one-to-one meetings, pro-active campaigns and inquiry and request handling). Such activities are sometimes conducted by IPAs' overseas offices, when they exist, thereby increasing budgets allocated to investment generation (Box 6.2).

Box 6.2. IPAs' overseas offices: An effective but costly investment promotion tool

In the MENA region, only IPAs in Tunisia (FIPA) and the Palestinian Authority have overseas offices or dedicated staff in another government agency abroad. AMDIE in Morocco recently closed its six offices abroad because the cost of operating the offices outweighed the benefits, according to the government. Most LAC IPAs do not operate overseas offices. In Southeast Asia, Indonesia's BKPM operates seven offices abroad and BOI in Thailand operates 16 offices, mostly spread in Asia and the Pacific. Three out of four OECD IPAs have their own offices abroad, meaning that they have personnel abroad, dedicated to investment promotion, on their payroll. The average OECD IPA has 34 offices abroad but with wide variations across economies. The Korean, Irish, and Czech IPAs have respectively 36, 19 and 10 offices abroad.

IPAs' overseas offices can make a difference for the agencies' ability to attract FDI but they also strongly weigh on agencies' finances. IPAs have different arrangements to operate their secondary offices overseas with reduced costs. As several OECD IPAs are part of broader agencies covering other mandates, their overseas offices can perform different functions (e.g. trade, investment and tourism promotion). As such, OECD agencies with over 50 overseas offices abroad combine investment with other mandates. Some agencies with offices abroad hire local staff in foreign offices to lower costs. Other agencies do not have their own offices abroad, but place staff in the foreign diplomatic representations or entirely delegate the investment promotion tasks to commercial attaches. There is no consensus on how effective this last approach is; some IPAs with overseas offices report that in their experience staff at embassies are not equipped with the skills to best conduct investment promotion.

Source: (OECD, 2018[3]) (OECD, 2019[11]) (OECD, 2020[6]) (OECD, 2021[7]) (Volpe Martincus and Sztajerowska, 2019[2]).

Investment facilitation efforts and evolving priorities

MENA governments dedicate sizeable resources to investment facilitation with the wider objective of improving the business climate. Investment facilitation starts when an investor shows interest in a location. It includes the way IPAs handle inquiries, and measures to reduce obstacles faced by investors once they have decided to invest. Facilitation is also about encouraging existing investors to expand, helping them overcome any operation challenges, and connecting them with suitable local suppliers. Aftercare measures such as structured troubleshooting, ombudsman, intervention, and conflict mitigation, can influence firms' decisions to stay in the country and reinvest.

Investment facilitation efforts are geared towards pre-establishment services…

MENA IPAs provide a wide range of investment facilitation services to investors, although most of them focus on pre-establishment services and less on aftercare and retention activities. This is coherent with objectives of cutting red tape and easing procedures to start a business, which is still a challenge in many MENA economies. The majority of IPAs offer assistance with business registration through their OSS, which are labour intensive but do not require high-skilled workers. The focus on labour-intensive services explains the large gap that exists between budget and personnel allocated to investment facilitation across most agencies (Figure 6.5). This gap is higher among MENA agencies compared to OECD and LAC IPAs, the majority of which do not run OSS.

Figure 6.5. Investment facilitation and retention: personnel and budget allocation

In % total personnel and budget allocated to the core functions, 2017

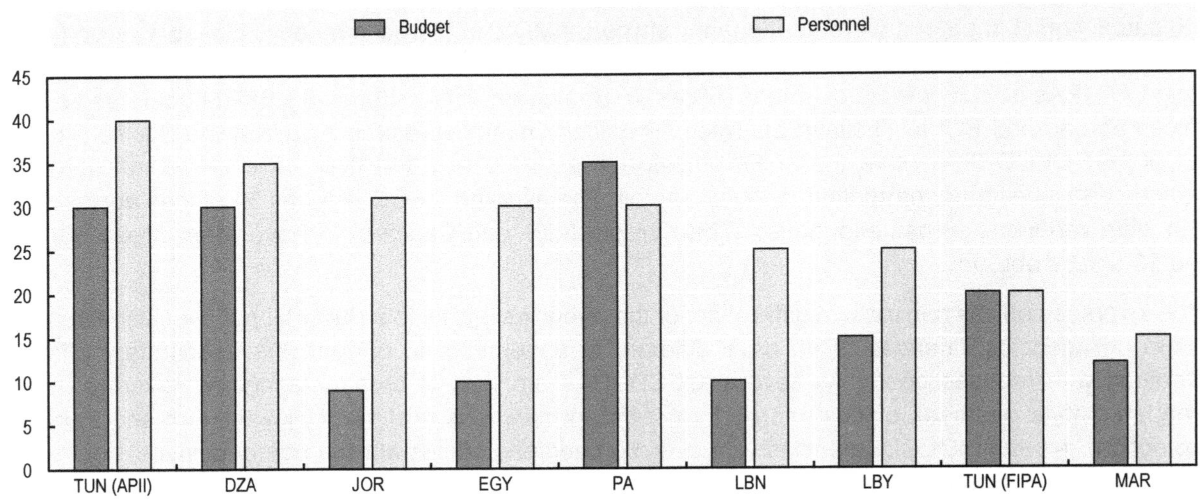

Note: The functions are image building, investment generation, investment facilitation, and policy advocacy.
Source: OECD-IDB survey of investment promotion agencies.

One MENA IPA with a strong focus on pre-establishment services is GAFI in Egypt. To address persistent doing business challenges, the IPA recently established investor services centres in different governorates of the country, offering a wide range of government services to incoming investors (Box 6.3). The Algerian agency allocates considerable resources to investment facilitation as it has an extensive network of subnational offices that support both foreign and domestic investors in establishing their business. The newly established TIA in Tunisia focuses on facilitating large investors' establishment and handling their incentives requests, and less on providing aftercare services than the other Tunisian IPA FIPA, although a better separation of the functions of each agency is still needed.

Box 6.3. One-stop-shops: The investor services centre in Egypt

One-stop shops (OSS) involve placing officials from different government agencies and ministries under the same roof to centralise administrative procedures and requirements for incoming investors. They are often established under the IPA and are frequently geared towards foreign businesses. OSS can reduce transaction costs for businesses if they are fully-functional but they can become "one-more stop" if officials from external ministries do not have sufficient decision power to issue themselves the permit and need to seek approval from their line ministry or ask the investor to directly contact the ministry. They can also be costly, as they force ministries to duplicate or multiply the number of officials to allow a presence in both their own administration and the OSS offices.

Egypt's Investors Services Centres (ISC) were set up in 2017 in several governorates to grant the approvals, certifications and licences that are necessary for establishing and operating a company. Depending on their level of development and geographic location, each ISC has a different number of external agencies and ministries represented. For example, 28 ministries and public agencies were represented in Alexandria's ISC as of 2018. The ISCs follow a number of good practices. First, they are not mandatory entry points for investors, providing an incentive for ISCs to remain efficient. Second, ISCs are equipped with a Customer Relationship Management system, which includes key performance indicators for monitoring performance. Third, the costs of the ISCs seem to be efficiently and equitably shared between GAFI and external ministries.

The ISCs have been welcomed by the business community but more time is needed to evaluate their long-term influence on the business environment. One of the main points is to ensure licensing decisions can be taken within the ISCs, without having to reach out to line ministries if a case is not straightforward. It is also important that the decisions to grant or refuse a business licence are based on transparent criteria and made publicly available, with a right of appeal for investors.

Source (OECD, 2020[4])

More specialised agencies such as Morocco's AMDIE and Tunisia's FIPA allocate fewer resources to investment facilitation and the gap between budget and personnel is smaller, probably reflecting the absence of a labour-intensive OSS service. In both countries, other bodies provide such assistance (e.g. the newly established TIA in Tunisia), potentially leaving more space for IPAs to offer more tailored business services. In addition, business registration procedures are more streamlined – both countries are in the top 50 in the World Banks' Doing Business ranking on the ease of starting a business – potentially reducing the need to set-up an OSS service.

...but during Covid-19 outbreak agencies focused on existing investors

The Covid-19 outbreak and the resulting health measures changed IPAs' modus operandi and the type of assistance required by clients. Immediate, short-term responses focused on existing clients and information provision (OECD, 2020[10]). Most MENA agencies set up crisis units to inform and communicate with existing investors, to respond to their queries and to follow up on production disruptions:

- GAFI in Egypt adopted new measures to facilitate the operations of the ISCs and set up electronic services to ensure that communication with investors was operational despite initial confinement measures.
- The Jordan IPA established a "Crisis Management Group" to communicate regularly with investors, discuss issues, devise solutions for the retention of investments, and provide support to investors as needed.
- The Lebanese IPA posted online all measures initiated to help businesses overcome the crisis, from tax incentives to targeted awareness campaigns, building on an earlier initiative to respond to the political and economic crisis Lebanon was facing prior to the pandemic. IDAL also created online legal and advisory services, free of charge, to support firms with health, financial and fiscal measures.
- AMDIE in Morocco set up a dedicated unit to provide information and aftercare services to investors and co-ordinate crisis responses with other institutions.
- FIPA in Tunisia created a crisis unit, including staff from overseas offices to inform on the situation and specific government measures, collect information on foreign investors' operations, co-ordinate with partners to respond to issues faced by investors, and support the implementation of solutions.

MENA IPAs' shift towards supporting existing investors and intense aftercare during the Covid-19 outbreak have pushed the agencies to develop new digital tools and innovative retention services that they were lacking before the crisis. As investment facilitation requires a whole-of-government approach, some IPAs had to intensify their co-ordination with other government agencies. MENA IPAs could consider operating some of these tools and services in the longer term, and adjust them to become permanent.

Monitoring and evaluation

Pressure on MENA IPAs to demonstrate success has been growing in the past few years, because of tighter budgets and uncertainties on the impact of FDI on inclusive and sustainable development (see Chapter 2 on FDI trends and benefits). Ensuring the efficiency and effectiveness of IPAs' actions is a constant preoccupation of governments in other parts of the world too. This trend is likely to accelerate following the Covid-19 outbreak as IPAs are more than ever pressed to attract FDI that can contribute positively to sustainable development. To ensure accountability, IPAs need to have accurate information about their activities and actions. Robust and formal monitoring and evaluation systems (M&E) are therefore required.

Before monitoring, there needs to be an evidence- and consensus-based decision on what is worth tracking, which is closely linked to the IPA's strategy; after that, it is necessary to define targets or key performance indicators (KPIs) (Sztajerowska, 2019[12]). According to the OECD-IDB survey, most IPAs in the MENA region report the existence of such target objectives. These targets are often not publicly available, however, nor is the strategy that underlies them. This may make it difficult to understand how targets are selected and defined and how objectives are linked to the IPA's overall strategy.

Some agencies such as IDA Ireland or CINDE Costa Rica devote an entire report to describe their strategy and how it translates to priorities and measurable targets. IDA's strategy includes quantified targets based on "a detailed assessment of the Global FDI marketplace, the outlook for sectors". The targets often relate to the amount of investment, the number of jobs created or spending on R&D. Although similarities exist with MENA IPAs strategies, such as the definition of key sectors, IDA and CINDE's reports are enriched with targets and a detailed action plan on how to attain them.

Most of the eight MENA focus economies report that their IPAs have an M&E unit and extensively use customer relationship management (CRM) tools to measure the agency's performance and impact on the economy. Such responses to the OECD-IDB survey are hard to reconcile with the fact that robust M&E is costly and difficult to implement, and thus often not well developed, including in OECD IPAs with higher budgets and more staff trained in evaluation techniques (OECD, 2018[3]). Qualitative discussions with MENA IPAs clarified that many agencies seem to have some sort of audit or quality control, but few have a proper horizontal unit dedicated to monitoring performance.

MENA agencies put more weight on monitoring how investment projects relate to development outcomes rather than monitoring their operational performance in providing adequate services. The majority monitor the number of jobs created and regional development, although some IPAs like PIB Libya report monitoring all outcomes, a response that contrasts with the resources of the agency and the type of FDI it receives (Table 6.1). Some agencies such as ANDI in Algeria or GAFI in Egypt require by law that investors granted tax incentives report on certain outcomes, such as the number of jobs created. This information allows them to take corrective action if investors do not deliver on their promises. MENA IPAs are more likely to take corrective action if investors do not deliver on their job creation promises than if they breach responsible business conduct (RBC) standards. This may differ for JIC in Jordan and AMDIE in Morocco as both IPAs host the National Contact Point (NCP) for RBC (See Chapter 10 for further details).

Another key aspect of the M&E organisational setting is the reporting process of the IPA to the government, and whether the reporting is publicly available. All agencies produce financial reports and most of them produce activity reports that are submitted to the government or the IPA board, although those reports are rarely available on the IPA's website. In the UK, the Department for International Trade includes in its annual report a dedicated performance section providing the list of objectives along with the key performance measures and a detailed assessment of its performance.

Table 6.1. Outcome indicators of MENA IPAs

		DZA	EGY	JOR	LBN	LBY	MAR	PA	Tunisia	
	% of OECD IPAs	ANDI	GAFI	JIC	IDAL	PIB	AMDIE	P PA	FIPA	TIA
Total FDI	81%	✓	✓	✓	✓	✓	✓	✓	✓	✓
Jobs	88%	✓	✓	✓	✓	✓	✓	✓	✓	✓
Wages	28%		✓			✓		✓		
Exports	34%	✓	✓			✓	✓	✓		
Innovation / R&D	53%	✓	✓			✓		✓		✓
Regional Development	41%	✓	✓	✓	✓	✓		✓	✓	✓
Tax Revenue	16%	✓				✓		✓		
Capacity of Domestic Firms	22%	✓			✓	✓		✓		✓
Trainings of MNEs to their staff or to local firms	n.a.	✓				✓		✓		
Investors Record on RBC	6%					✓		✓		✓
Green Investment	23%	✓	✓			✓		✓		✓
Sustainability	19%	✓	✓			✓		✓		✓

Source: OECD-IDB survey of investment promotion agencies.

Promoting and facilitating investment in regions and provinces

With the international fragmentation of production and services, investors are increasingly attracted to what they get from a specific city or region (Crescenzi, Di Cataldo and Giua, 2019[13]). Locations within the same borders can differ greatly in their attractiveness due to varying productivity levels, skills attributes and other local ecosystem characteristics. MENA economies are no exception and those with access to the Mediterranean Sea have considerable inequalities between coastal areas and inland regions, which has also fuelled social tensions. Governments have been seeking to attract investors to less developed regions but their attempts have focused on national policies such as tax incentives in specific regions and less on developing, together with local institutions, subnational investment promotion strategies, thereby not taking into account that each region is unique in the way it competes in national and global investment networks.

The degree of state centralisation influences the local dimension of investment promotion and facilitation

A government's institutional configuration influences the way it conducts investment policy at the local level. This configuration is determined largely by the level of centralisation of economic policy and the related governance mechanisms between central and subnational government bodies (region, state, province or city). Some countries choose to centralise investment promotion at the level of the national IPA, which may or may not have a network of subnational offices. Others, often with more decentralised governance or economic systems, establish subnational IPAs that are partly or fully independent from the central agency.

All MENA economies are unitary states with a strong history of centralisation.[4] Accordingly, most of them have a centralised approach to investment promotion and facilitation. Around a third of MENA IPAs never contact agencies at the subnational level and report difficulties working with local governments, which often lack the adequate skills. Only a few consult them to integrate local development plans into their national attraction strategy. IPAs work with their own local branches, when these exist, rather than with separate, decentralised entities. Branches focus on the provision of facilitation and aftercare services and sometimes run OSS services. Among the eight MENA focus economies, Tunisia's FIPA and Morocco's AMDIE are the only IPAs with no subnational offices. In Morocco, the national IPA cooperates with the recently reorganised regional investment centres, which are under the authority of governorates (*wilayas*) and coordinated, at central level, by the Ministry of Interior. The regional investment centres are autonomous agencies that provide single window services, conduct economic intelligence, promote the regions, and offer dispute settlement services.

Many other countries have a centralised system of national IPAs that interact with subnational branches, including emerging economies such as Thailand and OECD economies including Japan, Ireland or the Czech Republic (OECD, 2018[3]) (OECD, 2021[7]). The approach of many other IPAs is to share investment promotion and facilitation responsibilities with governorates and institutions or, in some, cases, fully rely on them. This has been the approach followed by almost half of OECD IPAs as well as countries like Viet Nam, where provincial authorities were empowered to improve their own investment climate and develop investment promotion tools (Box 6.4).

Box 6.4. Decentralised investment promotion and facilitation: the experience of Viet Nam

In Viet Nam, the Investment Law of 2005 (subsequently superseded by the Investment Law of 2014) transferred the authority to issue investment certificates and business registration certificates, among other things, to the 58 provinces of the country. Provincial authorities were formally empowered to improve their own investment climate. Teams were charged with facilitating FDI in each province and many provinces were able make significant changes in the rules and regulations governing business activities. Each province has a Department of Planning and Investment (DPI), which is responsible for investment-related activities and reports to the province's People's Committee.

Provincial DPIs perform various functions pertaining to investment attraction, such as marketing their location as an investment destination, conducting promotional missions in overseas markets and organising site visits for prospective investors. Some provinces also have dedicated Investment Promotion Centres, which are either located under the DPI or directly under the authority of the People's Committee. For example, the Investment and Trade Promotion Centre of Ho Chi Minh City provides local and foreign companies with required information and consulting services, and arranges match-making between domestic businesses and foreign affiliates. Some provinces, such as Hanoi City and Ho Chi Minh City, have opened representative offices overseas.

While provinces serve as the entry point for investors to establish businesses, their level of activity and efficiency in terms of investment promotion greatly depend on local capacities and resources. With decentralisation in place, peer learning among provinces helped to boost business climate reforms at the local level, although the decentralisation of investment promotion has also generated some opportunities for bribery and corruption.

Source: (OECD, 2018[14]).

After 2011, some MENA economies initiated reforms to address citizens' demands for more participative governance and more efficient public services at the local level, with regional development as a central objective. Morocco introduced the objective of regionalisation in the 2011 Constitution and undertook advanced regionalisation reforms in 2015 but outcomes have yet to meet expectations (OCDE, 2018[15]). Tunisia's 2014 Constitution dedicates a chapter to decentralisation and the government passed a decentralisation law and set up elected local councils in 2018. With the 2015 decentralisation law in Jordan, the country has undertaken a first step towards a bottom-up approach to the identification of service needs and policy priorities, based on the role of the new local councils. In Tunisia and Jordan, the creation of elected local bodies was not accompanied by a transfer of fiscal power, thereby limiting public action at the local level.

The rationale for conducting investment promotion activities at the local level

Investment promotion and facilitation should strike a balance between centralised strategic decision-making and sufficient leeway for subnational governments to exercise their power. The central government alone cannot foster economic attractiveness, suggesting the importance of a multi-level arrangement. At the same time, having a single point of entry for foreign companies and investors has demonstrated success (Pasquinelli and Vuignier, 2020[16]).

There are four main reasons for conducting investment promotion activities at a local level (Millenium Cities Initiative, 2009[17]):

- *Development objectives*: subnational bodies and the central government may have different economic development objectives and competitive advantages;
- *Knowledge of their location*: subnational bodies have greater knowledge of their area's strengths and weaknesses, and are thus better able to market them by providing accurate information to investors;
- *Facilitation on the ground*: as subnational bodies are closer to local decision-makers, they are better positioned to assist investors in their establishment and post-establishment phases; and
- *Attracting domestic investment*: for many regions, attracting companies from the same country can be as important as attracting foreign investors. Subnational bodies can apply the same principles and techniques as those used to promote FDI as well as more successfully link their operations to the local economy.

Whether there is a network of national IPAs with local branches or a system of independent subnational IPAs, MENA governments could give subnational bodies more room to conduct investment promotion and facilitation tasks. Evidence from the European Union's regions shows that FDI responds better to the activity of subnational IPAs operating in closer proximity to investors' operations (Crescenzi, Di Cataldo and Giua, 2019[13]). The experience of Viet Nam has shown that investment promotion measures carried out at the local level can help increase both domestic and foreign investment, and enhance the contribution of investment to local economic development. Some decentralisation of investment promotion has also provided Viet Nam's provinces with an incentive to become more efficient in their efforts to improve the investment environment (Box 6.4).

Even if the priority of subnational branches of MENA IPAs is to facilitate investors' establishment, developing more tailored investment attraction tools is equally relevant. The multiplicity of subnational investment promotion activities does not automatically lead to a race to the bottom between different locations. Evidence shows that neighbouring cities (or regions), including within the same country, can attract foreign investment from different geographical sources and in distinct economic activities or segments of the supply chain (Wall, 2019[18]). National investment promotion strategies often disregard their cities' specificities and competitors, and reflect the country's wider competitive advantages relative to other countries.

Casablanca and Cairo, for instance, do not necessarily compete over foreign investment because they attract different types of investors (Wall, 2019[18]). Casablanca's rivals are port cities spread over different continents and include Panama City, Danang (Viet Nam) and Valencia. Cairo's competitors are often cities like Algiers, Riyadh and Tunis. One reason Casablanca has global rivals is likely because the city is well anchored in global value chains and has access to maritime networks. Casablanca and its rivals compete over efficiency-seeking investment in automotive, business services and transport sectors. In Cairo, the world's 16th largest metropole, foreign investors are more interested in serving domestic consumers and in using the capital to reach the African or Middle Eastern market. Cairo and its city rivals, compete over FDI in real estate, energy and financial services.

Comparative information on city competitors can help MENA IPAs, with their subnational branches, or subnational agencies, craft investment promotion strategies tailored to the competitive strengths and potential of each territory. It can also help in developing policy tools that connect foreign investors with local suppliers. For instance, smaller cities may concentrate efforts in attracting large companies (e.g. by offering generous tax incentives) instead of focusing their promotion strategies and tools on prospecting smaller investors that they can realistically attract. Investment promotion tools to attract such second-tier firms might prove useful as these firms may forge stronger linkages with local companies than large companies, because of lower absorptive capacity gaps and higher labour mobility.

Sharing investment promotion responsibilities across different levels of government can bring a number of challenges. Some regions may resist foreign-funded projects that were directed to the region by the central agency because of perceived environmental risks to the local population or concerns that local firms may suffer from increased competition. At the same time, because of inter-regional competition, national IPAs can be deliberately excluded from locally identified opportunities or, on the contrary, become arbitrators (i.e. deciding to which region should they direct a foreign investor) and face difficult decisions.

Co-ordination tools party help to overcome these challenges. In Sweden, a code of conduct agreement among the national IPA and the regions was established to better communicate opportunities and encourage exchange of information. The French IPA has a formal information-sharing process to increase the efficiency of the collaboration with subnational IPAs. The agency created a "marketplace" of projects and shares information weekly with its regional partners about new foreign investment projects identified, and requests made at the regional level (OECD, 2018[3]). Thanks to this platform, partners can coordinate their responses and identify areas for joint action. This framework guarantees the impartiality and neutrality of Business France vis-à-vis all the regions (not favouring one over the other when bringing new projects.

References

Crescenzi, R., M. Di Cataldo and M. Giua (2019), "FDI Inflows in Europe: Does Investment Promotion work?", London School of Economics and Political Science, Institute of Global Affairs. [13]

Millenium Cities Initiative (2009), *Handbook for Promoting Foreign Direct Investment in Medium-size, Low-Budget Cities in Emerging Markets*, Millenium Cities Initiative, https://scholar.google.fr/scholar?hl=fr&as_sdt=0%2C5&q=Handbook+for+Promoting+Foreign+Direct+Investment+in+Medium-Size%2C+Low+Budget+Cities+in+Emerging+Markets&btnG= (accessed on 27 February 2021). [17]

Novik, A. and A. De Crombrugghe (2018), *OECD Investment Insights: Towards an International Framework for Investment Facilitation*, OECD. [8]

OCDE (2018), *Dialogue Maroc-OCDE sur les politiques de développement territorial: Enjeux et Recommandations pour une action publique coordonnée*, Éditions OCDE, Paris, https://dx.doi.org/10.1787/9789264302884-fr. [15]

OECD (2021), *OECD Investment Policy Reviews: Thailand*, OECD Investment Policy Reviews, OECD Publishing, Paris, https://dx.doi.org/10.1787/c4eeee1c-en. [7]

OECD (2020), *Investment in the MENA region in the time of COVID-19*, OECD, Paris, http://www.oecd.org/coronavirus/policy-responses/investment-in-the-mena-region-in-the-time-of-covid-19-da23e4c9/ (accessed on 27 February 2021). [10]

OECD (2020), *Investment promotion agencies in the time of Covid-19*, http://www.oecd.org/coronavirus/policy-responses/investment-promotion-agencies-in-the-time-of-covid-19-50f79678/ (accessed on 27 February 2021). [9]

OECD (2020), *OECD Investment Policy Reviews: Egypt 2020*, OECD Investment Policy Reviews, OECD Publishing, Paris, https://dx.doi.org/10.1787/9f9c589a-en. [4]

OECD (2020), *OECD Investment Policy Reviews: Indonesia 2020*, OECD Investment Policy Reviews, OECD Publishing, Paris, https://dx.doi.org/10.1787/b56512da-en. [6]

OECD (2019), *Mapping of Investment Promotion Agencies: Middle East and North Africa - OECD*, OECD, Paris, https://www.oecd.org/investment/investment-policy/mapping-of-investment-promotion-agencies-med.htm (accessed on 27 February 2021). [1]

OECD (2018), *Mapping of investment promotion agencies in OECD countries - OECD*, OECD, Paris, http://www.oecd.org/investment/Mapping-of-Investment-Promotion-Agencies-in-OECD-Countries.htm (accessed on 27 February 2021). [3]

OECD (2018), *OECD Investment Policy Reviews: Viet Nam 2018*, OECD Investment Policy Reviews, OECD Publishing, Paris, https://dx.doi.org/10.1787/9789264282957-en. [14]

OECD (202), *Investment Promotion in Eurasia: A Mapping of Investment Promotion Agencies*, OECD, Paris, https://www.oecd.org/eurasia/competitiveness-programme/Investment-Promotion-in-Eurasia-A-Mapping-of-Investment-Promotion-Agencies-ENG.pdf. [11]

Pasquinelli, C. and R. Vuignier (2020), "Place marketing, policy integration and governance complexity: an analytical framework for FDI promotion", *European Planning Studies*, Vol. 28/7, pp. 1413-1430, http://dx.doi.org/10.1080/09654313.2019.1701295. [16]

Sztajerowska, M. (2019), *OECD Investment Insights: Monitoring and Evaluation, a Brief Guide for Investment Promotion Agencies*, OECD, http://www.oecd.org/sti/ind/measuring- (accessed on 27 February 2021). [12]

Volpe Martincus, C. and M. Sztajerowska (2019), *How to Solve the Investment Promotion Puzzle: A Mapping of Investment Promotion Agencies in Latin America and the Caribbean and OECD Countries*, Inter-American Development Bank, http://dx.doi.org/10.18235/0001767. [2]

Wall, R. (2019), *The Geography of FDI in the Southern Mediterranean*, EU-OECD Programme on Promoting Investment in the Mediterranean. [18]

World Bank (2012), *Global Investment Promotion Best Practices 2012*, the World Bank Group, http://www.wbginvestmentclimate.org (accessed on 27 February 2021). [5]

Notes

[1] The Tunisian institutional landscape for investment promotion and facilitation includes other agencies such as the Agency for the Promotion of Industry and Innovation (API).

[2] IPAs do not structure their investment budgets into the four categories, therefore the budget breakdowns are based on estimates provided by agencies, and should be treated as approximations. Budget allocated to fiscal incentives is not taken into consideration. Chapter 7 provides an inventory of tax incentive policies in MENA economies.

[3] For instance, Egypt marketing campaign during the 2018 FIFA World Cup aimed at reinforcing the branding of the country as an entry door for foreign investors to the Africa market.

[4] Unitary states are states governed as a single power in which the central government is ultimately supreme. Iraq, which is not covered by this chapter, is the only MENA exception as it is a federal state.

7 Towards smarter use of investment incentives

MENA governments widely use tax and financial incentives to attract investment and direct it into certain sectors, activities and locations. This chapter presents original research mapping investment incentives granted in the eight MENA focus economies, including the types of instruments used and the extent to which they target certain sectors, activities and locations. It also explores the level of discretion involved in granting incentives. The results reflect tax and financial incentives detailed in national tax codes, investment laws, and in publicly-available documents published by investment promotion agencies, ministries of finance and economic zones. The chapter also draws on discussions with practitioners from investment promotion agencies and finance ministries in the region.

Summary and policy considerations

Governments in the Middle East and North Africa, as in most developing and emerging economies, widely use tax and financial incentives to attract private investment and direct it into certain sectors, activities and locations. Investment incentives are measures that seek to influence an investment project through favourable tax treatment or other benefits that affect the relative cost of the project. But the costs of incentives, particularly tax incentives, could outweigh the benefits. Tax incentives may subsidise firms that would have invested without favourable treatment and can constitute a significant cost for governments in terms of revenue forgone. However, carefully designed and targeted incentives may help correct market failures and advance certain development goals, such as supporting renewable energy or skills and technology upgrades, enhancing the positive impact of investment (Chapter 2). Many governments have recently sought to incentivise investment in the health sector to respond to the challenges of the Covid-19 pandemic. Better understanding the scope of incentives offered and how they are administered is essential to analyse their effectiveness and efficiency.

This chapter provides an overview of the types of investment incentives offered in the MENA region, the instruments used and their stated goals (targeting), as well as how they are governed. The eight MENA governments covered in this report (MENA focus economies) grant fiscal and financial incentives primarily to investors in agricultural, tourism and industrial sectors (broadly defined), export-oriented activities, and under-developed regions.[1] Also common are incentives to investors that advance environmental protection, as are fiscal benefits to hydrocarbon industries. Several of the focus economies give tax breaks or grants to firms that create jobs or enhance skills. Fewer give incentives to firms that use new technologies or support technology transfer and R&D activities, unlike OECD countries.

Benefits to eligible investors are often generous. Among the eight MENA focus economies, all offer tax holidays – total exemptions from corporate income tax (CIT) – to investors in certain sectors and locations. All but two countries (Jordan and Tunisia) offer permanent CIT exemptions to eligible investors, and half grant permanently reduced CIT rates. Several governments have taken steps to reduce the length of tax holidays and number of firms eligible for them. But profit-based incentives (tax holidays and CIT rate reductions) remain widespread and are often easy for firms to receive, with broad eligibility requirements. Investment incentives in the MENA focus economies are often open to interpretation and discretion of implementing authorities (in many cases investment promotion agencies or councils of investment composed of representatives from different ministries), increasing the risk of corruption and aggressive tax planning by firms.

Tax incentives to firms are one, and often not the determining, factor for their investment decisions. Some investors (such as those that are efficiency-seeking) may be more sensitive to incentives than others (such as market- or natural resource- seeking), but surveys suggest that most firms would invest even without incentives (IMF-OECD-UN-World Bank, 2015[1]) (James, 2013[2]). On average, MENA economies offer more permanent exemptions and longer tax holidays (14.6 years) than ASEAN countries (11 years), yet receive lower levels of FDI. This highlights the importance of the overall investment climate for attracting firms, and raises questions about the merits of generous, broad-based incentives.

MENA governments grant incentives through multiple pieces of legislation, decrees and executive orders, and often more than one agency is responsible for administering incentives. The spectrum of incentives is thus subject to frequent amendments. Many governments in the region plan to add or revise incentives to respond to the economic and social costs of the Covid-19 pandemic. Disruptions to supply chains and economic activity have prompted some governments to re-assess their investment promotion strategies. As governments seek swift measures to advance their economic recovery, assessments on the effectiveness and efficiency of incentives will be key to support already strained state budgets, and to ensure incentive design matches its goals.

Policy considerations

- Consider how widely to offer tax and financial benefits, if these incentives are necessary to attract investment, and if their costs – in terms of revenue forgone and economic distortions – outweigh their benefits. Cost-benefit analysis prior to introducing incentives, and monitoring ex-post, would help governments assess the extent to which, and at what cost, incentives meet their intended objectives. Such monitoring and evaluation is challenging, requiring data and resources that may not be available. In such cases, simple tax incentive reports, identifying and describing all available incentives, their policy goal, and legal reference, is an important first step to create accountability and transparency. Replacing permanent incentives with temporary benefits would also encourage evaluation.
- Consider moving gradually from broad-based tax holidays to more targeted, cost-based incentives in line with government priorities. The type and generosity of tax incentives play an important role in their effectiveness and efficiency. Profit-based incentives are more likely to be redundant than cost-based incentives. Because the latter reduces the costs of investment (rather than benefiting firms already profitable), it may make marginal investment profitable, increasing the chances of creating additional investment. The more targeted the incentive, the more likely it is to reach its stated goal.
- Ensure that incentives are specific, with clear eligibility criteria that reduce room for excessive discretion by implementing authorities. This will allow for more fair competition, lower corruption and easier evaluation. Investment incentives in the MENA focus economies often have vague eligibility criteria, while investment laws often note the option of undefined additional benefits to investors that meet unspecified criteria. This creates uncertainty for investors over what they are eligible to receive, and raises the risk of aggressive tax planning by firms, as well as the risk of corruption by administering authorities (see Chapter 11).
- Consolidate all tax incentives in tax laws – rather than in investment laws and executive regulations, legislation governing specific industries or one-off agreements with firms – to enhance transparency and reduce potential redundancies and confusion over the administering authority. The Ministry of Finance is often best placed to grant incentives and monitor their costs. Other ministries may be more inclined to offer fiscal benefits as they are not in charge of tax collection or necessarily aware of the state's fiscal needs.
- Assess whether the goals of tax incentives (directing investment in particular sectors or activities), align with investment promotion strategies and national development goals (see chapter 6 on promotion strategies). Simple tax incentive reports (described above), can help policymakers make this assessment, while more in-depth monitoring of firms compliance with the terms of the incentive (for example, jobs created, value of exports), can assist in determining if the incentive is contributing to development goals.

Investment incentive instruments

Statutory corporate income tax (CIT) rates are the first reference point for foreign and domestic investors when evaluating the tax treatment of a jurisdiction. But it is the entire tax regime – including various forms of tax incentives – which determines the tax liability of businesses or incentives to invest. The most common types of tax incentives used in the MENA focus economies, and in developing and emerging markets, are: corporate tax holidays (periods during which an investment is fully exempt from corporate taxation), reduced corporate tax rates, and tax deductions (or allowances) and credits (provisions to deduct certain expenditures from taxable income or directly from tax liability). Beyond incentives directly affecting corporate income taxes, exemptions from indirect taxes, including import and export duties and value added tax (VAT), are commonly used (OECD, 2019[3]).

The average statutory CIT rate in among the MENA focus economies is 21%, ranging from 15% (Palestinian Authority) to 25% (Tunisia) (Figure 7.1).[2] This is slightly lower than the average CIT rate in OECD (25%) and ASEAN countries (23%) (OECD, 2019[3]). Algeria and Jordan set different rates for different sectors and activities, and Morocco uses a progressive rate (between 10-31% depending on revenue).

Figure 7.1. Statutory CIT rates in MENA focus economies

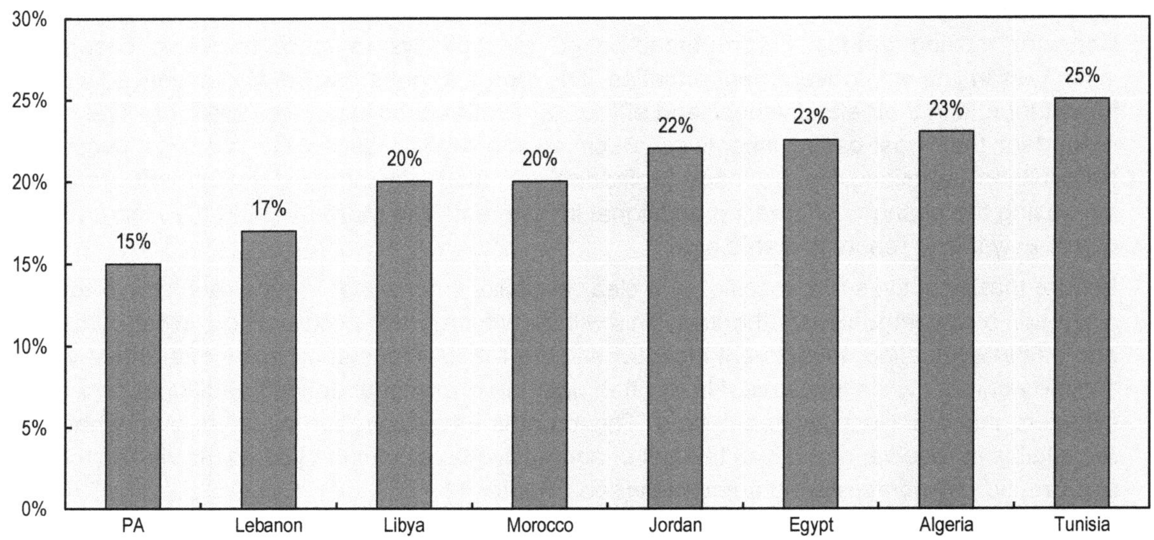

Note: Rates as of 2020. Standard CIT figures for Algeria and Jordan show the simple average of standard rates for different sectors (excluding rates that only apply to one sector), Morocco shows the simple average of progressive rates. PA: Palestinian Authority.
Source: OECD based on national legislation and (EY, 2020[4]).

All MENA economies provide income tax holidays

A corporate tax holiday is a complete exemption from taxation of corporate incomes, usually over a defined period of time, starting at the beginning of the investment lifecycle. The broad consensus among international institutions is that tax holidays are one of the most distortive tax incentives (IMF-OECD-UN-World Bank, 2015[1]) (OECD, 2015[5]). Along with corporate income tax reductions or partial income exemptions, tax holidays are profit-based incentives: they are determined as a percentage of profit and benefit firms that are already profitable. These firms are more likely than firms with a longer profit horizon to have invested without the incentive (IMF-OECD-UN-World Bank, 2015[1]). Profit-based incentives also support projects with low up-front costs, which tend to be mobile (i.e. able to easily change their location to seek better conditions), raising the risk of profit shifting. Profit-based incentives do not necessarily provide impetus for firms to stay and contribute positive spillovers to the economy (Klemm and Van Parys, 2012[6]). These incentives remain prevalent in part because they are easy to administer, and politically difficult to remove once in place.

All eight MENA focus economies offer tax holidays to eligible investors. All but two (Jordan and Tunisia) grant permanent CIT exemptions to select firms. Projects that are eligible for tax holidays include in agriculture (Algeria, Morocco and Palestinian Authority), export-oriented sectors or in free and economic zones (Algeria, Egypt, Lebanon and Libya), and capital risk, offshore and holding companies (Lebanon and Morocco). Excluding indefinite exemptions, the maximum length of tax holidays (including extensions) is similar across countries at around 10 years. Jordan offers the longest exemptions at 30 years (Figure 7.2). In comparison, tax holidays in ASEAN countries vary between four and 20 years (including extensions), though no countries offer permanent exemptions (OECD, 2019[3]).

All MENA governments (except the Palestinian Authority) grant tax holidays based on the location of the investment, including in under-developed areas, and, more frequently, in economic or free zones. The majority (except Egypt and Libya) offer tax holidays based on sector, and half of the countries grant holidays based on certain economic activities (e.g. skills development, R&D, environmental protection). Algeria, Lebanon and Morocco provide tax holidays based on all three criteria. Libya gives five-year tax holidays to all investors as part of its standard tax regime.

Figure 7.2. Length of CIT holidays in MENA focus economies (years)

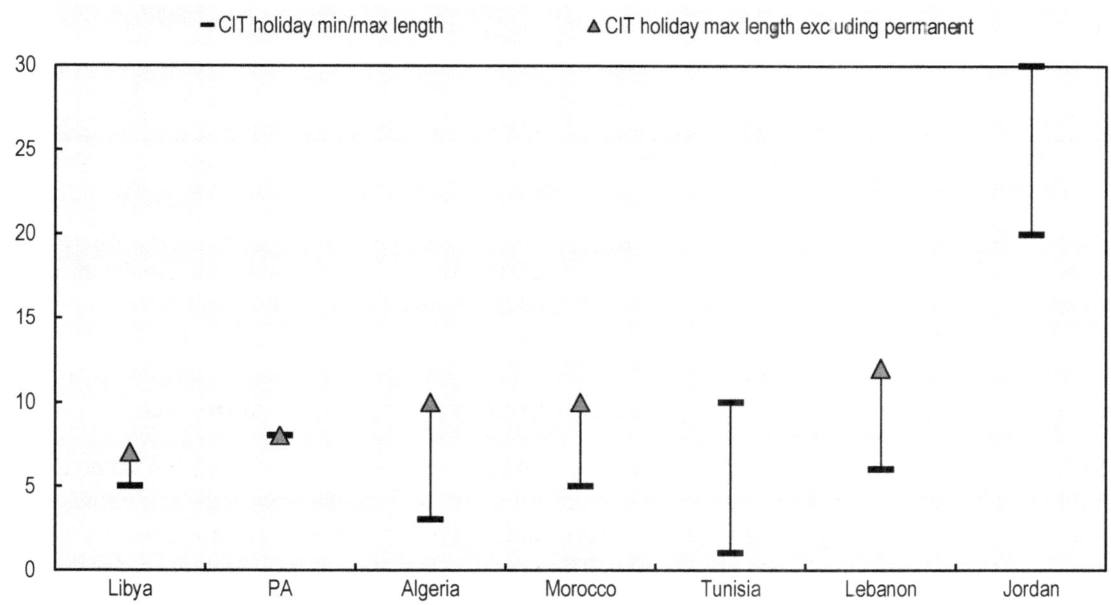

Note: Minimum and maximum lengths of CIT holidays offered to investors shown. Arrows indicate the country also grants permanent CIT exemptions to some investors. Only Tunisia and Jordan do not offer permanent CIT exemptions. Egypt gives permanent CIT holidays to some investors, with no minimum or maximum length, therefore is not included in the graph below. PA: Palestinian Authority.
Source: OECD based on national legislation.

CIT rate reductions in MENA economies are often permanent

Reduced CIT rates are preferential, non-zero tax rates below standard CIT rates. Often firms are eligible for reduced CIT rates after a tax holiday has expired. Five out of the eight MENA focus economies offer reduced CIT rates. Those that do tend to offer fewer tax holidays, and conversely, MENA countries that use tax holidays widely (such as Algeria, Lebanon and Libya) have fewer or no CIT reduction schemes. Generosity of reductions varies. Figure 7.3 shows the maximum and minimum reduced CIT rates offered to investors (i.e. the most and least generous CIT reduction the country grants) compared to the average standard rate in each country. These benefits are often permanent, or lengthy. Lebanon offers the shortest reductions at 5 years, compared to 20 years for certain investors in Morocco and Jordan. All of Tunisia's CIT reductions are permanent. Eligibility criteria are more varied than for tax holidays, with no discernible concentration in certain activities or sectors across the region.

Figure 7.3. Statutory and reduced CIT rates in MENA focus economies

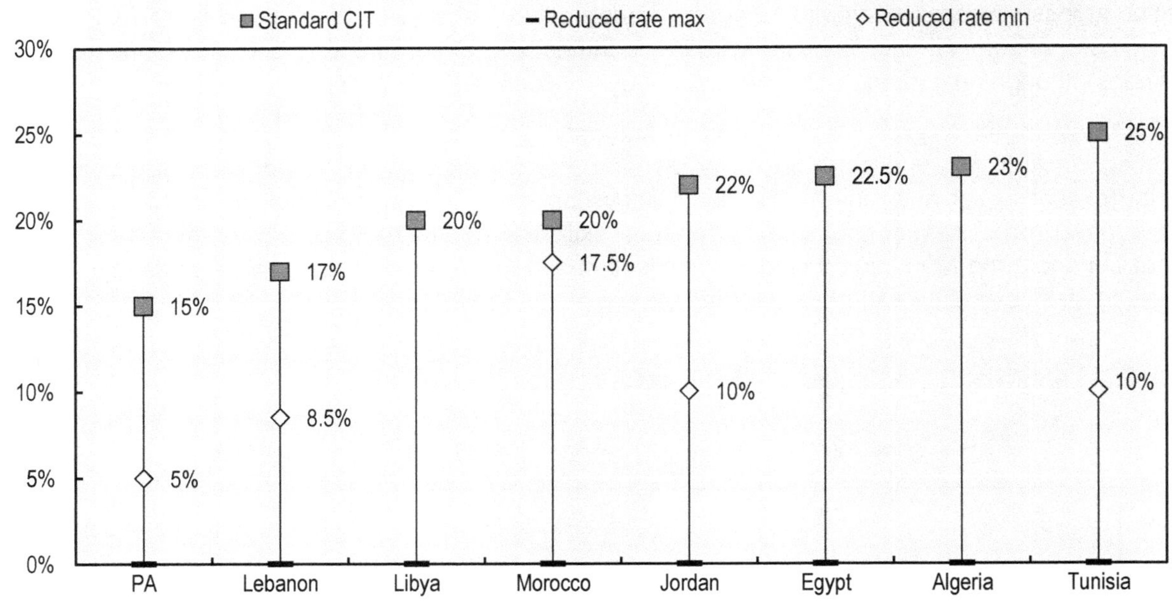

Note: Standard CIT figures for Algeria and Jordan show the average of standard rates for different sectors, Morocco shows the average of progressive rates. Minimum reduced rate depicts the least generous CIT reduction offered to investors. If none, the country does not offer CIT reductions less than 100%. All countries provide tax holidays, shown as maximum reduced rates. PA: Palestinian Authority.
Source: OECD based on national legislation and (EY, 2020[4]).

Tax deductions and credits used less frequently than profit-based schemes

Tax deductions (or investment allowances) allow firms to deduct certain expenditures from taxable income. Tax credits are similar but enable investors to deduct an expense directly from their tax liability (versus their taxable income), reducing the amount of taxes due. Unlike the profit-based incentives described above, tax deductions and credits are cost-based. They reduce the cost of the investment for firms, such as upfront expenses, profits reinvested or more targeted costs like training programmes and research and development (R&D) activities (IMF-OECD-UN-World Bank, 2015[1]) (James, 2013[2]).

Half of the MENA focus economies provide tax deductions to investors. Egypt for example revised its investment scheme in 2017 to adopt wider use of such cost-based incentives rather than tax holidays. It allows deductions of up to 50% of investment costs from taxable income for projects in areas most in need of development, and up to 30% for investment in specific sectors and activities (including renewable energy and labour-intensive projects) (OECD, 2020[7]). Tunisia offers the greatest number of tax deduction schemes, including for reinvested profits in agriculture, “innovative sectors” and exporting firms. Algeria gives unspecified tax deductions for investments in R&D. While most countries in the region allow for accelerated depreciation of assets and loss-carry-forward schemes (allowing firms to deduct losses made in a previous year from income made in a given fiscal period), these are often part of the general scheme applied to all investors, rather than used as an incentive, i.e. as a benefit to investments in a particular sector or activity. There is limited accessible information on these schemes, necessitating further research. Tax credits are used much less frequently across the MENA focus economies.

Overall, cost-based incentives are much less common in the MENA focus economies than profit-based benefits, as is the case in most developing and emerging economies. This may be due in part to higher administrative costs involved in granting such incentives (Andersen, Kett and Von Uexkull, 2017[8]). But cost-based incentives are less biased toward firms that are already profitable. They depend instead on the size of the investment or its use toward certain activities, so are more likely to encourage new business and specific policy objectives (OECD, 2019[3]). Recognising these benefits, other emerging countries like Thailand have initiated a gradual, albeit still moderate, move towards providing more targeted incentives based on the "merits" of the project (Box 7.1).

Box 7.1. Tax incentives in Thailand: adopting cost-based approaches

Tax incentives are at the core of the investment promotion strategy of Thailand. The incentive framework operated by the Board of Investment, the Thai investment promotion agency, consists of a basic scheme and, since 2015, a merit-based scheme. Basic incentives include CIT exemptions granted to nearly 300 sub-sectors specified in a list updated to reflect wider changes in government strategy (for instance new sub-sectors in the health industry were added following the Covid-19 crisis). The sub-sectors are grouped into five categories that set the generosity of the incentive. The most generous category includes sub-sectors of special importance to the economy and those with no or little existing investments in the country.

Merit-based incentives are additional tax incentives (i.e. on top of basic incentives) which are granted to stimulate investment or spending on activities that benefit the country or industry at large. These incentives are cost-based: businesses spending on skills development and R&D are eligible to include the investment value for CIT exemption (e.g. expenditures on in-house or joint R&D with overseas institutes, donation to technology or human capital development funds, or intellectual property acquisition/licensing fees). To promote business linkages, projects are granted additional incentives on taxable income for spending on the development of local suppliers in advanced technology through training and technical assistance.

Other merit-based incentives are granted with the objective of attracting investment in less developed regions of the country. These consist of enhanced tax deductions from the costs of transport, electricity and water supply for 10 years and additional 25% deductions of the investment cost of installation or construction of facilities.

Source: (OECD, 2021[9]).

Exemptions from other taxes, duties and fees widespread

MENA countries offer a broad range of exemptions on other taxes that do not directly affect CIT, but form part of the cost of investment. These include exemptions on customs duties, VAT, sales tax, and other fees, such as land registration, stamp duties, and work/residence fees.

All countries in the region offer incentives related to costs of trade, i.e., exemptions or reductions on import and export duties and other customs charges. These are sometimes specific to certain inputs, such as raw materials not available domestically. But in many cases MENA countries give blanket exemptions. For example, in Morocco large investment projects receive complete import duty exemptions for three years. These schemes are almost universal in free zones and economic zones designed to encourage exports and prevalent across the region. Two countries (Egypt and Libya) offer all investors reductions or exemptions on customs duties on imported machinery or other equipment required to execute the project. All countries but Libya offer exemptions or reductions on VAT or sales tax. Similarly, these benefits are ubiquitous in economic zones, and are often granted alongside customs duties exemptions.

The majority of MENA economies also provide certain investors with reductions or exemptions on other fees, most notably land and building registration fees, stamp duties and professional activity taxes. These benefits are often permanent. Algeria is one exception, offering benefits on customs duties and other taxes and fees to firms only during their set-up phase. It is also notable that legislation often does not specify the length of time firms can receive these incentives, allowing for the interpretation that they are permanent benefits.

Financial incentives offered in the majority of MENA economies

Though offered less frequently than tax incentives, financial benefits, such as grants for investment costs, are used throughout the region in an effort to attract investment in particular sectors, activities and locations.

Libya is the only of the focus economies that does not detail specific financial benefits in its legislation. All the other MENA focus economies offer grants for, for example, infrastructure costs, staff training, land/building or equipment costs, and/or utility expenses. With the exception of Tunisia, the specific details of these incentives – such as the amount of funds eligible firms can receive – are not specified in legislation. Most countries are also vague about eligibility requirements. For example, executive regulations often do not detail how investors can spend grants, such as for staff training, leaving them open to interpretation.

Several MENA economies offer financial support for investment costs in activities related to sustainable development, environmental protection or renewable energy (Tunisia, Morocco, Egypt and Algeria). Loan guarantees and interest subsidies are other financial incentive tools, used for example in Algeria to promote tourism projects, and in Lebanon for firms that relocate to underdeveloped areas.

Targeting of investment incentives

All of the MENA focus economies use incentive schemes to promote investment in certain sectors, activities and locations, and in so doing, encourage economic and social spillovers through investment. Notably, Algeria adopts a negative list approach to incentives; more than 100 sectors and activities are not eligible for tax benefits. In most MENA countries, the criteria to receive the incentive tend to be unspecific and broad, covering multiple sectors or categories such as industrial projects. Incentives that target specific investment expenditures (as opposed to profits), or certain, well-defined activities are more likely to attract investment that would not otherwise have been made, can help achieve specific policy goals, and make it more difficult for firms to conduct aggressive tax planning (IMF-OECD-UN-World Bank, 2015[1]). Any incentives scheme requires regular evaluation and review to limit abuse and market distortions.

This section summarises the extent to which incentives in the MENA focus economies are targeted to support economic and development goals. The majority of incentives offered seek to direct investment into certain locations, followed by key sectors, and types of activities (including export-oriented and job-creating projects). More than a quarter of incentives are eligible to firms that meet a combination of these criteria (for example, sector and location). Investment size is also often a requirement, though rarely the only one. MENA policymakers could consider whether these targets align with their investment promotion strategies and national development goals (Chapter 6). As for the types of incentives used, these largely depend on the country. Some countries, like Algeria, tend to use tax holidays broadly, whereas Morocco and Tunisia provide more grants to investors than other countries in the region. Incentives for investment in sectors, activities and locations are examined in turn.

Incentives target agriculture, tourism and industrial sectors

More than a third of incentives mapped across the eight MENA focus economies seek to direct investment into particular sectors. Among sector-specific incentives, a third are further targeted toward sectors in certain locations (excluding zones) and/or performing particular activities. Table 7.1 summarises the six sectors that receive the most tax and financial incentives in region: agriculture, hydrocarbons, information and communications technology (ICT), industry, renewable energy, and tourism.[3]

Some countries detail a specific list of priority sectors within executive regulations to investment laws or in tax codes, whereas others list broader categories. A notable example is the industrial sector; around 40% of all sector-specific incentives in the region target industrial projects. Investment legislation in Tunisia for example lists automotive manufacturing and pharmaceutical industries as among its targeted sectors, whereas Lebanon and the Palestinian Authority's Investment legislation and regulations refer more broadly to investments in industry.

More targeted incentives in specific segments of a sector could better support the expansion and upgrading of priority sectors in MENA economies. For instance, Thailand specifies around 280 sub-sectors that are eligible for tax incentives. They fall under a broader group of sectors considered to be strategic for the wider economy (Box 7.1) (OECD, 2021[9]).

Table 7.1. Incentives for investment in select sectors in MENA economies

	Agriculture	Hydrocarbons	ICT	Industrial	Renewables	Tourism
Algeria	Tax holiday, customs/sales tax exemption			Tax holiday		Tax holiday, customs/sales tax exemption
Egypt	Tax deduction, customs/sales tax exemption, grants	Tax deduction, customs/sales tax exemption		Tax deduction customs/sales tax exemption, grants	Tax deduction, customs/sales tax exemption, grants	Tax deduction, customs/sales tax exemption, grants
Jordan	Tax holiday, CIT reduction, customs/sales tax exemption	Tax holiday, CIT reduction	CIT reduction, customs/sales tax exemption	Customs/sales tax exemption	Customs/sales tax exemption	Tax holiday, CIT reduction, customs/sales tax exemption
Lebanon	Tax holiday, CIT reduction, land/property tax exemption		Tax holiday, CIT reduction, land/property tax exemption	Tax holiday, CIT reduction, land/property tax exemption		Tax holiday, CIT reduction, land/property tax exemption
Libya						
Morocco	Tax holiday	Tax holiday		Tax holiday, grants		Tax holiday, CIT reduction
PA	Tax holiday			CIT reduction, customs/sales tax exemption	CIT reduction, customs/sales tax exemption	CIT reduction, customs/sales tax exemption
Tunisia	Tax holiday, CIT reduction, customs/sales tax exemption, tax deduction	Tax deduction, customs/sales tax exemption	Grants	Grants	Grants	

Note: Does not include incentives granted to specific sectors in economic zones or free zones. *Tax holiday* = total income tax exemption over defined period; *CIT reduction* = corporate income tax reduction over defined period; *tax deduction* = deductions of certain expenses from taxable income; *customs/sales tax exemption* = exemption from import duties, export taxes, VAT or sales tax; *land/property tax exemption* = exemption from land/property registration fees, stamp duties; *grants* = financial support towards specific investment costs. Table does not include other categories of benefits.
Source: OECD based on national legislation.

In addition to the industrial sector – and with the exception of Libya, which does not use investment incentives to target specific sectors – all countries offer incentives for investment in the agricultural sector. Agricultural projects tend to be eligible for the most generous incentives, including permanent CIT exemptions in Algeria, Morocco and the Palestinian Authority. The tourism sector, however, is eligible for the greatest number of distinct incentives in the region. For example, Jordan, Lebanon and Morocco offer tax holidays followed by CIT reductions to tourism investments. Half the countries in the region offer incentives to renewable energy investments, and only Jordan, Lebanon and Tunisia provide specific incentives to the ICT sector. It is worth noting that other countries may promote these sectors indirectly through incentives that target certain activities. For example, firms that use new technologies or advance environmental protection are often eligible for separate incentives, described below.

Half of the countries in the region provide tax benefits to investment in hydrocarbons – though it is likely that the data presented vastly underrepresent the extent of fiscal support to the industry. This chapter only considers incentives explicit in tax codes and investment-related laws and regulations. Many oil and gas firms receive additional exemptions in specific contracts with national governments. For example, in Egypt, specific decrees govern each petroleum agreement, which override domestic law for tax purposes (PwC, 2017[10]). Studies and investor surveys consistently suggest that natural resource-based incentives are redundant; as the resource is location specific, it raises the question of the necessity of incentives in attracting extractive firms (IMF-OECD-UN-World Bank, 2015[1]) (James, 2013[2]).

All MENA economies incentivise export activities, many incentivise environmental protection

All of the eight MENA economies use investment incentives to target investment in certain activities, such as job creation, skills development, export, or environmental protection. These incentives are often designed to help advance the positive impact of investment on sustainable development (Chapter 2). Activity-specific incentives are only slightly less frequent than sector-specific incentives, and comprise around a third of all incentives offered by the focus economies. Similar to sectoral benefits, a third of these incentives target activities in specific sectors and/or locations.

As summarised in Table 7.3, exports are the most encouraged activity across the region. Every country offers incentives to investors that primarily export or seek to increase their share of exports. Table 7.2 includes incentives granted to firms in free zones that have minimum export requirements. But all of the MENA focus economies except Jordan also offer incentives to exporting firms irrespective of their location. In addition to trade tax exemptions, most countries offer tax holidays and/or CIT reductions to exporting firms.

Several studies suggest that exporters respond more to incentives than domestic market-seeking investors, due to high international competition to attract such firms and their demands to keep costs low (James, 2013[2]) (Andersen, Kett and Von Uexkull, 2017[8]). But this varies by country. In Jordan, a 2009 survey of investors found that exporters were only slightly more attracted by incentives than non-exporters: around a third of exporters reported that they would not have invested in the country without incentives, compared to 20% of non-exporters (James, 2013[2]). The survey found that the majority of investors would have entered the market regardless. Incentives to export-only firms may contribute to integrating the country in global value chains, but might not help forging linkages with local business (see the case of Tunisia Box 8.2 in Chapter 8). Moreover, tax benefits contingent on export performance may run counter to World Trade Organisation rules against export subsidies, raising concerns about their use (WTO, 2019[11]).

Also common across the MENA economies are incentives to investors that advance environmental protection. For example, Tunisia offers firms in recycling and waste treatment CIT rates at less than half the standard rate, and Libya and Algeria grant tax holidays to investments that preserve the environment and protect natural resources. Aside from these two trends, there is wide variation in activity targeting across the focus economies. Half provide incentives to firms that create jobs, usually with a specific threshold requirement, or enhance skills (though as noted above, other countries provide grants for skills training). The Palestinian Authority is one of the only governments to give tax benefits to firms that use local content in their production, a policy that could incentivise foreign investors to forge stronger business linkages with local SMEs (see Chapter 8 for more on linkages programmes). Few countries give incentives to firms that use new technologies or support technology transfer and R&D activities, unlike OECD countries, which primarily grant incentives for R&D activities. This may be because MENA governments focus more on attracting FDI in labour-intensive industries, but it may also reflect a broader trend in the MENA region, and indeed in many emerging economies, of targeting a wide range of investors.

Table 7.2. Incentives for investment in certain activities in MENA economies

	Environmental protection	Exports	Job creation / skills	Technology / R&D	Local sourcing
Algeria	Tax holiday, grants	Tax holiday	Tax holiday	Tax holiday, tax deduction, grants	
Egypt		Tax holiday, tax deduction, customs/sales tax exemption, grant	Tax deduction, customs/sales tax exemption, grant		
Jordan		CIT reduction, customs/sales tax exemption, land/property tax exemption			Customs/sales tax exemption
Lebanon		Tax deduction			
Libya	Tax holiday, customs/sales tax exemption, land/property tax exemption	Tax holiday, customs/sales tax exemption			
Morocco	Grants	Tax holiday, CIT reduction, customs/sales tax exemption	Grants	Grants	
PA	CIT reduction, customs/sales tax exemption	Unspecified			CIT reduction, customs/sales tax exemption
Tunisia	CIT reduction, customs/sales tax exemption, grants	CIT reduction, tax deduction, customs/sales tax exemption, land/property tax exemption, grant	CIT reduction, tax deduction, customs/sales tax exemption, grants	Tax deduction grants	

Note: Benefits to exporting firms include incentives given to firms in free zones with minimum export requirements. *Tax holiday* = total income tax exemption over defined period; *CIT reduction* = corporate income tax reduction over defined period; *tax deduction* = deductions of certain expenses from taxable income; *customs/sales tax exemption* = exemption from import duties, export taxes, VAT or sales tax; *land/property tax exemption* = exemption from land/property registration fees, stamp duties; *grants* = financial support towards specific investment costs. Table does not include other categories of benefits.
Source: OECD based on national legislation.

Location-based incentives most widely used in the region

The majority of incentives offered to investors in the MENA focus economies seek to direct investment into particular locations. Half of these incentives are reserved for investors in economic, development or free (trade) zones, geographically defined areas that often have special regulations, administration, fiscal incentives, and/or infrastructure. Zones often have other eligibility requirements, including specific sectors and activities (notably exports). The scale of location-based incentives offered is indicative of a zone-based development strategy in many MENA economies, and the shared aim of regional development. Table 7.3 lists the types of incentives offered to investors in underdeveloped areas, economic zones (including zones labelled development zones, industrial parks and special economic zones), and free zones. The latter tend to have special export requirements or offshore status and thus are separated from economic zones for analytical purposes, though some countries have zones that cross the boundary between the two categories (Libya and the Palestinian Authority).

Table 7.3. Incentives for investment in specific locations in MENA economies

	Areas for development	Economic Zones	Free Zones
Algeria	Tax holiday, customs/sales tax exemption, land/property tax exemption, grants		
Egypt	Tax deduction, customs/sales tax reduction, grants	Tax deduction, customs/sales tax reduction/exemption, grants	Tax holiday, customs/sales tax exemption
Jordan	Tax holiday, CIT reduction, customs/sales tax exemption	CIT reduction, customs/sales tax exemption, land/property tax exemption	CIT reduction, customs/sales tax exemption, land/property tax exemption
Lebanon	Tax holiday, CIT reduction, customs/sales tax exemption	Tax holiday, customs/sales tax exemption, land/property tax exemption	Customs/sales tax exemption
Libya	Tax holiday, customs/sales tax exemption, land/property tax exemption	Tax holiday, customs/sales tax exemption	
Morocco	Grants	Tax holiday, CIT reduction	Tax holiday, CIT reduction, customs/sales tax exemption
PA	CIT reduction, customs/sales tax exemption	CIT reduction, customs/sales tax exemption, grants	
Tunisia	Tax holiday, CIT reduction, tax deduction, grants		CIT reduction, tax deduction, customs/sales tax exemption

Note: Economic zones include Development Zones, Special Economic Zones (SEZs) and industrial parks/zones. Free Zones refer to zones with specific export requirements. *Tax holiday* = total income tax exemption over defined period; *CIT reduction* = corporate income tax reduction over defined period; *tax deduction* = deductions of certain expenses from taxable income; *customs/sales tax exemption* = exemption from import duties, export taxes, VAT or sales tax; *land/property tax exemption* = exemption from land/property registration fees, stamp duties; *grants* = financial support towards specific investment costs. Table does not include other categories of benefits.
Source: OECD based on national legislation.

Economic zones or free zones tend to provide the greatest number of different tax incentives available to firms. As discussed under activity-based incentives, free zones often have export requirements, and are indicative of an emphasis on promoting export-driven growth, although this objective is not always compatible with wider development goals (Box 7.2). Economic zones usually target certain activities, including manufacturing, or more specific industries such as textiles or finance. Every zone (free and economic) offers CIT reductions or exemptions. These range from permanent CIT exemptions (Egypt's Free Zones, Lebanon's Tripoli Economic Zone, Libya's Misurata and Taminhenet Free Zone) to permanent

CIT reductions (at 5% in Jordan's Aqaba Special Economic Zone) or temporary CIT reductions (at 5% for 5 years and 10% for 3 years in the Palestinian Authority's Industrial Parks). Nearly every free and economic zone offers trade tax and VAT exemptions, and most provide exemptions on land/property tax.

Box 7.2. Tax incentives in zones, exports and wider development goals: are they compatible?

Zone-based tax incentives may impede fair competition between firms inside and outside of zones. This can be particularly the case for zones providing CIT holidays, a type of incentive that raises two concerns. The first is that CIT holidays attract investors that are already profitable, and may have invested anyway, as described above. A second concern, which directly relates to the impact of zones on wider development, is the possibility for zone-based firms to sell to the domestic market while they enjoy a competitive advantage over peers outside of zones, due to tax relief. Countrywide productivity growth may be adversely affected by zone-based firms' sales on the domestic market. By having access to the domestic market, zone-based firms can avoid export markets and related competitiveness pressures while benefiting from tax incentives.

In Egypt, for instance, firms in free zones are awarded a wide array of tax breaks, including CIT holidays, conditional on their export performance – this practice also exists in Morocco's free zones and the offshore regime in Tunisia. The large amount of production sold by firms in free zones on the domestic market reveals zones' challenge in meeting their development objectives, however. Over the last five years, free zone projects in Egypt sold half of their production on the domestic market and the other half abroad, below the 80% export share requirement. There are several reasons behind these large domestic sales. Access to a large domestic market pushes firms to sell imported goods (instead of using imported inputs in the production process) or to discharge an excess of production that they cannot export. At the same time, the lack of competitiveness and adequate knowledge of foreign markets reduces the capacity of businesses in free zones to export.

The design of zone-based policy should consider the potential adverse impacts of zones on the wider economy. Zone-based policy could further shift from relying on CIT incentives to facilitating a more effective business environment that promotes competition, integrates targeted sectors with the rest of the economy, and adequately protects the environment. Governments may consider policy reforms that align the country's import tariffs, import procedures and corporate income tax incentives with those in zones to cut the detrimental comparative advantage gap between firms inside and outside of zones. Levelling the playing field between zones and the rest of the country may be an even more pressing priority in light of many MENA governments' strategy to expand the number of zones.

Some countries have successfully managed to address challenges inherited from their zone-based tax policies. Zones in Poland discriminated against SMEs. As a remedy, Poland aligned in 2018 zones' incentives with those granted in the rest of the territory and shifted criteria from geographical and investment scale to sustainability and innovation. The Dominican Republic phased out export share requirements related to CIT incentives in export-processing zones. With the country joining the Central American Free Trade Agreement (2004) and the WTO deadline to comply with the Agreement on Subsidies and Countervailing Measures (2015), it became necessary for the country to phase-out such incentives. Zones in the country remained attractive locations for exporters, with no impact on exports levels.

Source: (OECD, 2020[7])

All economies in the region offer incentives to investors that operate in less-developed regions of the country, outside of zones. The location of these areas are often specified in national decrees, though sometimes are listed in investment promotion laws. Most countries map areas of territory from less to least developed, offering progressively more generous incentives to firms in more underdeveloped areas. Jordan and Lebanon divide the whole country by level of development, providing incentives in nearly every location. Governments tend to require that the investor meet other criteria in more developed areas, such as listing shares on the national stock exchange (Lebanon). Benefits to firms in least developed regions tend to be the (or among the) most generous offered by the country. Algeria and Tunisia offer 10 year tax holidays to firms in designated areas, Jordan a 20 year holiday with possible extension of 10 years. Half of the focus economies also offer financial support, including grants for infrastructure and utilities (Algeria, Egypt, Morocco and Tunisia), and training and land costs (Egypt and Morocco).

Discretion in awarding incentives

An important element of incentive policy is the level of discretion involved in granting incentives to investors. That is, whether the details of the incentive, such as the generosity of the tax incentives or length of exemption, are made explicit in legislation, and whether eligibility criteria to receive the incentive are specific and automatic, or require interpretation or approval from an administering authority.

There is broad consensus among international organisations that consolidating all tax incentives in tax laws – rather than in investment laws, legislation governing specific industries or one-off agreements with firms – enhances transparency and reduces potential redundancies and confusion over the administering authority (IMF-OECD-UN-World Bank, 2015[1]). The Ministry of Finance is often best placed to grant incentives and monitor their costs. Indeed, other ministries or investment promotion agencies (IPAs) may be more inclined to offer fiscal benefits as their priority is to attract investors; they are not in charge of tax collection or necessarily aware of the state's fiscal needs (James, 2013[2]). In tax laws, any incentives offered should be specific, with clear eligibility criteria and little room for discretion by authorities. This reduces the risk of corruption as well as unfair competition between firms (IMF-OECD-UN-World Bank, 2015[1]).

The majority of the MENA focus economies grant investment incentives through investment laws and decrees. Only Morocco has consolidated most of its tax incentives in its tax code. Half of the countries list some benefits in the tax code or budget/finance laws (Algeria, Jordan and Lebanon) or publish amendments to the incentives regime in finance laws (Tunisia) – a step towards consolidation. In every country, the spectrum of incentives offered are dispersed in multiple pieces of legislation (including sectorial and SEZ laws), decrees and executive orders. This makes compiling a complete picture of incentives offered difficult, and may create confusion among investors regarding their entitlements. Not all MENA IPAs detail all incentives offered on their websites, for example. When incentives are granted in a range of laws (and administered by different authorities, see below), it may allow investors to shop around for incentives, while the government may lack a clear view of the full spectrum of incentives it provides.

A quarter of all incentives offered among the eight focus economies are not explicitly detailed in national legislation. That is, the law does not specify the length or amount of a tax exemption/reduction, amount of grant/financial support, or other details about the benefit. Often, both the conditions for receiving the incentives ("national interest") and the benefits available are imprecise. To receive these incentives, investors usually have to apply to the authority administering tax incentives (in the MENA region, often to the IPA or a council for investment, composed of representatives from relevant ministries). Some MENA IPAs (including in Lebanon and the Palestinian Authority) have wide discretion in determining which investors receive incentives and the generosity of the benefit. As IPAs' role is to attract investors, they may not take into account the cost of the incentive, in terms of foregone revenue to the state, or assess whether investors would have entered the market without the incentive (see chapter 6 for more on the implications of the wide range of responsibilities held by MENA IPAs).

Many incentives granted in MENA region, and indeed across countries, are given to firms on an ad-hoc, contract-based manner. Specificity in laws and regulations, rather than wording that allows open interpretation by officials, helps reduce opportunities for corruption (see chapter 11 for more on the corruption risk involved in administering incentives and during market entry). Moreover, rules that are applied in an ad hoc manner across taxpayers creates unfair competition. It is often not clear whether investors can appeal against an administrative decision not to grant the incentive. Uncertainty over eligibility, the cost of bribes, and scope for an uneven playing field all pose a deterrent to investors (OECD, 2020[7]).

References

Andersen, M., B. Kett and E. Von Uexkull (2017), "Corporate Tax Incentives and FDI in Developing Countries", in *Global Investment Competitiveness Report 2017/2018*, World Bank, http://dx.doi.org/10.1596/978-1-4648-1175-3. [8]

EY (2020), *Worldwide Corporate Tax Guide 2020*, EY, https://www.ey.com/en_gl/tax-guides/worldwide-corporate-tax-guide-2020. [4]

IMF-OECD-UN-World Bank (2015), *Options for Low Income Countries' Effective and Efficient Use of Tax Incentives for Investment*, A report prepared for the G-20 Development Working Group by the IMF, OECD, UN and World Bank., http://www.imf.org/external/pp/ppindex.aspx (accessed on 31 May 2019). [1]

James, S. (2013), *Tax and Non-Tax Incentives and Investments: Evidence and Policy Implications*, http://ssrn.com/abstract=2401905http://ssrn.com/abstract=2401905 (accessed on 31 May 2019). [2]

Klemm, A. and S. Van Parys (2012), "Empirical evidence on the effects of tax incentives", *International Tax and Public Finance*, Vol. 19/3, pp. 393-423, http://dx.doi.org/10.1007/s10797-011-9194-8. [6]

OECD (2021), *OECD Investment Policy Reviews: Thailand*, OECD Investment Policy Reviews, OECD Publishing, Paris, https://dx.doi.org/10.1787/c4eeee1c-en. [9]

OECD (2020), *OECD Investment Policy Reviews: Egypt 2020*, OECD Investment Policy Reviews, OECD Publishing, Paris, https://dx.doi.org/10.1787/9f9c589a-en. [7]

OECD (2019), *OECD Investment Policy Review of Southeast Asia*, OECD, Paris, https://www.oecd.org/investment/oecd-investment-policy-review-southeast-asia.htm (accessed on 28 May 2019). [3]

OECD (2015), *Policy Framework for Investment, 2015 Edition*, OECD Publishing, Paris, https://dx.doi.org/10.1787/9789264208667-en. [5]

PwC (2017), *Oil and Gas Tax Guide for Africa 2017*, PwC, https://www.pwc.com/gh/en/assets/pdf/oil-and-gas-tax-guide-for-africa-2017.pdf. [10]

WTO (2019), *Anti-dumping, subsidies, safeguards: contingencies*, Understanding the WTO: the Agreements, https://www.wto.org/english/thewto_e/whatis_e/tif_e/agrm8_e.htm (accessed on 12 June 2019). [11]

Notes

[1] This chapter presents original research mapping investment incentives granted in eight MENA economies, collected in mid-2019. The results reflect tax and financial incentives (defined as grants, loans or other expenditure to lower the cost of investment) detailed in national tax codes, investment laws, and in publicly-available documents published by investment promotion agencies, ministries of finance and economic zones. Tax guides from PwC, EY and Deloitte were also consulted. The data do not take into account any additional benefits firms may receive through one-off contracts with national governments, as these are not publicly available. It also does not reflect investment incentives taken in response to the COVID-19 pandemic.

[2] The calculation uses average rates of different sectors in Algeria and Jordan, and Morocco.

[3] This summary is not a complete picture of the extent of incentives received by specific sectors, as it does not take into account benefits granted to firms in economic or free zones. These incentives are summarised under location-based incentives and, in the case of free zones, also under activities.

8 Enabling SME linkages with foreign firms in global value chains

This chapter describes trends in MENA economies' participation in global value chains and provides measures of supply chain linkages between multinationals established in the region and domestic SMEs. It gives an overview of relevant policies and programmes in the eight MENA economies to enable SME linkages with foreign firms in global value chains. The chapter also sheds light on policy priorities and discusses policy options for MENA governments to support business relationships with higher sustainable development impacts.

Summary and policy considerations

One of the most notable traits of the global economy over the past few decades is the organisation of international production, trade and investment within global value chains (GVCs), where different stages of the production process of various goods are located across different countries. Many factors have driven the rise of GVCs, including the reduction of barriers to trade and investment, the increasing sophistication of MNEs' business strategies and the efforts by countries and industries to specialise in activities where they have or can develop a comparative advantage. The future of GVCs is driven by additional factors such as trade tensions and major disruptions brought about by Covid-19, which is leading companies and countries to reassess the benefits and costs of GVCs.

Taking advantage of GVCs is an important policy focus for countries aiming to raise productivity, create quality jobs, and acquire knowledge and technology that allow engaging in activities with higher levels of value added. Helping domestic firms, in particular micro, small and medium-sized enterprises (SMEs) to participate in GVCs is crucial in this regard, including by fostering linkages between SMEs and foreign companies. SMEs can plug into GVCs through the provision of inputs of goods and services to MNEs established in their countries. This enables them to create jobs, develop skills, improve workers' conditions, upgrade products or services to meet global standards, or adopt more sustainable production processes.

MENA countries' engagement in GVCs reflects the different compositions of their export baskets, their positioning in supply chains and other aspects such as trade and investment regulations, political stability, the quality of infrastructure and human capital. For example, Algeria's participation in GVCs is limited to oil exports and hindered by a challenging, albeit improving, business climate. The scenario is similar in Libya, although the situation is aggravated by political instability and conflict. Egypt, Jordan, Morocco and Tunisia rely more on foreign inputs to engage in GVCs and diversify their exports, given their larger private sectors and greater openness to trade and investment. However, gains from GVCs in those countries have been relatively limited in terms of knowledge and technology diffusion and engagement in higher value-added activities. GVC participation in Lebanon is also confined to trade in relatively low value-added goods and adversely affected by the socioeconomic instability over the past few years and months.

Foreign business has to some extent helped SMEs in the region integrate in GVCs. For instance, foreign manufacturers' sourcing of local inputs is relatively high in Egypt and Morocco, although it is not possible to infer whether this is the result of a proactive decision by the foreign firm or because of local content requirements. Overall, linkages between foreign and local businesses in the MENA economies covered in this report (MENA focus economies) mostly involve sourcing of low-skilled inputs rather than contractual arrangements for R&D or other upstream activities. Furthermore, in some countries, including Jordan and Morocco, sourcing relationships are dominated by foreign firms supplying intermediate inputs to other foreign firms hosted in the country, reflecting the fact that domestic SMEs face challenges in producing goods that meet international standards.

Policy efforts supporting greater and more resilient SME-MNE linkages can help MENA countries better engage in GVCs to support recovery from the Covid-19 crisis. Broader business climate reforms are pre-conditions for enabling business linkages, particularly in less diversified and competitive economies. For example, barriers to FDI in services in the region impede the deployment of foreign projects that are crucial for GVC participation and export diversification (Chapter 4). Openness to services can reduce input costs and improve the quality and availability of services. Targeted policy action is also required, for example to address the low levels of SME productivity, which reduce the propensity to promote transfers of technology and managerial expertise. Initiatives helping SMEs to establish business linkages to MNEs are particularly important in this regard. While MENA governments have deployed such initiatives, these often lack an overarching government strategy. Initiatives tend to be scattered across different institutions, implemented on an ad hoc basis and are not part of a specific, more explicit, linkages programme.

Policy considerations

- Assess and address barriers in the business environment preventing SME-MNE linkages. Priorities include improving legal security and property protection rights (e.g. investment, bankruptcy and intellectual property rights laws and regulations, and effective contract enforcement mechanisms) and reducing regulatory barriers hampering investment in sectors that are crucial for participating in increasingly digitised GVCs, particularly in the aftermath of the Covid-19 crisis. Active dialogue with the private sector is essential in this regard.
- Establish mechanisms to facilitate the flow of information on GVC opportunities for domestic firms and on local suppliers and SME partners for foreign investors. This requires collaboration between investment promotion agencies (IPAs), SME agencies, investors and private sector associations, among other actors.
- Foster the development of a market of business development services (BDS) for SMEs to establish linkages with MNEs in GVCs. This includes supplier development programmes such as those helping SMEs to form consortia (e.g. to respond to large orders from clients), improving quality, strengthening managerial and technical skills, etc. This also includes programmes to facilitate SME access to resources such as finance, technology, knowledge and skills. Co-operation between firms, SME agencies and BDS providers (e.g. incubators, private providers, associations, etc.) is important.
- Promote RBC standards as a means to signal safe local sourcing, a signal that can be particularly important for multinationals doing business in conflict-affected states. Governments with more established RBC standards could include RBC principles and standards in, inter alia, industry-specific training programmes as a way to build absorptive capacity of domestic SMEs.
- Move away from wide tax holidays to targeted tax deductions when firms forge R&D or other partnership agreements with local suppliers. Zone-based policies such as reduced VAT on deals between firms inside and outside zones can incentivise linkages, and be an alternative to local content requirements, but related administrative procedures should not discourage firms from using such tools.
- Further promote investment by diaspora, and their anchoring through linkages with local suppliers, by increasing outreach efforts and developing, in consultation with diaspora representatives, tailored attraction strategies and programmes.
- Support the efforts of firms to build more resilient GVCs and help them recover from Covid-19 crisis. This includes:
    - Collecting and sharing information on potential concentration and bottlenecks upstream, by developing stress tests for essential supply chains and by creating a conducive regulatory environment that is not a source of additional, policy-related, uncertainty.
    - Maintain, through IPAs' intensified and digitised aftercare services, close contact with foreign firms with established relationships with local suppliers to address challenges related to disruption in GVCs resulting from the Covid-19 pandemic.

SME internationalisation through GVCs and SME-MNE linkages

SMEs and entrepreneurs are widely acknowledged as major economic and social agents in all countries, contributing to important shares of employment and production and playing a significant role in innovation and value creation. For example, in the OECD area SMEs account for about 60% of employment and 50-

60% of value added (OECD, 2019[1]). In developing and emerging economies, SMEs and self-employment also play an important role, as they provide sources of income, goods and services to millions of people and act as a social buffer in the absence of adequate social security systems and other sources of jobs. A recent ILO study notes that formal and informal self-employment accounts for above 50% of total employment in low-income countries and for 60% in lower middle-income countries. If employment in micro firms (2-9 persons employed) is also taken into account, the figures are about 90% of employment in low-income countries and over 80% in lower middle-income countries. In the MENA region self-employed (formal and informal) and micro enterprises account for 70% of employment, just behind South Asia and Sub-Saharan Africa (80% in both) (ILO, 2019[2]).

Encouraging and facilitating the participation of SMEs in international markets is an important means to promote innovation, economic growth and higher productivity. Internationalisation gives SMEs access to opportunities for business expansion, increasing productivity and acquiring international knowledge and technology. Furthermore, given their economic and social importance, SMEs can also be particularly effective actors to address the polarising effects of a country's participation in global markets. Those effects include productivity and wage gaps between firms and industries, development gaps between geographical areas, inequalities of income, wealth and opportunities among social groups, etc.

SME participation in international markets can take several non-mutually exclusive forms. The most common are exporting directly to foreign countries and indirectly exporting by selling to other exporting firms. SMEs can also benefit from international markets by sourcing foreign goods, services, inputs, intellectual property and technology. Although a rarer practice, SMEs can also engage in joint ventures with foreign firms in their domestic market or in a foreign market. They can also participate in global value chains by focusing on specific segments of the production of a set of goods and services, for instance, by supplying a foreign firm in the host market with domestic inputs (goods or services).

Despite their importance in domestic economies, SMEs are generally under-represented in international markets. For example, in OECD countries SME contributions to overall exports is between 20-40% (OECD, 2019[3]). Those figures are lower in the MENA region: for example, in Egypt, a large and relatively open economy, only 6% of SMEs export and just 1.8% of enterprises with less than 20 employees are exporters (Helmy Elsaid et al., 2014[4]). Those figures are likely to be significantly lower if all enterprises, including informal ones, are considered.

The low levels of participation of SMEs in international markets are explained, to an important extent, by the inherent characteristics of small businesses. For example, SMEs concentrate in non-tradable sectors such as retail trade, construction and services (e.g. hairdressers, repair shops, restaurants, etc.). SMEs are also largely absent in internationally oriented sectors where scale matters and where large investments in tangible assets are the norm (e.g. commodities, heavy industry, large-scale manufacturing, etc.). There are other factors acting as barriers for SMEs with potential and drive to internationalise. Those include "internal" barriers such as low capacity to access information (e.g. on foreign markets) and lack of managerial and technical knowledge and skills (e.g. languages, finance, cultural norms, etc.). They also include "external" barriers such as burdensome regulatory procedures (in home and foreign markets), poor infrastructure, difficult business environments (e.g. corruption, weak property rights, etc.), among others.

The international fragmentation of production processes for certain goods reflected in GVCs, and other trends such as the increasing importance of digital technologies in the economy represent an opportunity to boost SME access to international knowledge and markets. Promoting the establishment of business linkages between (usually large and multinational) foreign firms established in a country and SMEs is an important tool to boost the participation of domestic actors in the global economy. It is also a practical alternative to mitigate the external and internal barriers to SME internationalisation by providing small business with direct access to international partners, knowledge and technology. Those SME-MNE linkages can take various forms of business partnerships, for example:

- Supply/manufacturing agreements, whereby an SME or group of SMEs provide goods and services to a foreign firm or MNE. These agreements do not involve directly exporting to a foreign market but rather supplying a MNE established domestically. Conversely, supply agreements also occur when SMEs buy goods or inputs from foreign MNEs based in their home country (OECD-UNIDO, 2019[5]).
- Licensing agreements, whereby an SME or group of SMEs acquire a license from an MNE to produce and sell goods under a brand or trademark or use patented technology.
- R&D agreements whereby the MNE and SMEs undertake joint research and development of a product, service or production method.

All MENA economies participate in GVCs but not in the same way

The organisation of international production, trade and investment within GVCs has become a dominant feature of globalisation. Participation in GVCs can offer new opportunities to integrate in the global economy by allowing firms to join global production networks rather than having to build their own from scratch. Firms participating in GVCs can use international, instead of national, knowledge, resources and inputs in their production. As a result, economic activity has become more interconnected and complex (Kowalski et al., 2015[6]). Factors such as the level of development, geographical location, stability and the policy environment shape countries' participation in GVCs. Sectoral specialisation is another key factor.

In the MENA region, firms' participation in GVCs has been promoted as a key way to achieve higher export diversification and eventually more sustainable and inclusive development models. The impact on sustainable development has been limited, however, reflecting countries' different compositions of export baskets or positioning in supply chains. For instance, Algeria and Libya participate in GVCs mainly because they are large exporters of commodities (Box 8.1). As a result, they need to use very few imported inputs in their exports, whereas countries with advanced levels of industrialisation and services rely highly on imported inputs for exports (e.g. OECD area). Large countries such as Egypt also rely on commodity exports to engage in GVCs but they have a higher domestic capacity for producing specific inputs and diversify their exports, such as in food supply, petrochemicals, electrical machinery and textiles.

Tunisia and Morocco participate in GVCs as light manufacturers and firms in the two countries use significant amounts of manufactured imports in their own exports. Besides textiles and garments, both economies are well embedded in supply chains of electrical, electronic, and to a lesser extent, ICT sectors that serve the EU market. Morocco has also successfully integrated into the global automotive value chain. Jordan and Lebanon are smaller countries that depend on imports of intermediate goods and services, notably in the garment and pharmaceutical supply chains in Jordan and in the processed food sector in Lebanon. But few countries use Jordanian and Lebanese goods and services as inputs into their own exports, thereby limiting the value-added of both countries' exports.

MNEs can help countries plug into higher-value added segments of the supply chain

Along with trade, the "GVC revolution" has been driven largely by MNEs through FDI. FDI is not only an important channel for exchanging capital across countries, it is also an essential vehicle for the international flow of goods, services, and knowledge and serves to link and organise production across countries. With the establishment of foreign affiliates of MNEs, investment can play a key role in fostering the recipient's country participation in GVCs. FDI motives shape the type and extent of GVC participation. FDI directed at establishing an export processing facility boosts backward linkages: MNEs' affiliates import large shares of intermediate products that are used in production and export (Kowalski et al., 2015[6]).

In most of the eight MENA focus economies, and as described in Chapter 2, FDI is concentrated in capital-intensive sectors (natural resources, real estate and construction) or light manufacturing activities with low propensity to promote transfers of technology and managerial expertise, making it more challenging for the region to benefit from participation in GVCs.

Box 8.1. Participation in GVCs in the MENA region: definitions and trends

GVCs reflect the foreign and domestic value added of a country's exports. For example, in a given set of products such as consumer electronics (TVs, mobile phones, etc.), some countries specialise in the R&D and design stages of the devices, others focus on the assembly of parts (which in turn can be produced in several countries), and yet others host logistics, marketing and aftersales services. GVC participation can be decomposed into backward participation and forward participation:

- **Backward participation**, or foreign value added as a share of exports, indicates to what extent countries' and companies' exports depend on imported products. For example, in the case of consumer electronics, a country can specialise in the assembly of the products with imported components, and with the implied imported R&D and design of those products. That country would have high backward participation and a low share of vale added in GVCs. Along those lines, a country that produces raw materials such as the minerals used in the electronics components would have low backward participation (minerals do not require high levels of imports) and also low shares of value added in the consumer electronics GVCs.
- **Forward participation**, or the exported value added incorporated in third-country exports, is the extent of relationships with foreign downstream buyers. Using the same example of the consumer-electronics value chain, countries specialising in the R&D and design stages of the value chain have a high forward and high value added participation with respect to those countries specialising in assembly.

Exports of commodities by MENA focus economies are behind the high forward participation rates of the region compared with OECD and other developed and developing economies (Figure 8.1). Commodities are used in downstream production processes that typically cross several borders. Relatively low backward participation in GVCs reflects MENA countries' limited use of imported inputs in their manufactured exports, whereas other developed and developing countries rely more on imported inputs for exports.

Figure 8.1. Participation in GVCs: MENA and selected economies, 2011-2018

In % of gross exports

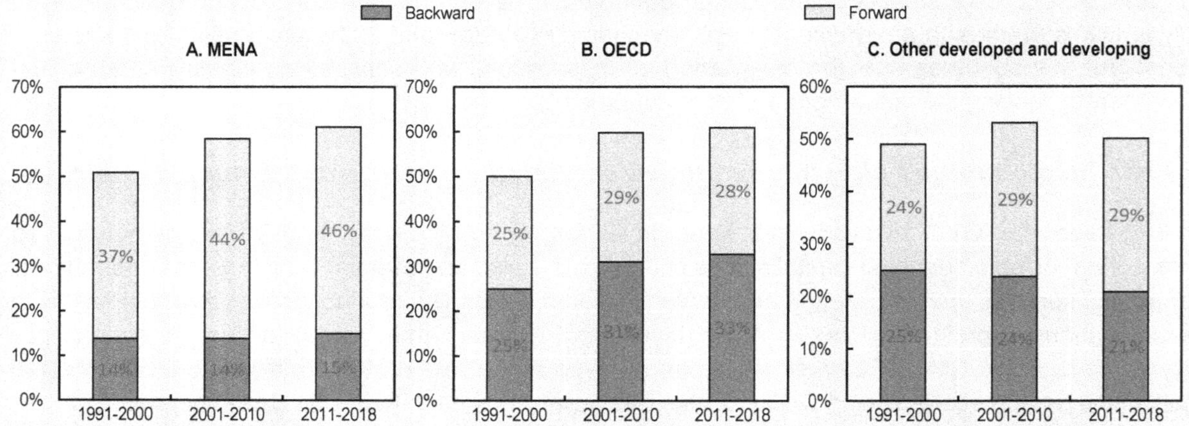

Source: OECD based on UNCTAD-EORA GVC database.

Jordan and Lebanon are the MENA countries that participate the least in GVCs despite high FDI stock-to-GDP ratio (Figure 8.2). In Jordan, the Qualified Economic Zone (QIZ) attracted large Asian textile MNEs that rapidly turned a country without a clothing industry into a leading regional garment exporter. However, the affiliates of MNEs did not invest in upstream segments of the textile industry in Jordan (e.g. R&D or clothing design), thereby limiting the value-added generated from exports and their sustainability (Azmeh and Nadvi, 2014[7]).

Figure 8.2. FDI and GVC participation in MENA economies, 2011-2018

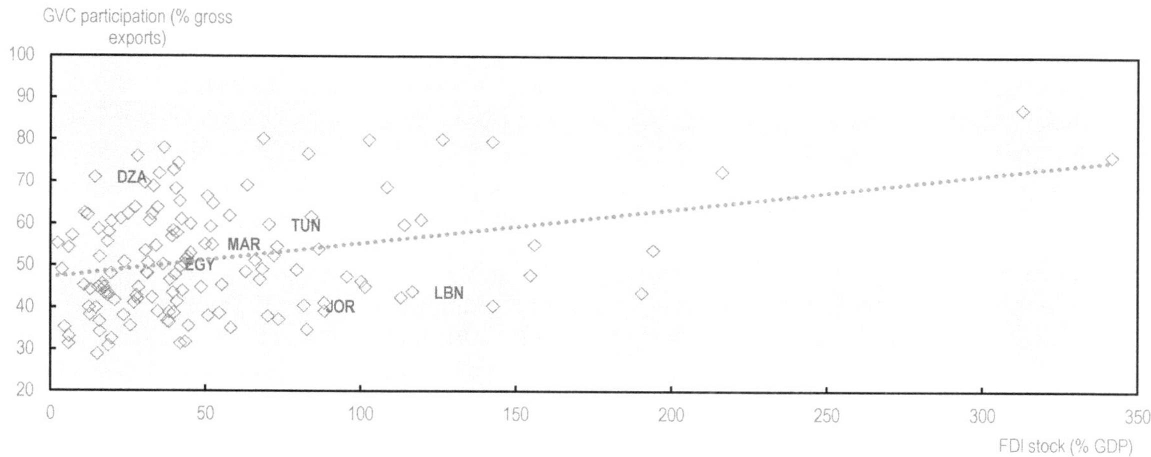

Source: OECD based on UNCTAD-EORA GVC database and UNCTAD.

Tunisia, Morocco and, to a lesser extent, Egypt combine both higher FDI stock-to-GDP and GVC participation ratios in comparison with other countries. Besides the presence of an industrial base, generous tax incentives and trade facilitation measures given to foreign exporting firms, such as the offshore regime in Tunisia or free zones in Egypt, has driven participation in GVCs. Territorial disparities and high unemployment among young people and higher education graduates have nonetheless highlighted the limited impact of those countries' participation in GVCs. Both Morocco and Tunisia report, for instance, a low demand for local skills in their GVC exports (UNECA, 2016[8]).

MNE affiliates in Algeria and Libya increase domestic value-added in exports as they focus on processing natural resources but help only to a small extent to plug these countries into new segments of the supply chain. Overall, the sectors that receive the bulk of FDI in these countries and the wider MENA region, e.g. real estate and petroleum activities, are also those with the least segmented or shorter supply chains, i.e. few intermediate inputs are needed to produce the final good.

While critical, there is little evidence on the use of services in GVCs in the MENA region. With increasingly digitalised GVCs, access to high quality services – particularly telecommunications, transport and specialised business services – is becoming all the more important. Almost half of value-added inputs to exports are service-sector activities, as most manufacturers require services for their exports (UNCTAD, 2013[9]). In addition, a significant part of the international production networks of MNEs are geared towards providing services inputs, as indicated by the fact that more than 60% of global FDI stock is in services activities. Evidence for Morocco and Tunisia, which are part of the OECD Trade-in Value Added Database (OECD TiVA), indicates that both countries use fewer services inputs in manufacturing GVCs in comparison with OECD member states.

GVC disruptions due to the Covid-19 pandemic has created challenges and opportunities for MENA economies (Box 8.2). Those disruptions affect MNE decisions to reorganise the geographical and sectoral spread of their production activities, providing possible opportunities for the MENA region. The region should seize potential opportunities if European MNEs seek to shorten their supply chains and reduce the distance between suppliers and clients (nearshoring). Similarly, some firms may diversify their supply networks to increase resilience to shocks, which will involve divestments from some locations but expansion in others.

Box 8.2. GVC disruptions during Covid-19 crisis and recovery: challenges and opportunities

Covid-19 has re-ignited the debate about the supply chain risks associated with international production, although there is no evidence that countries would have fared better in the absence of GVCs, as lockdowns have also affected the supply of domestic inputs. The pandemic has revealed both the strengths and weaknesses of GVCs, including for the supply of essential products. Past experience shows that global production networks can be disrupted and play a role in the propagation of shocks across countries and sectors. But they also help firms and countries to recover faster.

Ensuring sufficient supply of goods and services needed to fight the pandemic has been the immediate priority for policymakers. Pharmaceuticals, medical supplies and equipment, and healthcare provision depend much more on GVCs and international investment than in the past. Immediate urgencies at home are sometimes at odds with global objectives and the smooth functioning of GVCs, as suggested by the spread of export curbs on medical supplies introduced by numerous governments in Spring of 2020, including by MENA countries. These distortionary measures should remain temporary tools to mitigate the crisis, not permanent fixtures in the world trade system.

GVC disruptions have adverse impacts on the MENA region but also offer opportunities. Thanks to their proximity and trade ties with Europe, countries in MENA may benefit from the restructuring efforts of European MNEs, which may reconsider their dependence on Chinese manufacturing and shorten supply chains through nearshoring or onshoring. For instance, automotive manufacturers could create stronger business linkages in the region, as these manufacturers may aim to produce closer to their primary markets by investing in countries with favourable industry policies and low input costs.

In Morocco, for instance, both Renault and PSA dominate the auto manufacturing industry with well-developed supply chains throughout the country. In April 2020, Renault announced plans to exit the Chinese passenger car segment and relocate some production, along with its aim to increase its localisation rate (the percentage of value-added that is sourced locally) in Morocco from 50% in 2018 to 80% at the end of 2020. The entire value chain of Groupe PSA Kenitra's plant is in Africa, particularly in Morocco where its ecosystem involves a network of 62 Moroccan suppliers. In Egypt, Fiat Chrysler Automobiles and PSA are also producing vehicles either through partnerships or contracts with domestic companies and are also expected to create stronger regional supply.

MENA governments and private sector associations can support firms' efforts to build more resilient GVCs by collecting and sharing information on potential concentration and bottlenecks upstream, developing stress tests for essential supply chains, and creating a conducive regulatory environment that is not a source of additional, policy-related, uncertainty. Governments and the private sector can also work with SMEs to assess potential opportunities to participate directly or indirectly in relocating GVCs to the region in the aftermath of the crisis.

Source: (OECD, 2020[10]); (OECD, 2020[11]); (OECD, 2020[12])

Integrating SMEs in GVCs: the extent of linkages with foreign investors

Leveraging FDI to integrate SMEs in GVCs can be an opportunity for MENA countries to adopt a more inclusive development trajectory. Given the performance premium of foreign firms over domestic ones (see Chapter 2), supply chain relationships should positively support SMEs, depending on the extent and intensity of linkages, absorptive capacity of SMEs and the sector of activity. Local sourcing of MNEs, when not the result of restrictive trade policies such as high tariffs or local content requirements, can generate optimal demand for host economy firms and lead to productivity-enhancing knowledge spillovers. It can enable SMEs in the MENA region to export, develop managerial skills, upgrade products or services to international norms, innovate, reduce costs, improve working conditions, or produce more sustainably.

Manufacturing MNEs' sourcing of local inputs is relatively high in the region

Foreign manufacturers present in some of the MENA focus economies source significantly from local producers (Figure 8.3).[1] MNE affiliates in Egypt, Morocco and Jordan source more than half of their inputs from firms (both domestic and foreign) that produce locally. MNEs in Tunisia rely more on imported inputs. This mirrors, to some extent, the various ways MENA countries participate in GVCs – Egyptian exports rely less on foreign inputs than other MENA exporters do. Overall, linkages between manufacturing MNEs and local firms mostly involve sourcing of low-skilled inputs, rather than contractual arrangements for R&D or other upstream activities.

Figure 8.3. Foreign manufacturers' sourcing from local intermediates

Foreign manufacturers' composition of intermediates sourcing, by origin

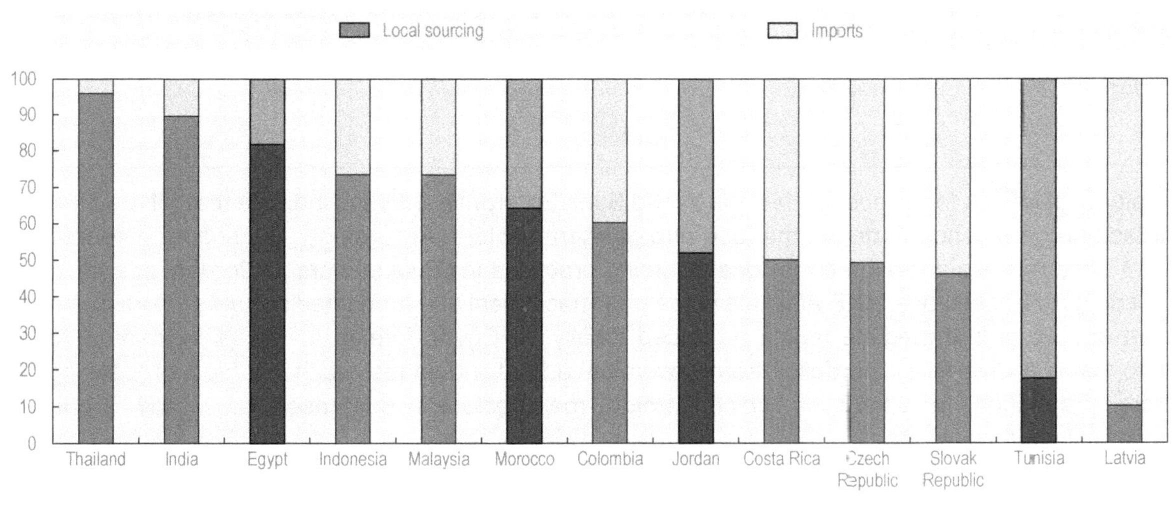

Note: The indicators in this figure include averages for manufacturing as a whole. It does not include services.
Source: OECD estimates based on OECD-UNIDO (2018) and World Bank Enterprise Surveys.

Differences in the sectoral structure of the economy, positioning within specific value chains, and policy factors can explain variation across countries. For instance, significant local sourcing can reflect a high local capacity for producing specific inputs, which may explain the higher share of local sourcing by foreign manufacturers in countries like Thailand, where advanced local supplier capabilities exist in some key sectors such as motor vehicles and machinery and equipment (OECD-UNIDO, 2019[5]).

Different shares of local sourcing by foreign investors can also be the result of restrictions to imports or legal and regulatory requirements to source from local and foreign suppliers. In Egypt, for instance, local content requirements (LCRs) in specific sectors like in the automotive industry (45% of localised content) or in Free Zones, combined with lengthy procedures on imports, result in higher shares of local sourcing by foreign firms (OECD, 2020[13]). In Tunisia, export-only firms belonging to the offshore regime have little sourcing or subcontracting activities with domestic, onshore firms due to taxation and burdensome administrative custom procedures (Box 8.3). The limited sourcing reduces potential spillovers from the offshore regime to the wider Tunisian economy.

Box 8.3. Foreign offshore firms in Tunisia and their linkages with local suppliers

The progress of Tunisia in GVCs is linked to foreign companies in the offshore regime – they account for nearly half of all offshore enterprises. Offshore companies are exempt from customs duties on imports and exports, benefiting from a reduced tax rate and especially simplified administrative procedures and better access to transport services. They can sell 30% of their turnover on the local market with prior payment of customs duties.

Opportunities for spillovers or technological externalities related to FDI are limited in the Tunisian manufacturing sector. Foreign offshore companies have few economic ties with the rest of the economy. Taxation, administrative and customs procedures constitute a barrier to the development of subcontracting relationships between foreign and local businesses and, more generally, to the training and technology transfer effects of offshore foreign companies on the Tunisian economy.

Offshore firms can get supplies on the local market and, in this case, are exempt from VAT. In practice, local sourcing is limited. Similarly, an onshore firm selling products to an offshore company should be able to be reimbursed for the VAT paid on its intermediate consumption. In practice, tax authorities reimburse businesses once a year, creating cash flow problems for some firms, especially small ones. In addition, requests for VAT credit lead sometimes to control checks by tax officials, which often discourage subcontracting.

Source: (Joumard, Dhaoui and Morgavi, 2018[14])

In the majority of MENA focus economies, the World Bank Enterprise Surveys indicate that MNEs affiliates in manufacturing are concentrated in the food and garment sectors. Accordingly, the shares presented in Figure 8.3 often represent foreign firms' local sourcing practices in these sectors. In Jordan, in addition to the food and garment sectors, MNE affiliates in the pharmaceutical and fabricated metals sectors purchase significant shares of intermediate inputs produced locally. In Egypt, foreign investors in manufacturing appear to have a diversified portfolio, from low-value added industries, such as food processing, to machinery production, a sector in which foreign manufacturers purchases of locally produced intermediates is relatively high.[2]

MNE affiliates are a key source of revenue for local suppliers but not necessarily SMEs

In terms of market size, MNE affiliates can represent a large source of revenue for local suppliers. This is the case in Morocco and Jordan, where foreign firms buy more than half of the locally produced intermediates (Figure 8.4, panel A). But local sourcing in the two countries is mostly driven by foreign firms supplying intermediates to other foreign firms hosted in the same country (Figure 8.4, panel B). This is often observed when lead firms establish in host economies and large international first-tier suppliers – companies that provide parts and materials directly to a manufacturer of goods – locate affiliates in their proximity (OECD-UNIDO, 2019[5]). This could be occurring in higher-tech industries such as the automotive sector in Morocco or the pharmaceutical sector in Jordan, and where domestic SMEs face challenges in producing goods that are up to the foreign firms' international standards. The purchase of local intermediate goods by foreign manufacturers matters less for producers in Egypt and Tunisia than in other countries.

Nonetheless, SMEs[3] and large firms jointly account for almost all intermediates supplied to foreign MNEs in the two countries, in sharp contrast with what is observed in Morocco and Jordan.

Figure 8.4. Foreign MNEs are an important market for some MENA SMEs

Panel A. Share of foreign firms in purchases of locally-produced intermediate goods

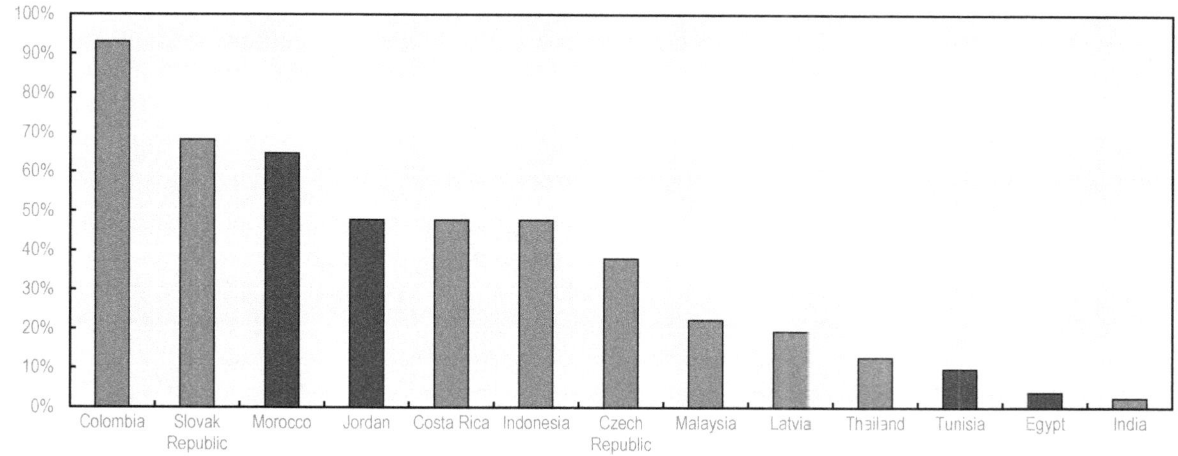

Panel B. Foreign firms purchases of locally-produced intermediate goods, by supplier type (in %)

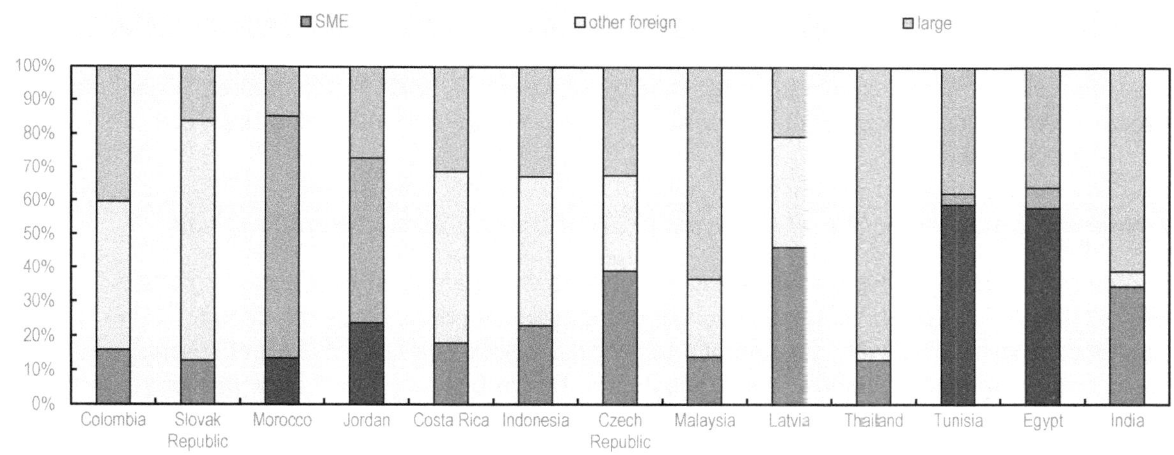

Note: The indicators in this figure include averages for manufacturing as a whole. It does not include services.
Source: OECD estimates based on OECD-UNIDO (2018) and on World Bank Enterprise Surveys.

Improving investment and business environments for SME participation in GVCs

A conducive investment and business environment is a crucial ingredient for anchoring foreign investors into the domestic economy through deep linkages with SMEs. It is also essential to materialise the latent development gains from GVCs, beyond the more immediate objective of allowing domestic firms to participate in global production networks without developing the full range of capabilities required to produce a product or service. Factors such as trade openness, well-functioning finance supply and markets, intellectual property rights protection, a conducive innovation infrastructure, flexible labour market policies and competition rules that facilitate market entry and exit, need to be in place for countries to enable SME-MNE linkages and enhance knowledge and technology diffusion. This section focuses on two business climate areas that are priorities for enabling business linkages in MENA focus economies: addressing restrictions to FDI in sectors that are vital for GVCs and guaranteeing contract enforcement.

Opening up to FDI in services can increase the potential for MNE-SME linkages

Legal and regulatory restrictions on FDI limit market access and thereby reduce the potential for linkages between foreign investors participating in GVCs and domestic enterprises, including SMEs. As such, re-thinking FDI restrictions and reforming them when relevant is a basic step to promote stronger linkages between the global and the domestic economy (OECD-UNIDO, 2019[5]). The pace of investment liberalisation in MENA countries has contributed to some extent to attracting FDI to the region (Chapter 4). For example, the recent decision of Algeria to ease foreign ownership restrictions may help the country attract more FDI in the manufacturing sector and thus support export diversification.

MENA economies in general display moderate levels of FDI restrictions in the manufacturing sector, which is an important element in GVCs. Yet, compared with OECD countries – and with the exception of Morocco – FDI restrictions remain high in services sectors particularly vital to GVCs, namely wholesale and retail, transport, and financial and business services (see Chapters 4 and 9). Similarly, while most countries have made progress in removing barriers to goods trade, restrictions in services trade are still high (Karam and Zaki, 2015[15]). Along with trade barriers, FDI restrictions in services may impede the deployment of foreign investment in sectors such as infrastructure and logistics that are crucial for further GVC participation and strengthened business linkages (it is worth noting that construction is also an activity with high barriers to FDI in the region).

Further openness could help raise efficiency (and reduce input costs) in sectors dominated by large state monopolies and improve the quality and availability of services. Openness in services may also be particularly important for the competitiveness and productivity of small manufacturers throughout the MENA region. SMEs often rely more on high quality backbone services and other services provided by upstream, external providers.

Guarantees of legal security and investor protection can strengthen linkages

MNEs, when contemplating engaging in business linkages with domestic firms, including SMEs, need to be reassured that their business interests, such as property rights will be protected throughout the lifespan of the contracts. Investors take into consideration the transparency and predictability of policies, as well as guarantees of legal security. Well-designed investment, bankruptcy and intellectual property rights laws and regulations are crucial to strengthen investor protection and contract enforcement. Since they increase confidence among parties, they also facilitate the establishment of business linkages in the form of partnerships, contractual arrangements, technology licenses, franchises, and research collaborations.

MENA economies have taken steps to improve regulation and facilitate the upscaling and development of linkages between MNEs and SMEs. Most of the focus economies have introduced changes in their legal and regulatory investment regime and have made sustained efforts to move closer to achieving a more transparent and enabling investment climate, with modern dispute settlement provisions and strong guarantees of property rights protection (see Chapters 3 and 5).

The effectiveness of contract enforcement and dispute resolution in business is fundamental for SMEs to participate in GVCs, and good enforcement procedures are indeed associated with higher levels of business linkages (Amendolagine et al., 2019[16]) (OECD-UNIDO, 2019[5]). In the MENA region, albeit the ease of enforcing contracts varies widely across economies, all of them are below the OECD average (Figure 8.5). Enforcing contracts is harder in Egypt, Lebanon, Libya and the Palestinian Authority than in the average non-OECD economy. When enforcing contracts is cumbersome or when contract disputes cannot be resolved in a timely and cost-effective manner, foreign investors may refrain from engaging with local businesses. Therefore, guaranteeing legal security not only promotes linkages between foreign investors and local SMEs but also makes technology transfers more likely.

Figure 8.5. Ease of enforcing contracts in MENA economies

(100: best performance; 0: lowest performance)

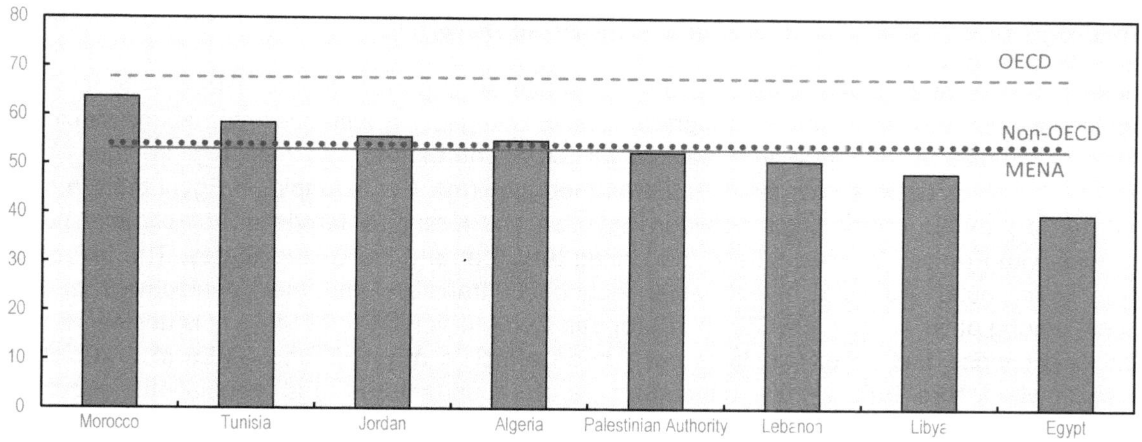

Note: In Doing Business, "Distance to frontier" measures the distance of an economy from the best performance observed in all years and all economies since 2005. The overall score for enforcing contracts is a simple average of the scores for (1) days to resolve a commercial dispute through the courts; (2) attorney, court and enforcement costs as a share of claim value; and (3) use of good practices promoting quality and efficiency. MENA represents the average of the eight MENA focus economies in the figure.
Source: OECD based on www.doingbusiness.org/data/exploretopics/enforcing-contracts.

Modernising dispute settlement mechanisms is also key to supporting an enabling environment for foreign investment. Measures can include adopting e-justice systems to facilitate the management of the judiciary caseload, and organising the judicial system along key areas of specialisation, for example by creating specialised commercial courts, intellectual property courts, and land courts. Meanwhile, alternative dispute resolution mechanisms, including arbitration, mediation and conciliation, are increasingly used for resolving commercial and investment disputes. International investment agreements (IIAs) may provide an additional layer of security to covered investors, including by offering recourse to international investment arbitration to resolve investor-state disputes (See Chapter 5 on Investment Disputes and Management).[4]

Policies and programmes for SME-MNE linkages in GVCs

Broadly speaking, linkages and partnerships among enterprises are initiatives to create opportunities and synergies, and address common problems. For example, SMEs can undertake joint actions to increase the quality of their offer, achieve economies of scale and scope by creating consortia, stimulate the supply of business support services and promote technology transfers, among others. Linkages and partnerships can be especially important for SMEs given their limited resources. As noted earlier in this chapter, when undertaken between foreign and local firms, partnerships and linkages can also enhance the positive impacts of FDI, such as increased business opportunities and employment in domestic enterprises.

There are a number of concrete actions that government agencies such as Investment Promotion Agencies (IPAs) and SME Agencies, private sector associations, MNEs, business development services providers and many other actors can take to foster the participation of SMEs in global value chains through linkages with MNEs based in their domestic markets. Those actions include disseminating information among SMEs and MNEs of opportunities for business linkages, the creation of databases of products, suppliers and buyers, programmes for the formation of SME consortia to supply large orders, supplier development programmes and several other initiatives. Actions can also include support to SMEs and MNEs to engage in responsible business conduct, and helping small businesses to take advantage of other tools such as participating in special economic zones and leveraging the financial and networking resources of diaspora investors. This section provides an overview of those actions and actors and their relevance to the MENA region.

Reinforcing business associations and enterprise networks

Enterprise networks and business associations constitute an important tool to disseminate information about business opportunities in GVCs through SME-MNE linkages. For instance, international or binational chambers of commerce are present in several MENA countries and can help explore and establish business partnerships between domestic SMEs and foreign firms. For example, in Egypt there a number of initiatives to promote partnerships between Egyptian and foreign enterprises, notably joint business associations with France, Germany, Italy, the United Kingdom and the United States. The aim of those initiatives is to foster industrial investments, technology transfers and the development of human resources, among other actions (OECD/The European Commission/ETF, 2014[17]). It is unclear, however, to what extent those and other initiatives have been effective at integrating SMEs in GVCs through partnerships with MNEs. Furthermore, although there are abundant business associations, especially at the national and sub-national levels across the MENA region, it is not clear to what extent those organisations are representative of the interests of SMEs (OECD/European Union/ETF, 2018[18]).

Transnational or multilateral initiatives to promote business partnerships can also prove useful to establishing SME-MNE linkages in the MENA region. For example, the Enterprise Europe Network (EEN) is a multinational initiative sponsored by the EU Programme for the Competitiveness of SMEs (COSME) and bringing together chambers of commerce and industry, technology poles, innovation support organisations, universities and research institutes, regional development organisations, and other groups. The EEN operates in over 60 countries and coordinates more than 3 000 experts and 600 member organisations providing business development services to SMEs, in particular in the areas of innovation, international growth and international partnerships. Of the MENA economies covered in this report, only Egypt, Jordan and Tunisia participate in the EEN.[5] The EEN provides an extensive database of business opportunities, including but not limited to SME-MNE linkages – at the time of writing, no SME-MNE specific opportunities were found in MENA economies, although there were many partnership possibilities for accessing foreign technologies and brands.[6]

Other initiatives promoting Euro-Mediterranean economic co-operation can also provide useful platforms for strengthening SME-MNE linkages, particularly given the important presence of European direct investment in several economies in the MENA region. For example, ANIMA Investment Network promotes the development of investment, business partnerships and clusters in Europe, the Middle East and Africa to promote innovation, entrepreneurship and the internationalisation of enterprises (OECD/The European Commission/ETF, 2014[17]). This network brings together 70 organisations, including public and private and business development services providers to support SMEs and entrepreneurs and to promote the development of business support organisations in the Southern Mediterranean.[7]

Providing business development services for SMEs to engage in linkages with MNEs

Given their small resource base, SMEs rely more on services supplied by external providers than larger firms do. Those services range from supporting day-to-day business functions (e.g. accounting, legal, logistics, human resource management, etc.) to developing longer-term and strategic capabilities (e.g. management counsel, human resource development, access to technology, access to markets, etc.). The first category of services (business support) is important since it allows SMEs to focus on their core competences and externally contract functions that the firm has no capacity or strategic wish to perform.

The second category (business development services) is essential for SMEs to build new competencies and achieve longer-term objectives such as increased sales, productivity, reaching new markets, and/or developing new products, services or processes.

Business development services (BDS) can provide important means to help small businesses to identify and engage in linkages with foreign firms in the context of GVCs. The markets for BDS, however, differ importantly among MENA economies in terms of diversity of services available and actors providing them. For example, Jordan has a relatively diverse BDS market, with public and private actors active in the provision of support to SMEs. These include the SME agency, JEDCO (Jordan Enterprise Development Corporation) which provides tailor-made support to firms with growth potential to undertake business diagnostics, address barriers to expansion and obtain coaching. Another actor in Jordan is the Local Enterprise Support Project (LENS), implemented by the US Agency for International Development (USAID) to encourage the growth of small businesses in target sectors, the development of private or non-government BDS providers, and to help SMEs to connect with industry associations, chambers of commerce and BDS providers. In addition, other public and private actors also implement a number of BDS programmes (OECD, 2019[19]).[8]

Other economies with diverse BDS markets include Morocco. The country relies on a solid presence of public and private actors and implements a number of flagship initiatives to provide strategic direction to economic development policy. At the other end of the spectrum is Algeria, with a less diversified BDS market and with fewer flagship initiatives mostly led by the public sector, reflecting lower levels of private sector development in the country (OECD/European Union/ETF, 2013[18]).[9]

The diversity of BDS and their suppliers in several MENA countries has not been decoded into comprehensive and structured databases allowing SMEs and entrepreneurs to search and filter specific programmes responding to their potential needs – including opportunities to establish SME-MNE linkages to participate in international value chains. In other terms, BDS markets remain fragmented into a wide but disconnected series of offers, hence limiting the reach and impact of such measures. To address such fragmentation, MENA governments and private sector actors could establish electronic BDS databases where suppliers and users could upload and consult available support.[10]

Furthermore, MENA countries could also draw inspiration from some BDS support schemes used to promote the participation of SMEs in public procurement, such as the electronic dissemination of procurement opportunities by MNEs in the domestic market (akin to the publication of public procurement opportunities in e-procurement platforms). This could be done by public actors such as SME agencies or IPAs, or by private associations, such as chambers of industry and commerce, or associations of SMEs and MNEs. Electronic portals could include up-to-date procurement opportunities by MNEs and electronic registries of suppliers.

Other BDS programmes used in public procurement could also prove valuable for SME-MNE linkages, by helping small suppliers to form consortia to source large orders of goods and services, and comply with certain standards and increase quality. In addition, measures to ensure that payments by MNEs to supplying SMEs are made in time, could also prove essential in avoiding cash flow stress in small firms and a *de facto* financing of larger firms by SMEs.

Unfortunately, most MENA governments do not implement any of those procurement programmes. However, SME-MNE linkages could provide an opportunity to develop such practices first in the context of GVCs and then extend them to public procurement markets.

Investment promotion agencies can also use a variety of tools to connect businesses

National investment promotion agencies (IPAs) can also use policy tools such as targeted supplier development programmes, matchmaking services and high-quality supplier databases. Training and supplier development initiatives offer funding to MNEs that support local SMEs in acquiring skills or technology, or in meeting specific requirements. Other possible initiatives include the creation of SME or business development centres to help SMEs upgrade their capabilities.

IPAs are often the lead agency for implementing business linkages programmes or share that responsibility with other institutions, such as ministries of industry, trade and innovation, or SMEs agencies and BDS providers. Often, linkages programmes target priority sectors that IPAs promote. MENA IPAs, along with other government agencies and private sector associations, could further contribute to the formulation of an adequate set of linkage policies and to the implementation of supplier development programmes (see Chapter 6 on investment promotion and facilitation strategies).

MENA IPAs have at their disposal some tools to promote business linkages. For instance, all agencies offer foreign investors matchmaking services with local suppliers. They also all have a local supplier database, or rely on one run by another government agency, that allows MNE affiliates to connect with relevant suppliers. But tools to promote linkages are often implemented on an ad hoc basis, and are not part of a specific, more explicit, linkages programme. IPAs that wish to be more active in supporting the creation and forging of linkages may need to have a clear mandate to provide investors with accurate and timely information on local suppliers and SME partners, and ensure co-ordination with ministries and other agencies (OECD, 2019[20]).

The quality of supplier databases differs across MENA economies. For instance, not all MENA IPAs are equipped with databases that list certifications held by local suppliers. Databases are also not publicly available online, which requires potential foreign investors to contact the IPA to enquire about the existence and features of local suppliers. In Tunisia, the foreign investment promotion agency, FIPA, provides matchmaking services but relies on the local supplier database of another agency, APII, the Agency for the Promotion of Industry and Innovation. The database is available online, includes both companies in manufacturing and services and provides information at the product level. It also lists certified companies, i.e. businesses with a specific quality certification.

Some MENA IPAs offer capacity building for local suppliers (Algeria, Lebanon, Palestinian Authority, and Tunisia). These IPAs have in common a mandate to promote domestic investment in addition to foreign investment. A minority of MENA IPAs provide assistance in recruiting and training programmes for local staff, which is similar to OECD IPAs (OECD, 2018[21]). Training local staff is often carried out by other agencies, such as SME development agencies, whether in the MENA region or elsewhere. Co-ordination across agencies is thus crucial to ensure good implementation of linkages policies.

An example of an IPA that has managed to promote business linkages is Czech Invest, notably thanks to the Supplier Development Programme, which offered an online access to a database of local suppliers in specific sectors and matchmaking and negotiation services (Box 8.4). Other effective programmes include Thailand's Board of Investment Unit for Industrial Linkage Development (BUILD), which illustrates that linkage promotion needs to be part of a longer-term development plan that is coordinated across multiple actors. BUILD flexibly and informally coordinates linkages activities with other government bodies, the private sector and academic institutions (OECD-UNIDO, 2019[5]).

Box 8.4. Czech Invest Supplier Development Programme

Czech Invest launched the Supplier Development Program in 1999, with a focus on electronics, the Czech Republic's fastest growing sector and its second largest FDI sector after automotive. The programme aimed to boost Czech suppliers' competitiveness but also improve the communication between local companies and MNEs. It consisted of targeting specific local businesses to participate in training and technical assistance programmes to heighten their product quality and improve their absorptive capacity, providing matchmaking services by setting up meetings between MNEs and selected producers and providing assistance during negotiations. The agency also provided financial intermediation for businesses expansion, notably by giving an affidavit to a lending bank or when the MNE as a partner can guarantee the contract for supplies.

The Czech IPA also operates an online database of local suppliers to ease communication between foreign investors and suppliers. The database serves as an effective tool for identifying and categorising suppliers in the Czech Republic and as a means of clearly presenting individual industrial sectors. The database is intended primarily for foreign investors entering the Czech Republic and those that are already operating there, as well as for other foreign and domestic companies that are interested in obtaining supplies from the Czech Republic. It also allows searches for suppliers according to first, second and third tier.

Promote safe business linkages through responsible business conduct

RBC principles and standards set out an expectation that all businesses contribute to sustainable development, and avoid and address adverse impacts of their operations. This entails integrating and considering environmental and social issues within core business activities, including in the supply chain and business relationships (see Chapter 10). MNEs increasingly base their decisions about where to invest on the ability to ensure predictable and reliable supply chains, capable of delivering effectively at each stage. Costs of delays due to, for example, labour unrests or environmental damage, can be substantial. Ensuring efficiency of supply chains has become even more relevant in the aftermath of the Covid-19 outbreak as they have become more vulnerable to disruptions generated by the pandemic.

Clearly communicating RBC priorities and expectations, including to the private sector, would help promote linkages with MNEs, and hence maximise the development impact of FDI in the MENA region. Suppliers of MNEs may find that following RBC principles and standards gives them an advantage over businesses that do not, as they are able to address concerns that may come up in due diligence efforts of the MNE. Governments could also use RBC as a tool for MNE-SME matchmaking. RBC expectations should be included in FDI facilitation efforts and may help attract MNEs that are more inclined to source locally. For instance, one element of supplier databases and matchmaking events could be RBC. Governments could also include RBC principles in industry-specific training programmes as a way to build absorptive capacity of domestic firms. This could encompass supporting cost-sharing efforts within and among industries for specific due diligence tasks, participation in initiatives on responsible supply chain management and cooperation between industry members who share suppliers.

Smart incentive regimes and zone-based policies can support deeper linkages

MENA economies widely use tax and non-tax incentives to promote and encourage investment activities that enable economic and social spillovers (see Chapter 7). They are also one of the tools available to governments to influence MNEs' sourcing decisions, and can consist of tax deductions to subtract certain expenses or reward firms for training their local suppliers (e.g. on training programmes, R&D activities, capacity building of SMEs, and environmental protection). Tax incentives (particularly tax holidays) can impose significant fiscal costs on the countries using them. Targeted approaches should be preferred

Most MENA economies target wide sectors or regions, either via special incentive provisions for less developed regions or additional zone-based incentives. Only a few countries, such as Morocco, have a more targeted approach to incentives, with specific incentives to promote skills, R&D, and high-tech activities. Outside of the region, several countries use targeted incentives to support SME engagement with foreign companies. For instance, projects in Thailand are granted expenditure deduction from taxable income incurred for spending on the development of local suppliers through training and technical assistance. More broadly, incentives on linkages could include the expenditures of lead firms in assisting and auditing their suppliers to adhere with the company's quality, environmental, health and safety standards (Galli, 2017[22]).

MENA economies participation in GVCs is in part driven by the setup of exclusive zone-based regimes (e.g. Tangier free zone in Morocco, the Suez Canal Special Economic Zone in Egypt) or special exporting regimes (offshore regime in Tunisia, the QIZs in Jordan). Often, the objectives of these regimes is spurring new investments and trade, creating jobs and fostering economic opportunities. While such regimes have managed to attract investment and foster trade, notably by offering generous tax incentives and adequate services, their positive impact and spillovers on the local economy is not clear-cut. For example, the zone of Tangier, which attracted global leaders in the automotive and aeronautic sector, only partially succeeded in connecting local SMEs to zone producers and to upgrade their capabilities to plug in new segments of GVCs (IFC, 2019[23]).

To promote linkages, some governments exempt MNEs in exclusive regimes from paying value added tax (VAT) on locally purchased inputs. VAT exemptions can help compensate for possible cost disadvantages of local products compared to foreign supply. It can also level the playing field between local suppliers and imports in cases where imports by MNEs are also exempt from VAT (Sabha, Liu and Douw, 2020[24]). Some MENA economies introduced such VAT incentives but their expected impact on linkages has not always materialised. For instance, in Tunisia, firms with an exporting status (offshore regime) are exempt from VAT on local supplies. Similarly, an onshore firm selling products to an offshore company can be reimbursed for the VAT paid on its intermediate consumption. In practice, few linkages exist between the two, notably due to cumbersome administrative procedures (Box 8.3).

Non-tax incentives can be as important as tax incentives to promote linkages, if not more so when the regulatory environment is complex. For instance, Egypt eased the regulatory and administrative procedures on local firms that supply businesses in zones, which have duty-free regimes. Although products and services sold to these zones are treated as exports and therefore subject to the same trade rules, some administrative incentives are given to local suppliers in specific sectors. These suppliers do not need to obtain the approval from the trade control authority to source some goods that are usually subject to quality control (OECD, 2020[13]).

Linkages policy is framed in some MENA economies as a local-content requirement (LCR), which sometimes can discourage foreign investors and potentially confine relationships to low-skilled activities to meet the requirements. Incentives to forge proactively meaningful relationships with local suppliers can be a better alternative for host countries to reap the sustainable development benefits of FDI (Box 8.5). For instance, in Jordan, the government envisaged setting a LCR on renewable energy investment, which would have increased the cost of inputs for downstream power producers (OECD, 2016[25]). As an alternative, the government could provide tax deduction to power producers financing the upgrading of local suppliers so that they can produce renewable energy components that are not available locally.

Box 8.5. Targeted incentives represent an alternative to local content requirements

Local content requirements may discourage FDI by establishing hard conditions to achieve local requirements that restrain competition from imports, which might contribute to higher production costs and ultimately higher prices to downstream industries and consumers. Potential short-term gains in the targeted industry can therefore act as a drain on the rest of the economy. The costs in terms of forgone investments is not necessarily compensated by improved local development outcomes, if any, such as increased employment, investment and technology transfer (OECD, 2020[26]).

The literature on the potential effects of LCR is extensive, and while there may be situations where these policies could potentially increase domestic welfare depending on market characteristics (e.g. potential learning and technological spillovers, economies of scale etc.), the overall evidence suggests that they tend to lead to a suboptimal allocation of resources (Stone, Messent and Flaig, 2015[27]). The inefficiencies arising in other sectors due to the LCR can also reduce job growth, undermining the original goals for imposing the LCR. They can also cause a decline in trade, including for the imposing economy.

In pursuing such objectives, proactive tax tools incentivising meaningful linkages between foreign investors and local SMEs, such as targeted tax incentives, can offer an alternative to LCR policies. Targeted incentives generate less negative economy-wide effects and their long-term benefits on upgrading the capacity of suppliers can be higher, even if they are more costly and require stronger institutional capacity to be effectively implement. When LCR exist, local suppliers are mostly hired for lower value, site-specific operations such as construction, support services and non-productive functions. This is often done to meet the requirements rather than leveraging comparative advantages (Bamber et al., 2014[28]). In the best of cases, LCRs should dovetail with the interest of investors in reducing costs by procuring goods and services locally, but local content targets need to be both realistic and flexible and must be accompanied by broader policies supporting business linkages.

Diaspora investors can forge enhanced linkages with local business

MENA economies have large diaspora scattered worldwide that can positively influence cross-border investment flowing to their origin countries. Diaspora investors are also more likely to forge linkages with local suppliers than non-diaspora foreign investors (Amendolagine et al., 2019[16]). Chinese or Indian diaspora, for instance, have strongly contributed to the integration of both countries in GVCs, especially through investment (Buckley et al., 2007[29]). The diaspora can stimulate investment by reducing transaction and information costs as they often have links to local networks (Chen, Chen and Ku, 2004[30]). They can also circumvent challenges in remote or risky areas and provide a positive signal about the region. As with MNE affiliates, diaspora firms have higher productivity levels and better export performance relative to domestic firms (Boly et al., 2014[31]).

Evidence on investment by MENA diaspora in their home countries is limited. According to one survey, diaspora investors from MENA economies are doubtful that local businesses would be willing and able to work with them (Malouche, Plaza and Salsac, 2016[32]). They also believe that they do not benefit from the same preferential treatment accorded to foreign investors and do not expect much support from their governments to help them invest. A study on Tunisia reveals that potential diaspora investors often report not being aware of investment incentives offered to foreign investors (UNDP, 2016[33]). Existing Tunisian diaspora investors do not forge more partnerships with local businesses than other foreign investors, and their overall impact on jobs and wages is weaker than the impact of foreign firms. Tunisian diaspora investors are more present in remote or rural regions than foreign firms are, however.

MENA governments could further promote investment by diaspora, and their anchoring through linkages with local suppliers, by increasing outreach efforts and developing, in consultation with diaspora representatives, tailored attraction strategies and programmes. Lebanon developed several initiatives to attract greater investment from its diaspora (Box 8.6). The Moroccan government is active in attracting diaspora investors through regional investment centres and the Houses of Moroccans Living Abroad, a program that provides information to expatriates. Governments could also collect micro-level data on diaspora investors, as for instance API in Tunisia, to compare them with non-diaspora investors and monitor differences in trends and impacts (UNDP, 2016[33]).

Box 8.6. Promoting diaspora investment in Lebanon

Several government ministries and agencies are involved in attracting Lebanese diaspora investors and anchoring them through linkages with local SMEs. One of the objectives of the Lebanese IPA is to identify concrete investment opportunities across all regions of Lebanon and actively promote them locally and internationally among diaspora members. The Lebanon SME Strategy aims to facilitate linkages between the SMEs and MNEs, as well as with the diaspora, and share success stories of Lebanese expatriates.

The Ministry of Foreign Affairs and Emigrants is engaged in the promotion of diaspora investment through its foreign embassies and consulates. For instance, the Lebanese Diaspora Energy initiative, launched by the Ministry in 2014, has among its objectives to establish linkages between the diaspora and residents to provide opportunities for sharing experiences and establishing business and social connections. The initiative also aims to explore opportunities for Lebanese residents and expatriates to work together to restore the image of country and trust in the economy.

Source: (UNCTAD, 2018[34]).

References

Amendolagine, V. et al. (2019), "Local sourcing in developing countries: The role of foreign direct investments and global value chains", *World Development*, Vol. 113, pp. 73-88, http://dx.doi.org/10.1016/j.worlddev.2018.08.010. [16]

Azmeh, S. and K. Nadvi (2014), "Asian firms and the restructuring of global value chains", *International Business Review*, Vol. 23/4, pp. 708-717, http://dx.doi.org/10.1016/j.ibusrev.2014.03.007. [7]

Bamber, P. et al. (2014), "Connecting Local Producers in Developing Countries to Regional and Global Value Chains: Update", *OECD Trade Policy Papers*, No. 160, OECD Publishing, Paris, https://dx.doi.org/10.1787/5jzb95f1885l-en. [28]

Boly, A. et al. (2014), "Diaspora investments and firm export performance in selected sub-Saharan African countries", *World Development*, Vol. 59, pp. 422-433, http://dx.doi.org/10.1016/j.worlddev.2014.02.006. [31]

Buckley, P. et al. (2007), "The determinants of Chinese outward foreign direct investment", *Journal of International Business Studies*, Vol. 38/4, pp. 499-518, http://dx.doi.org/10.1057/palgrave.jibs.8400277. [29]

Chen, T., H. Chen and Y. Ku (2004), *Foreign direct investment and local linkages*, http://dx.doi.org/10.1057/palgrave.jibs.8400085. [30]

Galli, R. (2017), "The role of investment incentives for structural transformation a comparative analysis of investment incentives legislations in Sub-Saharan African, South-Asian and", *ILO Working Papers*, No. 994955393402676, International Labour Organisation, https://ideas.repec.org/p/ilo/ilowps/994955393402676.html (accessed on 27 February 2021). [22]

Helmy Elsaid, H. et al. (2014), *Small and Medium Enterprises in Egypt: New Facts from a New Dataset Small and Medium Enterprises Landscape in Egypt: New Facts from a New Dataset* *, http://www.academicstar.us (accessed on 27 February 2021). [4]

IFC (2019), "Creating Markets in Morocco: A Second Generation of Reforms-Boosting Private Sector Growth, Job Creation and Skills Upgrading", https://elibrary.worldbank.org/doi/abs/10.1596/32402 (accessed on 27 February 2021). [23]

ILO (2019), *Small Matters: Global evidence on the contribution to employment by the self-employed, micro-enterprises and SMEs*, ILO, http://www.ilo.org/global/publications/books/WCMS_723282/lang--en/index.htm (accessed on 27 February 2021). [2]

Joumard, I., S. Dhaoui and H. Morgavi (2018), "Insertion de la Tunisie dans les chaines de valeur mondiales et role des entreprises offshore", *Documents de travail du Département des Affaires économiques de l'OCDE*, No. 1478, Éditions OCDE, Paris, https://dx.doi.org/10.1787/546dbd75-fr. [14]

Karam, F. and C. Zaki (2015), "Trade volume and economic growth in the MENA region: Goods or services?", *Economic Modelling*, Vol. 45, pp. 22-37, http://dx.doi.org/10.1016/j.econmod.2014.10.038. [15]

Kowalski, P. et al. (2015), "Participation of Developing Countries in Global Value Chains: Implications for Trade and Trade-Related Policies", *OECD Trade Policy Papers*, No. 179, OECD Publishing, Paris, https://dx.doi.org/10.1787/5js33lfw0xxn-en. [6]

Malouche, M., S. Plaza and F. Salsac (2016), *Mobilizing the Middle East and North Africa Diaspora for Economic Integration and Entrepreneurship Mariem Mezghenni Malouche*, The World Bank, Washington, DC., https://openknowledge.worldbank.org/handle/10986/26307 (accessed on 27 February 2021). [32]

OECD (2020), *COVID-19 and global value chains: Policy options to build more resilient production networks*, OECD, Paris, http://www.oecd.org/coronavirus/policy-responses/covid-19-and-global-value-chains-policy-options-to-build-more-resilient-production-networks-04934ef4/ (accessed on 27 February 2021). [10]

OECD (2020), *Investment in the MENA region in the time of COVID-19*, OECD, Paris, http://www.oecd.org/coronavirus/policy-responses/investment-in-the-mena-region-in-the-time-of-covid-19-da23e4c9/ (accessed on 27 February 2021). [11]

OECD (2020), *OECD investment policy responses to COVID-19*, OECD, Paris, http://www.oecd.org/coronavirus/policy-responses/oecd-investment-policy-responses-to-covid-19-4be0254d/ (accessed on 27 February 2021). [12]

OECD (2020), *OECD Investment Policy Reviews: Egypt 2020*, OECD Investment Policy Reviews, OECD Publishing, Paris, https://dx.doi.org/10.1787/9f9c589a-en. [13]

OECD (2020), *OECD Investment Policy Reviews: Indonesia 2020*, OECD Investment Policy Reviews, OECD Publishing, Paris, https://dx.doi.org/10.1787/b56512da-en. [26]

OECD (2019), "Fostering greater SME participation in a globally integrated economy", in *Strengthening SMEs and Entrepreneurship for Productivity and Inclusive Growth: OECD 2018 Ministerial Conference on SMEs*, OECD Publishing, Paris, https://dx.doi.org/10.1787/400c491d-en. [3]

OECD (2019), *Mapping of Investment Promotion Agencies: Middle East and North Africa - OECD*, OECD, Paris, https://www.oecd.org/investment/investment-policy/mapping-of-investment-promotion-agencies-med.htm (accessed on 27 February 2021). [20]

OECD (2019), *OECD SME and Entrepreneurship Outlook 2019*, OECD Publishing, Paris, https://dx.doi.org/10.1787/34907e9c-en. [1]

OECD (2019), *SME Policy Effectiveness in Jordan User Guide 1: Reinforcing SME policy co-ordination and public-private dialogue*, OECD, Paris, https://www.oecd.org/mena/competitiveness/sme-policy-effectiveness-in-jordan-user-guides.htm (accessed on 27 February 2021). [19]

OECD (2018), *Mapping of investment promotion agencies in OECD countries - OECD*, OECD, Paris, http://www.oecd.org/investment/Mapping-of-Investment-Promotion-Agencies-in-OECD-Countries.htm (accessed on 27 February 2021). [21]

OECD (2016), *OECD Clean Energy Investment Policy Review of Jordan*, Green Finance and Investment, OECD Publishing, Paris, https://dx.doi.org/10.1787/9789264266551-en. [25]

OECD/CAF (2019), *Latin America and the Caribbean 2019: Policies for Competitive SMEs in the Pacific Alliance and Participating South American countries*, SME Policy Index, OECD Publishing, Paris, https://dx.doi.org/10.1787/d9e1e5f0-en. [35]

OECD/European Union/ETF (2018), *The Mediterranean Middle East and North Africa 2018: Interim Assessment of Key SME Reforms*, SME Policy Index, OECD Publishing, Paris, https://dx.doi.org/10.1787/9789264304161-en. [18]

OECD/The European Commission/ETF (2014), *SME Policy Index: The Mediterranean Middle East and North Africa 2014: Implementation of the Small Business Act for Europe*, SME Policy Index, OECD Publishing, Paris, https://dx.doi.org/10.1787/9789264218413-en. [17]

OECD-UNIDO (2019), *Integrating Southeast Asian SMEs in global value chains: Enabling linkages with foreign investors - OECD*, https://www.oecd.org/industry/inv/investment-policy/integrating-southeast-asian-smes-in-global-value-chains.htm (accessed on 27 February 2021). [5]

Sabha, Y., Y. Liu and W. Douw (2020), *Investment Linkages and Incentives IN FOCUS Promoting Technology Transfer and Productivity Spillovers from Foreign Direct Investment (FDI)*, World Bank, http://www.worldbank.org (accessed on 27 February 2021). [24]

Stone, S., J. Messent and D. Flaig (2015), "Emerging Policy Issues: Localisation Barriers to Trade", *OECD Trade Policy Papers*, No. 180, OECD, Paris, https://www.oecd-ilibrary.org/trade/emerging-policy-issues_5js1m6v5qd5j-en (accessed on 27 February 2021). [27]

UNCTAD (2018), *Investment Policy Review of Lebanon*, UNCTAD, Geneva, https://investmentpolicy.unctad.org/publications/1196/investment-policy-review-of-lebanon (accessed on 27 February 2021). [34]

UNCTAD (2013), *World Investment Report 2013, GLobal Value Chains: Investment and Trade for Development*, UNCTAD, https://worldinvestmentreport.unctad.org/wir2013/ (accessed on 27 February 2021). [9]

UNDP (2016), *Case Study : Assessing the impact of diaspora investments in Tunisia*, UNDP, https://www.undp.org/content/undp/en/home/librarypage/poverty-reduction/case-study---assessing-the-impact-of-diaspora-investments-in-tun.html (accessed on 27 February 2021). [33]

UNECA (2016), *Promoting Regional Value Chains in North Africa*, UNECA, Addis Ababa, https://repository.uneca.org/handle/10855/23016 (accessed on 27 February 2021). [8]

Notes

[1] The measures focus on the manufacturing sector.

[2] There are not enough observations for Morocco and Tunisia to include firms in the machinery sector (e.g. automotive sector).

[3] SMEs are defined here as firms with less than 100 employees.

[4] Along with dispute settlement provisions contained in the legislation and in IIAs, the adherence of all MENA economies to international conventions, such as the New York Convention on the Enforcement and Recognition of Foreign Arbitral Awards, also provides a guarantee that contracts will be enforced smoothly, in the event a dispute is brought before an arbitral panel rather than before domestic courts.

[5] According to the latest edition of the SME Policy Index for the Middle East and North Africa, Morocco was part of the EEN; however, that country does not appear in more recent lists of EEN contact points (OECD/European Union/ETF, 2018[18]).

[6] See https://ec.europa.eu/easme/en/enterprise-europe-network.

[7] See https://anima.coop/en/ and http://ebsomed.eu/.

[8] See, for example, the Business Development Centre, the Young Entrepreneurs Association, Injaz, the Crown Prince Foundation, the King Abdullah Fund for Development, the SME Association, Endeavor, and Oasis 500 (OECD, 2019[19]).

[9] For a more complete overview of the BDS markets in the MENA region refer to the SME Policy Index for the Mediterranean Middle East and North Africa editions 2014 and 2018 (OECD/The European Commission/ETF, 2014[17]) (OECD/European Union/ETF, 2018[18]).

[10] For example, the SME and entrepreneur portals and websites established in some Lain American countries providing up to date and structured search engines for small businesses to search for support to access markets, technology, finance, etc. (OECD/CAF, 2019[35]).

9 Enhancing connectivity through infrastructure investment

This chapter examines the current context of infrastructure investment in the MENA region with a focus on transport, ICT and energy sectors. It reviews the challenges of infrastructure development and provides an overview of recent reforms to boost infrastructure investment and financing, including through public-private partnerships. It also provides policy considerations to address the legal and institutional frameworks for investment in infrastructure.

Summary and policy considerations

High-quality infrastructure is a crucial input for inclusive and sustainable growth. Transport, energy and ICT infrastructure are vital for facilitating investment and promoting connectivity, industrial development and economic diversification in the MENA economies covered in this report (MENA focus economies). Yet, several shortcomings persist across all infrastructure sectors. While the MENA focus economies have made progress in developing basic physical infrastructure, the performance of transport infrastructure (including ports, roads and airports) remains low, causing delays and raising the cost of trade. Poor logistics affects trade and investment more than the lack of infrastructure. On average, 24% of manufacturing firms in the MENA focus economies identify transport issues as a major constraint to their business operations.[1]

MENA economies face bottlenecks in transport infrastructure, including railways, a lack of multi-modal transport, and a fragmented port system. In the wider MENA region[2], this will require investment of at least USD 100 billion annually over the next five to ten years to maintain existing and build new infrastructure (World Bank, 2020[1]). Financing gaps are present across all infrastructure sectors, but more prevalent in cross-border infrastructure, road transport and energy.

While ICT infrastructure is relatively well developed across the MENA region, significant investment in fixed and mobile broadband capacity is required to further facilitate domestic and foreign investment. Key factors limiting the development of the ICT sector include the lack of effective competition and appropriate regulation (Gelvanovska, Rogy and Rossotto, 2014[2]). Many countries still face high barriers to internet accessibility, hindering business operations. Currently, only 8% of SMEs in the wider MENA region have an online presence (compared to 80% in the US) and only 1.5% of the region's retailers are online (McKenna, 2017[3]).

Infrastructure is mainly provided by the public sector through state-owned enterprise (SOEs), with relatively little private sector participation. Public-private partnerships (PPPs) are limited but they are an important avenue through which private sector resources and expertise can be leveraged. In recent years, some MENA governments have boosted efforts to build a credible environment for PPPs by updating their PPP laws and setting up PPP agencies or specialised units within existing institutions (e.g. Jordan, Morocco, Tunisia and Egypt). While the regulatory and institutional environments governing PPPs differ, there is growing political support for PPPs across most MENA economies. Greater private sector involvement in infrastructure through PPPs could not only improve the efficiency of infrastructure and bring new technologies and skills, but also reduce the fiscal burden on public budgets.

Improving infrastructure governance could also attract more private investment. MENA focus economies could improve the management and efficiency of public investment, as well as transparency of procurement and appraisal processes. Planning infrastructure development in a holistic way, following good practices for infrastructure governance, can help alleviate some of the challenges in the region and boost investment.

Policy considerations

- Clarify the regulatory framework for infrastructure investment to provide potential investors with clear, transparent, predictable and consistent policies and regulations. Often, the PPP laws coexist with other procurement modes for infrastructure such as public utilities legislation and a number of sector-specific laws.
- Ensure that infrastructure strategies are well aligned with overall national and regional trade and development strategies, including investment, logistics development and broader governance reforms. MENA economies have often developed hard infrastructure without the accompanying trade and business regulatory reforms or have not adopted a multi-modal approach to deliver the expected results.
- Undertake more pro-competition reforms in the ICT sector to further level the playing field between new entrants and incumbents. Similar to other key sectors, the ICT sector is typically dominated by a few incumbent firms and SOEs, limiting entry of new investors. Reforms should include lifting some entry barriers in the telecommunications sector.
- Streamline or remove restrictions to foreign investment in the energy and transport sectors. Currently, the eight focus economies impose higher restrictions than the OECD average in maritime and air transport, construction and telecom sectors but also in some cases in electricity distribution and generation. In cases where such policies are considered necessary to address national development objectives, governments should ensure that they are not more restrictive than needed (see Chapter 4).
- Foster dialogue between the public and private sectors. There is significant scope for the private sector to become more engaged in infrastructure development in the region. The public sector should work more closely with private stakeholders to address bottlenecks in the investment climate and build appropriate domestic regulations that foster competitiveness, particularly in backbone service sectors.
- Strengthen capacity and co-ordination across ministries and related entities involved in infrastructure planning and prioritisation. Infrastructure in the region is often developed in silos and not always integrated with other types of policies such as industrial development strategies

Key infrastructure challenges affecting investment in the MENA region

Infrastructure that improves the connectivity of the eight focus economies in the MENA region is an essential element of policies to promote inclusive and sustainable growth. With a population that is expected to grow by 40% to 586 million by 2030, accelerated urbanisation in the coming decades, and a rapidly growing middle class, the region faces increasing strains on its existing infrastructure (Kandeel, 2019[4]). The economic fallout caused by the Covid-19 pandemic is also creating the need for technologically advanced, sustainable and resilient infrastructure that can support the economic recovery. Infrastructure – including transport, energy and ICT and associated services – is vital for facilitating investment, promoting industrial development and economic diversification of the focus economies in the MENA region. Yet, several shortcomings across all infrastructure sectors currently limit the potential for further investment and the contribution made by infrastructure to sustainable and inclusive growth.

The quality of hard and soft infrastructure in the MENA region remains low

While the region has made progress in developing basic physical infrastructure in recent years, the performance of transport infrastructure (e.g. ports, roads and airports) remains low, causing delays and raising the cost of trade. According to the World Bank's *Logistic Performance Index,* the performance of infrastructure varies considerably across the eight focus economies (Figure 9.1). Egypt has advanced most in the region in the past decade thanks to a boost in investment, while Morocco's performance has worsened. Morocco's performance is partly inhibited by weaknesses in customs services and tracking and tracing consignments (Chauffour, 2018[5]). Algeria has also improved its performance since 2010, while in Tunisia and Lebanon there is significant scope for improvement. Overall, the region still faces important infrastructure shortcomings, including in transport, ICT and energy, as reflected in various international indicators (Annex 9.A).

Figure 9.1. The World Bank's Logistic Performance Index, Infrastructure Indicator

Score from 1 to 5 (best)

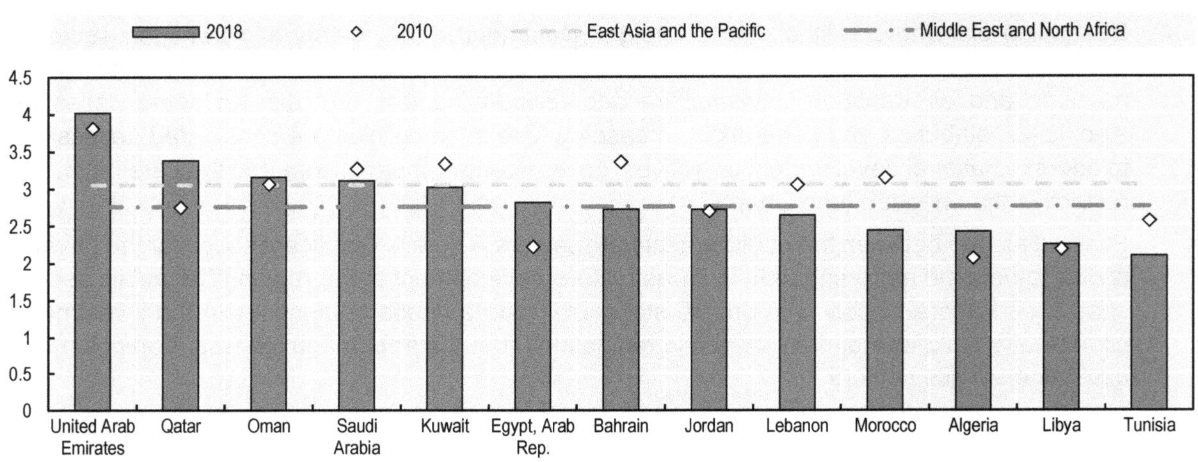

Note: Data for Morocco is from 2012. The Infrastructure Indicator is one of the six dimensions of the logistics supply chain of the World Bank Logistics Performance Index (LPI), which is based on a worldwide survey of logistics operators on the ground, providing feedback on the logistics "friendliness" of the countries in which they operate and those with which they trade. It measures performance along six dimensions of the logistics supply chain, including: 1) Efficiency of the clearance process (i.e., speed, simplicity and predictability of formalities) by border control agencies, including customs; 2) Quality of trade and transport related infrastructure (e.g., ports, railroads, roads, information technology); 3) Ease of arranging competitively priced shipments; 4) Competence and quality of logistics services (e.g., transport operators, customs brokers); 5) Ability to track and trace consignments; 6) Timeliness of shipments in reaching destination within the scheduled or expected delivery time.
Source: World Bank Logistics Performance Index database

Across the MENA region, poor logistics affects trade and investment more than the actual lack of infrastructure, making the economies relative outliers compared to other regions in terms of their logistics performance. Logistics challenges can be widespread. The cost of port facilities in North African economies are around 40% above the global norm, with long container dwell times, lengthy documentation processing, and delays in vessel traffic clearance (AfDB, 2019[6]). As a result, 70% of delays in cargo is due to extra time in ports. Less than 7% of global intraregional merchandise trade occurs within the region, compared to 40% in East Asia and 50% in Europe. Public sector monopolies in transport infrastructure in most of the MENA economies has undermined incentives to reform (World Bank, 2020[1]).

Transport connectivity

The poor quality of connectivity infrastructure constrains the manufacturing sector

Bottlenecks in logistics and transport infrastructure in the MENA region are a major constraint to more trade and investment, limiting the growth of manufacturing firms in particular. In a number of the focus economies, firms identify transport issues as a major constraint to their business operations (Figure 9.2). According the World Bank Enterprise Survey, this is particularly a challenge in Jordan, Morocco and Tunisia. Exporting firms also often face higher transport constraints than domestic firms, particularly in Tunisia, Jordan and the Palestinian Authority.

Figure 9.2. Exporting firms identifying transport costs as a major constraint

As % of manufacturing firms

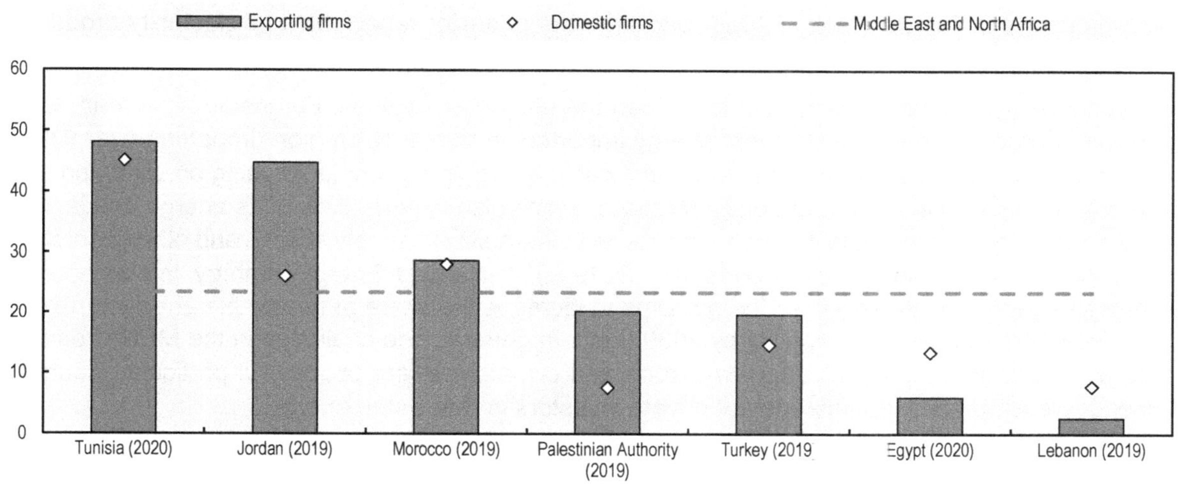

Note: Exporting firms include firms with direct exports with 10% or more of sales; domestic firms include non-exporters. MENA average for the 8 focus economies except Algeria and Libya due to an absence of data.
Source: World Bank Enterprise Surveys for 2019 and 2020

The maritime networks in the MENA region are fragmented

In contrast to other transport sectors, port infrastructure has received significant public investment by MENA governments. Many economies have developed port infrastructure aimed at accessing European markets but there is also scope to enhance regional trade. Only 5% of cargo traffic in the Mediterranean region passes between MENA countries, while it is 70% between European ports, and 15% between Europe and North Africa (IMF, 2019[7]). The number of inter-port links or port pairs across the Mediterranean has actually declined, from 2,279 in 2009 to 1,532 in 2016. For instance, Tunisia has direct links only to its closest European trade partners (Arvis et al., 2019[8]). There are very few direct lines of sea transport among Maghreb countries, which transport their intraregional goods through third-country ports, such as Marseille, Almeria or even Rotterdam. These locations generate additional costs and limit the price competitiveness of traded products.

Many ports in the region offer significant opportunities for foreign manufacturers looking for locations near markets in Europe, the Middle East and Africa, but this potential is not realised in many countries. According to the IMF, only a few ports are competitive by international standards, with Morocco leading the way with its Tangier port, which became a logistical hub for the region and is considered the biggest container port in Africa in terms of turnover. In Egypt, the expansion of the Suez Canal in 2015 and the establishment of the Suez Canal Economic Zone to offer more competitive services for global shipping lines and investors are also expected to capture up to 25% of Egypt's containerised Mediterranean trade (Arvis et al., 2019[8]).

Energy and ICT connectivity

Many countries in the region are well endowed with renewable energy resources but have not sufficiently diversified their power supply

The MENA focus economies are well endowed with renewable energy sources such as solar and wind, but the share of renewables in the energy mix varies among countries (see also Chapter 2 on FDI trends and development benefits). Such resources could lower the price of renewable energy and add significant generating capacity. Yet, the share of renewable energy in final energy consumption varies significantly among countries, from 0.1% in Algeria, between 5 and 5.5% in Egypt and Jordan, and between 10 and 12% in Morocco and Tunisia (IEA, 2020[9]). Similarly, the share of renewables in electricity production ranges from 35% in Morocco and 8.5% in Egypt.

Some countries have shown commitment to deepen the use of renewables. For instance, Jordan, which together with Morocco is one of the largest energy importers in the MENA region (importing over 93% of its total energy supplies), has launched a large renewable energy programme focusing on wind and solar (Abu-Rumman, Khdair and Khdair, 2020[10]). Morocco, which also imports 93% of its energy needs, aims to increase the share of renewable energy to reduce its vulnerability to supply shocks and other disruptions caused by the heavy dependence on imports (IFC, 2019[11]). Its National Energy Strategy, implemented by the Moroccan Agency for Sustainable Energy, aims to increase the share of renewable energy to 52% of total installed energy generating capacity by 2030 (ibid). In general, one challenge in the MENA region is to create an environment conducive to low-carbon and climate resilient options. In particular, countries need to encourage competition and entry of private investors in renewable energy.

ICT infrastructure has been expanding fast but businesses in the region still face high costs

ICT infrastructure is relatively well developed across the wider MENA region, thanks to investment by the government as well as by the private sector. According to the 2019 Mobile Connectivity Index[3], which measures the performance of countries against the key enablers of mobile internet adoption – infrastructure, affordability, consumer readiness, content and services – many of the MENA focus economies are "transitioners".[4] Lebanon has the highest score among the focus economies, followed closely by Tunisia and Morocco; Jordan, Egypt, and Algeria rank slightly lower on the index (GSMA Intelligence, 2020[12]). Mobile technologies and services account for 4.5% of GDP in the wider MENA region, supporting 1 million jobs directly and indirectly, and contributing to over USD 18 billion of taxes. Overall, mobile technology and services generated USD 191 billion of value added, which is expected to exceed USD 222 billion by 2023. 4G technology is expected to surpass 3G in the region by 2021 (ibid).

Yet, to keep up with growing demand, significant investment is necessary to increase the fixed and mobile broadband transmission capacity of the eight focus economies. Key factors limiting the development of the ICT sector in Algeria, Egypt, Morocco, Libya, Tunisia and Jordan include the lack of effective competition and appropriate regulation (Gelvanovska, Rogy and Rossotto, 2014[2]). In Jordan, lack of competition has led to low quality of service and one of the highest prices of mobile and fixed internet in the region. Better ICT infrastructure could further facilitate investment, including by making it easier for companies to access local and international markets, and allowing frequent and uninterrupted communication with the headquarters (Latif et al., 2018[13]).

A more competitive ICT sector would allow companies to enter new markets and contribute to the digitalisation agenda of the focus governments in the region. Like many other sectors, the ICT sector is generally dominated by incumbent firms, private sector or state-owned, making it difficult for other firms to enter the market (World Bank, 2019[14]). Enhanced broadband services would allow all sectors to take advantage of a more modern digital economy (ibid). It would also create new trade opportunities for SMEs, allowing them to reach to new markets.

Many countries still face high barriers to internet accessibility. Currently, only 8% of SMEs in the wider MENA region have an online presence (compared to 80% in the US) and only 1.5% of the region's retailers are online (McKenna, 2017[3]). Excluding the high-income countries from the average, the MENA region has 100 mobile phone subscriptions per 100 inhabitants on average. Morocco and Tunisia surpass the average (128 and 124 per 100 inhabitants respectively), while other countries are below the average: Lebanon (64) and Jordan (88) (WEF, 2019[15]).

The infrastructure gap in the MENA region

Investment gap in infrastructure amounts to 7% of regional GDP

The wider MENA region needs over 100 billion a year (7% of the annual regional GDP) over the next five years to maintain existing and create new infrastructure, according to the World Bank[5] (Figure 9.3). Developing oil exporting countries will need to commit 11% of their GDP annually. Oil importing countries and GCC oil exporters need approximately 6% and 5% of their GDP in infrastructure investments, respectively. The gaps are present across all sectors, but are more prevalent in cross-border infrastructure, road transport and energy. Transport and electricity account for around 43% of total needs, followed by ICT (9%) and water and sanitation (5%). The electricity needs alone will require 3% of annual regional GDP. Oil importing countries will also need to spend around USD 86 billion to upgrade transport networks. Not only is new infrastructure needed, but also proper maintenance and quality control of the existing assets.

Figure 9.3. Annual infrastructure investment needs in MENA

By sector, investment as % of estimated GDP

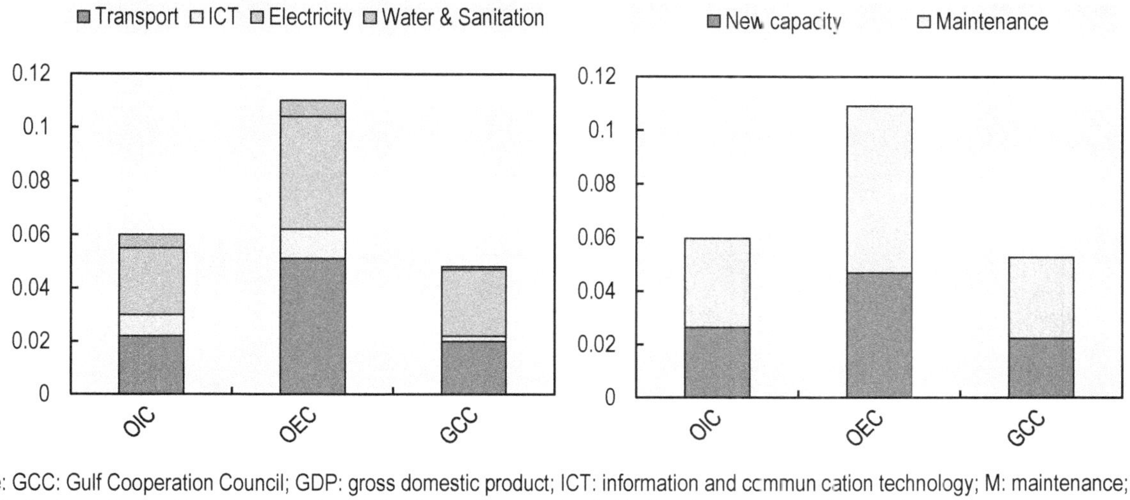

Note: GCC: Gulf Cooperation Council; GDP: gross domestic product; ICT: information and communication technology; M: maintenance; MENA: Middle East and North Africa; N: new capital; OIC: Oil importing country; OEC: Developing oil exporting country.
GCC includes: Bahrain, Kuwait, Oman, Qatar, Saudi Arabia, UAE; OEC includes Algeria, Iran, Islamic Rep., Iraq, Libya, Syrian Arab Republic, Yemen, Rep.; OIC includes: Egypt, Jordan, Lebanon, Morocco, Tunisia.
Source: World Bank estimations based on (Freund and Ianchovichina, 2012[16]).

The Global Infrastructure Hub recently estimated that Egypt, Morocco and Tunisia together need USD 997 billion of investment in infrastructure until 2040 (GIHub, 2017[17]). The largest gap is in Egypt, which, under a growth assumption of 4% of GDP each year, will need to spend USD 675 billion (or 5% of GDP) on average until 2040. Given the current levels of spending, this translates to an investment gap of 1.7% of GDP. Morocco has a USD 37 billion infrastructure gap (or 0.90% of GDP under a 3.6% growth assumption). More recent estimates suggest that total investment needs range from 11.5%-18.3% depending on three scenarios of low-growth, business-as-usual, or high-growth) (IFC, 2019[11]). Similarly, Tunisia will also need to spend USD 75 billion (or 4.4% of GDP) on average on infrastructure until 2040.

The MENA region lags behind other regions in terms of private financing

Since the early 2000s, private investment in infrastructure has been increasing steadily across most regions with the exception of MENA. In several MENA countries, private sector infrastructure investments declined sharply in 2010-12. While investment has since recovered to pre-2010 levels, this is primarily due to a few large projects concentrated in the electricity sector in Morocco. The transport and water sectors have seen very limited activity over the past five years (Figure 9.4). Private investment in infrastructure over the past three years has been highly concentrated geographically. Two-thirds of the number of projects have taken place in Jordan, partly a result of the country's programme promoting renewable energy, particularly solar PV plants. In terms of capital expenditure however, almost 75% has gone to Morocco due to the Noor I and II large concentrated solar power projects in Ouarzazate, and a 1360 MW coal-fired power plant in Safi, Southwest Morocco (OECD, 2017[18]).

The principal sources of infrastructure project finance in the MENA region over the past three years have been multilateral and bilateral lenders with the EIB, EBRD, and Islamic Development Bank, being among the most active players. Bilateral lenders come from a wide range of countries and include France, Germany and Japan, among others. Support from multilateral and bilateral lenders has almost exclusively been in the form of debt. International banks have also participated in a number of projects though always in conjunction with a multilateral lender or a major bilateral lender. Local commercial banks have only played a marginal role with the exception of the Agadir desalination plant in Morocco, where they have been the only source of debt finance (OECD, 2017[18]).

Figure 9.4. Private investment in infrastructure in MENA, 2000-2019 (by sector)

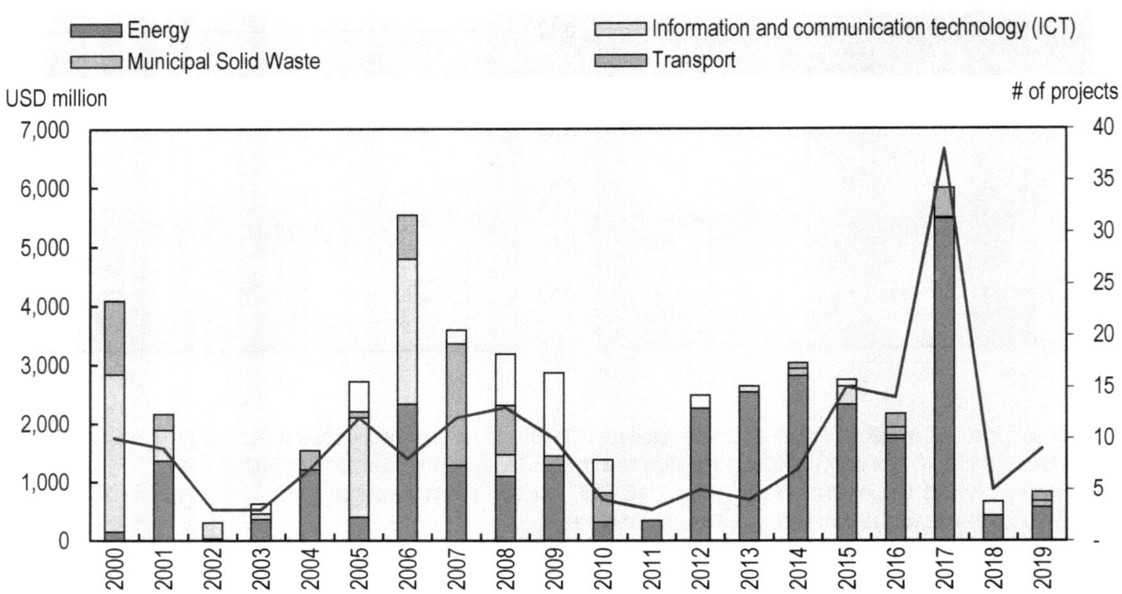

Source: World Bank PPIA, PPI project database

Establishing an enabling environment for investment in infrastructure

In order to attract more private sector participation in infrastructure, governments in the region need to ensure that infrastructure priorities are an integral part of economic development strategies and supported by a clear accompanying regulatory and institutional framework. There are often cases when hard infrastructure is developed without the appropriate trade and business regulatory reforms, or where it has lacked the necessary multi-modal approach to deliver the expected results. Overcoming such a fragmented approach is critical for strengthening the investment climate and leveraging the positive spillovers from regional connectivity.

Infrastructure development strategies and financing instruments

In MENA countries that have traditionally relied on natural resource revenues for infrastructure financing, low oil prices will require governments to reconsider their investment strategies and plans for the long term (Rice, 2015[19]). The social and political upheavals over the past decade, coupled with the Covid-19 pandemic, have created additional challenges, including the need to improve governance to give confidence to the private sector to invest in infrastructure.

Infrastructure development is high on the region's agenda. Many focus economies have launched national strategies that stress the need for upgrades in infrastructure to promote sustainable development. Two specific projects that have successfully combined infrastructure investment with an industrial policy agenda are the expansion of the Suez Canal and the Development of the Suez Canal Economic Zone and the Tanger Med Port of Morocco (Box 9.1). In Egypt, plans to increase connectivity are laid out in Egypt's Vision 2030, which aims to increase the capacity of the transport sector and boost Egypt's share in international and regional transport volumes. The Economic Pillar of Vision 2030 includes mega projects such as the Suez Canal and Suez Canal Economic Zone. At the sectoral level, the Transport Master Plan 2027 aims to achieve multi-modal transport chains between national, regional and gateway centres, but also to enhance the role of the private sector in investing and participating in transport projects.

In Morocco, all infrastructure sectors have developed investment plans with ambitious targets and long time horizons for increasing both stocks and quality. For instance, the 2040 Rail Strategy (Plan Rail Maroc) aims to develop the rail network and its various components across the country by 2040 and contribute to territorial development (ONCF, 2020[20]). The National Port Strategy 2030 also aims to consolidate Morocco's ports to increase cargo output and port capacity at a total investment of USD 6 billion, primarily from the public sector (Rensma and Hamoumi, 2018[21]).

Box 9.1. Selected Infrastructure Projects in MENA

Important investments in a number of the MENA focus economies have been a driving force in the region's infrastructure development. The two most prominent examples are the new transhipment hub of the Suez Canal Development Project and Tanger-Med Port and, which continue to facilitate internal and cross-border transport and trade, and have an important role not only for the economic development of Egypt and Morocco, but also for the Mediterranean region.

The Suez Canal Area Development Project

The Suez Canal Area Development Project comprises three main components aimed at reinforcing the position of the Suez Canal as a global maritime trade route, and exploiting its potential for investment attraction and export-oriented growth:

- The "New Suez Canal", involving a major expansion to increase capacity and allow ships to navigate in both directions at the same time, which will decrease waiting hours from 18 to 11 for most ships and double the capacity of the Canal from 49 to 97 ships a day. This project is expected to lead to enlarged transit capacity and increased industrial activity in the area, which will raise the international profile of Egypt as an international logistical and industrial hub.

- The "East Port Said" development project, involving the construction of a 9,5-km side channel bypassing the Suez Canal entrance, port expansion works, a new industrial zone and logistics centre as well as four new East-West tunnels to increase cross-canal connectivity and link the Sinai Peninsula to Egypt's mainland.
- The "Suez Canal Economic Zone" (SCZone) established on 461 km² of land and six maritime ports strategically located along the international waterway with direct access to ports, to serve as an international logistics hub and areas for light, medium and heavy industry as well as commercial and residential developments.

Tanger MED

Situated 40km east of Tangier, Morocco, Tanger Med is the largest cargo port in the Mediterranean and in Africa by capacity. The port represents a major logistics and industrial hub and a gateway for Morocco's imports and exports, connecting to 186 ports worldwide. The first phase of the project (Tanger MED 1) entered into service in 2007 with an initial capacity of over 3.5 million shipping containers, while the second phase (Tanger MED II) was completed in 2019 at a cost of USD 1.5 billion and increased capacity to 9 million containers. The project is part of Morocco's diversification plan to attract new investment and create jobs by offering various investment incentives, access to free trade agreements, skilled labour, as well as well-connected logistics to firms willing to relocate their production. Tanger MED currently hosts around 900 companies in four industrial zones around port facilities creating over 70,000 jobs overall. Nearly half of these companies are European and are linked to the automotive sector, making Tanger MED the largest manufacturing hub of autos in Africa and MENA. Today, automotive sector is Morocco's largest exporting sector. Two most influential car companies are Renault Tanger Med and Peugeot, which are now assembling new vehicles and engines to export to EU and African markets.

Source: (Bank of Alexandria, 2014[22]), (N Gage Consulting, 2016[23]), (EuroMesco, 2019[24]), Suez Canal Authority Website, www.suezcanal.gov.eg.

Infrastructure development is also high on Algeria's policy agenda. The 2015-2019 Investment Plan aimed to support development of various connectivity projects, including rail systems, roads, airport modernisation and ports (Oxford Business Group, 2017[25]). Given that the vast majority of the country's trade is moved through its 11 commercial ports (95% of imports arrive by sea), an important priority is to upgrade ports to increase capacity to handle large vessels and make Algeria a Mediterranean hub (ITA, 2019[26]). Another priority is to expand the rail network to reduce road congestion and increase rail freight domestically and with neighbours. The push for regional connectivity is also driven by the opening of a rail line linking Annaba with Tunisia (Oxford Business Group, 2017[25]).

Jordan's 2025 National Vision and Strategy stresses the role of infrastructure to achieve economic transformation based on export development (Harake, 2019[27]). The infrastructure priorities are laid out in the Jordan Economic Growth Plan 2018-22 for each sectors. In the transport sector, the Plan has several objectives, including to complete and upgrade the transport networks such as airports and ports, enhance the capacity of the land cargo system, and develop a multimodal transport system. In particular, the government aims to establish a cargo-based rail network connecting the main industrial cities and logistical centres domestically, as well as to connect with neighbouring countries and Europe (Jordan Economic Policy Council, 2018[28]). The investment required for such a network is estimated at USD 2.1 billion, which the government hopes to allocate through partnerships with the private sector (ibid).

Mobilising the necessary resources for infrastructure investment in the region requires effective planning and prioritisation of projects. Numerous projects are set up in different infrastructure strategies across countries. Often, the allocation of budget for projects is done on an annual basis. MENA governments need a medium-term planning and funding allocation to increase stability for infrastructure projects. So far, Algeria and Jordan have introduced a medium-term budgetary framework that could allow for multiyear sectoral planning to ensure that investment expenditures are driven by policy priorities and fiscal objectives (World Bank, 2013[29]). Better co-ordination between different ministries would also allow for better prioritisation of investment projects.

Improving the regulatory framework for investment in infrastructure

In order for the private sector to participate in infrastructure projects, an adequate regulatory framework is required. This involves removing administrative bottlenecks and improving regulations (see Chapter 3). In recent years, some governments across the MENA region have boosted efforts to build a credible environment for public-private partnerships (PPPs) by updating their PPP laws and setting up PPP agencies or specialised units within existing institutions (e.g. Jordan, Morocco, Tunisia and Egypt). These improvements have led to a growth in PPPs in recent years. Greater private sector involvement in infrastructure could not only improve the efficiency of such investment, bring new technologies and skills, but also reduce the fiscal burden on public budgets.

The legal frameworks for public-private partnerships can bring important financing solutions for infrastructure projects

The regulatory and legal frameworks vary significantly across different countries with some countries clearly separating PPPs from other forms of procurement, while in others PPPs are treated as a dimension of a wider procurement policy. A number of countries in the region, including Jordan, Morocco, Tunisia and Egypt, have recently updated their PPP laws and set up a new PPP agency or unit to bring further clarity and transparency to their PPP regimes in line with good practices (Table 9.1) (OECD, 2016[30]). In Jordan, PPP investments have equalled 2% of GDP per year over the last five years and a revised PPP law las been submitted to the Parliament. Egypt's revised PPP law streamlined PPP contracts, particularly by cutting the time to issue tenders for PPP projects and introducing new mechanisms for private sector contracting (Enterprise, 2019[31]).

Table 9.1. International practices for PPP projects

Preparatory Stage of PPPs	Procurement Stage of PPPs	Contract Management Stage
The Ministry of Finance or central government budget authority approves the long-term financial implications of the project	The bid evaluation committee meets the minimum technical qualifications	The procuring authority has a system to manage the implementation of the PPP contract, including a contract management team in the project starting at the procurement stage
PPP projects have a specific accounting/reporting framework	The procuring authority publishes the procurement notice online, allowing potential bidders at least 30 days to submit proposals	The procuring authority establishes a system for tracking progress and completing construction works under a PPP contract, with relevant information made publicly available
PPP projects are assessed and prioritised along with all other public investment projects in the context of wider national public investment plans	Foreign companies are allowed to take part in PPP procurements	Monitoring and evaluation systems are in place to oversee the implementation of the PPP contract after the construction stage, with relevant information publicly available.

Assessment results of PPPs and tender documents are made publicly available online	The tender documents set the selection criteria in a transparent manner, and the procuring authority organises a pre-bid conference to disseminate information	Foreign companies are not prohibited from repatriating the income generated by the operation of a PPP project.
The PPP project are adequately justified in the light of socioeconomic, fiscal, financial, environment and risk assessments	Award notice of the winning bidder and the grounds for selection is made publicly available	Any changes in the structure of the private partner are expressly regulated, requiring the replacing entity to be at least as qualified as the original private partner.
The procuring authority prepares a draft and makes the draft contract publicly available before approval	A standstill period after the intended award of the contract is allowed for other bidders to challenge the award decision	Modification and renegotiation of the contract are expressly regulated to reduce incentives to use these changes opportunistically by either the private partner or the procuring authority.
To guarantee consistency and efficiency, the procuring authority has standardised PPP model contracts	The signed PPP contract and amendments is made publicly available	Dispute resolution mechanisms should be in place, and specific circumstances (e.g., setbacks in implementation, refinancing, changes in law) should be accounted for with the grounds of a termination of contract and its consequences clearly laid out

Source: based on (World Bank, 2018[32]).

Yet, a large proportion of private investment in the region has been in sectors where financial sustainability is easier to attain, such as for example power generation projects. For sectors other than energy such as water, it is more challenging to attract investment because projects are generally less bankable and offer fewer prospects for future cash flows. In Jordan, most PPP investments focused on renewable energy. A revamped PPP framework is needed to help facilitate projects in sectors where more extensive government support is required to attract private investment, such as in toll roads. Egypt has a general PPP framework that coexists with alternative channels for procuring infrastructure projects, such as the system of public economic entities, public utilities legislation and a number of sector- specific or project-specific laws (EBRD, 2018[33]).

In Morocco, while the PPP law (Law 86-12) offers a framework for PPPs, it has not replaced other specific laws, which create overlapping legislation for private investment in infrastructure and uncertainty regarding which laws apply to what contracts. The sector-specific laws allow for contracting with private parties in a number of sectors such as ports, renewable energy, electricity generation, desalination, and airports. This has created misalignment on contract selection, preliminary evaluation of projects, minimum clauses, and guarantees. Moreover, SOEs involved in infrastructure, which often receive subsidies (around 0.5% of GDP) from the public budget for investment or operations, can directly select private partners for joint ventures under the commercial law and can invest in private operators even when they compete against them in the market. To address such shortcomings, the Ministry of Finance has taken steps to streamline the market participation of SOEs but with mixed results, while the Ministry of Economy is currently preparing an amendment to the PPP law.

There is growing political support for PPPs across most MENA economies. PPP laws and regulations could create an environment that protects both the public and private sector. When PPPs are used, it is important that, among other principles, the process is transparent and predictable, with a level playing field for all bidders (Box 9.2). Adopting PPPs is not straightforward. It takes time for governments to build capacity to implement credible PPP programmes. But there is strong commitment and multilateral support to help countries deliver and manage PPPs, which can lead to more infrastructure that enhances regional connectivity.

Box 9.2. OECD Principles for Public Governance of Public-Private Partnerships

The 2012 Recommendation of the OECD Council on the Principles for Public Governance of Public-Private Partnerships provides concrete guidance to policy makers on how to make sure that public-private partnerships represent value for money for the public sector.

Establishing clear, predictable, and legitimate institutional frameworks that are supported by competent and well-resourced authorities

1. Political leaders should raise public awareness of the relative costs, benefits and risks of PPPs and conventional procurement. All stakeholders, including end-users should be included in the design and quality control of PPP projects.
2. The role of relevant institutions should be clearly defined and maintained. Procuring authorities, PPP units, Central Budget Authorities, auditors, and sector regulators should have clear mandates and sufficient resources to ensure effective procurement and accountability.
3. Regulatory frameworks that affect PPPs should be clear, transparent, and enforced.

Maximising value in the selection of PPPs

1. Governments should set and pursue strategic goals regarding infrastructure development on the highest political level. PPPs should not be a subject to any institutional, procedural or accounting bias.
2. Prospective infrastructure projects should be assessed for their key characteristics and risks to determine the investment method with most value for money. A procurement option pre-test can help governments to determine whether to investigate PPPs as a further option.
3. Risks should be defined, identified, measured and allocated to the party most able to carry and mitigate them.
4. Procuring authorities should be ready for the operational phase of a PPP, which requires vigilance and effort similar to the pre-project phase.
5. In the event of renegotiation, the public sector should only consider compensations to the private sector partners if conditions have changed due to discretionary public policy decisions.
6. The government should ensure a level playing field and a sufficient amount of competition throughout the tendering process.

Using the budgetary process transparently to minimise fiscal risks and maintain the integrity of the procurement process

1. The Central Budget Authority should ensure that the PPP project is affordable within the framework of wider fiscal policy.
2. Transparency should be maintained throughout the budgeting process. All costs and contingent liabilities should be disclosed.
3. The government should maintain the integrity of the procurement process by guarding against waste and corruption.

Source: OECD Principles for Public Governance of Public-Private Partnerships

Re-thinking restrictions to foreign investment in sectors relevant to connectivity

While some MENA economies are fairly open to foreign investment, some restrictions are still relatively high compared to the OECD average, particularly in infrastructure services and the construction sector. According to the OECD FDI Regulatory Restrictiveness Index (Chapter 4), the MENA focus economies have higher restrictions in maritime and air transport and construction sectors than the average OECD countries (Figure 9.5). Algeria has the highest restrictions in all relevant sectors (with the exception of surface transport). Jordan also has relatively high restrictions in the transport sector. In Morocco, several sectors including in maritime and air transport face restrictions on foreign ownership. For instance, foreign investment in air transport companies is limited to 49% of capital, while in maritime transport, for a vessel to fly the Moroccan flag, it must be 75% Moroccan owned or the majority of the board of directors or the supervisory board must be Moroccan citizens.[6]

Egypt also only allows foreign investments in the maritime sector in the form of joint venture companies in which foreign equity does not exceed 49%. In transport, provision remains dominated by the public sector, with some private concessions in ports and airports. The Construction Law (1992) also restricts foreign investment to joint-ventures in which foreign equity does not exceed 49%. In addition, foreign participation in electrical wiring and other building completion and finishing services is restricted to projects valued over USD 10 million.[7] Such restrictions affect competition in the market and limit the quality of service provision.

Figure 9.5. OECD FDI Regulatory Restrictiveness Index in selected infrastructure sectors (2019)

Closed=1; Open=0

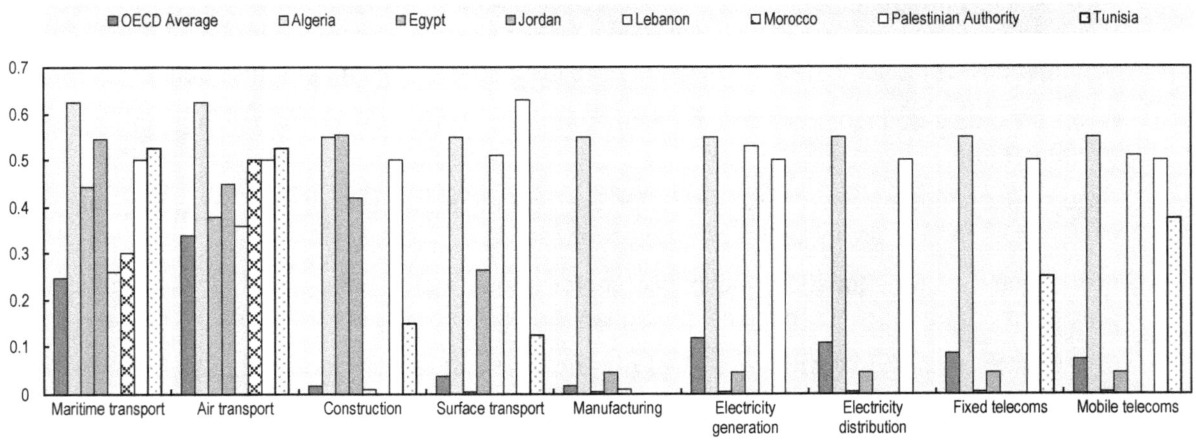

Source: OECD FDI Restrictiveness Index

Beyond removing restrictions, improving the governance of infrastructure could also attract more private investment

Good governance and strategic vision can improve the management of infrastructure projects and create the basis for increasing private sector participation in funding, construction and operation. For a number of countries in the region, developing infrastructure has come at high levels of capital expenditure, while the efficiency of public investment could be improved. Areas of public management improvement include strengthening the procurement, transparency, and appraisal and selection processes. Planning of infrastructure development in a holistic way following the OECD's key principles for infrastructure governance can help ensure efficient use and allocation of resources (Box 9.3).

In Algeria, while the efficiency of public investment for large projects has improved in the past decade, reducing delays in project completion and cost overruns, it is still lower than in other oil exporters in the region and well below the global average (IMF, 2018[34]). Such inefficiencies have led to costly public investment projects. Algeria's unit cost of road construction projects is about 34% higher than in most countries in the region. According to one estimate, with stronger public investment management institutions, the same amount of investment could have funded 60% more infrastructure projects (ibid).

Box 9.3. OECD Draft Recommendation on the Governance of Infrastructure

The OECD Draft Recommendation on the Governance of Infrastructure developed by the Public Governance Committee reflects the experience, needs and aspirations of the global infrastructure governance at large.

To ensure the efficient use and allocation of resources, the Draft Recommendation develops ten comprehensive policy recommendations:

1. develop a long-term strategic vision for infrastructure
2. guard fiscal sustainability, affordability, and value for money
3. ensure efficient and effective procurement of infrastructure projects
4. ensure systematic and effective stakeholder engagement
5. co-ordinate infrastructure policy across levels of government
6. promote a legitimate, coherent, efficient and predictable regulatory framework
7. implement a whole of government approach to manage threats to integrity
8. undertake evidence-informed infrastructure decision making
9. make sure the asset performs throughout its life
10. strengthen critical infrastructure resilience

The recommendations take into account high-level policy directions in order to underline the specific work areas for Member and non-Member States adhering to the projects (Adherents). The Draft Recommendation on the Governance of Infrastructure will be a basis for OECD reviews and an available Toolkit that Adherents would be able to use in order to plan, make decisions, and monitor the delivery of public infrastructure.

Source: (OECD, 2020[35]).

References

Abu-Rumman, G., A. Khdair and S. Khdair (2020), "Current status and future investment potential in renewable energy in Jordan: An overview", *Heliyon*, Vol. 6/2, p. e03346, http://dx.doi.org/10.1016/j.heliyon.2020.e03346. [10]

AfDB (2019), *African Economic Outlook 2019*, African Development Bank, Abidjan, https://www.afdb.org/fileadmin/uploads/afdb/Documents/Publications/2019AEO/AEO_2019-EN.pdf. [6]

Arvis, J. et al. (2019), *Maritime Networks, Port Efficiency, and Hinterland Connectivity in the Mediterranean*, World Bank Group, Washington, DC, http://dx.doi.org/10.1596/978-1-4648-1274-3. [8]

Bank of Alexandria (2014), *Egypt Country Report: On the Road to Recovery*, Bank of Alexandria, https://www.alexbank.com/document/documents/ALEX/Retail/Research/Country-Profile/AR/Egypt-Country-Report-2014.pdf. [22]

Chauffour, J. (2018), *Morocco 2040: Emerging by Investing in Intangible Capital*, World Bank Group, Washington, DC, http://dx.doi.org/10.1596/978-1-4648-1066-4. [5]

EBRD (2018), *Public-Private Partnership Assessment 2017-2018 Review: Egypt*, European Bank for Reconstruction and Development, https://ppp-ebrd.com/review.php?country=Egypt. [33]

Enterprise (2019), *Egypt's Finance Ministry finalizes PPP law amendments*, Enterprise, https://enterprise.press/stories/2019/06/20/egypts-finance-ministry-finalizes-ppp-law-amendments/. [31]

EuroMesco (2019), *Infrastructures and Power in the Middle East and North Africa: The Crossroads of Regional and Global Geopolitics*, EuroMesco, Rome, https://www.euromesco.net/wp-content/uploads/2020/02/Report-28-Infrastructures-and-Power.pdf. [24]

Freund, C. and E. Ianchovichina (2012), *Infrastructure and Employment Creation in the Middle East and North Africa*, World Bank Group, https://openknowledge.worldbank.org/handle/10986/10853. [16]

Gelvanovska, N., M. Rogy and C. Rossotto (2014), *Broadband Networks in the Middle East and North Africa: Accelerating High-Speed Internet Access*, World Bank Group, Washington, DC, http://dx.doi.org/10.1596/978-1-4648-0112-9. [2]

GIHub (2017), *Global Infrastructure Outlook: infrastructure investment needs, 50 countries, 7 sectors to 2040*, Global Infrastructure Hub, Oxford Economics, https://gihub-webtools.s3.amazonaws.com/umbraco/media/1530/global-infrastructure-outlook-factsheet-24-july-2017.pdf. [17]

GSMA Intelligence (2020), *The Mobile Economy: Middle East and North Africa 2019*, GSMA Intelligence, https://www.gsma.com/mobileeconomy/wp-content/uploads/2020/03/GSMA_MobileEconomy2020_MENA_Eng.pdf. [12]

Harake, W. (2019), *Strategic Assessment : The 2019 Project Pipeline for Jordan and Investment Opportunities*, World Bank Group, https://documents.worldbank.org/en/publication/documents-reports/documentdetail/445051554135426057/strategic-assessment-the-2019-project-pipeline-for-jordan-and-investment-opportunities. [27]

IEA (2020), *Data and statistics: Renewable share in final energy consumption*, IEA, https://www.iea.org/data-and-statistics?country=ALGERIA&fuel=Renewables%20and%20waste&indicator=SDG72 (accessed on 12 February 2021). [9]

IFC (2019), *Creating Markets in Morocco: A second generation of reforms boosting private sector growth, job creation and skills upgrading*, IFC, https://www.ifc.org/wps/wcm/connect/d0c0f18c-26b7-4861-b4c5-14896aaba7f1/201910-CPSD-Morocco-EN.pdf?MOD=AJPERES&CVID=m-LGA3X. [11]

IMF (2019), "Economic Integration in the Maghreb : An Untapped Source of Growth", *Developmental Paper Series*, No. No. 19/01, IMF, https://www.imf.org/en/Publications/Departmental-Papers-Policy-Papers/Issues/2019/02/08/Economic-Integration-in-the-Maghreb-An-Untapped-Source-of-Growth-46273. [7]

IMF (2018), *Algeria: Selected Issues. Country Report NO. 18/169*, IMF, Washington, DC, https://www.imf.org/en/Publications/CR/Issues/2018/06/13/Algeria-Selected-Issues-45987 (accessed on 15 February 2021). [34]

ITA (2019), *Algeria: Public Works, Infrastructure Development, and Water Resources*, International Trade Administration (ITA), US Department of Commerce, https://www.stopfakes.gov/article?id=Algeria-Public-Works-Infrastructure-Development-and-Water-Resources. [26]

Jordan Economic Policy Council (2018), *Jordan Economic Growth Plan: 2018-2022*, Jordan Economic Policy Council, http://extwprlegs1.fao.org/docs/pdf/jor170691.pdf. [28]

Kandeel, A. (2019), *Freshwater Resources in the MENA Region: Risks and Opportunities*, Middle East Institute, https://www.mei.edu/publications/freshwater-resources-mena-region-risks-and-opportunities#:~:text=In%202018%2C%20the%20region%20had,1.7%20percent%20as%20of%202017.&text=The%20region's%20population%20is%20projected,and%20731%20million%20by%202050. [4]

Latif, Z. et al. (2018), "The dynamics of ICT, foreign direct investment, globalization and economic growth: Panel estimation robust to heterogeneity and cross-sectional dependence", *Telematics and Informatics*, Vol. 35/2, pp. 318-328, http://dx.doi.org/10.1016/j.tele.2017.12.006. [13]

McKenna, J. (2017), *The Middle East's start-up scene: explained in five charts*, World Economic Forum, https://www.weforum.org/agenda/2017/05/what-you-need-to-know-about-the-middle-easts-start-up-scene-in-five-charts/. [3]

N Gage Consulting (2016), *The Suez Canal Economic Zone: A Strategic Location and Modern Day Innovation*, N Gage Consulting, https://www.ngage-consulting.com/downloads/SuezCanal%20report%20July%202016-NGAGE%20CONSULTING.pdf. [23]

OECD (2020), *OECD Recommendation on the Governance of Infrastructure*, http://www.oecd.org/gov/infrastructure-governance/recommendation/. [35]

OECD (2017), *Supporting the Development of the Suez Canal Economic Zone: Identifying Priority Actions for a Dynamic and Sustainable Economic Zone*, OECD, Paris. [18]

OECD (2016), *Strengthening governance and competitiveness in the MENA region for stronger and more inclusive growth*, Better Policies, OECD Publishing, Paris, https://dx.doi.org/10.1787/9789264265677-en. [30]

ONCF (2020), *Plan Rail Maroc 2040*, ONCF, https://www.oncf.ma/en/Development/Strategy/Morroco-s-2040-rail-strategy. [20]

Oxford Business Group (2017), *Algeria focuses on transport infrastructure and housing*, Oxford Business Group, https://oxfordbusinessgroup.com/overview/building-possibilities-focus-remains-transport-infrastructure-and-housing. [25]

Rensma, M. and S. Hamoumi (2018), *Dutch business opportunities: Transport & Logistics sector Morocco*, Ministry of Foreign Affairs of the Netherlands, Barendrecht/Casablanca, https://www.rvo.nl/sites/default/files/2018/05/Transport-and-Logistics-sector-Morocco.pdf. [21]

Rice, J. (2015), *Why infrastructure is key to a stable Middle East*, World Economic Forum, https://www.weforum.org/agenda/2015/05/why-infrastructure-is-key-to-a-stable-middle-east/. [19]

WEF (2019), *Global Competitiveness Report 2019: How to end a lost decade of productivity growth*, World Economic Forum, https://www.weforum.org/reports/how-to-end-a-decade-of-lost-productivity-growth. [15]

World Bank (2020), *Convergence: Five Critical Steps toward Integrating Lagging and Leading Areas in the Middle East and North Africa*, World Bank, Washington, DC, http://dx.doi.org/10.1016/978-1-4648-1450-1. [1]

World Bank (2019), *MENA Economic Update: Reaching New Heights: Promoting Fair Competition in the Middle East and North Africa*, World Bank, http://dx.doi.org/10.1596/978-1-4648-1504-1. [14]

World Bank (2018), *Procuring Infrastructure PPPs 2018*, World Bank Group, Washington, DC, https://ppp.worldbank.org/public-private-partnership/library/procuring-infrastructure-ppps-2018. [32]

World Bank (2013), *Beyond the Annual Budget : Global Experience with Medium-Term Expenditure Frameworks*, World Bank, Washington, DC, http://dx.doi.org/10.1596/978-0-8213-9625-4. [29]

Annex 9.A. Comparative infrastructure indicators across MENA

	Egypt	Morocco	Saudi Arabia	Tunisia	United Arab Emirates	Algeria	Jordan	Libya	Lebanon	Palestinian Authority	Middle East and North Africa*
Electricity											
Access to electricity (% of population) 2017	100.0	100.0	100.0	100.0	100.0	100	100	70.1	100	100	97.8
Electric power transmission and distribution losses (% of output) 2014	11	15	7	15	7	17	11	70	10	-	14
Quality of electricity supply (1-7 (best), WEF 2017-2018	5.0	5.6	6.2	5.1	6.5	4.2	5.7	N/A	1.7	-	5.1
ICT											
Mobile telephone subscriptions (per 100 people) 2018	95	124	123	128	209	112	88	91	64	90	106
Individuals using the internet (% of population) 2016	47	65	93	64	98	49	67 (2017)	22 (2017)	78	64	43
Fixed broadband subscriptions (per 100 people) 2018	6.7	4.3	20.2	8.8	31.4	7.26	4.01	4.83	0.14	7.49	9.6
Transport											
Quality of road infrastructure, 1-7 (best), WEF 2019	5.1	4.7	5.2	3.6	6.0	4.0	4.2	N/A	2.6	-	-
Quality of railroad infrastructure, 1-7 (best), WEF 2017-2018	3.3	3.9	3.3	2.8	-	3.4	2.2	-	-	-	-
Liner shipping connectivity index (maximum value in 2004 = 100)³ 2019	66.7	58.2	63	7.8	71.5	12.8	33.9	14.7	38.5	-	-
Efficiency of seaport services, 1-7 (best), WEF 2019	4.8	5.1	4.8	3.4	5.5	3.9	4.4	-	3.6	-	-
Efficiency of air transport services, 1-7 (best), WEF 2019	5.1	5.3	5.4	3.6	6.0	4.0	5.2	-	4.3	-	-

Note: * The average for the MENA region includes: Algeria, Bahrain, Djibouti, Egypt, Iran, Iraq, Israel, Jordan, Kuwait, Lebanon, Libya, Malta, Morocco, Oman, Qatar, Saudi Arabia, Syrian Arab Republic, Tunisia, United Arab Emirates, West Bank and Gaza, and Yemen.
Source: World Bank World Development Indicators database, World Economic Forum Competitiveness Index (2018).

Notes

[1] Based on responses to the World Bank Enterprise Surveys; average excludes Algeria and Libya due to absence of data.

[2] Unless specified otherwise, the wider MENA region in this chapter refers to the eight focus economies as well as Bahrain, Djibouti, Iran, Iraq, Kuwait, Oman, Qatar, Saudi Arabia, Syria, United Arab Emirates and Yemen.

[3] The Mobile Connectivity Index is an input index that measures the performance of 163 economies – representing 99% of the global population – of a range of metrics that are essential to create an effective enabling environment for mobile internet adoption. The corresponding output measure is the number of people accessing the internet via mobile. The GSMA includes the following economies in the MENA average: GCC Arab States (Qatar, UAE, Bahrain, Kuwait, Libya, Lebanon, Saudi Arabia), North Africa (Tunisia, Morocco, Israel, Iran, Algeria), Other Arab States (Egypt, Oman, Turkey, Jordan, Mauritania), and others (Syria, Iraq, Sudan, Palestinian Authority, Yemen, Somalia, Comoros, Djibouti).

[4] Transitioners (score above 50) perform well on at least two enablers and generally have mobile internet penetration rates between 30% and 50%.

[5] These estimates are based on a study of (Freund and Ianchovichina, 2012[16]), which are still considered valid today.

[6] See OECD National Treatment Instrument, 2017: https://www.oecd.org/daf/inv/investment-policy/nationaltreatmentinstrument.htm.

[7] See OECD National Treatment Instrument, 2017: https://www.oecd.org/daf/inv/investment-policy/nationaltreatmentinstrument.htm.

10 Promoting responsible business conduct as a strategic choice

Promoting and enabling responsible business conduct (RBC) is key to attract and retain quality investment and ensure that business activity contributes to broader value creation and sustainable development. This chapter reflects on achievements and challenges in MENA economies in promoting and enabling RBC.

Summary and policy considerations

Promoting and enabling responsible business conduct (RBC) is central to ensure that business activity contributes to broader value creation and sustainable development. RBC principles and standards set out an expectation that all businesses avoid and address negative impacts of their operations, including throughout the supply chain and business relationships, on the environment and society, while contributing to sustainable development where they operate. RBC is an integral part of a quality investment climate, and in recent years has been a priority policy area in the international economic agenda.

The impetus to promote RBC among MENA businesses is not only a social matter but also an economic one. As demands for RBC are growing, companies that participate in global supply chains must be aware of international expectations of RBC. Some of the key trading partners of the eight MENA economies covered in this report (MENA focus economies), such as the EU, have integrated RBC principles and standards in their policies and legislations. This makes promoting RBC particularly important for MENA countries to ensure integration in supply chain networks. Businesses that implement RBC principles and standards are also better equipped to sustain supply chain and operational shocks, and ultimately build resilience and long-term value. This is notable in the context of the Covid-19 pandemic and its impact on supply chains as well as occupational safety at work.

The notion that businesses should contribute to society is prevalent throughout the MENA region. In line with global trends, awareness and understanding of RBC in the region is growing and increasingly moving from approaches based on philanthropy and social investments towards a more comprehensive approach that looks at how core business operations affect society. Promising initiatives driven by businesses and other stakeholders could be leveraged to communicate clear expectations on RBC and support a common understanding of RBC among businesses of all sizes and types.

All MENA governments promote sustainability as a development objective and important commitments towards RBC have been made, although approaches differ across economies. Among the eight MENA focus economies, four governments – Egypt, Jordan, Morocco, and Tunisia – have adhered to the OECD *Declaration on International Investment and Multinational Enterprises*, thus committing to promote the OECD *Guidelines for Multinational Enterprises* (the *Guidelines*) and to establish a National Contact Point (NCP) to further their effectiveness. NCPs are agencies established by governments to promote the *Guidelines*, and to handle cases as a non-judicial grievance mechanism. Notably, Morocco's NCP has taken an active role in the promotion of RBC. In many cases though, this mechanism has been under-utilised and should be strengthened to fulfil its mandate and support the sound design and implementation of RBC policies in the region.

MENA economies have every interest in building on existing strengths to promote wide implementation of internationally recognised RBC standards. An opportunity exists to ensure that businesses conduct due diligence to identify, prevent and mitigate environmental and social risks, and address RBC issues that are prevalent in specific industries. Implementing RBC standards requires broad engagement with businesses but also with all stakeholders, including relevant government ministries and agencies, NGOs and trade unions. MENA governments could do more to create an environment that enables all stakeholders to contribute to the design and implementation of RBC standards. MENA governments have a practical opportunity to lead by example in their role as economic actors and could be more proactive in integrating RBC standards in state-owned enterprises (SOEs). Communicating in a clear and transparent manner what RBC policies are in place in SOEs could send a signal to the business community and incentivise RBC. Developing overarching frameworks on RBC such as National Action Plans (NAP), in line with good practice, could be one avenue to enable greater stakeholder engagement, promote policy coherence on RBC, and signal to international partners and domestic constituencies commitments to improving the overall business environment.

Policy considerations

- Develop National Action Plans on RBC in all MENA economies, in line with international good practice and in wide consultation with stakeholders. The development of NAPs would help build multi-stakeholder support for RBC and advance reforms needed to ensure an adequate legal framework that protects the public interest and underpins RBC.
- Leverage existing collaborative initiatives to actively promote and disseminate RBC due diligence instruments among businesses in key industries. In particular, there is an opportunity to build on existing collaborative initiatives to facilitate dialogue and support application of the OECD *Due Diligence Guidance for Responsible Supply Chains in the Garment and Footwear Sector*, as a way to improve industrial relations and enhance competitiveness of the garment sector in MENA economies.
- Facilitate meaningful stakeholder engagement in the design and implementation of RBC policies and processes. Particular attention should be paid to ensuring meaningful engagement in the early stages of policy development, and prioritising reforms to ensure that stakeholders are empowered to participate in consultative processes.
- Implement RBC standards in state-owned enterprises (SOEs). The Guidelines, together with the OECD *Guidelines on Corporate Governance of State-Owned Enterprises* and the *UN Guiding Principles*, provide a comprehensive framework for addressing RBC in SOEs. As a first step, MENA governments could consider communicating in a clear and transparent manner the RBC policies that their SOEs have in place.
- Strengthen NCPs capabilities in Egypt, Jordan and Tunisia and pursue ongoing efforts in Morocco. This may involve ensuring that NCPs are provided with adequate human and financial resources to fulfil their mandate. NCPs could also engage with peers in the region and beyond to share experience and build their capacity. Voluntary peer reviews could also be considered to assess practical aspects of NCP functioning and identify opportunities for further improvements.

Scope and importance of responsible business conduct

RBC means that businesses should make a positive contribution to sustainable development, while avoiding and addressing adverse impacts of their operations, including throughout their supply chains and business relationships. Risk-based due diligence – a process through which businesses identify, prevent and mitigate their actual and potential adverse impacts and account for how those impacts are addressed – is a key element of RBC.

Many businesses, governments and stakeholders are familiar with the term corporate social responsibility (CSR), which is often used to describe business interactions with society. CSR tends to be considered alongside RBC and Business and Human Rights (BHR), with some using the terms interchangeably (e.g. the European Union). All these concepts reflect the expectation that businesses should consider the impact of their operations and supply chains on people, the planet and society as part of their core business operations and not as an add-on. A key characteristic of CSR, RBC and BHR is that they refer to corporate conduct beyond simply complying with domestic law. They call on business to contribute positively to sustainable development while managing risks and any harm that may result from their activities and from that of their suppliers and partners. These concepts should not be understood to be equivalent to philanthropy (OECD, 2015[1]).

While it is the role of businesses to act responsibly, governments have a duty to protect the public interest and a role in providing an enabling framework for RBC. Governments can support RBC in several ways (Box 10.1). When governments provide an enabling environment for businesses to act responsibly and meet their duty to protect the public interest from potential negative impacts of business activities, they are more likely to keep and attract responsible investors. They are also more likely to minimise the risks of potential adverse impacts of investments and ensure broader value creation and sustainable development (OECD, 2015[1]).

Box 10.1. Role of governments in promoting and enabling responsible business conduct

Governments can promote and enable RBC in several ways, as outlined in the OECD Policy Framework for Investment:

Regulating: establishing and enforcing an adequate legal framework that protects the public interest and underpins RBC, and monitoring business performance and compliance;

Facilitating: clearly communicating expectations on what constitutes RBC, providing guidance with respect to specific practices and enabling enterprises to meet those expectations;

Co-operating: working with stakeholders in the business community, workers' organisations, civil society, general public, across internal government structures, as well as other governments to create synergies and establish coherence with regard to RBC;

Promoting: demonstrating support for best practices in RBC;

Leading by example: setting the example as an economic actor.

Source: (OECD, 2015[1])

RBC expectations are affirmed in international principles and standards, as well as increasingly in national legislation (Box 10.2, see also Chapter 3 on the domestic legal framework for investment). The main OECD instrument for promoting and enabling RBC is the OECD *Guidelines for Multinational Enterprises* (the *Guidelines*) (OECD, 2011[2]) As noted in the introduction to this chapter, the *Guidelines* are part of the OECD *Declaration on International Investment and Multinational Enterprises* (the *Declaration*), which is a policy commitment to provide an open and transparent investment environment and to encourage the positive contribution businesses can make to economic and social progress (OECD, 2011[3]).

The *Guidelines* are practical recommendations from governments to businesses on how to act responsibly. They cover all areas of business responsibility, including information disclosure, human rights, employment and labour, environment, anti-corruption, science and technology, competition, taxation, and consumer interests. Their purpose is to ensure that business operations are in harmony with government policies, strengthen the basis of mutual confidence between businesses and the societies in which they operate, improve the foreign investment climate, and enhance the contribution of the private sector to sustainable development (OECD, 2011[2]). Together with the *UN Guiding Principles on Business and Human Rights*, the fundamental International Labour Organisation (ILO) conventions and ILO MNE Declaration, the *Guidelines* are one of the major international instruments on RBC. The *Guidelines* do not aim to introduce differences of treatment between multinational and domestic enterprises, but to reflect good practice for all. Adherents to the *Declaration* encourage observance of the *Guidelines* to the fullest extent possible, including among SMEs, while acknowledging that these businesses may not have the same capacities as larger enterprises.

To support implementation of the *Guidelines*, the OECD has developed due diligence guidance, which provides practical recommendations to businesses on how to identify and respond to the risks of adverse impacts associated with particular products, regions, sectors or industries.[1]

To date, all 37 OECD members and 12 additional economies – including, in the MENA region, Egypt, Jordan, Morocco and Tunisia – have adhered to the *Guidelines*. Governments that adhere make a binding commitment to implement the *Guidelines* and encourage their use. The *Guidelines* have a unique implementation mechanism, the National Contact Points (NCPs), which are agencies established by governments. Their mandate is twofold: to promote the *Guidelines* and related due diligence guidance, and to handle cases (referred to as "specific instances") as a non-judicial grievance mechanism. Adhering governments have an obligation to establish a NCP to further the effectiveness of the *Guidelines*. (OECD, 2020[4]).

Promoting RBC in MENA can help attract quality FDI and participate in trade

The impetus to promote RBC among MENA businesses is not only a social matter but also an economic one. Companies that participate in global supply chains must be aware of international expectations of RBC (Box 10.2). The UK, which is one of the top ten sources of FDI to the MENA focus economies, requires companies of a certain size to prepare an annual report on steps taken to ensure the absence of modern slavery and human trafficking in supply chain or business operations.[2] The EU, which is the second most important regional source of FDI to the MENA focus economies, has integrated RBC principles and standards in a number of policies, legislations and economic instruments.[3] For example, the EU Trade for All policy includes objectives to reinforce CSR initiatives and due diligence across the production chain (European Commission, 2015[5]). All EU Free Trade Agreement negotiations since 2011 include binding sustainability provisions (OECD, 2020[4]).

To date, seven out of the eight MENA focus economies have concluded Association Agreements with the EU, including reciprocal free trade agreements essentially limited to trade in goods (Algeria, Egypt, Jordan, Lebanon, Morocco, Palestinian Authority, and Tunisia)[4]. Since 2011 negotiations are ongoing to widen existing agreements through the establishment of Deep and Comprehensive Free Trade Areas with Egypt, Jordan, Morocco and Tunisia.[5] In this context, any supplier to EU businesses that integrates internationally-recognised RBC instruments like the *Guidelines* will have a comparative advantage over those that do not. These firms can more easily address concerns about environmental, social, human rights or labour issues that may arise in the due diligence processes of MNEs assessing country and supplier risks (OECD, 2020[4]).

Various studies have also demonstrated that implementing RBC principles and standards can enhance financial performance. Empirical evidence from a study led by the OECD on 6,500 companies showed that the "social score" – a measure of a company's capacity to generate trust and loyalty with its workforce, customers and society – had a positive effect on companies' return on equity and return on assets (OECD, 2017[6]). The business case is often confirmed when looking at index performances. For example, on the Egyptian stock exchange, a comparison the between the EGX100 and the S&P EGX ESG shows that on average over the last 10 years responsible companies tend to perform better[6] (OECD, 2020[4]). A recent study analysing the impact of CSR practice on the financial performance of a sample of 61 Jordanian companies listed on the Amman stock exchange over the period 2012-2016 concluded that on average CSR had a positive impact on firms' return on assets (Al Qaisi, 2019[7]).

The COVID-19 health and economic crisis has shown that RBC can also help business build resilience and create long-term value. Businesses that observe RBC standards and implement due diligence might be in a better position to respond and recover from supply chain and operational shocks. Information from supply chain due diligence, for example on origin of raw materials, can be used to understand short- and medium-term vulnerabilities in the supply chain, and support continuity planning to manage disruptions

(OECD, 2020[8]). Applying RBC standards throughout the supply chain can reduce the negative impacts of enterprises' activities, improve the reputation of these enterprises and the locations where they operate, and decrease supply chain disruptions (OECD, 2018[9]).

Box 10.2. Rising international expectations on RBC

The financing needs for achieving the SDGs, as well as the essential role of the private sector as a driver of economic growth and job creation, have placed businesses at the centre of the global development agenda. High-level commitments from UN member states and the G20 and G7 have made it clear that RBC is a priority on the international agenda.

G20 Ministers of Labour and Employment committed in 2018 to promote due diligence and transparency in global supply chains, and encouraged businesses to consider the 2018 OECD *Due Diligence Guidance for Responsible Business Conduct*. G20 Leaders committed in 2017 to foster the implementation of labour, social and environmental standards and human rights in line with internationally recognised frameworks, including the *Guidelines*.

RBC expectations are also reflected in domestic legislation. Several countries, including the UK, Australia, France and the US, have passed laws to strengthen due diligence requirements to address supply chain and sustainability risks. RBC is also frequently referenced in trade, investment and co-operation agreements. Any company that wishes to integrate in the global economy through trade and investment must be aware that their buyers, clients and partners may have various RBC obligations. RBC is also an entry point for any company that wishes to contribute to the SDGs or achieve specific economic and sustainability outcomes (see Chapter 2).

Source: (OECD, 2019[10])

Awareness and understanding of RBC in the MENA region is growing

The notion that businesses should contribute to society is prevalent throughout the MENA region. One of the five pillars of Islam is *zakat*, an obligation of charity that is common practice among organisations and individuals in the region. A corporate philanthropy concept, *waqf*, dates back to the 11th century and is a charitable endowment under Islamic law that involves donating assets for religious or charitable purposes (Jamali, 2017[11]). While philanthropy and social investments tend to be the main form of RBC engagement by businesses in the MENA region, governments' and firms' understanding of RBC is gradually evolving towards a more comprehensive approach that looks at how core business operations affect society (OECD, 2020[4]) (OECD, 2013[12]) (OECD, 2012[13])

A survey of 638 businesses, primarily listed entities, was carried out in 2018 to understand the degree of awareness and integration of CSR/RBC practices in 18 MENA economies, including 6 of the MENA focus economies (Algeria, Egypt, Jordan, Lebanon, Morocco, Tunisia, and the Palestinian Authority)[7]. The results show that a majority of businesses surveyed (64%) integrate environmental or social considerations in some form. Among them, 31% report having a holistic strategy in place to address sustainability topics across the entire organisation and in consideration of all stakeholders (Sustainable Square, 2019[14]).

Progress on firms' awareness of and commitment to RBC is exemplified in businesses participation in the UN Global Compact Network, which supports companies to act responsibly and advance social goals. The network counts 96 companies in Egypt and 51 participants in Tunisia in 2020. Participation is lower in Jordan and Morocco; each have fewer than 25 firms in the Network (UNGC, 2020[15]). Various business associations and chambers of commerce take an active role to promote RBC in the region. In Morocco, the main business association, the *Confédération Générale des Entreprises du Maroc*, has issued a CSR label since 2006 in recognition of companies' engagement and strategic inclusion of CSR issues in operation. There are currently over 100 companies under the label.[8] The Confederation of Tunisian Citizen Enterprise launched a CSR promotion programme in 2011 and a CSR label in 2018. In Egypt, the Federation of Egyptian Industries, in cooperation with the ILO, also established a unit dedicated to CSR in 2015 to provide its members with expertise and technical assistance.

Important progress has been made in the region on advancing RBC principles in the financial sector. Stock exchanges in Amman, Casablanca, Tunis, Cairo and Alexandria are part of the Sustainable Stock Exchanges Initiative (SSEI), a UN Partnership Programme that supports enhanced firm performance on environmental, social and corporate governance issues. With the exception of *Bourse de Tunis*, all of these exchanges also provide written guidance to firms on reporting on sustainability performance (SSE, 2020[16]). Morocco's *Bourse de Casablanca*, for example, details how to promote corporate social responsibility among publicly traded companies (Bourse de Casablanca and Autorite Marocaine du Marche des Capitaux, 2017[17]). In 2018, the Amman Stock Exchange published two sustainability brochures to provide businesses with guidance on sustainability reporting and sustainable business practices.[9] At the regional level, the Hawkamah Institute for Corporate Governance and S&P Dow Jones Indices jointly launched in 2011 the S&P/Hawkamah ESG Pan Arab Index – a regional index tracking the performance of 50 stocks leading on a set of ESG criteria in Bahrain, Egypt, Jordan, Lebanon, Kuwait, Morocco, Oman, Qatar, Saudi Arabia, Tunisia, and the United Arab Emirates (S&P Dow Jones Indices, 2020[18]).

While the number of initiatives related to RBC in the MENA region has increased, they tend to be more prevalent among large business and multinational enterprises than smaller firms. RBC expectations apply to all businesses – regardless of their legal nature, size, ownership structure, or the sector of the economy in which they operate.

Important commitments towards RBC have been made

MENA governments vary substantially in their approach towards RBC. As adherents to the OECD *Guidelines for Multinational Enterprises*, Egypt, Jordan, Morocco and Tunisia have committed to support responsible business practices, including by improving domestic policies to enable RBC. Each has made a binding commitment to establish a National Contact Point to promote and help implement the *Guidelines* (see below on the status of NCPs in the four MENA economies). All four countries also participate in annual exchanges with representatives from the 50 governments that adhere to the *Guidelines* to share experiences on RBC (OECD, 2019[10]).

Most countries in the MENA region have national sustainable development strategies, which often cite RBC principles, though not always explicitly. Egypt's Sustainable Development Strategy (Vision 2030), recognises the important role of the private sector in achieving the SDGs (Government of Egypt, 2017[19]). The Palestinian National Policy Agenda prioritises creating permanent employment opportunities, ensuring a safe working environment, and environmental sustainability (Palestinian Authority, 2016[20]). Jordan's 2025 National Vision and Strategy highlights CSR goals (Government of Jordan, 2014[21]). Many MENA economies also outline social and environmental goals in investment legislation. Algeria, Egypt and Tunisia all stress the aim that investment should contribute to sustainable development in recent revisions to Investment Laws (see Chapter 3 for more details on recent legislative reforms in the MENA region).

Steps have been taken to enhance the enabling framework for RBC. Most MENA economies have notably undertaken reforms to encourage sound governance practices and increase transparency. For example, corporate governance codes have been developed in all MENA focus countries since 2005 (OECD, 2019[22]). A 2017 report by the Hawkamah Institute found that listed companies in the MENA region had significantly improved transparency and disclosure levels since 2007.[10] Important challenges persist however, notably in the disclosure of beneficial ownership and related party transactions (OECD, 2019[22]).

There is also an opportunity to enhance disclosure on environmental, social and governance aspects, which remains relatively limited in the region (Ould Daoud Ellili, 2020[23]).

Some MENA governments have also supported awareness-raising forums on CSR. Egypt has held annual CSR forums since 2015 to integrate efforts by the government, business community and civil society organisations to promote CSR in Egypt (OECD, 2020[4]). The Lebanese government also supports a business network to promote sustainability practices among private sector firms in the country. Such initiatives could be scaled up and leveraged to support wide dissemination of internationally-recognised RBC standards such as the *Guidelines* and OECD due diligence instruments.

MENA economies face challenges in implementing RBC principles and standards

While nearly all MENA governments recognise sustainability as a development objective, more could be done to create an environment that fosters a positive contribution of the private sector to development objectives. This section highlights areas where MENA governments could focus their efforts to improve the enabling environment for RBC and support implementation of RBC principles and standards by businesses.

Advancing human and labour rights

States have a primary duty to protect against human rights abuses. At the same time, businesses are expected to respect human rights independently of the state's ability or willingness to fulfil its human rights obligations. The eight MENA focus economies are parties to most of the core UN human rights treaties, although only Morocco has ratified all core instruments.[11] International organisations continue to raise concerns in particular about the protection of human rights defenders in all of the MENA focus economies. Specific concerns common to all MENA focus economies include the repression of peaceful protests and online dissent, including arrests and prosecution of activists (Amnesty International, 2020[24]) (OECD, 2018[25]).

Human rights defenders play a critical role in the due diligence process, in enabling companies to understand the concerns of stakeholders that may be adversely impacted by business operations. Affected stakeholders include workers, local communities, unions, journalists, activists or consumers and have to be engaged taking into account their particularities and pre-existing vulnerabilities.

Every country in the region could do more to ensure that workers and civil society organisations can take part in policy design and due diligence processes. Creating an environment where stakeholders are empowered to express their views and actively participate in policy design is essential for RBC. The *Guidelines* recommend that enterprises participate in private or multi-stakeholder initiatives and social dialogue on responsible supply chain management. For human rights impacts in particular, the *Guidelines* recommend that companies consult and engage workers, workers' representatives and trade unions to gather information on adverse impacts and risks. Where directly consulting with stakeholders is not possible, reasonable alternatives such as consulting credible, independent expert resources, including human rights defenders, trade unions and civil society groups could be considered (OECD, 2018[25]).

Stronger labour rights are often associated with higher foreign investment (Busse, Nunnenkamp and Spatareanu, 2011[26]) (Kucera, 2002[27]). Multinational companies may shy away from investing in countries with low labour standards because of reputational risks and to fulfil international standards on RBC. Most MENA focus economies have ratified all or seven of the eight fundamental ILO conventions – which cover fundamental principles and rights at work, such as the right to collective bargaining and elimination of forced labour – and three of the four of the governance conventions – which cover labour inspections, employment policy, and tripartite consultations (Table 10.1). These commitments show MENA governments' intent to align legal frameworks with international standards.

There are concerns about the application of these standards in practice, however, including complaints raised to the ILO, primarily for alleged violations of Freedom of Association rights. In Algeria for example, there is an active complaint by a trade union in the energy sector alleging "a systematic crackdown on its officers and members", and failure of the government to secure their trade union rights (ILO, 2018[28]). Other cases raised to the ILO over the past decade include allegations by five trade unions in Egypt of "serious and systematic violations of the right to freedom of association", and claims in Jordan that the country's labour legislation and regulations are "not in conformity with the principles of freedom of association" (ILO, 2015[29]) (ILO, 2012[30]). International human rights organisations report that freedom of association of workers has worsened in Egypt following amendments to the Trade Unions Law in 2017. Violent dispersal of trade union and labour demonstrations is common in many countries in the region (Amnesty International, 2020[24]).

Table 10.1. Ratifications of ILO Conventions

Country (member since)	Fundamental (8)	Governance (4)	Technical (178)	Total (190)
Algeria (1962)	8	3	49	60
Egypt (1936)	8	3	53	64
Jordan (1956)	7	3	16	26
Lebanon (1948)	7	2	42	51
Libya (1952)	8	2	19	29
Morocco (1956)	7	4	54	65
Tunisia (1956)	8	3	52	63

Note: Palestinian Authority not included. ILO Conventions are all legally binding international treaties that may be ratified by ILO member states. If it is ratified, a Convention generally comes into force for that country one year after the date of ratification. The ILO Governing Body has identified eight "fundamental" Conventions, covering subjects that are considered to be fundamental principles and rights at work, and has also designated another four Conventions as governance (or priority) instruments, thereby encouraging member States to ratify them because of their importance for the functioning of the international labour standards system. Technical Conventions are also legally binding once ratified and encompasses all of the other international labour standards in the ILO scope of work.
Source: (ILO, 1919-2020[31])

Supporting industry initiatives

Ensuring wide dissemination and active promotion of internationally recognised RBC due diligence instruments such as OECD *Due Diligence Guidance for Responsible Business Conduct* and OECD sector-specific due diligence guidance can help promote a common understand among businesses, governments and stakeholders as to what RBC entails. RBC due diligence guidance provide practical support to enterprises on the implementation of RBC principles and standards. Implementing these recommendations can help enterprises avoid and address adverse impacts related to workers, human rights, the environment, bribery, consumers and corporate governance that may be associated with their operations, supply chains and other business relationships.

Such measures are often more easily implemented and effective if undertaken collectively. This is particularly true to address issues that cannot be solved by one actor alone. For example, poor business practices among buyers in the value chain can play a role in decisions to require excessive or forced overtime and subcontract illegally (OECD, 2020[8]). A 2017 survey of 1,454 companies by the ILO highlighted the role that buyers can play, by imposing extreme pressure on suppliers' price quotes. Across all sectors, 39% of suppliers reported having accepted orders whose price did not allow them to cover their production costs. The textile sector was an outlier in this survey with such an outcome reported for 52% of suppliers (ILO, 2017[32]). Practices including abrupt suspensions of contracts and cancellation of orders had significant effects on workers globally during the COVID-19 crisis (OECD, 2020[8]).

The garment sector is an important driver of growth in some of the MENA focus economies and provides an example of how industry players can organise themselves and collaborate to promote RBC. For example, the Better Work programme – an ILO/IFC partnership that aims to improve working conditions and boost the competitiveness of apparel businesses – is active in Egypt and Jordan. In 2019, the Better Cotton Initiative (BCI), the largest cotton sustainability programme in the world, launched a pilot programme in Egypt in partnership with the Cotton Egypt Association to create a sustainable supply chain supporting the welfare of cotton workers and the environment. BCI also has members in Tunisia.

MENA governments could benefit from convening, engaging and supporting such initiatives. They could also leverage them to actively disseminate guidance on RBC tailored to the specific needs of the industry, such as the OECD *Due Diligence Guidance for Responsible Supply Chains in the Garment and Footwear Sector* (OECD/FAO, 2016[33]).

Promoting RBC standards in the garment and footwear sector, where women often represent a large majority of the workforce, can go a long way in promoting gender equality, which remains a challenge in the MENA region. Gender equality can generate positive economic outcomes (see Chapter 2). An Egyptian factory participating in a programme initiated by Levi Strauss to build a network of better-run factories reported that the programme had a four-to-one return on investment, largely because of interventions focused on women (Fry, 2017[34]).

RBC challenges are not limited to one particular sector and examples in the garment and footwear sector could be replicated and expanded to other industries, including those covered by OECD sectoral due diligence instruments. These include, the OECD *Due Diligence Guidance for Responsible Supply Chains of Minerals from Conflict-Affected and High-Risk Areas*, the OECD-FAO *Guidance on Responsible Agricultural Supply Chains*, and the *Due Diligence Guidance for Meaningful Stakeholder Engagement in the Extractive Sector*.

Improving environmental protection

The *Guidelines* call on enterprises to take account the need to protect the environment. This entails, among other responsibilities, establishing and maintaining appropriate environmental management systems; assessing and addressing the environmental impacts associated with the processes, goods and services of the enterprise over their full life cycle; improving environmental performance; and being transparent about environmental impacts and risks. Governments should set clear expectations to business enterprises in this regard.

MENA governments have taken steps to promote protection of the environment and natural resources. Several countries offer tax incentives or grants to investment projects that advance environmental protects. For example, Tunisia offers firms in recycling and waste treatment corporate income tax rates of less than half the standard rate, and Libya and Algeria grant tax holidays to investments that preserve the environment and protect natural resources. Egypt, Jordan, the Palestinian Authority and Tunisia also offer fiscal or financial incentives for investment in renewable energy (See Chapter 7 on Investment Incentives).

There is scope for further progress on environmental protection, evidenced by the relatively low ranking of some MENA economies according to the 2020 Yale Environmental Performance Index, which ranks 180 countries on environmental health and ecosystem vitality. The index provides a gauge at a national scale of how close countries are to established environmental policy targets. Jordan (48) ranks top of its peers, followed by Tunisia (71), Lebanon (78), Algeria (84), Egypt (94), and Morocco (100) (Yale Center for Environmental Law and Policy, 2018[35]). High-energy emitting industries, including fossil fuels and mining, remain an important driver of investment in Egypt, Algeria, Libya, Morocco and Tunisia.

Tackling corruption

An important aspect of RBC is fighting bribery and corruption. Corruption discourages investment, increases inequality, undermines the trust in governments and erodes the rule of law. Further reforms are required to lower the incidence of corruption in the public and private sector in the MENA region. The MENA focus economies rank among the bottom 50% on international indices measuring perceptions of corruption. None of the focus economies score above a passing grade according to Transparency International's Corruption Perception Index, and all but Jordan receive a negative score on the World Bank's Control of Corruption Index (see Chapter 11 on Integrity for more on progress in curbing corruption in the region and remaining challenges).

Promoting policy coherence on RBC

Despite important commitments made towards RBC, MENA countries could do more to promote and implement RBC standards, including by developing an overarching framework defining objectives and actions (through National Action Plans), leading by example in their own economic activities, and increasing awareness among business communities.

National action plans can help strengthen RBC

Business operations can affect society through a spectrum of policy areas, including labour and human rights, environment, anti-corruption and consumer interests. To strengthen coherence among all relevant laws and policies relating to RBC, many governments have developed National Action Plans on Business and Human Rights (NAP). NAPs articulate government priorities and can promote coordination among state agencies. The UN recommends that all governments develop NAPs, and that they be updated regularly (OHCHR, 2020[36]).

In the MENA region, only Morocco and Jordan have adopted or are in the processes of developing NAPs. Morocco included a chapter on business and human rights in its national Action Plan for Democracy and Human Rights 2018-2022. It encourages businesses to adopt policies to promote human rights and outlines plans to raise awareness and build capacity among businesses on the subject. The government aims to develop a full NAP in line with international standards on RBC (Government of Morocco, 2018[37]).

Jordan also includes a section on business and human rights in its Comprehensive National Plan for Human Rights 2016-2025. The Kingdom commits to review legislation related to labour contracts and establishment of unions, and to implement awareness programmes for the public and private sector on environmental sustainability (Government of Jordan, 2016[38]). The government said it developed the plan in cooperation with civil society institutions and professional associations in line with international best practices (Jordan Times, 2016[39]).

Indeed a key element of the NAP process is multi-stakeholder engagement. Greater participation of stakeholders in policy design and implementation leads to better targeted and more effective policies. Ensuring buy-in from a variety of actors is essential to address complex and systemic challenges that may lead to negative impacts of business operations.

Governments should implement RBC in their own economic activities

When the state acts as an economic actor (e.g. as an employer, procurer, shareholder, or through the enterprises it owns or controls), governments are expected to not merely behave responsibly, but to exemplify RBC in their own role in the economy. This is a question of policy coherence as well as credibility, as the state should not ask less of companies that are closely associated with it than it asks of private businesses.

State-owned enterprises (SOEs) play a fundamental role in MENA economies. They operate across a wide range of sectors, including extractive industries, electricity and gas, telecommunications, finance, transportation, as well as manufacturing and property development. In the MENA region as a whole, governments are majority shareholders in over a third of the region's 100 largest companies listed on stock exchanges.[12] The state is a minority shareholder in an additional third (OECD, 2019[22]).

Ensuring that SOEs operate in accordance with good governance practices and RBC principles is fundamental to encourage their positive contribution to society and convey political commitment to RBC. MENA countries could consider strengthening RBC considerations in policies that apply to SOEs. This is all the more important as like any private enterprise, SOEs may have adverse impacts on a range of human rights, social and environmental issues. Likely impacts of SOEs in the region include environmental, health and safety issues, as well as treatment of workers.

Governments in the region could, as a first step, consider communicating in a clear and transparent manner the RBC policies that their SOEs have in place. The *Guidelines*, together with the OECD *Guidelines on Corporate Governance of State-Owned Enterprises* and the UN *Guiding Principles*, provide a comprehensive framework for addressing RBC in SOEs (Box 9.4) (OECD, 2015[40]).

Box 10.3. SOE Guidelines: provisions on stakeholder relations and responsible business

The OECD *Guidelines on Corporate Governance of State-Owned Enterprises* (SOE Guidelines) outline good practice standards for enhancing engagement with stakeholders on SOE ownership. The text of Chapter V on stakeholder relations and responsible business is as below:

The state ownership policy should fully recognise SOEs' responsibilities towards stakeholders and request that SOEs report on their relations with stakeholders. It should make clear any expectations the state has in respect of responsible business conduct by SOEs.

- Governments, the state ownership entities and SOEs themselves should recognise and respect stakeholders' rights established by law or through mutual agreements.
- Listed or large SOEs should report on stakeholder relations, including where relevant and feasible with regard to labour, creditors and affected communities.
- The boards of SOEs should develop, implement, monitor and communicate internal controls, ethics and compliance programmes or measures, including those which contribute to preventing fraud and corruption. They should be based on country norms, in conformity with international commitments and apply to the SOE and its subsidiaries.
- SOEs should observe high standards of responsible business conduct. Expectations established by the government in this regard should be publicly disclosed and mechanisms for their implementation be clearly established.
- SOEs should not be used as vehicles for financing political activities. SOEs themselves should not make political campaign contributions.

Source: (OECD, 2015[40])

Beyond its role as a shareholder of companies, MENA governments also play a key economic role in public procurement of goods, services and works. In the MENA region as a whole, governments spend approximately 18% of their GDP on public procurement (OECD, 2016[41]). If used strategically, public procurement policies and processes offer an important avenue for governments to incentivise RBC. Governments could use RBC criteria, such as environmental impact or labour standards, in the tender process, selecting partners that follow RBC standards. Several of the MENA focus economies have taken steps to integrate non-financial considerations into their public procurement processes. For example, Morocco requires that public procurement comply with the rules for the protection of the environment. Tunisia's public procurement rules provide that tender specification should consider environmental and social aspects and take into account global sustainable goals (OECD, 2016[41]).

Strengthening MENA National Contact Points

National Contact Points for Responsible Business Conduct (NCPs for RBC) have a twofold mandate: to promote the OECD *Guidelines for Multinational Enterprises*, and related due diligence guidance, and to handle cases (referred to as "specific instances") as a non-judicial grievance mechanism. To date, 50 governments, all adherents to the *Guidelines* and thus including Egypt, Jordan, Morocco and Tunisia, have an NCP for RBC. All governments adhering to the Guidelines have a legal obligation to set up an NCP. Governments have flexibility in how they set up their NCP, provided all NCPs meet basic criteria laid out in the Procedural Guidance to the *Guidelines* (Box 9.4) (OECD, 2011[2]).

Box 10.4. Structures and criteria for National Contact Points

Core criteria laid out in the Guidelines for NCPs are visibility, accessibility, transparency and accountability (OECD, 2011[2]). The *Guidelines* also spell out guiding principles for the handling of specific instances, namely impartiality, predictability, equitability and compatibility with the *Guidelines*. Finally, the *Guidelines* contain a number of additional criteria with regard to the practical organisation of the NCP and functioning of the NCP, in particular:

- Have sufficient human and financial resources;
- Develop and maintain relations and confidence with social partners and stakeholders;
- Be headed by a senior person;
- Collaborate and engage in peer learning with other NCPs;
- Report to the Investment Committee.

In practice, four main types of NCP structures have been set up by adhering governments:

- Single agency NCP: The NCP is composed of one individual in a single ministry, or by a group of individuals belonging to the same service in the same ministry.
- Inter-agency NCP: The NCP is composed of a group of representatives from several ministries or government agencies.
- Multipartite NCP: The NCP is composed of a group of government officials and stakeholder representatives.

Expert-based NCPs: The NCP is composed of experts who are appointed by, but external to, the government.

Source: (OECD, 2011[2]), (OECD, 2011[42])

NCPs can build relations with and involve stakeholders in a variety of ways. Multipartite NCPs include stakeholder representatives in the main institutional body of the NCP, whereas other NCPs may create an advisory body composed of stakeholders' representatives that provide advice and support to the NCP. Inclusion of stakeholders in NCP structures has been shown to be a major factor for building and retaining the necessary relationship of confidence between the NCP and stakeholders (OECD, 2019[43]).

Table 10.2. Key organisation and activity data for MENA NCPs

	Structure	Location	Active website	Dedicated budget	Promotional events	Cases since adhesion	RoP online	Number of staff	Full time staff	Turnover	Dedicated budget	Attended NCP meetings	Peer review
Egypt	Single agency, no advisory body	Formerly: Ministry of Investment and international cooperation	No	No	0	0	No	0	0	Yes	No	Yes	No
Jordan	Single agency, no advisory body	Investment promotion agency	No	No data	No data	0	No	No data	No data	No data	No data	No	No
Morocco	Inter-agency, no advisory body	Investment promotion agency	Yes	Yes	16	4	Yes	2	0	No	Yes	Yes	No
Tunisia	Multipartite	Ministry of Development, Investment and International Cooperation	No	No	2	0	No	2	1	Yes	No	Yes	Committed 2022

Source: NCP annual reports to the OECD and OECD case database.

Table 10.2 outlines MENA NCPs' organisation and activity in 2019. In terms of structure, the four MENA NCPs are fairly diverse, with three different models represented (single agency, inter-agency, multipartite), though only Tunisia's NCP includes stakeholders in its structure. The Tunisian NCP was re-established in 2018 after a period of hiatus and the composition of its multi-partite structure is still under construction, as it is currently in the process of inviting relevant organisations to become members.

All MENA NCPs are either located in an investment promotion agency (IPA) or in a ministry responsible for investment or economic affairs. The proximity of some NCPs with investment promotion portfolios has sometimes raised questions regarding the perception of impartiality of these NCPs. Stakeholders have questioned whether conflicts of interest might emerge between, for example, the NCP's role in handling a case, and the wider role of the IPA or ministry to promote investment within the country (OECD, 2019, p. 5[44]). It is therefore important that governments clearly delineate boundaries between the work of the NCP and investment promotion activities (See Chapter 6 for more details on MENA IPAs' functions and activities).

Of note is the low level of activity across NCPs of the MENA region, except for the Moroccan NCP. As indicated, one of the main activities in the NCP mandate is to disseminate and promote the *Guidelines* and related due diligence guidance with businesses and other stakeholders. This can be done in many ways, including distributing promotional materials or responding to enquiries from the public about RBC. To maximise their promotional impact, NCPs also regularly organise informational or training events on various RBC themes, or make presentations at such events organised by other actors. For example, in February 2020, the Moroccan NCP organised an information workshop for professionals from the textile sector on the OECD Due Diligence Guidance in the Garment on Footwear Sector (NCP for RBC Morocco, 2020[45]). Other MENA NCPs have been largely inactive as regards to NCP promotion in recent years. NCP cases are also low in the region, as only the Moroccan NCP has handled cases (4) since its creation.

This low level of activity may partly be explained by the low level of resources available to MENA NCPs. While the Moroccan NCP has a dedicated budget that allows it to maintain a good level of activity, other MENA NCPs have to request funding for all their activities from the general budget of the ministry or agency where they are located. Low numbers of staff, high reliance on part-time staff and high turnover have been flagged as issues limiting the activity of NCPs across the entire NCP network. Turnover in particular prevents the building of long-term relations with stakeholders, damages institutional memory, and diminishes the expertise available to the NCP, as incoming staff typically have to be trained for several months before becoming fully operational.

Given the small number of cases handled by the MENA NCPs, there is little data to analyse the extent to which they comply with the *Guiding Principles* for the handling of specific instances (impartiality, equitability, predictability and compatibility with the *Guidelines*). In terms of predictability, it should be noted that only the Moroccan NCP has made its Rules of Procedure publicly available. For all other NCPs, submitters and companies involved in cases do not know in advance how their case will be handled, thereby reducing predictability. As indicated above, the location of all MENA NCPs in IPAs or ministries responsible for investment and other economic affairs without clear separation from the investment promotion portfolio may diminish the perception of impartiality of potential case submitters.

In terms of visibility and transparency, only the Moroccan NCP has an active, state-of-the-art website.[13] Other NCPs either have no website or very limited information available.

The interrelated challenges highlighted above (resources, low level of activity, low number of cases, limited visibility, reduced relations with stakeholders) are not unique to MENA NCPs, but seem to affect MENA NCPs particularly severely, the Moroccan NCP being a notable exception. Governments should ensure that NCPs have the resources and support they need, but also that NCP structures are conducive to stakeholder confidence (OECD, 2019[44]).

NCP strengthening may occur through active participation in peer learning activities offered by the OECD or by other NCPs, or by undergoing a peer review. Egypt and Morocco attended both NCP network meetings organised at the OECD in 2019, while Tunisia attended one, and Jordan none. In terms of peer learning activities organised by NCPs themselves, the Moroccan NCP organised and hosted a peer learning workshop in Rabat in October 2019 on 'Managing specific instances in the context of the OECD Guidelines', also led by the Consensus-Building Institute (CBI) and attended several peer learning events organised by other NCPs. The Egyptian and Tunisian NCPs attended peer learning events organised by other NCPs, and no data exists for the Jordanian NCP. Finally, in 2017, the OECD Secretariat and the Moroccan NCP conducted a peer-learning mission with the Jordanian NCP.

There seems to be willingness on the part of MENA NCPs to engage in peer learning, but resources (notably travel budget) may be a limiting factor. Regarding peer reviews, no MENA NCP has to date undergone a peer review, though Tunisia has committed to having its NCP undergo one in 2022. As adherents to the OECD *Guidelines*, the governments of Egypt, Jordan, Morocco and Tunisia should commit to having their NCPs peer reviewed by 2023.

References

Al Qaisi, F. (2019), "Corporate social responsibility effect on firms financial performance in Jordan", *International Journal of Monetary Economics and Finance*, Vol. 12/4, pp. 325-342, http://dx.doi.org/10.1504/IJMEF.2019.101942. [7]

Amnesty International (2020), *Human rights in the Middle East and North Africa: Review of 2019*, Amnesty International, London, https://www.amnesty.org/en/documents/mde01/1357/2020/en/ (accessed on 1 June 2020). [24]

Bourse de Casablanca and Autorite Marocaine du Marche des Capitaux (2017), *Guide sur la Responsabilité Sociétale des Entreprises et le reporting ESG*, https://www.casablanca-bourse.com/BourseWeb/UserFiles/File/2017/Mai/Guide%20RSEESGVersion%20soumise%20consultation.pdf (accessed on 19 May 2020). [17]

Busse, M., P. Nunnenkamp and M. Spatareanu (2011), "Foreign direct investment and labour rights: a panel analysis of bilateral FDI flows", *Applied Economics Letters*, Vol. 18/2, pp. 149-152, http://dx.doi.org/10.1080/13504850903559500. [26]

European Commission (2015), *Trade for All. Towards a more responsible trade and investment policy*, http://trade.ec.europa.eu/doclib/docs/2015/october/tradoc_153846.pdf. [5]

Fry, E. (2017), "Can Levi's Make Life Better for Garment Workers?", *Fortune*, https://fortune.com/2017/09/08/levis-change-the-world/ (accessed on 13 October 2020). [34]

Government of Egypt (2017), *Sustainable Development Strategy: Egypt Vision 2030*, http://sdsegypt2030.com/economic-dimension/economic-development-pillar/?lang=en&lang=en. [19]

Government of Jordan (2016), *Comprehensive National Plan for Human Rights: For the years 2016-2025*, http://jordanembassy.or.id/_2file_obj/pdf/Comprehensive-National-Plan-for-Human-Rights.pdf (accessed on 29 May 2020). [38]

Government of Jordan (2014), *Jordan 2025: A National Vision and Strategy*, http://inform.gov.jo/Portals/0/Report%20PDFs/0.%20General/jo2025part1.pdf (accessed on 29 May 2020). [21]

Government of Morocco (2018), *Le plan d'action national en matière de démocratie et des droits de l'Homme (2018-2021)*, http://didh.gov.ma/fr/planification-et-suivi/politiques_publiques/le-plan-daction-national-en-matiere-de-democratie-et-des-droits-de-lhomme-2018-2021/ (accessed on 29 May 2020). [37]

ILO (2018), *Interim Report No 386, June 2018, Case No 3210 (Algeria) - Complaint date: 26-APR-16 - Active*, https://www.ilo.org/dyn/normlex/en/f?p=1000:50002:0::NO:50002:P50002_COMPLAINT_TEXT_ID:3950204 (accessed on 19 May 2020). [28]

ILO (2017), "Purchasing practices and working conditions in global supply chains: Global Survey results", *INWORK Issue Brief* 10, https://www.ilo.org/wcmsp5/groups/public/---ed_protect/---protrav/---travail/documents/publication/wcms_556336.pdf. [32]

ILO (2015), *Definitive Report - Report No 375, June 2015; Case no 3025 (Egypt) - Complaint date: 17-May-13 - Closed*, https://www.ilo.org/dyn/normlex/en/f?p=1000:50002:0::NO:50002:P50002_COMPLAINT_TEXT_ID:3241132 (accessed on 19 May 2020). [29]

ILO (2012), *Case No 2977 (Jordan) - Complaint date: 22-May-12*, https://www.ilo.org/dyn/normlex/en/f?p=1000:50001:0::NO::P50001_COMPLAINT_FILE_ID:3074665:NO (accessed on 19 May 2020). [30]

ILO (1919-2020), *International Labour Organisation Conventions and Recommendations*, https://www.ilo.org/dyn/normlex/en/ (accessed on 19 May 2020). [31]

Jamali, D. (2017), *Comparative Perspectives on Global Corporate Social Responsibility*, IGI Global, Hershey PA, USA. [11]

Jordan Times (2016), "King urges full implementation of human rights plan", *Jordan Times*, https://www.jordantimes.com/news/local/king-urges-full-implementation-human-rights-plan (accessed on 29 May 2020). [39]

Kucera, D. (2002), "Core labour standards and foreign direct investment", *International Labour Review*, Vol. 141/1-2, pp. 31-69, http://dx.doi.org/10.1111/j.1564-913x.2002.tb00230.x. [27]

NCP for RBC Morocco (2020), *Seminar on due diligence in the garment and footware sector*, https://pcnmaroc.ma/en/ncp-news/seminar-on-the-due-diligence-in-the-garment-and-footwear-sector-on-february-26th-2020/. [45]

OECD (2020), *COVID-19 and responsible business conduct*, OECD Policy Responses to Coronavirus (COVID-19), http://www.oecd.org/coronavirus/policy-responses/covid-19-and-responsible-business-conduct-02150b06/ (accessed on 20 July 2020). [8]

OECD (2020), *OECD Investment Policy Reviews: Egypt*, OECD Publishing, Paris, https://doi.org/10.1787/9f9c589a-en. [4]

OECD (2019), *Annual Report on the OECD Guidelines for Multinational Enterprises 2018*, OECD, https://www.oecd.org/daf/inv/mne/annualreportsontheguidelines.htm (accessed on 29 May 2020). [10]

OECD (2019), *Corporate governance in MENA: Building a Framework for Competitiveness and Growth*, OECD Publishing, https://doi.org/10.1787/20776535. [22]

OECD (2019), *Guide for National Contact Points on Structures and Activities*, http://mneguidelines.oecd.org/Guide-for-National-Contact-Points-on-Structures-and-Activities.pdf. [43]

OECD (2019), *Progress report on National Contact Points for Responsible Business Conduct*, http://www.oecd.org/mcm/documents/NCPs%20-%20CMIN(2019)7%20-%20EN.pdf. [44]

OECD (2018), *OECD Due Diligence Guidance for Responsible Business Conduct*, OECD, Paris, https://www.oecd.org/investment/due-diligence-guidance-for-responsible-business-conduct.htm (accessed on 1 June 2020). [25]

OECD (2018), *OECD Due Diligence Guidance for Responsible Supply Chains in the Garment and Footwear Sector*, OECD Publishing, Paris, https://dx.doi.org/10.1787/9789264290587-en. [9]

OECD (2017), *Responsible business conduct for institutional investors: Key considerations for due diligence under the OECD Guidelines for Multinational Enterprises*, https://mneguidelines.oecd.org/RBC-for-Institutional-Investors.pdf. [6]

OECD (2016), *Stocktaking report on MENA Public Procurement Systems: MENA-OECD Network on Public Procurement*, OECD, https://www.oecd.org/governance/ethics/Stocktaking_MENA_Public_Procurement_Systems.pdf (accessed on 19 May 2020). [41]

OECD (2015), *OECD Guidelines on Corporate Governance of State-Owned Enterprises, 2015 Edition*, OECD Publishing, Paris, https://dx.doi.org/10.1787/9789264244160-en. [40]

OECD (2015), *Policy Framework for Investment, 2015 Edition*, OECD Publishing, Paris, https://dx.doi.org/10.1787/9789264208667-en. [1]

OECD (2013), *OECD Investment Policy Reviews: Jordan 2013*, OECD Investment Policy Reviews, OECD Publishing, Paris, https://dx.doi.org/10.1787/9789264202276-en. [12]

OECD (2012), *OECD Investment Policy Reviews: Tunisia 2012*, OECD Investment Policy Reviews, OECD Publishing, Paris, https://dx.doi.org/10.1787/9789264179172-en. [13]

OECD (2011), *Decision of the Council on the OECD Guidelines for Multinational Enterprises C/M(2011)11/PROV*, https://legalinstruments.oecd.org/en/instruments/OECD-LEGAL-0307. [42]

OECD (2011), *Declaration and Decisions on International Investment and Multinational Enterprises, 2011 Edition*, OECD, Paris, https://www.oecd.org/investment/investment-policy/oecddeclarationanddecisions.htm (accessed on 12 May 2020). [3]

OECD (2011), *OECD Guidelines for Multinational Enterprises, 2011 Edition*, OECD Publishing, https://doi.org/10.1787/9789264115415-en (accessed on 12 May 2020). [2]

OECD/FAO (2016), *OECD-FAO Guidance for Responsible Agricultural Supply Chains*, OECD Publishing, https://doi.org/10.1787/9789264251052-en. [33]

OHCHR (2020), *State national action plans on Business and Human Rights*, United Nations Office of the High Commissioner on Human Rights, https://www.ohchr.org/EN/Issues/Business/Pages/NationalActionPlans.aspx (accessed on 29 May 2020). [36]

Ould Daoud Ellili, N. (2020), "Environmental, Social, and Governance Disclosure, Ownership Structure and Cost of Capital: Evidence from the UAE", *Sustainability*, Vol. 12/18, p. 7706, http://dx.doi.org/10.3390/su12187706. [23]

Palestinian Authority (2016), *State of Palestine: 2017-22 National Policy Agenda*, https://planipolis.iiep.unesco.org/sites/planipolis/files/ressources/palestine_draft_final_npa.pdf (accessed on 19 May 2020). [20]

S&P Dow Jones Indices (2020), "S&P/Hawkamah ESG Indices methodology". [18]

SSE (2020), *Sustainable Stock Exchange Initiative*, https://sseinitiative.org/exchanges-filter-search/ (accessed on 19 May 2020). [16]

Sustainable Square (2019), "The 2018 State of Sustainability and CSR in the MENA region", https://sustainablesquare.com/wp-content/uploads/2019/05/2018-STATE-OF-SUSTAINABILITY-AND-CSR-IN-THE-MENA-REGION.pdf. [14]

UNGC (2020), *Our Participants | UN Global Compact*, United National Global Compact, https://www.unglobalcompact.org/what-is-gc/participants/search?utf8=%E2%9C%93&search%5Bkeywords%5D=&search%5Bsort_field%5D=&search%5Bsort_direction%5D=asc (accessed on 19 May 2020). [15]

Yale Center for Environmental Law and Policy (2018), *Environmental Performance Index 2018*, https://epi.envirocenter.yale.edu/epi-report-2018/executive-summary (accessed on 19 May 2020). [35]

Notes

[1] OECD RBC Due Diligence instruments are: the OECD Due Diligence Guidance for Responsible Supply Chains of Minerals from Conflict-Affected and High-Risk Areas, the OECD-FAO Guidance on Responsible Agricultural Supply Chains, the Due Diligence Guidance for Meaningful Stakeholder Engagement in the Extractive Sector, the OECD Due Diligence Guidance for Responsible Supply Chains in the Garment and Footwear Sector and the OECD Due Diligence Guidance for Responsible Business Conduct.

[2] The UK is the seventh largest investor to the eight focus economies based on announced greenfield investment between 2003-2019. It is the largest foreign direct investor in Egypt, based on FDI inflows

[3] In addition to the examples listed, EU Directive 2014/95/EU on non-financial disclosure requires that certain companies disclose non-financial and diversity information, and encourages businesses to rely on relevant frameworks such as the Guidelines to provide this information. See: https://eur-lex.europa.eu/legal-content/EN/TXT/?uri=CELEX%3A32014L0095

[4] For a complete list of Euro-Mediterranean Association Agreements, see: https://eur-lex.europa.eu/legal-content/EN/TXT/?uri=LEGISSUM:r14104

[5] For an overview of FTA and other trade negotiations, see: https://trade.ec.europa.eu/doclib/docs/2006/december/tradoc_118238.pdf

[6] The Egyptian stock exchange tracks 8 indices, namely the EGX30, EGX50 EWI, EGX20 Capped, EGX70, EGX100, the Banks Sector Index, the Nile Index and the S&P EGX ESG. The rationale for comparing the S&P EGX ESG with the EGX100 is that it is includes a broader range of companies both in terms of sector and size. The EGX100 combines constituents of the EGX30 and EGX70. In addition, the list of current constituents indicated that as of today, all the 30 constituents of the S&P EGX ESG are also constituents of the EGX100. Therefore, the S&P EGX ESG as it stands today could be understood as a selection of the 30 best performing companies in terms of ESG among the 100 companies listed in the EGX100. By comparison, the ESG30 can be understood as the top 30 companies by liquidity and activity among the 100 listed in the EGX100.

[7] The survey included business organisations from the United Arab Emirates, the Kingdom of Saudi Arabia, Egypt, Morocco, Tunisia, Algeria, Qatar, Oman, Kuwait, Lebanon, Bahrain Jordan, Mauritania, Yemen, Libya, Iraq, Palestinian Authority and Sudan. The survey results are based on the responses of 638 business organisations operating in 16 sectors, with 71% of listed-companies and 84% are privately-owned. Respondents were operating in the following sector: finance and banking, manufacturing, media and telecommunication, food and beverage, oil and gas, tourism, retail, personal household goods, construction, healthcare, transport and logistics, services, automotive, chemicals, utilities and conglomerate.

[8] For more information, see: http://rse.cgem.ma/label-rse.php

[9] For more information on the Sustainable Stock Exchanges Initiative, see: https://sseinitiative.org/stock-exchange/ase/

[10] The study compared several categories of disclosure, including disclosure of non-financial information, among the 50 largest and most liquid companies listed on 11 MENA markets: Bahrain, Egypt, Jordan, Lebanon, Kuwait, Morocco, Oman, Qatar, Saudi Arabia, Tunisia and UAE.

[11] The nine core international human rights instruments cover civil, political, economic, social and cultural rights; children's rights; rights of persons with disabilities; elimination of discrimination by race and against women; elimination of torture and other cruel, inhuman or degrading treatment; protection of rights of migrant workers and families; and protection against enforced disappearance. The full list of core international human rights treaties is available at www.ohchr.org/EN/ProfessionalInterest/Pages/CoreInstruments.aspx

[12] Figures for MENA governments' ownership of publicly-listed firms covers the wider MENA region, that is Algeria, Bahrain, Djibouti, Egypt, Iraq, Jordan, Kuwait, Lebanon, Libya, Mauritania, Morocco, Oman, Palestinian Authority, Qatar, Saudi Arabia, Tunisia, United Arab Emirates and Yemen (OECD, 2019[22]).

[13] See https://www.pcnmaroc.ma/.

11 Integrity for sustainable investment

This chapter explores how the adoption and promotion of anti-corruption and integrity measures by MENA governments and the private sector can contribute to more sustainable investment, and in turn inclusive economic development. It reviews the link between corruption, integrity and investment and analyses corruption risks and occurrence across the investment process. To advance the integrity agenda, MENA governments should enhance the connection between investment and anti-corruption frameworks and strategies at the domestic level and rely further on international conventions and instruments on anti-corruption. The private sector also has a central role to play in the fight against corruption.

Summary and policy considerations

Enhancing integrity for investment is of utmost importance for MENA economies. Integrity in business and transparency are critical to attract quality investment and advance sustainable development. Despite variations across the MENA economies covered in this report (MENA focus economies), corruption perception levels remain high in the region, negatively affecting investors' confidence and the business environment. In recent years, corruption has progressively moved to the forefront of reform agendas in the region: new legislation and national strategies have been conceived in a number of economies, notably in Morocco and Tunisia, and specialised anti-corruption institutions have emerged, for example in Jordan. However, corruption remains a prevalent issue, as demonstrated by the large-scale protests that took place in the past year in Lebanon and Algeria, and is a clear threat to the political stability, economic development and social cohesion of MENA economies.

Governments have a variety of policy options and strategies to curb corruption across the investment process. Yet most MENA focus economies so far have addressed the objectives of integrity and sustainable investment separately. Some governments have actively pursued policies to promote and facilitate investment in an effort to generate jobs, revenue and productive growth, among other objectives. Several focus economies have also reinforced their legal and institutional anti-corruption framework recently. But the links between integrity and sustainable investment call for a more holistic approach in both the policy and the institutional framework. Investment and anti-corruption agencies and policy-makers need to coordinate more closely to advance their respective agendas in a mutually reinforcing manner.

MENA governments could rely further on anti-corruption instruments and standards adopted at the international and regional levels, and should ensure progressive convergence of their national regulatory framework to these instruments. In particular, the United Nations *Convention against Corruption* (UNCAC), ratified by all of the MENA focus economies, requires the establishment of a comprehensive strategy to prevent and combat corruption. The OECD *Convention on Combatting Bribery of Foreign Public Officials in International Business Transactions* criminalises bribery of foreign public officials by private companies in international business transactions with strong enforcement and monitoring mechanisms. While MENA focus economies have not adhered to the OECD *Anti-Bribery Convention*, these standards can guide governments to advance integrity. In addition, the provisions in this Convention impact foreign firms operating in the region, as companies are bound to abide by the obligations set out in their home jurisdictions when doing business abroad. Implementing these standards will signal to international and domestic investors that MENA governments support a level playing field for all businesses.

Last, a culture of integrity cannot be achieved through public regulation alone: complementary and mutually supportive actions by the private sector also play a crucial role. It is vital that MENA governments involve the private sector in the prevention of corruption through good business practices, adoption of corporate anti-bribery policy and related compliance measures. The private sector has a key role to play in improving corporate integrity and accountability to create trust in business. Existing multi-stakeholder initiatives to promote a clean business environment should also be supported, and new and innovative opportunities for public-private collaboration should be further explored. By strengthening their integrity frameworks and acting in concert, firms and governments can provide strong signals that they support a business-friendly environment to enhance investment in the MENA region.

Policy considerations

- Enhance the connection between integrity and investment frameworks at the domestic level. Investment promotion bodies and anti-corruption agencies should develop tools and practices that allow them to coordinate and communicate effectively on shared goals. Investment attraction goals could be better embedded in anti-corruption strategies. Likewise, investment policies must prioritise integrity and good governance across the investment process.
- Rely on international and regional conventions and standards in the fight against corruption and related instruments. MENA economies can benefit from the proper implementation of the anti-corruption instruments they have adhered to, as this sends a strong signal to foreign investors of convergence to international standards. Moreover, other international instruments to which MENA economies have not yet adhered can provide guidance to inspire domestic efforts to promote integrity in business transactions.
- Collaborate with the private sector and promote multi-stakeholder initiatives to encourage integrity in business. Governments and businesses have a shared responsibility. It is vital to involve the private sector in the prevention of corruption through good business practices, in particular stronger compliance frameworks at the firm level, and collective efforts to prevent corruption and address bribe solicitation problems industry-wide.

Investment, integrity and the fight against corruption

Challenges and state of play in the MENA region

Estimates suggest that around 2.5% of world GDP is lost annually in corruption, an amount equivalent to the size of the French economy (OECD, 2017). In developing countries, bribery is estimated to account for around 10% of the total cost of doing business (UNPRI, 2016). Corruption decreases investor confidence, produces welfare losses, misallocates resources, and can have a significant negative impact on basic public services like health and infrastructure. It affects the quantity and efficiency of investments by increasing costs of production and project uncertainty, hence reducing returns and increasing risks. Corruption also negatively affects the quality of investment, threatening its durability and its positive externalities on growth, innovation and technological progress.

Fighting corruption is a priority in the economic development agendas of the MENA focus economies. Studies specific to the region highlight the significant negative effect of corruption on GDP growth and foreign direct investment (FDI) inflows (Al-Khouri and Khalik, 2013; Awdeh and Hamadi, 2019). Higher business integrity in MENA economies is found to improve the positive impact of FDI on economic development, pointing to the important synergies between the fight against corruption and the promotion of quality FDI (Hakimi and Hamdi, 2017).

Although integrity levels vary across the region, the overall picture remains bleak when considering the main international corruption indicators. In both 2018 and 2019, no MENA focus economy received a score above a "passing grade" of 50 (on a scale from zero indicating high corruption to 100 indicating high integrity) according to the Corruption Perception Index (CPI) of Transparency International (2018a). The index ranks economies based on how corrupt a country's public sector is perceived to be by experts and business executives. Similarly, the World Bank's Control of Corruption Index (CCI) gives all economies in the region, except Jordan, a negative score (World Bank, 2020).

Libya and, to a lesser extent, Lebanon and Algeria, suffer from particularly negative perceptions of corruption (Figure 11.1). Jordan, Tunisia and Morocco, on the other hand, fare relatively well vis-à-vis their peers. When looking at the evolution of corruption perceptions over time, Morocco and Egypt have advanced their scores the most since 2007. Broadly, however, perception of corruption in the MENA focus economies do not seem to have considerably improved over the past decade. Recent demonstrations of social discontent across the region, including in economies that saw fewer large-scale protests in 2011, such as Lebanon, are a case in point. Popular mobilisation expresses clear dissatisfaction with the lack of economic opportunities, weak and unaccountable forms of government, as well as widespread corruption.

Figure 11.1. Evolution of CPI scores in MENA focus economies (2007-2019)

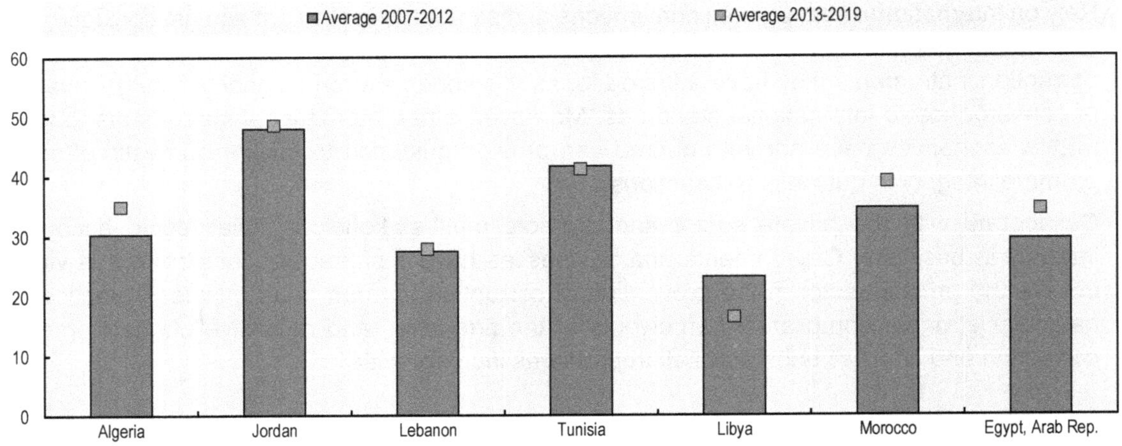

Note: The CPI methodology employed by Transparency International was updated in 2012. Accordingly, CPI scores prior to 2012 were multiplied by 10 to be visually comparable to scores of subsequent years. CPI scores for the Palestinian Authority not available.
Source: Author's figure based on data of Transparency International, Corruption Perception Indexes

These dynamics are particularly evident when comparing the average scores of MENA focus economies with those of ASEAN[1] members (Figure 11.2). In 2008, ASEAN members were perceived as more corrupt than MENA focus economies on average. In the following years, however, this relationship was overturned, with international observers and firms increasingly deeming ASEAN economies less corrupt than MENA ones. This is mainly due to a stable improvement of the scores of ASEAN, while those of MENA stagnated and in certain cases worsened.

Figure 11.2. Average CPI scores for MENA and ASEAN economies (2007-2019)

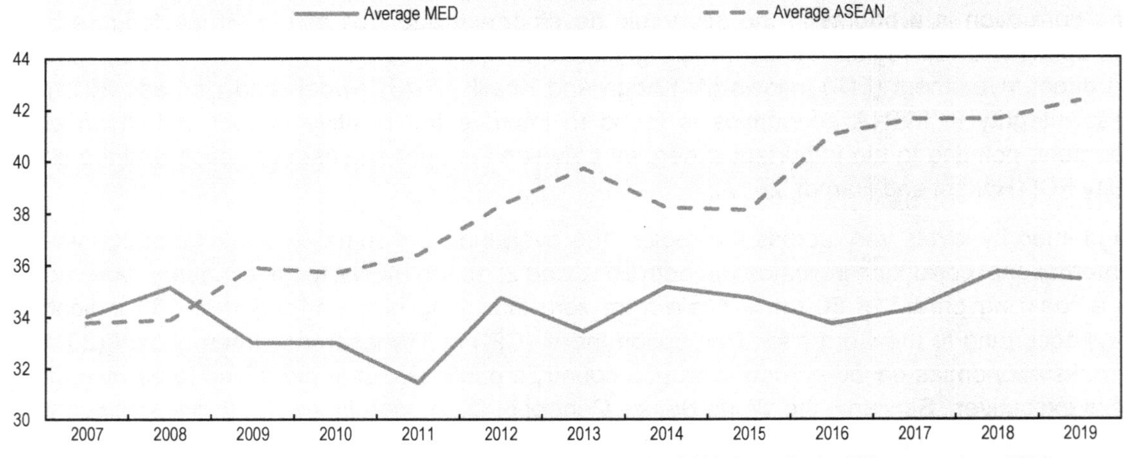

Note: The CPI methodology employed by Transparency International was updated in 2012. Accordingly, CPI scores prior to 2012 were multiplied by 10 to be visually comparable to scores of subsequent years. CPI scores for the Palestinian Authority not available.
Source: Author's calculations based on data from Transparency International, Corruption Perception Index.

Enhancing integrity to promote the trust of international investors and maximise the positive impact of FDI on the economy is a priority for MENA governments. The promotion of sustainable investment and the fight against corruption are processes that reinforce each other and should be considered as such by investment and anti-corruption policymakers. MENA governments are actively pursuing policies to promote and facilitate investment in an effort to generate jobs, revenue and productive growth in the local economy. Investment promotion agencies (IPAs) have been established to attract investment and better capture its benefits (Chapter 6). A number of economies of the region have recently introduced strategies to strengthen the anti-corruption framework and promote business integrity, and have established dedicated anti-corruption bodies.

Yet, governments have not addressed these challenges in a holistic and concerted manner. For instance, efforts to tackle corruption have mainly pertained to the sphere of domestic bribery and criminal legislation, rather than being addressed as limits to economic development and international investment. Conversely, strategies to promote investment in the region have focused on creating a business-friendly regulatory framework, and less on strengthening integrity in this domain – as a dimension of a better investment climate. As presented below, concrete corruption risks occur at several stages of the investment process. This and the links between integrity and sustainable investment call for a holistic and whole-of-government approach towards both the policy and the institutional frameworks governing integrity and investment.

Trust in government, strong and effective institutions and good governance all contribute to increasing international investors' confidence and perception of integrity. Figures from Transparency International (2019) point to low trust in government across the MENA region, albeit with variations across economies.[2] Levels of trust in public institutions are particularly low in Lebanon and the Palestinian Authority, where 80% and 50% of respondents reported having little to no trust in government, respectively, and notably higher in Jordan, where 60% of responded indicated they had trust in the government.

Institutional effectiveness, quality and capacity, are also important pre-conditions to ensure clean business transactions and promote integrity. Strong institutions play an essential part not only in maintaining a predictable and transparent business environment, but also in increasing the likelihood of detection and prosecution, and deterring corruption. There is evidence that structural reforms, including rationalisation of state functions, reliance on market pricing, and a sound regulatory environment contributed to a substantial and significant reduction of corruption in transition economies (Abed and Davoodi, 2000).

Corruption risks across the investment process

An investor may resort to corruption in order to enter a foreign market; obtain or retain a government contract, licence or customs clearance; access raw materials or foreign currency; or to receive specific incentives or tax benefits. In order to combat and prevent corruption among foreign investors, it is therefore important to understand where and how corruption risks can materialise. Several stages of the international investment process that are particularly exposed to corruption risks are presented below.

Market entry

In entering a foreign market, international investors are required to go through a number of administrative and contractual procedures. Depending on the type of FDI (greenfield investment or M&A), as well as its destination (both geographical and sectoral), these may include screening and approval procedures, investment licensing, enterprise registration, capital requirements, customs clearance, as well as public procurement contracts (Box 11.1).

Market entry is a high-risk stage in the investment process. OECD (2017) analysis of foreign bribery data obtained from law enforcement authorities shows that 76% of the bribes considered were paid in connection to administrative procedural requirements at the investment entry stage. In particular, 57% of them were paid to obtain public procurement contracts, 12% to obtain customs clearance, 6% to receive a licence or other authorisation, and 1% for travel visa purposes. Among all public servants who took bribes, 11% were customs officials, 3% procurement officials, and 1% immigration officials.

These figures attest to the importance of streamlining market entry rules, making them predictable and publicly available to foreign investors (Chapter 4). Clear and unambiguous market entry rules and requirements are a prerequisite to reduce opportunities for officials' discretion over the provision of licences, permits or public contracts.

In the MENA focus economies, the legal framework for the entry of foreign investors is not always legible and transparent. Often details on discriminatory measures are not available in English or involve lengthy and frequently updated lists of open sectors, making it difficult for investors to understand prevalent rules. A more transparent and predictable approach involves a "negative list", whereby all foreign investment projects are authorised without discriminatory conditions, except specific sectors or sub-sectors clearly outlined in the negative list. Among the MENA focus economies, Jordan has a negative list, and Tunisia and Algeria are in the process of adopting this approach.

Most of the MENA focus economies have also established one-stop-shops (OSS) to reduce steps required to start a business and, in some cases, procedures can be completed online (e.g., the investor service centres in Egypt). This should help reduce the risk of bribery, although it is not yet clear to what extent OSS offices (and online portals) in MENA economies are fully functional (Chapter 6).

Box 11.1. Case study: corruption in entering a foreign market through public procurement

In 2016, the National Court of Spain found the Spanish transport and infrastructure companies Elecnor, Assignia and Rover Alcisa guilty of money laundering and corruption of foreign public officials in relation to their international operations in Algeria. Through a dense criminal network, the companies bribed Algerian officials around EUR 3 million to win projects concerning the construction of tramway rails and a desalination plant in the southern and northern regions of the country, respectively. The payments were made by a Dutch company located in the Netherlands to a consulting firm owned by Algerian counterpart, as well as by a Spanish intermediary through Western Union transfers to family members of Algerian officials residing in France.

Source: Transparency International (2018b)

Emergency processes put in place by governments in the context of Covid-19 health and economic crisis have increased the risks of corruption in public procurement. Many countries used emergency procedures to contain the spread of the virus, or in some cases, to import medical equipment and supplies. OECD data shows that many of the recently detected cases of foreign bribery have occurred in the health industry. Other risks and potential integrity violations arise from the unprecedented economic and fiscal measures being implemented to respond to the ongoing economic crisis. These measures may be exploited and represent a test for public financial management systems. Governments should ensure that public integrity is not compromised in the management of the economic stimulus packages and that these packages produce their intended benefits (OECD, 2020).

Protection of property rights

The protection of property and land use rights in the host economy is essential for the confidence of international investors. Instances of corruption in this domain include public officials soliciting bribes in exchange for access to land, or investors resorting to corrupt practices in order to secure and maintain property rights.

Legal clarity and predictability, notably against arbitrary expropriation, as well as transparency in land registration and administration (for example through the proper maintenance of public registers), can contribute to reducing corruption risks by improving information asymmetries (Chapter 3). Moreover, the distribution of land through market mechanisms and market pricing, rather than through centralised procedures relying on considerable red tape, can decrease corruption risks by limiting the opportunities for arbitrary decisions of public officials. In this respect, digitalisation can play a particularly positive role.

Regarding the institutional setting, better co-ordination and a clearer division of responsibilities between central government and local land authorities can enhance reporting, knowledge sharing and improve resource allocation (OECD, 2015).

Taxation and investment incentives

Tax collection and incentive allocation are particularly exposed to corruption risks. This is not only due to the complexity and opacity of the processes that underpin them, but also to the level of potential profits at stake. High levels of corruption are often associated with low government revenues (IMF, 2019b).

Weak policy design, lack of transparency, and cumbersome tax administration are all factors that increase the potential for bribery in fiscal matters. Cross-country analysis suggests that fiscal institutions play an important role for the control of corruption, with evidence indicating that the more complex fiscal laws are, the higher the risk of corruption will be (IMF, 2019a). Similar correlations are found when factoring in the number of tax payments required, the amount of time spent for tax auditing and VAT refunds, and the level of administrative burden (both in terms of time and procedures). On the contrary, more tax transparency and higher degrees of digital government stand out as key features of a healthier, cleaner business environment (ibid.).

Lack of transparency in the design and allocation of investment incentives is also the main cause of corruption at this stage of the investment lifecycle (Chapter 7). Where eligibility criteria are unclear, public authorities have more room to exercise discretion and more opportunities for corruption arise. In order to avoid misconduct, it is important that tax and financial incentives offered to international investors, and eligibility criteria to receive them, are clear and specific, and that vague wording and ad hoc rules are reduced to the minimum. Additionally, granting incentives based only on tax law can limit scope for corruption as well as aggressive tax planning by international firms (World Bank, 2017).

Access to finance, foreign exchange and profit repatriation

Like public administrations, banking institutions in host economies can impose burdensome requirements or bureaucratic procedures on investors seeking to obtain loans or other financial services. Access to foreign exchange can also be challenging. Overly restrictive conditions and unclear exchange control rules leave room for discretionary decisions by authorities, and may in turn create higher incentives to resort to corruption. Automation and reliance on market mechanisms and pricing, rather than on the discretion of authorities, can help curb risks.

Investors can resort to corruption in repatriating capital or profits in order to overcome restrictions and foreign control rules still in force in a number of MENA economies, avoid transfer pricing rules, or evade taxes. Where illicit financial flows (tax avoidance, money laundry schemes, terrorism financing, etc.) are at play, investors may offer bribes to avoid scrutiny. Risks can be mitigated through adequate auditing and tax compliance processes, and co-operation with relevant financial and governmental institutions.

Policy options to enhance integrity for sustainable investment

Governments have a variety of policy options and strategies to curb corruption across the investment process. Three important approaches are considered: enhance the connection between investment and anti-corruption frameworks and strategies at the domestic level; rely on and implement international conventions and standards on integrity, and converge toward international standards and good practices in this domain; and benefit from the crucial contribution of the private sector in the fight against corruption.

Enhancing the connection between integrity and investment frameworks at the domestic level

The fight against corruption and the promotion of sustainable investment are mutually beneficial policy priorities and should therefore be tackled through a holistic approach. Policymakers should further connect the domestic legal and institutional frameworks for investment and anti-corruption. Occasional instances of such connection exist in the MENA region, but more can be done.

Concerning the investment legal framework, for example, integrity provisions are hardly mainstreamed in the investment laws of the eight economies. Egypt is the only MENA focus economy to explicitly reference corruption issues in its Investment Law, stipulating that any investment project set up through corrupt means is exempt from all guarantees and incentives stipulated in the law.

Meanwhile, national anti-corruption strategies often do not note the economic benefits of a corruption-free business climate. Notable exceptions include the Egyptian National Anti-Corruption Strategy 2019-2022 and the Moroccan National Strategy against Corruption 2017-2025, which explicitly indicate corruption as a threat to the country's attractiveness to international investors. National strategies can be effective tools to engage investors and investment policymakers in the fight against corruption, notably in terms of inter-institutional co-operation between national investment and anti-corruption bodies, as well as between public and private actors.

With regard to inter-institutional cooperation, the Moroccan strategy gives the Ministry of Industry, Trade, Investment and Digital Economy the responsibility to co-ordinate projects on digitalisation of public administration. Similarly, according to the proposed Palestinian 2020-2022 Anti-Corruption Strategy, the Ministry of National Economy is expected to collaborate with the Anti-Corruption Commission to apply codes of conduct in targeted public institutions and enhance corporate governance rules (Palestinian Anti-Corruption Commission, 2020). Finally, in the Tunisian National Strategy for Good Governance and the Fight against Corruption 2016-2020, the Ministry of Investment and International Co-operation is co-responsible for activities on private sector capacity building and co-operation with international peers (Instance Nationale de la Lutte Contre la Corruption, 2019a).

Concerning the engagement of the private sector, the 2016 Moroccan National Anti-Corruption Strategy includes a dedicated programme on business integrity. The General Confederation of Moroccan Enterprises (CGEM) is responsible for the implementation of activities on improving transparency in the private sector, promoting adherence to ethical codes and corporate social responsibility certification processes, and reducing private-sector driven corruption opportunities (Commission Nationale Anti-Corruption, 2016). Similarly, the Egyptian National Anti-Corruption Strategy 2019-2022 commits the government to cooperate and co-ordinate with all relevant stakeholders, including the private sector and civil society. In this respect, a number of capacity building activities to prevent and fight corruption in the private sector are considered, including courses, seminars, and tools facilitating access to relevant information (Sub-Coordinating Committee, 2019).

The Tunisian and Jordanian anti-corruption strategies also plan and encourage co-operation and dialogue between the public and the private sectors. Practically, this takes the form of collaboration in drafting and implementing activities related to good governance and integrity in the domains of education, science and culture in Tunisia, and of structured and regular consultation sessions for Jordan.

Beyond national strategies, other instances of inter-institutional co-operation between authorities responsible for investment and integrity are present in the region. The Egyptian Administrative Control Authority (ACA), the main national anti-corruption body, supported Egypt's Investment Promotion Agency, the General Authority for Investment (GAFI), in the introduction of investor services centres (ISCs) for foreign investors. These aim to curb corruption by simplifying registration procedures and decreasing person-to-person contact (Administrative Control Authority, 2015).

Other institutions opted for structured co-operation with their counterparts through joint agreements or memoranda of understanding. This is the case between the Palestinian Ministry of National Economy and the Anti-Corruption Commission (Palestinian Anti-Corruption Commission, 2015), the Tunisian Ministry of Investment and International Co-operation and the National Authority for the Fight against Corruption (Instance Nationale de Lutte Contre la Corruption, 2019b), as well as between the Jordanian anti-corruption body, the Integrity and Anti-Corruption Commission, the Aqaba Special Economic Zone and the Jordan Chamber of Industry (Jordan Integrity and Anti-Corruption Commission, 2018; 2019).

International conventions and standards in the fight against corruption

A number of instruments have been adopted both at the international and regional level to fight corruption and promote integrity. While some of these aim to generally promote a corruption-free environment, others seek to specifically combat corruption in international business transactions. MENA governments could greatly improve their image as sustainable investment destinations by showing their willingness to converge towards international standards. The section below offers an overview of the main international and regional conventions against corruption, as well as relevant OECD instruments on integrity. Box 11.2 examines how MENA economies have starting including specific provisions on anti-corruption in their international investment agreements, and Table 11.1 provides an overview of MENA focus economies' policy measures to fight corruption and promote integrity.

International instruments

The United Nations Convention against Corruption (UNCAC) is the most widespread legally binding international instrument for the fight against corruption. In force since 2005, the Convention has near universal coverage currently comprising 187 parties – including all MENA, EU and OECD economies. Although it does not explicitly target investment transactions, the UNCAC sets up a comprehensive strategy to prevent and combat corruption from a multilateral perspective. Its standards cover both the supply and demand sides of corruption: public and private bribery. Its declared objective is to promote and strengthen measures to prevent and fight corruption, facilitate international co-operation and technical assistance, and promote integrity, accountability and proper public management.

To this end, parties to the convention are required to adopt a number of measures corresponding to an important area of anti-corruption, namely: prevention, criminalisation, international co-operation, asset recovery, technical assistance and information exchange, and implementation. Requirements include the obligation to criminalise a number of corruption-related offences (e.g. bribery, embezzlement, diversion of funds, money laundering, and obstruction of justice) and establish independent national anti-corruption bodies. In particular, article 5 of the UNCAC requires governments to have anti-corruption strategies.

In addition to UNCAC, the OECD Convention on Combating Bribery of Foreign Public Officials in International Business Transactions (OECD Anti-Bribery Convention) is the first and only international instrument to specifically tackle the supply side of corruption, that is to say the offering (or promising) of bribes from companies to public officials as defined in the Convention. It is also the only instrument of its kind that specifically aims to fight corruption in international business, making it particularly relevant to inspire efforts in promoting integrity in FDI transactions and international trade.

The OECD Anti-Bribery Convention (entered into force in 1999), currently has 44 parties: all OECD countries and seven non-OECD countries. Parties to the Convention agree to establish bribery of foreign public officials as a criminal offence under their laws and to investigate, prosecute and sanction this offence. They must hold both individuals and companies responsible for foreign bribery. The Convention contains a host of related measures to fight corruption, including a peer-review mechanism in the context of the OECD Working Group on Bribery in International Business Transactions (a specialised OECD body where all States Parties are represented), entrusted with monitoring and promoting full implementation of the Convention.

Although no MENA government has adhered to the OECD Convention, it has important implications for the region. Indeed, foreign businesses coming from adherent countries and operating in a MENA economy are bound by the obligations set out in their home jurisdictions when doing business abroad. Throughout the years, this seems to have helped deter the international supply of bribes. OECD research shows that investors from signatories to the OECD Convention are significantly less likely to invest in economies perceived as having high corruption levels, due to the fear of being prosecuted in their country of origin (Blundell-Wignall and Roulet, 2017). This has significant consequences in view of the weight of OECD companies in terms of international trade and investment, including in the MENA region. Indeed, the 44 Parties to the Convention cover together 81% of the global outbound FDI stocks and over 66% of the world's exports (OECD, 2018).

Box 11.2. Integrity promotion in international investment agreements: evidence from MENA economies

Some of the MENA focus economies have started including specific provisions on corruption in their international investment agreements (Chapter 5). While such provisions are often mere reiterations of broad commitments to the fight against corruption (such as in the Preamble of the US-Libya Trade and Investment Framework Agreement), others have gone further, introducing international co-operation mechanisms or obliging the contracting parties to exclude corrupt international investors from bidding procedures.

The EU-Algeria Association Agreement of 2002, for example, calls for co-operation on the basis of the relevant international legal instruments to combat corruption in international business transactions by, *inter alia*, "taking effective practical measures against all forms of corruption, bribery and illicit activities of every sort" and "providing mutual assistance in criminal investigations into acts of corruption" (Article 91). The Agreement also encourages technical assistance between the two parties for the "training of officials and magistrates responsible for tackling corruption" (Article 91).

Similar measures are present in Article 18 of the Free Trade Agreement between the Morocco and the United States of 2008 (in force), which also calls on the parties to declare corrupted international investors ineligible for participation in public procurement processes (Article 9), as well as to cooperate and support relevant initiatives in international fora (Article 18).

The Investment Co-operation and Facilitation Agreement between Morocco and Brazil goes even further in the scope of co-operation. It binds the two parties to improve the transparency of their activities in the fight against corruption and extortion, abstain from engaging in corruption, keep accurate records and accounts that cannot be used for the concealment of illicit transactions, and adopt internal mechanisms for the prevention and detection of corruption. To ensure compliance, under Article 14, the Agreement establishes a Joint Committee charged with the monitoring the implementation of these measures.

Regional instruments

The Arab Anti-Corruption Convention (entered into force in 2013), issued by the League of Arab States is a regional legal instrument to support the international fight against corruption. It comprises 22 signatories, including all of the MENA focus economies. The aim of the instrument is to repress and prevent corruption through promoting Arab co-operation in this domain. Its content is similar to the provisions of the UNCAC, and includes the requirement to criminalise specific corruption offences, promote technical assistance, and ensure international co-operation including concerning stolen asset recovery. The Convention also introduces monitoring elements, notably by establishing a Conference of State Parties with the aim of exchanging information, cooperating with international fora, reviewing implementation and adopting recommendations.

The African Union Convention on Preventing and Combating Corruption is the main instrument of the African Union in this domain. It comprises 49 signatories, including Algeria, Egypt, Libya and Tunisia. Similar to the other international instruments outlined, its chapters cover aspects related to the prevention and criminalisation of corruption, asset recovery, and implementation mechanisms. The Convention seeks to fight both public and private corruption. To this end, it requires adherent countries to criminalise private sector bribery and private sector embezzlement (considered optional measures under the UNCAC). An Advisory Board elected by the African Union Executive Council is responsible for the follow-up of the Convention and it is required to submit regular reports on the progress of States Parties in implementing the provisions. Additionally, States Parties themselves are required to report their progress to the Advisory Board on an annual basis.

Other OECD instruments promoting a clean business environment

The OECD Guidelines for Multinational Enterprises comprise a comprehensive set of international standards on responsible business conduct (Chapter 10). The Guidelines cover a number of areas, including human rights, labour rights, environment, and anti-corruption. In particular, Chapter VII focuses directly on "Combating Bribery, Bribe Solicitation and Extortion", detailing, *inter alia*, the responsibility of MNEs to not offer or promise any type of pecuniary and non-pecuniary bribes to public officials or business partners, as well as to improve transparency, awareness, internal controls and risk assessments in this respect.

Table 11.1. Overview of MENA focus economies' policy measures to fight corruption and promote integrity

	UNCAC	OECD Anti-Bribery Convention	OECD Guidelines on MNE	AU Convention on Preventing & Combating Corruption	Arab Convention Against Corruption	Existence of national anti-corruption legislation	Specialised Anti-Corruption Body	National Anti-Corruption Strategy
Algeria								
Egypt								
Jordan				N/A				
Lebanon				N/A				
Libya								
Morocco								
Palestinian Authority				N/A				
Tunisia								

Note: Blue refers to adherence to the instrument or existence of legislation, body or strategy. White refers to non-adherence to the instrument or absence of legislation, body, or strategy. Grey refers to strategies under development but not yet implemented.
Source: Author's own elaboration based on national and international measures and instruments.

Additionally, the Principles for Enhancing Integrity in Public Procurement, approved by OECD member countries in 2008 based on international best practices from OECD and partner countries, aims to enhance integrity across the entire public procurement cycle, from needs assessment to contract management and payment. It responds to the high corruption risks to which, as explored above, procurement practices are exposed.

Role of businesses: promoting strong corporate compliance measures and multi-stakeholder initiatives to prevent corruption

The aforementioned international instruments have prompted many countries to adopt stricter anti-corruption legislation to repress and prevent corruption in the private sector. The private sector – as both actor and victim of corruption – is increasingly realising the adverse effects of corruption on its economic health, viability and long-term stability. It is therefore vital to consider the role and potential of the private sector in promoting integrity.

Robust anti-bribery compliance procedures are essential for ensuring that businesses can prevent, detect, and respond to bribery, domestically and in international business. A growing number of OECD and EU companies investing in the MENA region have adopted strong anti-corruption compliance systems, in accordance with international standards, including the *2009 OECD Good Practice Guidance on Internal Controls, Ethics, and Compliance*. Various factors have been driving private sector companies to design systems to prevent, detect and respond to the risk of corruption. These factors include enforcement and reputational risks, in addition to legal and regulatory requirements. MENA companies must also be encouraged to meet such compliance standards.

The mobilisation of the private sector has also led to the emergence of collective anti-corruption actions involving several companies from the same sector or field of activity working together to promote greater business integrity on a voluntary basis. This has in turn led to the establishment of common standards and the definition of fair rules between competitors in different sectors of activity to fight corruption collectively. Some of the collective actions launched by private sector actors have gradually involved governments and civil society representatives, evolving into multi-stakeholder initiatives for promoting integrity.

The practice of collective action has emerged in different parts of the world, including in the MENA region. In Morocco, pilot initiatives have been launched in the energy, health and transport sectors under the aegis of the *Confédération Générale des Entreprises du Maroc* (CGEM) and in accordance with the National Strategy against Corruption.

Another example of collective action is the Egypt Integrity Network Initiative initiated in 2015 by the Egyptian Junior Business Association in partnership with the Foundation for the Global Compact and the United Nations Global Compact to encourage Egyptian SMEs to commit to advancing their anti-corruption practices (Egyptian Junior Business Association Integrity Network, 2018). Similar initiatives have been emerging in other economies in the region, especially in the financial and construction sectors, and among SMEs, notably in Egypt and Tunisia, but also in Libya.

Finally, in order to avoid disputes with investors arising from governmental misconduct, many countries are setting up investment dispute prevention mechanisms, which favour, at early stages of investment-related disputes, the dialogue and the non-jurisdictional resolution of potential conflicts with enterprises, including cases involving bribery. An increasing number of MENA governments have introduced such mechanisms, through early alerts and after-care services for investors (Chapter 5). Egypt set up an inter-ministerial committee for investment dispute resolution and GAFI, the investment promotion agency, put in place a mediation and grievance mechanism to address investors' complaints as well as dispute arising between investors. The Jordan Investment Commission also established an Investment Grievance Mechanism.

References

Abed, G. and Davoodi, H. (2000), “Corruption, Structural Reforms, and Economic Performance in the Transition Economies,” *IMF Working Paper No. 00/132.* Available at: https://www.imf.org/en/Publications/WP/Issues/2016/12/30/Corruption-Structural-Reforms-and-Economic-Performance-in-the-Transition-Economies-3697.

Administrative Control Authority *(2015). Applied one stop shop to eradicate corruption.* Available at: http://www.aca.gov.eg/english/News/ACANews/Pages/News29720152.aspx.

Al-Khouri, R. and Khalik, M. (2013), “Does Political Risk Affect the Flow of Foreign Direct Investment into the Middle East North African Region?,” *Journal of Global Business and Technology,* Vol. 9 No. 2, pp. 47-59. Available at: http://search.ebscohost.com/login.aspx?direct=true&db=bth&AN=92620570&site=ehost-live.

Awdeh, A. and Hamadi, H. (2019), "Factors hindering economic development: evidence from the MENA countries," *International Journal of Emerging Markets*, Vol. 14 No. 2 pp. 281-299. https://doi.org/10.1108/IJoEM-12-2017-0555.

Blundell-Wignall, A. and Roulet, C. (2017), "Foreign direct investment, corruption and the OECD Anti-Bribery Convention", *Documents de travail de l'OCDE sur l'investissement international*, n° 2017/01. Available at: https://doi.org/10.1787/9cb3690c-en.

Commission National Anti-Corruption (2016). *Strategie nationale de lutte contre la corruption.* Available at: https://www.mmsp.gov.ma/uploads/file/Strategie Nationale de lutte Corruption_SNLCC_FR_2016.pdf.

Egyptian Junior Business Association Integrity Network (2018). *Implementing Collective Action Initiatives against Corruption in the Middle East and Africa.* Available at: https://www.baselgovernance.org/sites/default/files/2019-02/ini_collective-action_outcome-report_resized.pdf.

Hakimi, A. and Hamdi, H. (2017), “Does Corruption Limit FDI and Economic Growth? Evidence from MENA countries,” *International Journal of Emerging Markets,* Vol. 11 No. 3, pp. 550-571. Available at: https://doi.org/10.1108/IJoEM-06-2015-0118.

IMF (2019a), *Fiscal Monitor: Curbing Corruption*. Available at: http://dx.doi.org/10.5089/9781498302180.089.

IMF (2019b), "The Cost of Corruption: Graft results in lost tax revenue, but it also takes a social toll," *Finance & Development*. Available at: https://doi.org/10.5089/9781498316040.022.

Instance National de la Lutte contre la corruption (2019a). *Plan d’action 2019-2020 de la Stratégie Nationale de Bonne Gouvernance et de la Lutte Contre la Corruption.*

Instance Nationale de Lutte Contre la Corruption (2019b). *La signature d'une convention de partenariat entre l'INLUCC et le ministère du Développement, de l’Investissement et de la Coopération internationale*. Available at: http://www.inlucc.tn/www.inlucc.tn/index.php?id=121&L=1&tx_ttnews%5Btt_news%5D=1682&cHash=6560008886b430e95aa46d6968df874d.

Jordan Integrity and Anti-Corruption Commission (2018). *Memorandum of Understanding Singed between the Integrity and Anti-Corruption Commission and Jordan Chamber of Industry*. Available at: http://jiacc.gov.jo/en/news/79/Memorandum-of-Understanding-Singed-between-the-Integrity-and-Anti-Corruption-Commission-and-Jordan-Chamber-of-Industry--.

Jordan Integrity and Anti-Corruption Commission (2018). *Memorandum of Understanding between Integrity and Anti-Corruption Commission and the Aqaba Authority*. Available at: http://jiacc.gov.jo/en/news/910/Memorandum-of-Understanding-between-Integrity-and-Anti-Corruption-Commission-and-the-Aqaba-Authority.

OECD (2020), *Policy measures to avoid corruption and bribery in the COVID-19 response and recovery*, OECD Publishing, Paris, https://read.oecd-ilibrary.org/view/?ref=133_133216-hn3bqtlvkw&title=Policy-measures-to-avoid-corruption-and-bribery-in-the-COVID-19-response-and-recovery

OECD (2020), Stocktaking Report on Immediate Public Procurement and Infrastructure Responses to COVID-19, OECD Publishing, Paris, https://read.oecd-ilibrary.org/view/?ref=132_132982-9i47fud8xb&title=Stocktaking-Report-on-Immediate-Public-Procurement-and-Infrastructure-Responses-to-COVID-19.

OECD (2020), *Global Lessons on Collective Action Against Corruption – The Case of Morocco,* OECD Publishing, Paris, https://www.oecd.org/mena/competitiveness/Global-lessons-on-collective-action-against-corruption-Case-of-Morocco.pdf

OECD (2017), *OECD Business and Finance Outlook 2017*, OECD Publishing, Paris, https://doi.org/10.1787/9789264274891-en.

OECD (2015), *Policy Framework for Investment 2015 Edition,* OECD Publishing, Paris, *http://dx.doi.org/10.1787/9789264208667-en*

OECD (2014), OECD Foreign Bribery Report, An Analysis of the Crime of Bribery and Foreign Public Officials, OECD Publishing, Paris, https://www.oecd-ilibrary.org/docserver/9789264226616-en.pdf?expires=1594053043&id=id&accname=ocid84004878&checksum=C867832E87E6F4A74578D6C0DE5437CA

OECD (2018) Snapshot of 20 years of implementation and enforcement of the Anti-Bribery Convention by the OECD Working Group on Bribery. http://www.oecd.org/corruption/anti-bribery/anti-briberyconvention/oecdworkinggrouponbriberyininternationalbusinesstransactions.htm

Palestinian Anti-Corruption Commission (2015). هيئة مكافحة الفساد الفلسطينية. Available at: https://www.pacc.ps/Blog/Post/303.

Palestinian Anti-Corruption Commission (2020). هيئة مكافحة الفساد الفلسطينية. Available at: https://www.pacc.ps/strategy/.

Sub-Coordinating Committee for the Prevention and combating of corruption (2019). *Egyptian National Anti-Corruption Strategy*. Available at: https://www.aca.gov.eg/arabic/AntiCorruption/PublishingImages/Pages/nationalstrategy/English.pdf.

Transparency International (2019a). *Corruption Perception Index 2019*. Available at: https://www.transparency.org/cpi2019.

Transparency International (2018). *Exporting Corruption - Progress Report 2018: Assessing Enforcement of The OECD Anti-Bribery Convention.* Available at: https://www.transparency.org/whatwedo/publication/exporting_corruption_2018.

Transparency International (2019b). *Global Corruption Barometer Middle East and North Africa 2019 - Citizens' Views and Experiences of Corruption.* Available at: https://www.transparency.org/files/content/pages/2019_GCB_MENA_Report_EN.pdf.

UN (2000), *Le coût de la corruption*. Available at: https://www.un.org/french/events/10thcongress/2088bf.htm.

UNPRI (2016), *Engaging on anti-bribery and corruption*. Available at: https://www.unpri.org/esg-issues/governance-issues/corruption.

World Bank (2017), *Global investment competitiveness report 2017-2018: foreign investor perspectives and policy implications.* Available at: http://documents.worldbank.org/curated/en/169531510741671962/Global-investment-competitiveness-report-2017-2018-foreign-investor-perspectives-and-policy-implications.

World Bank (2018), *Privilege-Resistant Policies in the Middle East and North Africa*. Available at: http://documents.worldbank.org/curated/en/516331538648238168/Privilege-Resistant-Policies-in-the-

Middle-East-and-North-Africa

World Bank (2020), *Open Trade and Competitiveness Data - Control of Corruption*. Available at: https://tcdata360.worldbank.org/.

Notes

[1] Association of Southeast Asian Nations

[2] Data only available for Jordan, Morocco, Palestinian Authority, Lebanon and Tunisia.

12 Investment policy in fragile contexts

Fragility and crises are pervasive elements in some parts of the MENA region, weakening the potential of some countries to attract investment. This chapter discusses how the different dimensions of fragility affect investment in the focus economies, and outlines policy considerations to overcome challenges in attracting and retaining FDI. It presents the main drivers of fragility and explores their complex relationship with FDI. While fragility and crises may discourage investors, FDI is a crucial source of growth and financing to strengthen resilience in fragile scenarios.

Summary and policy considerations

Foreign direct investment (FDI) can be an important source of financing, driving job creation, technological advancement and private sector development in the MENA economies covered in this report (MENA focus economies). This chapter analyses the fragility challenges that some of the focus economies face, and provides policy considerations for overcoming barriers to attracting and retaining quality investment. Given the diversity in the region – from higher levels of fragility in Libya, Syria, the Palestinian Authority (PA), and increasingly Lebanon, to greater stability elsewhere – the implementation of these policy considerations would vary across the MENA focus economies.

Fragility is a multidimensional concept that affects the focus economies in different ways, to different degrees. While only two of the focus economies (Libya and the PA) appear among the most fragile 57 contexts on the OECD fragility framework, all governments are to some extent faced with fragility issues[1]. Analysis of the OECD's five dimensions of fragility indicates that the political and societal dimensions of fragility are the most salient across the focus economies, while the economic, environmental, and security dimensions affect them to varying degrees.

More broadly, the larger Middle East and North Africa (MENA) region[2] is one of the most fragile regions in the world, second only to Sub-Saharan Africa, and these security and fragility risks can bleed out to affect risk perceptions throughout the region. Macroeconomic and political instability, high levels of popular discontent, movements of forcibly displaced people, the social and economic effects of desertification and environmental degradation are problems that most governments in the region have had to confront in recent times.

The relationship between fragility and investment is complex. In affecting the return and risk considerations of foreign investors, fragility can have serious negative implications for FDI inflows and retention, and can encourage the concentration of FDI in heavily protected enclaves, distinct from the national economy. Fragility is costly for investors, even in the absence of outright conflict. At the same time, investment can help to address some of the underlying drivers of fragility by providing necessary sources of financing and contributing to inclusive and sustainable economic and social development. However, FDI in the focus economies is largely concentrated in low-productivity and low-employment sectors, limiting its ability to contribute to economic and social resilience (Chapter 2). On some occasions, certain investment projects can even exacerbate fragility risks, especially in cases where monitoring and regulatory enforcement capacities are low (Chapters 10 and 11).

Nevertheless, government policy and private sector investments can affect whether and how fragility risks negatively affect FDI, and the degree to which investment positively contributes to stability. Fragility analysis can be an opportunity to support FDI: the appropriate response depends on the nature and degree of fragility in a given context, and should be tailored as such. An understanding of fragility also reinforces the importance of priorities – such as improvement of the policy environment for investment and responsible business conduct (RBC) – that are outlined in other chapters.

In implementing policy responses, governments should adopt approaches that reflect the complementarity between investment promotion, resilience and inclusive development priorities, and – where relevant – seek support from development partners. Risk mitigation tools can help overcome some of the risks that constrain investment attraction. In this regard, blended finance approaches, as well as political risk insurances provided by public and private bodies (from development partners to export credit agencies), are relevant. Promoting business linkages between domestic and international firms, integrity and responsible business conduct can also contribute to decreasing risks and enhancing investors' trust (Chapters 8, 10 and 11). Governments supporting FDI in the face of fragility can develop tailored approaches to investment promotion, notably with respect to investor and sectoral targeting, but also by elaborating strategies based on proactive approaches, effective communication, efficient after-care services and grievance mechanisms (Chapter 6).

Policy considerations

- Enhance the overall investment environment using a fragility lens, recognising the complementarity between attracting investment and promoting resilience and inclusive development. Policymakers can adopt approaches that address the different dimensions of fragility, and align investment strategies and objectives with national development priorities, resilience and inclusiveness. Development partners can be recruited to assist governments in addressing the linkages between FDI and fragility in a holistic way.
- Demonstrate political commitment to legal stability, while laying the foundations for a sound legal investment framework. Solid and transparent investment protection provisions are ever-more essential to address investors' concerns in economies that are exposed to fragility. The international legal investment framework can also bring additional guarantees to investors, but breaches have increased during periods of instability, leading to complex and costly investor-State disputes. Governmental awareness of these risks, institutional co-ordination and investment dispute management and prevention mechanisms are needed to address the sensitive and complex issues of investment protection.
- Consider the adoption of measures and tools that contribute to mitigate real and perceived risks to investment. Promoting business linkages, integrity and responsible business conduct are key to increase the familiarity, penetration of foreign investors, and decrease uncertainty, while contributing to the overall positive impact on the economy and society. Additional tools include risk transfer mechanisms like political risk insurance and export credit finance, as well as blended finance approaches crowding-in private funding through public guarantees, PPPs, equity investment or debt instruments.
- Develop investment promotion approaches tailored to fragility. This includes adopting proactive mechanisms centred on institutionally strong and well-resourced IPAs, targeting investors that are more familiar with fragility and the national context, as well as prioritising strategic sectors with positive social and developmental effects that may help in mitigating the drivers of fragility itself.

The complex relationship between fragility and FDI

By increasing the risks and costs faced by international investors, fragility can discourage investment decisions, FDI inflows, reinvestment, and retention. Fragility is multidimensional and affects the focus economies in different ways, with some dimensions of fragility – for example, political and economic fragility – appearing to have a greater effect on FDI than others.

Yet, investors do invest in even highly fragile economies, and investment and fragility interact in complex ways. While FDI can be an important positive contributor to development and stability, there are cases where individual investment choices appear to exacerbate fragility and do not respect RBC. With the right policies and private sector actions, there are opportunities for investment to contribute to stability and resilience through positive developmental, technological and human capital spillovers.

This first section presents the framework that the OECD uses to assess fragility, outlines the relevance of fragility and synthesises the main fragility challenges present in the focus economies and the MENA region more broadly.

Fragility is multidimensional and affects the focus economies to different degrees

Fragility can be measured in many ways, and historically has often been perceived in terms of the presence or absence of conflict. Increasingly, however, fragility is seen as a multidimensional set of issues that affect all economies and countries in varying ways (Box 12.1) (Desai and Forsberg, 2020[1]).

It is important to stress that fragility is not a binary concept between "fragile country" and "non-fragile country". The OECD characterises fragility as "the combination of exposure to risk and insufficient coping capacities of the state, system and/or communities to manage, absorb or mitigate those risks" (OECD, 2020[2]). In this sense all countries and economies are fragile in some way, to some degree.

Fragility can lead to negative outcomes including violence, poverty, inequality, displacement, and environmental and political degradation. Identifying these risks, even before the outcomes are apparent, can help inform the ways in which governments and other actors can bolster resilience, with positive impacts for the investment climate.

Using the OECD fragility framework, fragility is measured on a spectrum of intensity across the economic, environmental, political, security and societal dimensions. A sixth dimension – human capital – will be added to the framework in 2022. Each dimension is represented by 8-12 indicators – 44 in total across all 5 dimensions – that measure fragility risks and government coping capacities to manage or mitigate these risks (Desai and Forsberg, 2020[1]). In doing so, the OECD multidimensional fragility framework captures the intersection of fragility, risk and resilience to inform where and how the root causes of fragility in each dimension can be addressed over time.

Globally, 175 economies have been analysed against the 2020 edition of the fragility framework.[3] Among the focus economies, Libya and the PA are among the most fragile 57 countries and territories – referred to as contexts – that are profiled in the *States of Fragility 2020* (OECD, 2020[2]). Of these 57 contexts, 13 are extremely fragile and 44 (including Libya and PA) are other fragile contexts. While most of the MENA focus economies are not among these 57 contexts, all exhibit some aspects of fragility. This fragility analysis, discussed here and shown in the Annex, has revealed useful findings to inform policies across the focus economies. Recent events, such as the political and economic crisis in Lebanon, have further revealed aspects of fragility in the region not fully captured in this data, the majority of which is from 2018. The Covid-19 health and economic crisis has exacerbated all dimensions of fragility around the world, with rising food insecurity, social inequalities (UN Women, 2020[3]; UNDP, 2020[4]), political violence and breaches of democratic norms and standards, especially in fragile contexts (Edgell et al., 2020[5]). Globally, an estimated 150 million people will be pushed into extreme poverty by 2021 (World Bank, 2020[6]).

Box 12.1. Fragility is about more than just conflict, economic performance or governance

The OECD's fragility framework analysis reveals that the drivers of fragility are much more complex and diverse than just conflicts, weak governance, or poor economic performance. They encompass a range of factors exacerbating stability and undermining sustainable development. While the economic dimension is an important factor in fragility, evidence shows that moving up the income ladder does not necessarily reduce entrenched fragility, nor does strengthening government institutions alone (OECD, 2018).

For example, while more than 80% of the world's poorest could be living in fragile contexts by 2030, 30 out of the 57 economies included in the 2020 OECD States of Fragility report are classified as middle income. And not all fragile contexts have active, or even recent, conflicts (OECD, 2020). There are no one-size-fits all solutions for fragility, so to be effective, approaches need to take account of the types of fragility seen in each context.

Fragility and investment interact in complex ways

FDI can be an important source of financing, job creation, technological advancement and private sector development for economies in the MENA region. It can help to mitigate fragility and promote inclusive social and economic development. Nevertheless, private investment should not be seen as a panacea. Fragility can stand in the way of achieving sustainable, quality investments by increasing the costs and risk exposure of international investors. If policymakers do not take account of the potential risks, investments hence miss the opportunity to contribute to development, or even exacerbate fragility.

Investment can help to mitigate elements of fragility

FDI can play a pivotal role in providing necessary financing to address fragility across its different dimensions. This is especially relevant considering the macroeconomic constraints, limited domestic private investment levels, and in some cases ODA dependence, that many economies face.

Increasing foreign investment is not purely about volumes of financing to the private sector, it should also promote economic resilience and inclusiveness. The sectoral distribution of FDI is thus particularly important: FDI can increase jobs, local income and productivity, and advance social goals, including through investment into sectors such as healthcare, education, and digital services. Using data from the Social Progress Index of social and environmental health of societies, Deloitte (2015[7]) found a positive relationship between FDI per capita and social progress across a sample of 132 countries, though the nature of this relationship varies according to country and sector. Additionally, input-output linkages with the local economy, including with local SMEs, can strengthen economic resilience by promoting private sector development.

Governments should therefore concentrate their efforts on attracting investment that can have a higher development impact by targeting sectors that contribute to creating a suitably skilled-workforce, and encouraging spill overs. Foreign companies should also act responsibly to generate higher impact for the host economy. Insights from private sector activities in the most fragile and conflict-affected contexts show that there is a positive business case for responsible investment in these economies, although this requires companies to see the benefit in adapting their core operations to manage the risks fragility presents and improve their impact on society (WEF, 2016[8]). When this is indeed the case, it may generate returns for the companies, local communities, and governments alike (*ibid.*).

Fragility and conflict, where present, can limit FDI and encourage FDI enclaves

Instability and conflict can reduce investor confidence and further compound protracted economic and political fragilities. This is particularly, though not exclusively, relevant in economies showing relatively high fragility in the security dimension, such as Libya and PA (see Annex A.) For example, based on the World Bank Group's classification of Fragile and Conflict-Affected Situations (FCS),[4] the IFC (2019[9]) found that even though the potential for FDI in FCS is lower than in more stable contexts due to small markets and low levels of trade, under conditions of peace and stability FDI flows to FCS would be at least twice as high as is currently the case.

Nevertheless, even severe fragility and conflict do not affect all investors alike, depending on the stage in the investment cycle or the sector (Barry, 2018[10]). Evidence suggests, for example, that resource-seeking FDI (e.g., in natural resource-intensive and extractives industries) is not particularly deterred by political instability or even conflict. FDI in natural resources is relatively insensitive to political instability (Chapter 2), driven in the region by a few mega-projects. Analysis using the Fragile States Index of the Fund for Peace showed that among countries with the highest level of fragility, FDI as a proportion of GDP was highest among resource-dependent countries, higher even than the average in low- and middle-income countries (Jensen, 2020[11]). Alongside natural endowments and global commodity prices, resource-seeking FDI in such situations is more likely to be determined by the extent to which production facilities and export infrastructure can be protected from current and future conflict, whether in offshore processing facilities or through onshore security measures (Jensen, 2020[11]; Multilateral Guarantee Agency, 2011[12]).

In some of these cases, however, overall positive FDI figures may hide its limited impact on resilience and sustainable development due to its structural and sectoral composition. While the employment outlook is varied and may be more positive in minerals, renewables, and agriculture, some natural resource investments – for example in mining and oil – may effectively operate in FDI enclaves with few linkages to the rest of the economy, generating relatively few jobs. This risk may be higher where investments are capital intensive rather than labour intensive (as is the case for most energy investments), require specialist training that local populations do not have access to, where they require few inputs from the local economy or local companies may not be set up to act as suppliers (UNCTAD, 2012[13]; Cordes, Östensson and Toledano, 2016[14]; Thompson, 2020[15]).

Fragility is costly for investors, even in the absence of conflict

Even in the absence of open conflict, fragility can discourage investment decisions, FDI inflows and retention by increasing the risks – actual and perceived. Studies indicate that some aspects of fragility have a greater negative impact on investment than others (Thompson, 2020[15]). Besides economic upheaval, political risk[5] can heighten investor concerns, whether due to increased protectionism, regulatory instability, policy uncertainty around Covid-19, or concerns about governments' ability to fulfil sovereign and contractual obligations or maintain currency convertibility (Kher and Chun, 2020[16]). FDI inflows also appear to be reduced by factors like low institutional quality (Alfaro, Kalemlio-Ozcan and Volosovych, 2008[17]) and high levels of corruption (Wei, 2000[18]).

Managing and mitigating these risks through, for example, political risk insurance (see below), increases the cost of doing business. Indeed, a global survey of international investors shows that political risk is the most important factor affecting investment entry decisions (Kher and Chun, 2020[16]). This includes fears on sudden political changes, uncompensated expropriations, breach of contracts, unfair treatments or discriminatory measures, abrupt regulatory changes (e.g., on licensing, tax, environmental requirements, etc.) and lack of transparency.

Recent studies show that investment in the MENA region is particularly sensitive to fragility in its political and security dimensions (Caccia, Baleix and Paniagua, 2018[19]; Dimitrova and Triki, 2018[20]). Moreover, quantitative analysis shows that higher political risk, especially in relation to conflict and institutional quality, increases the cost of equity capital for firms operating in the MENA region (Belkhira, Boubakrib and Griraa, 2017[21]).

On some occasions, investments can exacerbate risks to stability that need to be managed

The positive contributions of FDI to resilience, economic and social development are important, but not automatic. Investment is not a panacea, and its positive impact on sustainable development depends on a number of factors, including good policies, strong institutions and appropriate human resources (Li and Tanna, 2019[22]). Where State monitoring and regulatory enforcement mechanisms are weak, the possibility arises for FDI to have a negative impact on stability, whether through communal violence, poor working conditions, environmental degradation or increased corruption opportunities.

There have been cases globally where investments have been linked to increased fragility, especially in the extractives sectors. In sub-Saharan Africa, for example, (Christensen, 2018[23]) mining investments double the risk of protests and riots around the site, which are more likely when commodity prices increase, and in environments where the state is absent in negotiations between mining companies and local/host communities. In the Democratic Republic of Congo, even during conflict, the proximity of an AngloGold Ashanti mining site to a peace-keeping operation helped provide reassurance for the resumption of mining exploration. But this also involved engagement with and payments to the militia involved in the conflict, and the company was accused by Human Rights Watch of indirectly fuelling the ongoing conflict (Multilateral Guarantee Agency, 2011[12]).

Government policy and responses to fragility can help to determine whether FDI exacerbates fragility risks or reinforces coping capacities. High societal and security risks, high levels of unemployment and social instability may lead governments to adopt, willingly or not, behaviours that are even more detrimental for investors and increase this negative impact (WEF, 2019[24]). Christensen (2018[23]) argues that poor information flow can lead to mismatched expectations between the investing firm and the local population, which governments can help mitigate through greater transparency and institutions that can mediate between local communities and investors. In the case of Liberia, geo-spatial analysis supported the governments' decision to use a 'development corridor' approach, whereby agglomeration affects and the provision of public goods ensured that mining concessions support positive economic growth and development in the surrounding areas, even in the face of high levels of fragility (Bunte et al., 2018[25]).

The concrete risk that international investors could exploit a lack of state capacity has inspired international efforts to promote due diligence and responsible business conduct, particularly in sensitive sectors (Chapter 10). The OECD Due Diligence Guidance for Responsible Supply Chains of Minerals from Conflict-Affected and High-Risk Areas, for example, provides recommendations on how companies can avoid contributing to conflict through their mineral purchasing operations in these contexts. Recently, the OECD Due Diligence Guidance inspired EU due diligence obligations for importers of minerals originating in high-risk areas, effective as of January 2021.[6]

The five dimensions of fragility in the focus economies

Among the focus economies, Libya and the PA are among the most fragile contexts profiled in the 2020 OECD States of Fragility report. Egypt was profiled in the 2018 States of Fragility report but has increased its resilience and decreased fragility since then. Egypt reduced its fragility in every dimension except in the security dimension, achieving significant declines in political and societal fragility (OECD, 2020[2]).

In terms of aggregate regional fragility, the larger MENA region, excluding high income countries[7] is one of the most fragile regions in the world, second only to Sub-Saharan Africa (OECD, 2020[2]). Since 2011, the outbreak of the Syrian conflict has had unprecedented economic and political repercussions in the region with 5.6 million refugees flowing to neighbouring countries, including Lebanon and Jordan (UNHCR, 2020[26]). This situation has further compounded pre-existing fragilities in refugee-hosting countries, especially in Lebanon, which has experienced a profound economic and political crisis in 2020.

Fragility remains highly relevant to investment policymakers in the focus economies, even those with lower levels of fragility. For example, the macro-economic issues symptomatic of economic fragility – such as high levels of debt or aid-dependency – are common to several countries in the region. Almost all governments in the region have been confronted by political instability, movements of forcibly displaced people, the social and economic effects of desertification and environmental degradation and high levels of popular discontent. In terms of security, a surge of violence or conflict elsewhere in the MENA region can prejudice perceptions throughout the region (Caccia, Baleix and Paniagua, 2018[19]). Using the OECD's multidimensional framework, Figure 12.1 provides an aggregate indicator of fragility across the focus economies. Indicators for Iraq, the MENA regional average (excluding high income economies) and a global average are included for comparison purposes.

Figure 12.1. Fragility varies across the focus economies

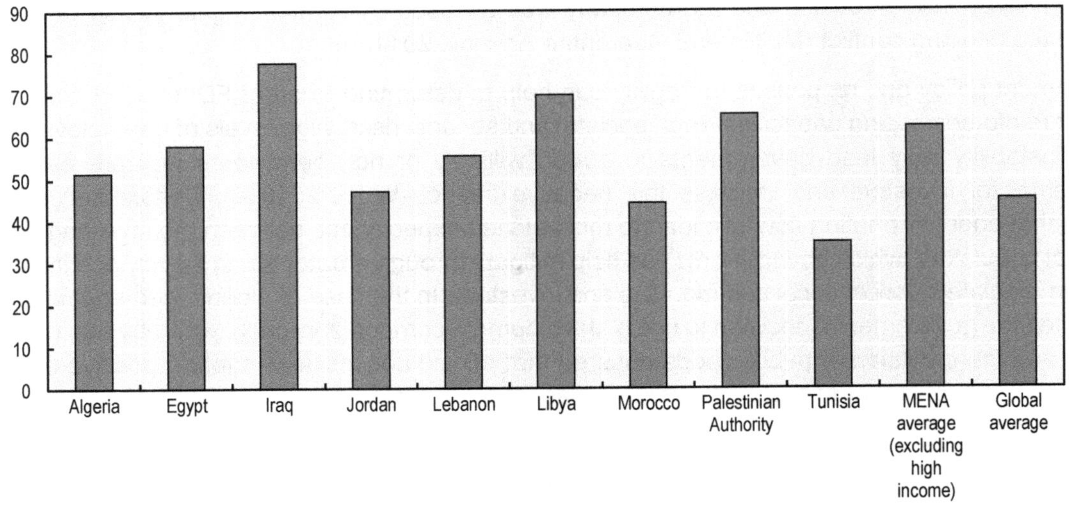

Note: This indicator has been scaled, with 0 indicating and 100 indicating the lowest and highest values of fragility, respectively. Figures for Iraq, the MENA average (excluding high income) and the global average are included for comparison purposes.
Source: Desai and Forsberg (2020). Data provided directly to the authors.

The OECD's multidimensional framework covers the five inter-related dimensions of economic, environmental, political, security and societal fragility. While each focus economy is unique, OECD quantitative analysis indicates that the political and societal dimensions of fragility are the most salient in the focus economies (Figure 12.2). The following sections look further across the five dimensions and their relevance to investment policymakers in the focus economies.

Figure 12.2. Political and societal dimensions of fragility are the most salient in the focus economies

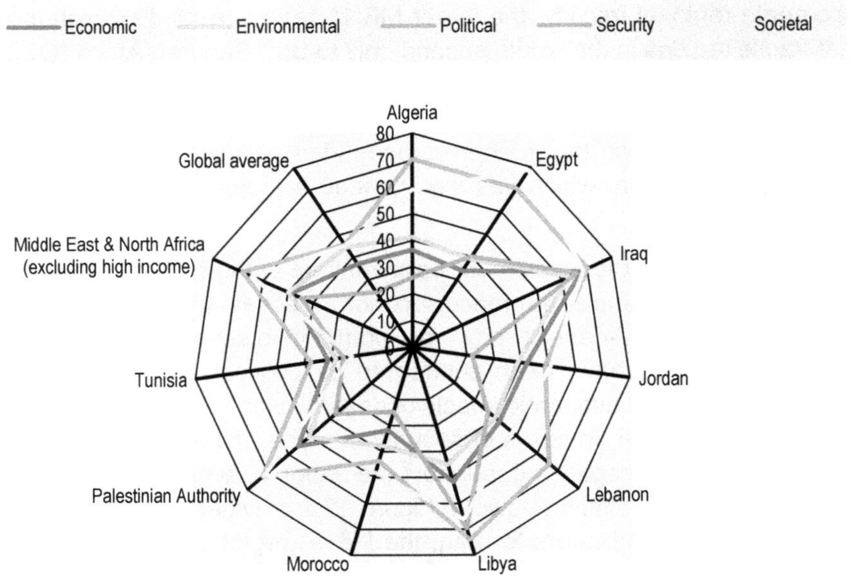

Note: 0 and 100 indicate the lowest and highest values of fragility, respectively.
Source: Desai *and Forsberg (2020). Data provided directly to the authors.*

The political dimension of fragility

The political dimension of fragility encompasses a country's mechanisms for mediating economic and social relationships – including those relevant for investment – and its capacity to strengthen accountability and transparency. Political fragility affects other dimensions by shaping the institutions that are key to supporting a sound investment climate, as well as inclusive societies. Indicators of the political dimension of fragility include clientelism and corruption, government effectiveness, division of power, constraints against the executive, physical integrity, voice and accountability, and women's participation in parliament. Political fragility can mean that the legal and regulatory context for international investment can be unstable and bring additional risk for investors.

The greater MENA region exhibits the highest level of political fragility among all regions of the world (OECD, 2020[2]). This is mirrored by data pointing to low trust in governments in the region. In Lebanon and the PA, for example, 80% and 50% of respondents to a recent survey reported have little to no trust in government (Transparency International, 2019[27]). Political fragility can be caused by endogenous factors, like lack of voice and accountability, social unrest, terrorism and poor institutional quality, as well as exogenous factors like conflict in neighbouring countries.

In the aftermath of the 2011 uprisings, some governments in the region have experienced major political transitions, including constitutional reforms. While some focus economies have increased their relative stability in this respect, political stability goes beyond stable and highly centralised states. The functioning of regional governance for example (i.e., the presence, level of autonomy, and effectiveness of elected public officials at the subnational level), as well as appropriate legislative and judicial constraints on the executive play, can play an important role in mitigating political fragility by promoting pluralism, local accountability, and mediating potential conflicts.

Among the focus economies, political fragility remains one of the most salient dimensions of fragility. Demonstrations of popular discontent in Algeria, Lebanon, Egypt, Morocco and Tunisia in particular have made increasingly clear that widespread corruption and territorial inequalities on the one hand, and accountability on the other, are intrinsically linked to the political dimension of fragility. Although corruption levels vary, international indicators point that none of the focus economies received a "passing grade" of 50/100 in terms of integrity (Chapter 11).

The societal dimension of fragility

The societal dimension of fragility comprises a country's vulnerability to risks affecting social capital and cohesion, especially in relation to inequality and access to opportunity, as well as the institutional capacity to mitigate these risks. Societal fragility exacerbates economic, political, and social exclusions and contributes to worsen the situation of marginalised communities.

In this dimension again, the greater MENA region excluding high income countries presents the highest level of fragility compared to other regions (OECD, 2020[2]). Youth unemployment is particularly severe across most of the focus economies: 50% in Libya, 41.6% in the PA, 36% in Tunisia, and 36% in Jordan (World Bank, 2020[28]). Although the total unemployment rate is estimated to be relatively low in Lebanon (6.3%), this is three times as high among young people (*ibid.*). High levels of unemployment, especially among youth and women, represent a major threat to social cohesion (ILOSTAT, 2020[29]). Globally, poverty and a lack of socio-economic opportunities are especially common among internally displaced people and refugees, which the focus economies host in large numbers (OECD, 2019[30]).

In the greater MENA region, the proportion of young people who are not in education, employment, or training (NEET) exceeds those in all other regions of the world (OECD, 2018[31]). Low scores on women's participation in the labour force, and on the proportion of NEET are common across the focus economies, with NEET rates among women surpassing 40% in Egypt, Jordan, PA and Tunisia (Dimova, Elder and Stephan, 2016[32]).[8]

The societal dimension of fragility is also exacerbated by low levels of social protection, for which public spending averages to barely 1% of GDP in the wider MENA region, against 20% in OECD countries (World Bank, 2018[33]). Low levels of social safety nets, along with low overall coverage and high informality are especially worrying factors in view of the present pandemic and economic shock it has precipitated (Box 12.2). The societal dimension of fragility affects both the economic dimension of fragility as well as political stability: popular mobilisations across the region point to the clear dissatisfaction with a lack of economic opportunities and socio-economic inclusion.

Box 12.2. Covid-19 is exacerbating the dimensions of fragility

Even in economies with relatively low rates of infection, lockdowns and other measures have had a range of socio-economic impacts (ACAPS, 2020[34]). The pandemic and resulting global recession have already exacerbated risks and weakened coping capacities, across the economic, environmental, and societal dimensions of fragility:

- Economic dimension: Extreme poverty will likely increase. According to the IMF's October estimates, the Gross Domestic Product (GDP) of the average fragile context will decline by 4% in 2020 (IMF, 2020[35]). Economic contractions in some MENA countries could be substantially greater, with some estimates suggesting GDP growth to contract by 19-25% in Lebanon and by 40-67% in Libya, though estimates are subject to high degrees of uncertainty (World Bank, 2020[36]).
- Societal dimension: Women and children will feel these effects disproportionately. Before the pandemic, the extreme poverty rate for women was expected to decline by 2.7% between 2019 and 2021. However, estimates now suggest a 9.4% increase following the pandemic (UN Women, 2020[3]). School closures left 384.5 million children – in mid-July – out of school, and many of these children are unlikely to return (UNESCO, 2020[37]; UNDP, 2020[4]).
- Environmental dimension: Food insecurity is likely to rise. Recent estimates suggest that 83-132 million people globally could fall into chronic hunger by the end of the year (FAO, 2020[38]). For example, in July, approx. 9.6 million people were experiencing crisis or worse levels of food insecurity in Sudan, more than at any time in Sudan's history (IPC, 2020[39]). At the end of October, one in five children under five years old in the southern parts of Yemen are acutely malnourished, which is the highest ever recorded and reflects a confluence of violent conflict, economic decline, funding shortfalls in food assistance, and Covid-19's impact (FAO, UNICEF, and WFP, 2020[40]).

Lockdowns and other restrictions on movement also impact the political and security dimensions of fragility. For example, there is the risk that Covid-19 measures could violate democratic norms and standards for emergency measures, which may lead to democratic backsliding. (Edgell et al., 2020[5]).

The economic dimension of fragility

The economic dimension of fragility comprises an economy's vulnerability to shocks and its capacities to address them. Indicators of the economic dimension of fragility include GDP growth, debt, regulatory effectiveness, resource dependence, economic remoteness and labour market measures. High economic fragility negatively affects households' ability to exit poverty and improve their socio-economic conditions. Economic fragility is closely associated with social and political challenges.

Since 2011, the greater Middle East region has been characterised by stagnating growth. The concurrent impact of the Covid-19 pandemic and oil price shocks has dramatically worsened macroeconomic outlooks, with an average GDP contraction of 5.3% projected for 2020 across the focus economies, except for Libya and Lebanon, which are expected to experience a particularly dramatic downturn in GDP growth, by -40% and 19% respectively in 2020, due to aggravated political, social and security dynamics, though forecasts are subject to high degrees of uncertainty (World Bank, 2020[36]). Current account and fiscal balances also suffered from a steep decline in both oil-importers and oil-exporters in 2020, and they are expected to remain negative in 2021 (IMF, 2020[35]).

While all of the focus economies have long faced high debt levels, the current economic contraction represents a major threat to the debt sustainability of those focus economies with particularly high debt levels. This is the case for Lebanon – which in March 2020 defaulted on the payment of a USD 1.2 billion in Eurobonds – and to a lesser extent for Jordan, whose credit rating was revised from stable to negative (FitchRatings, 2020[41]).

More generally, widening deficits will constrain the ability of governments to implement measures in support of public health and local economies, at a time when sources of private financing, including FDI and household remittances are falling globally. For countries like Algeria and Libya, resource dependence contributes to economic fragility by weighing on other issues present across the region like inflation rate fluctuations, exchange rate weakening and constrained public revenues. High dependence on oil and gas revenues contribute to creating rentier regimes, low economic complexity, lagging productivity, and limit economic diversification and innovation (Malik, 2017[42]).

Foreign aid can, for some countries, serve as an additional financial buffer but for PA, Lebanon and Jordan, aid dependence carries the risk of exposure in the event of cuts in foreign assistance. Low regulatory quality – defined as governments' lack of capacity to formulate and implement sound policies to cope with economic fragility– also affects several MENA countries, notably Algeria, Libya and Egypt, as well as, to a lesser extent, Tunisia and Morocco (World Bank, 2019[43]). Finally, as noted above, unemployment rates in the region have remained high (ILOSTAT, 2020[29]).

The environmental dimension of fragility

The environmental dimension of fragility encompasses a country's vulnerability to climate and health risks affecting citizens' livelihoods, as well as the presence of the institutions that can mitigate such environmental and food insecurity risks. Environmental fragility can affect the distribution of resources, increase inequality as well as the risk of conflict.

All of the focus economies are familiar with the challenges of desertification, soil degradation and water scarcity both due to their geographical location and a variety of human factors that exacerbate these phenomena. Climate change is leading to increasing temperatures, decreased rainfall, rising sea levels and economic damage in the focus economies. For example, 96% of the territory of Tunisia is threatened by desertification, and the overall cost of environmental deterioration is estimated around 2.5% of the country's GDP (ITES, 2017[44]). These worrying developments threaten food security across the greater MENA region, where only 5% of the land area is arable and where total agricultural production is expected to decrease by 21% by the end of the century compared to 2000 (OECD/FAO, 2018[45]). The quality and quantity of groundwater, the most important source of water in the region, has been considerably deteriorating in recent years (Hamed et al., 2018[46]).

Demographic factors, urbanisation and industrial growth will keep increasing the demand for scarce water resources, potentially weighing on social and security dynamics. There are already some indications that the densely populated Nile delta and coastlines of Algeria and Morocco are high-risk areas for climate-induced forced displacement (IOM, 2015[47]). Waste management is also a widespread issue, worsening land, water and air pollution and the associated health risks for the local population. The series of protests that took place in Lebanon in 2015 over the government's failure to dispose over 20 000 tons of garbage in and around the capital is just one example of how these environmental and health issues can feed and trigger social discontent and instability.

The security dimension of fragility

The security dimension of fragility encompasses a country's vulnerability to violence, crime and conflict, as well as the presence of institutions to prevent and mitigate it. The security dimension of fragility can cause societal and economic disruption, as well as damage to infrastructure and supply chains, which can be particularly problematic for investors. Insecurity can erode cohesion and social capital, cause mass displacement, and is a human and personal tragedy for millions of people globally.

The greater MENA region, excluding high income countries, exhibits the highest level of security fragility among all regions of the world, by significant margin (OECD, 2020[2]). Exposure to conflict in MENA has increased from 6% in 2007 to 19.4% in 2017, with one in five people now living in close proximity to conflict (Corral et al., 2020[48]). The 2011 uprisings led to conflicts and inter-communal violence taking an incalculable toll in Syria, Yemen, Libya and Iraq.

Some of the focus economies have been significantly affected by these security developments. Conflicts have severed trade ties, decelerated private investment and strongly affected the tourism sector. For example, studies estimate that the Libyan crisis was responsible for 24% of the deceleration of economic growth of Tunisia between 2011 and 2015 (ESCWA, 2017[49]). Lebanon, Jordan, Egypt and Tunisia have also experienced considerable inflows of forcibly displaced populations from Syria and Libya. Transnational terrorism, moreover, continues to embody a concrete threat for most of the focus economies, albeit to different degrees, forcing governments to channel public expenditures into the national security apparatus and posing a security risk to businesses, deterring investors or requiring them to incur the cost of private security. Across the region, territorial disputes represent a source of tension and instability, notably in the case of the PA and Lebanon, as well as, to a different degree, Morocco. Finally, illicit cross-border trade and smuggling of arms, drugs, oil and humans from the Sahel region into Algeria, Morocco and Libya, caused by limited or weaker state capacity in the southern regions, has historically fuelled transnational crime networks and armed clashes (Ralston, 2014[50]).

Policy considerations to improve investment outcomes in the face of fragility

Despite the challenges outlined above, FDI can and does take place in the face of fragility, and can help address some of the underlying drivers of fragility by providing necessary sources of financing and contributing to inclusive and sustainable economic and social development. The impact of FDI depend on the level and nature of fragility, and the level of conflict. Conflicts deter investment, but post-conflict situations where reconstruction is needed can attract investors.

While more research is needed on how policymakers can integrate fragility analysis into investment policy, evidence from the region and beyond provides useful policy considerations to attract FDI and enhance its impact on the dimensions of fragility. Governments could consider adopting co-ordinated national strategies and measures alongside development partners to address fragility's impact on FDI; promoting risk mitigation measures and tools; and developing tailored investment promotion mechanisms. Implementation of these policies would vary among MENA focus economies as fragility affects them in different ways, to different degrees.

Enhancing the investment environment in a fragility context

Towards a holistic approach to investment, resilience and inclusive development

The complex interaction between fragility and investment underscores that inclusive development and quality investment attraction are complementary. OECD (2019[51]) has measured the extent to which FDI can affect specific aspects of sustainable development, pointing to a broad positive impact on economic and environmental sustainability. Although further work is needed to fully understand FDI's contribution to advancing SDGs, the institutional and policy context are pivotal in determining its eventual positive or negative economic, social and environmental impacts (*ibid.*). These findings suggest the adoption of holistic approaches to investment, resilience and inclusive development, where FDI is assessed against the wider framework of a country's policy priorities and long-term development vision. In some of the more fragile contexts, this means that improving framework conditions needs to keep pace with more direct actions to increase FDI.

National development strategies can hence be a useful tool to promote economic growth and attract investment, while integrating vulnerability considerations and strengthening societal resilience. For example, efforts to increase skills of youth, women and refugees can improve the enabling environment for FDI (Purfield et al., 2018[52]). The region is progressively integrating social objectives in its strategies: e.g., Egypt's Vision 2030 measures the achievement of sustainable inclusive growth based on an increased female labour force participation, while the Jordan National Vision and Strategy for 2025 ties together regulatory reforms of SME policy, training and rehabilitation programmes for women and youth employment. However, results on these objectives have been mixed and a renewed, long-term commitment to implement inclusiveness objectives is needed.

Laying the institutional and legal bases for a sound investment framework

In the most fragile contexts of the region, it is challenging to undertake investment climate reforms, especially when the priorities are on enhancing overall governance or de-escalating conflict (e.g. the Libyan Political Dialogue Forum). Limited state capacity and room for policy manoeuver may require careful prioritisation of specific measures that carry the largest benefits. As economies move out of conflict and unrest, additional steps can be taken towards institutional and legal reforms, serving as the basis for a future investment framework. The OECD-Iraq project provides some lessons on the importance of taking a tailored, flexible, and conflict-sensitive approach to such reforms (Box 12.3).

Box 12.3. Promoting investment in a fragile context: The OECD Iraq Project

Between 2007 and 2016, the OECD supported the government of Iraq in improving its investment climate. Tangible outcomes included: the amendment of the 2006 Investment Law; policy advice and capacity building on arbitration law and bilateral investment agreements; training of national and provincial investment commissions in developing and presenting investment marketing material, handling investor inquiries, and formulating investment opportunities. It also represented a unique and independent platform for public-private dialogue and allowed for the participation of high-level Iraqi policy-makers in the regional networks of the MENA-OECD Competitiveness Programme.

The Project had to react and adapt to the realities of a fragile and conflict-affected environment, with high levels of violence and insecurity, a deep sense of mistrust between the various ethnic, religious and political factions of the country, the surge of the so-called "Islamic State" and the collapse of oil prices in 2014-15.

Based on the OECD Principles for Good International Engagement in Fragile States and Situations, the Project identified five key lessons:

- Do no harm: The project ensured that the selection and involvement of Iraqi stakeholders in the project activities did not add to or exacerbate existing political tensions. The project conducted a Conflict Sensitivity Analysis and a Stakeholder Analysis ensuring a wide and balanced representation of stakeholders and increasing acceptance, ownership and thus impact.
- Consistent monitoring and flexible approach: As political priorities often change fast in fragile environments, only a flexible project approach can respond adequately to stakeholders' demands and bring tailored solutions that produce results, while maintaining donors' support.

The Project conducted bi-annual impact assessments to determine the suitability of its policy advice. The donor (the Swedish International Development Cooperation Agency - Sida) showed a flexible implementation approach, often entailing a significant rebalancing, notably in view of the 2014 Islamic State offensive and its drastic implications.

- Integration of cross-cutting development perspectives: In a fragile context, economic policy reform is also likely to affect political, security and development objectives. Understanding local dynamics and sensitivities, the project analysed how its activities related to the cross-cutting development issues of poverty reduction, gender mainstreaming and conflict sensitivity.
- Frequent consultations and project ownership: In a fragile context often characterised by weak institutions, building strong relationships with individual stakeholders is as important as building relationships with institutions. The Project built relationships with key stakeholders and engage into an inclusive approach, strengthening sense of ownership, which translated into mutual trust and fruitful communication
- Public-private dialogue: PPD can be a powerful instrument for strengthening the quality of economic policy reforms and is considered particularly important in fragile and conflict-affected contexts, as it can improve transparency, quality and effectiveness of public policies and thus help build more resilient systems. The Project engaged non-public Iraqi stakeholders, as well as foreign firms investing in Iraq.

Source: (OECD, 2016[53])

Improving legal stability is one of the priorities governments should consider when faced by fragility. Fragility can increase the risk, or perceived risks, of expropriation, breach of contract and capital transfer restrictions, which in turn leads investors to withdrawing existing investments or cancelling planned investments (Kher & Chun, 2020). Reforms to support solid and transparent investment provisions on non-discrimination, fair compensation for expropriation, profit repatriation guarantees and property rights could help. When designing these measures, it is crucial that governments consider concrete steps needed to ensure their adequacy to recognised international standards.

International investment agreements (see Chapter 5) may provide an additional level of protection to foreign investors engaging in fragile contexts by granting protections alongside domestic laws.[9] At the same time, low implementation capacity, unforeseeable events, political and societal vulnerability and lack of inter-institutional co-ordination can potentially lead to involuntary breaches in fragile contexts (Kher and Chun, 2020[16]). In the midst of social and political turmoil in 2011, the region saw an increase of investor-state disputes, with Egypt and Libya being involved respectively in 24 and 16 known cases of international arbitration (UNCTAD, 2020[54]).

Effective implementation and enforcement of reforms aiming at improving legal stability in fragile contexts is equally relevant. This requires the establishment of bodies in charge of investment policy design and implementation, as well as co-ordination between them. For instance, a supporting institutional framework to deal with investors' disputes is still lacking in Libya, the PA and Lebanon (Chapter 5). Overall, in contexts where state monitoring and enforcement capacities are lacking and institutions are weak, investment policy remains scattered across several institutions and agencies. This can further raise the risk for inefficiency and inconsistencies.

Development actors can support private sector development and help improve the investment environment in fragile contexts

Development partners can help improve the investment environment in fragile contexts, both through technical cooperation, for instance on how to better manage and prevent investment disputes (e.g. the

World Bank Investor Grievance Management Mechanism), and financial pledges to support private sector development. Private sector development as an enabler of political, societal and economic resilience has been central to donor approaches in MENA. Various conferences (e.g., the 2016 London Syria conference, the 2017 and 2018 Brussels conferences for Syria and the region, and the 2018 Kuwait conference for Iraq, the 2020 Conference in support to the Lebanese people) resulted in financial pledges to support countries requiring post-conflict reconstruction assistance (Iraq and Syria) or facing large refugee inflows (Jordan) in the form of so-called "compacts" (Box 12.4).

More generally, development actors have been increasingly providing significant financial support to the most fragile contexts, which have limited capacity and funding. In recent years, financing for the most fragile contexts has reached record volumes: in 2018, bilateral donors spent USD 76 billion in the 57 most fragile contexts covered by the OECD fragility framework, the highest number ever recorded.

Box 12.4. Addressing the refugee crisis through the Jordan Compact

In 2016, the Government of Jordan, with the support of the international community, committed to improving the living conditions, prospects and resilience of Syrian refugees and Jordanian citizens and supporting the economy.

The three objectives of the Jordan Compact are: a) turning the refugee crisis into an opportunity to attract new investments, opening up to the EU market, and creating jobs for Jordanians and Syrian refugees; b) rebuilding the resilience of host communities by adequately financing; and c) supporting the Jordanian macroeconomic financing needs over the next three years, in the context of a new IMF programme.

The government introduced special work permits for Syrian refugees working in 18 new special economic zones (SEZs). Firms established and operating in these SEZs benefitted from concessional loans provided by the World Bank and preferential trade access to the EU if they sourced at least 15% of their workforce among Syrian refugees (EU Decision on relaxation of rules of origin). In parallel, the government committed to improve its investment climate to attract domestic and international investments through promotion, facilitation and reforms of business licensing and regulations.

Results, however, have been limited. As of February 2019, only 16 companies had applied for registration to export under the EU preferential scheme and 13 were approved. Collectively, these employed 280 Syrians – a figure that dwarfs the 300,000 working-age refugees registered in Jordan. Unattractive wages in SEZs and low levels of greenfield FDI have been pointed to as the main obstacles.

Nevertheless, this approach showed how displaced population can be seen as assets, rather than liabilities, and has been replicated in other contexts (i.e. Ethiopia). It also demonstrates an innovative example of how policies can be designed to strengthen societal resilience, while also providing new investment and market access opportunities.

Source: (Dettoni, 2019[55]); (Ali Slimane et al., 2020[56]); (World Bank, 2016[57]); (Government of Jordan, 2016[58]); (Barbelet, Hagen-Zanker and Mansour-Ille, 2018[59]).

Mitigating the risks that fragility poses for investors

Blended finance and risk transfer mechanisms

Though not replacing wider business climate reforms, a number of concrete and temporary instruments are available to insure investors against specific types of risk, in particular political risk. They include blended finance approaches and risk transfer mechanisms like export credit and political risk insurance. However, these tools are not a panacea. They are most effective alongside, rather than instead of, policy reforms (Basile and Neunuebel, 2019[60]). They require a case-to-case analysis that needs to integrate fragility considerations and appropriate safeguards and monitoring. Avoiding engaging government institutions, or focusing only on short-term "easy wins", could exacerbate fragility in the long run (Williams, Burke and Wille, 2014[61]).

The OECD defines blended finance as the strategic use of development finance to mobilise additional finance towards sustainable development in developing countries. Blended finance can take many forms, including the use of public guarantees, PPPs, debt instruments, equity investment, as well as innovative social-impact investment (Basile and Neunuebel, 2019[60]). OECD official statistics show that private finance mobilised by official donor interventions reached USD 48.4 billion globally in 2018, much of it concentrated in emerging markets (OECD, 2020[62]). Almost two thirds of these amounts were mobilised in economic infrastructure and financial services, mostly by guarantees, syndicated loans and direct investment in companies and special purpose vehicles (ibid.).

Blended finance can catalyse investment in fragile contexts by transferring some risks away from investors. In 2016, 15 of the largest development finance institutions (DFIs) invested a total of USD 1.3 billion in fragile contexts. IFC (2019[9]) accounted for one-third of this amount and committed to increase the share of its investments in fragile contexts and low-income countries to 40% by 2030. As for MIGA, 12% of its outstanding guarantee portfolio is in fragile contexts, accounting to USD 2.7 bn.

Interest in blended finance approaches has picked up in the last decade, including through dedicated funds and facilities. Based on recent data from the OECD's Blended Finance Funds and Facilities Survey – which includes 198 funds and facilities managed by both public and private organisations – has captured around USD 74.5 billion of assets under management globally. Of this, an estimated around 2.7 billion targets the focus economies, the majority (USD 1.5 billion) in Egypt (Dembele, Vilalta and Bangun, forthcoming[63]).

Development finance institutions (DFIs), development partners and export credit agencies (ECAs) can support investors through risk-mitigation instruments and financing. DFIs generally mitigate risks, real or perceived, of private investment undertaken at commercial or quasi-commercial terms (Miyamoto and Chiofalo, 2015[64]). Tools offered by DFIs include financial and technical support to private companies (e.g., project preparation services), including foreign investors, and mobilisation of private investment for activities with a developmental purpose. Instruments include long-term loans, equity capital, mezzanine finance and guarantees (both full and partial), as well as investment in local banks or on-lending to private companies (ibid.). The Islamic Development Bank Group (IsDBG) is a prominent example of DFI active in 57 shareholding economies in the wider MENA, including all focus economies. The Islamic Corporation for the Insurance of Investment and Export Credit (ICIEC), within the IsDBG, offers political risk insurance (PRI) covering issues such as transfer and convertibility, expropriation, and war and civil disturbance. With the objective of facilitating FDI, ICIEC's country risk insurance covers equity and non-equity investment under the condition that the investment is Sharia-acceptable.

Development partners can also offer a variety of risk-transferring tools to help mobilise private investment in fragile contexts. MIGA's Conflict-Affected and Fragile Economies Facility (CAFEF), for example, issues guarantees to eligible projects that provide an initial loss layer insurance. These cover loans, equity investments and future earnings against currency inconvertibility and transfer restriction, expropriation, breach of contract, war and civil disturbance. In 2010, the IFC added fragility to its strategic priority areas and established a Fragile and Conflict-affected States Coordination Unit. In MENA, the IFC invests and provides advisory services to international private investors and public institutions through its Conflict Affected States in Africa Initiative. For example, Scatec Solar ASA, an independent solar power producer listed on the Oslo Stock Exchange, has secured guarantees with MIGA in March 2020 to cover its equity investment in six Egyptian solar power plants. The guarantees cover 90% of investments by Scatec Solar for up to 15 years against the risks of transfer restrictions and convertibility.

ECAs are financial institutions, either private or government-sponsored, that support domestic exporters through short-term trade financing in the form of credit, insurance and guarantees or project-specific long-term financing (e.g. in infrastructure). ECA support among OECD countries is co-ordinated through the Arrangement on Officially Supported Exports Credit and the Working Party on Export Credits and Credit Guarantees, which serves as an important framework for the setting of minimum interest rates, risk fees and maximum repayment terms, as well as environmental and integrity standards.

Overall, despite of the wide variety of options available, penetration of risk mitigation mechanisms in the region seems to be relatively low and could be strengthened. A recent report of the US International Development Finance Corporation (DFC) highlights that, despite the high risk for foreign companies in some MENA contexts, tools like political risk insurance remain underexploited (OPIC, 2019[65]). According to the report, when asked for the reasons why they did not make use of political risk insurance, investors responded that they either did not believe the level of risk warranted for the adoption of such instruments, that the costs of coverage were too high or that they were simply unaware of this possibility (ibid.), suggesting that additional promotion and facilitation of risk mitigation options could, to some degree, bring benefits.

Promoting linkages between foreign firms and domestic businesses

Strengthening links between international investors and domestic businesses can also play a key role in mitigating potential risks for investors. Linkages with local businesses in domestic supply chains can mitigate operational risks thanks to their knowledge of the local context and their higher risk tolerance (World Bank, 2018[66]). Joint ventures or alliances with local companies are the most common strategies chosen by international investors to mitigate political risks in emerging markets (MIGA, 2014[67]). However, this can be particularly difficult to achieve for investors in fragile contexts due to insecurity, market fragmentation, a lack of sectoral linkages and under-developed business clusters (ibid.). IPAs can play a pivotal role in developing tailored strategies or programmes in this respect, focusing first and foremost on strategic and attractive sectors (Chapter 8).

Linkages between multinational enterprises and local firms, particularly SMEs, also increase employment and training opportunities, development of human capital, as well as knowledge and technology transfers. In the case of Libya, the OECD (2016[68]) has analysed the pivotal role that SMEs can play in the reconstruction of the country, reviewing the current national framework and identifying recommendations that can contribute to pave the way for post-conflict recovery once the situation has stabilised.

Promoting integrity and responsible business conduct

Governance risks, in particular corruption, represent a major financial, legal and reputational risk for international investors (Chapter 11). Corruption, as well as poor state capacity and weak monitoring and enforcement mechanisms, reduce FDI inflows (Wei, 2000[18]) Studies specific to the region highlight that integrity improves the positive impact of FDI on economic development (Hakimi and Hamdi, 2017[69]). On the investors' side, responsible business practices can reinforce the investment climate in fragile contexts, through accountable behaviours and increased transparency, especially in sensitive sectors such financial and extractives sectors (Chapter 10). In MENA focus economies, no IPA with the exception of the Moroccan one prioritises investors with a good RBC track record (Chapter 6).

Developing investment promotion strategies tailored to fragility

Sectoral focus

Adopting a sectoral focus for FDI promotion in fragile contexts can help achieve two concurrent objectives: identifying and exploiting an economy's comparative advantages, and supporting specific sectors in line with development, reconstruction and resilience strategies, as well as people and business needs. For example, research suggests that FDI in sectors like infrastructure, energy, agribusiness, retail and social services can contribute to peace consolidation and often offers high returns (WEF, 2016[8]). In post-conflict environments, evidence shows that, together with services, construction is the fastest-growing sector (World Bank, 2018[66]). Promoting FDI in infrastructure can further strengthen and support post-conflict or disaster rebuilding efforts, while also enhancing connectivity with regional and global markets (Box 12.5). For example, plans for the reconstruction of the Port of Beirut, together with a reform of the Lebanon port sector, is an opportunity to stimulate trade and economic growth.

As previously observed, most FDI in the region is channelled into capital-intensive sectors, which have contributed little to productivity and job creation, key to sustainable economic growth. Between 2003 and 2019 the majority of greenfield investment in the focus economies went to real estate and construction projects (35%) and extractive industries (26%). Investment in manufacturing has increased in recent years, but the sector attracts a relatively small amount of overall investment in the focus economies, and the service sector even less. Only 5% of greenfield FDI in Libya has gone to manufacturing since 2003 (Chapter 2).

Box 12.5. Infrastructure to attract FDI while boosting diversification and connectivity

Fragility poses additional strains on the existing infrastructure in a number of focus economies in the region and makes it even more difficult to attract much-needed investment to increase connectivity with the global economy (Chapter 9). Poor infrastructure, particularly prolonged power outages and water supply shortages, are severe challenges faced by businesses in fragile contexts (IFC, 2019[9]). For example, firms reported losses due to electrical outages over one firth of their annual sales in PA (*ibid.*). In Libya, the civil war led to a degradation in the availability of infrastructure services such as water for the population, while in Lebanon, electricity is the second biggest obstacle for firms and the quality of infrastructure is among the poorest in the world (EBRD, EIB, & World Bank, 2016[70]).

Infrastructure projects, whether in the transportation, energy, water or telecommunications sectors, are central in a post-crisis context to address reconstruction and rehabilitation needs, provide basic services to refugees and support the resilience of host communities through economic development and job creation (OECD, 2018[71]; Rubaba et al., 2015[72]). They are also instrumental in ensuring the continuity and viability of trade routes connecting countries to regional and global markets.

In Egypt, for example, the government initiated a number of mega-projects to increase economic resilience through better participation in global value chains. It invested over USD 335 billion, across real estate, transport and energy infrastructure (Flanders Investment & Trade, 2018[73]). Egypt has also doubled its level of electricity generation capacity over the last six years and is now in a situation of power surplus (Magdy, 2020[74]). In Jordan, the influx of over 1.3 million refugees from Syria put significant pressure on its infrastructure, particularly water supply. The 2025 National Vision and Strategy recognises the key role of infrastructure to achieve economic transformation and resilience based on export development (Harake, 2019[75]). Jordan is seeking to become a regional logistics hub, notably for electricity and transport networks.

Governments and IPAs in the region are aware of the need for diversifying the economy and prioritising investment in more productive and labour-intensive sectors. All but one IPA in the focus economies prioritise investments in certain sectors (Chapter 6). For example, the Palestinian National Policy Agenda includes the objective to attract FDI in the priority sectors of construction, tourism, agriculture and ICT. An assessment of the economy's competitiveness, in line with the needs to address fragility, is a relevant initial strategy to target specific sectors or projects (Whyte and Griffin, 2014[76]).

Targeting investors

Investment promotion tailored to very fragile countries may be aided by a strategy targeting specific investors that are more likely to engage in such contexts. This could include investors with prior experience in fragile contexts, with the capacity to deal with potential associated risks, or investors that were present before a period of instability, who may be willing to re-engage (Whyte and Griffin, 2014[76]). Investors from neighbouring countries or from diaspora communities are also likely to have good knowledge and understanding of the national context, can build and use their networks, and potentially take advantage of underutilised value chains. They may operate at a smaller scale but build stronger business linkages with the local economy. Preliminary evidence suggests, for example, that in fragile contexts, investors are more likely to come from other developing countries than are investors into more stable developed countries (Basile and Neunuebel, 2019[60]).

Targeting regions

Identifying geographical areas with relatively higher levels of security where investors can safely operate in very fragile contexts has been identified as a potentially useful, if temporary, strategy (World Bank, 2018[66]). Special Economic Zones (SEZs), free zones and industrial clusters are increasingly common in many developing economies. They can help to partly neutralise the effects of an otherwise less favourable business climate by offering differentiated treatment or services to investors, such as through tax or administrative incentives or better infrastructure than in the rest of the country. The creation of zones is often a reflection of the need to offset a negative impact of stringent import protection on trade or challenges in accessing secured land under the inland regime (OECD, 2020[77]).

However, impact of zone-based strategies in fragile contexts has been mixed. While zones can attract FDI and help boost exports, their expected benefits in terms of economic development are not necessarily positive or automatic but are greatly contingent on the local business environment. More problematic, they may be impeding fair competition between firms inside and outside of zones, and risk creating economic enclaves. They also bear a certain cost on government revenues as the incentives, particularly corporate income tax holidays, granted to firms reduce the fiscal base. Further analysis on the impact of SEZs in MENA fragile contexts on investment attraction and enterprise activities (e.g. Tripoli Special Economic Zone in Lebanon or the Misrata Free Zone in Libya) would allow to build lessons and good practices.

In some economies, involving subnational IPAs in promotion and facilitation mechanisms may also be useful to channel investment to specific regions (see chapter 6). In principle, IPAs may contribute to ease operations at the sub-regional level in large countries, attract investment to safer areas in conflict-affected economies, balance economic development across the territory, and facilitate dialogue with local communities. For example, Iraq built a network of 15 Provincial Investment Commissions with some being proactive in attracting investment (OECD, 2016[53]).[10] However, caution is once again necessary. Potentially low capacities of local institutions and lack of co-ordination with the central level may complicate administrative procedures and increase transaction costs and corruption risks.

References

ACAPS (2020), *Covid-19 Government Measures Dataset*, ACAPS, https://www.acaps.org/covid-19-government-measures-dataset. [34]

Alfaro, L., S. Kalemlio-Ozcan and V. Volosovych (2008), "Why doesn't capital flow from rich to poor countries? An empirical investigation", *The Review of Economics and Statistics*, Vol. 90/2, pp. 347-368, https://www.jstor.org/stable/40043150. [17]

Ali Slimane, M. et al. (2020), *New economic opportunities for Jordanians and Syrian refugees*, https://blogs.worldbank.org/arabvoices/new-economic-opportunities-jordanians-and-syrian-refugees. [56]

Barbelet, V., J. Hagen-Zanker and D. Mansour-Ille (2018), *The Jordan Compact: Lessons learnt and implications for future refugee compacts*, https://data2.unhcr.org/en/documents/download/61932. [59]

Barry, C. (2018), "Peace and conflict at different stages of the FDI lifecycle", *Review of International Political Economy*, Vol. 25/2, https://doi.org/10.1080/09692290.2018.1434083. [10]

Basile, I. and C. Neunuebel (2019), *Blended Finance in Fragile Contexts: Opportunities and risks*, OECD Publishing. [60]

Belkhira, M., N. Boubakrib and J. Griraa (2017), "Political risk and the cost of capital in the MENA region", *Emerging Markets Review*, Vol. 33, Pages 155-172, https://www.sciencedirect.com/science/article/pii/S1566014116301832?via%3Dihub. [21]

Bunte, J. et al. (2018), "Natural resource sector FDI, government policy, and economic growth: Quasi-experimental evidence from Liberia", *World Development*, Vol. 107, pp. 151-162, https://doi.org/10.1016/j.worlddev.2018.02.034. [25]

Caccia, F., J. Baleix and J. Paniagua (2018), "FDI in the MENA Region: Factors that Hinder or Favour Investments in the Region", *IEMed Mediterranean Yearbook 2018*, https://www.iemed.org/observatori/arees-danalisi/arxius-adjunts/anuari/med.2018/FDI_MENA_region_Carril_Milgram_Paniagua_Medyearbook2018.pdf. [19]

Christensen, D. (2018), "Concession Stands: How Mining Investments Incite Protest in Africa", *International Organization*, Vol. Volume 73/Issue 1, Winter 2019, pp. 65 - 101, https://doi.org/10.1017/S0020818318000413. [23]

Cordes, K., O. Östensson and P. Toledano (2016), "Employment from mining and agricultural investments: How much myth, how much reality?", Columbia Center on Sustainable Investment, Columbia University, http://ccsi.columbia.edu/files/2014/11/Employment-impact-mining-and-ag-Executive-summary-CCSI-2016.pdf. [14]

Corral, P. et al. (2020), *Fragility and Conflict : On the Front Lines of the Fight against Poverty*, World Bank, https://openknowledge.worldbank.org/handle/10986/33324. [48]

Deloitte (2015), *Foreign Direct Investment and Inclusive Growth: The impacts on social progress*, https://www2.deloitte.com/bd/n/pages/about/pages/about-deloitte/articles/fdi-and-inclusive-growth.html. [7]

Dembele, F., D. Vilalta and V. Bangun (forthcoming), *Blended Finance Funds and Facilities: 2020 Survey Results*, OECD Publishing, Paris. [63]

Desai, H. and E. Forsberg (2020), "Multidimensional Fragility in 2020", *Development Cooperation Working Paper*, No. 79, OECD Publishing, Paris, https://www.oecd-ilibrary.org/docserver/b4fbdd27-en.pdf?expires=1606489083&id=id&accname=ocid84004878&checksum=76A4C8D3131FD832F80C3F8D2A543C92. [1]

Dettoni, J. (2019), *Can free zones fix the global refugee crisis?*, https://www.fdiintelligence.com/article/75843. [55]

Dimitrova, A. and D. Triki (2018), "Does state fragility matter for foreign direct investment? Evidence from Southern and Eastern Mediterranean countries", *Management Decision*, Vol. 56/8, pp. 1787-1803, https://doi.org/10.1108/MD-03-2017-0252. [20]

Dimova, R., S. Elder and K. Stephan (2016), *Labour market transitions of young women and men in the Middle East and North Africa*, ILO, https://www.ilo.org/wcmsp5/groups/public/---ed_emp/documents/publication/wcms_536067.pdf. [32]

EBRD, EIB, & World Bank (2016), *What's Holding Back the Private Sector in MENA? Lessons from the Enterprise Survey*, The World Bank. [70]

Edgell, A. et al. (2020), *Pandemic Backsliding: Democracy During Covid-19 (PanDem), Version 4*, Varieties of Democracy Institute, http://www.v-dem.net/en/our-work/research-projects/pandemic-backsliding/. [5]

ESCWA (2017), *Impact of the Libyan crisis on the Tunisian economy An estimation of the macroeconomic and fiscal impacts of the Libyan crisis on the Tunisian economy*, https://www.unescwa.org/publications/impact-libyan-crisis-tunisian-economy. [49]

FAO (2020), *State of Food Security and Nutrition in the World*, Food and Agriculture Organisation, Rome, Italy, http://www.fao.org/3/ca9692en/online/ca9692en.html. [38]

FAO, UNICEF, and WFP (2020), *Malnutrition surges among young children in Yemen as conditions worsen*, Food and Agriculture Organisation of the United Nations/UN Children's Fund/World Food Programme, https://reliefweb.int/report/yemen/malnutrition-surges-among-young-children-yemen-conditions-worsen. [40]

FitchRatings (2020), , https://www.fitchratings.com/research/sovereigns/fitch-revises-jordan-outlook-to-negative-affirms-at-bb-08-05-2020. [41]

Flanders Investment & Trade (2018), *Megaprojects in Egypt*, https://www.flandersinvestmentandtrade.com/export/sites/trade/files/market_studies/2018%20-%20Egypt%27s%20Mega%20Projects.pdf. [73]

Government of Jordan (2016), *The Jordan Compact: A New Holistic Approach between the Hashemite Kingdom of Jordan and the International Community to deal with the Syrian Refugee Crisis*, https://reliefweb.int/report/jordan/jordan-compact-new-holistic-approach-between-hashemite-kingdom-jordan-and. [58]

Hakimi, A. and H. Hamdi (2017), "Does corruption limit FDI and economic growth? Evidence from MENA countries", *International Journal of Emerging Markets*, Vol. 12/3, pp. 550-571, https://doi.org/10.1108/IJoEM-06-2015-0118. [69]

Hamed, Y. et al. (2018), "Climate impact on surface and groundwater in North Africa: a global synthesis of findings and recommendations", *Euro-Mediterranean Journal for Environmental Integration*, Vol. 3/25, https://doi.org/10.1007/s41207-018-0067-8. [46]

Harake, W. (2019), *Strategic assessment: The 2019 Project Pipeline for Jordan And Investment Opportunltles*, World Bank, http://documents1.worldbank.org/curated/en/445051554135426057/pdf/Strategic-Assessment-The-2019-Project-Pipeline-for-Jordan-and-Investment-Opportunities.pdf. [75]

IFC (2019), *Generating Private Investment in Fragile and Conflict-Affected Areas*, IFC, Washington DC, https://www.ifc.org/wps/wcm/connect/07cb32dd-d775-4577-9d5f-d254cc52b61a/201902-IFC-FCS-Study.pdf?MOD=AJPERES&CVID=mzeJewf. [9]

ILOSTAT (2020), *International Labour Statistics*, https://ilostat.org/. [29]

IMF (2020), *World Economic Outlook (October 2020)*, International Monetary Fund, Washington D.C., https://www.imf.org/en/Publications/WEO/Issues/2020/09/30/world-economic-outlook-october-2020. [35]

IOM (2015), *Europe and Africa*, https://environmentalmigration.iom.int/europe-and-africa. [47]

IPC (2020), *Sudan: IPC Acute Food Insecurity Analysis June – December 2020 : Issued in July 2020*, Integrated Food Security Phase Classification, https://reliefweb.int/report/sudan/sudan-ipc-acute-food-insecurity-analysis-june-december-2020-issued-july-2020. [39]

ITES (2017), *Revue stratégique de la sécurité alimentaire et nutritionnelle en Tunisie*, http://www.onagri.nat.tn/uploads/Etudes/securite%20alimentaire.pdf. [44]

Jensen, L. (2020), *Foreign Direct Investment And Growth In Fragile And Conflict Affected Countries*, United Nations Development Programme, New York, https://www.undp.org/content/undp/en/home/librarypage/transitions-series/foreign-direct-investment-and-growth-in-fragile-and-conflict-aff.html. [11]

Kher, P. and D. Chun (2020), *Policy Options to Mitigate Political Risk and Attract FDI*, World Bank, Washington, DC, https://openknowledge.worldbank.org/handle/10986/34380?locale-attribute=fr. [16]

Li, C. and S. Tanna (2019), "The impact of foreign direct investment on productivity: New evidence for developing countries", *Economic Modelling*, Vol. 80/C, pp. 453-466, https://doi.org/10.1016/j.econmod.2018.11.028. [22]

Magdy, M. (2020), *Egypt in Talks Over Plan to Sell Power to Europe and Africa*, https://www.bloomberg.com/news/articles/2020-09-07/egypt-in-talks-over-plan-to-sell-surplus-power-to-europe-africa. [74]

Malik, A. (2017), *Rethinking the Rentier Curse*, Brill Publishers. [42]

MIGA (2014), *World Investment and Political Risk 2013*, MIGA, World Bank Group, http://dx.doi.org/doi:10.1596/978-1-4648-0039-9. [67]

Miyamoto, K. and E. Chiofalo (2015), "Official Development Finance for Infrastructure: Support by Multilateral and Bilateral Development Partners", http://dx.doi.org/10.1787/5jrs3sbcrvzx-en. [64]

Multilateral Guarantee Agency (2011), *World Investment and Political Risk 2010*, World Bank, Washington D.C., http://hdl.handle.net/10986/2538. [12]

OECD (2020), *Amounts mobilised from the private sector for development*, https://www.oecd.org/dac/financing-sustainable-development/development-finance-standards/mobilisation.htm. [62]

OECD (2020), *OECD Investment Policy Reviews: Egypt 2020*, OECD Investment Policy Reviews, OECD Publishing, Paris, https://dx.doi.org/10.1787/9f9c589a-en. [77]

OECD (2020), *States of Fragility 2020*, OECD Publishing, https://doi.org/10.1787/ba7c22e7-en. [2]

OECD (2019), *FDI Qualities Indicators: Measuring the sustainable development impacts of investment*. [51]

OECD (2019), *Financing for refugee situations*, https://www.oecd-ilibrary.org/development/financing-refugee-situations_02d6b022-en?mlang=fr. [30]

OECD (2018), *States of Fragility 2018*, https://www.oecd.org/dac/states-of-fragility-2018-9789264302075-en.htm. [71]

OECD (2018), *Youth Engagement and Empowerment: In Jordan, Morocco and Tunisia*, https://www.oecd.org/mena/governance/youth-engagement-and-empowerment-report.pdf. [31]

OECD (2016), *Promoting Investment in a Fragile Context: The OECD Iraq Project*, MENA-OECD Competitiveness Programme, https://www.oecd.org/mena/competitiveness/2016_06_Project_Insight_final.pdf. [53]

OECD (2016), *SMEs in Libya's Reconstruction: Preparing for a Post-Conflict Economy*, The Development Dimension, OECD Publishing, Paris, https://dx.doi.org/10.1787/9789264264205-en. [68]

OECD/FAO (2018), *OECD-FAO Agricultural Outlook 2018-2027*, OECD Publishing, https://doi.org/10.1787/agr_outlook-2018-en. [45]

OPIC (2019), *The challenge of mitigating political risk for investments in MENA*, https://www.dfc.gov/sites/default/files/2019-08/middle_east_insurance_review_may_2010_opic.pdf. [65]

Pohl, J. (2018), "Societal benefits and costs of International Investment Agreements : A critical review of aspects and available empirical evidence", *OECD Working Papers on International Investment*, No. 2018/1, OECD Publishing, Paris, https://dx.doi.org/10.1787/e5f85c3d-en. [78]

Purfield, C. et al. (2018), *Opportunity for All: Promoting Growth and Inclusiveness in the Middle East and North Africa*, IMF, https://www.imf.org/en/Publications/Departmental-Papers-Policy-Papers/Issues/2018/07/10/Opportunity-for-All-Promoting-Growth-and-Inclusiveness-in-the-Middle-East-and-North-Africa-45981. [52]

Ralston, L. (2014), *Trafficking and Fragility in West Africa*, World Bank Group, https://openknowledge.worldbank.org/handle/10986/20638. [50]

Rubaba, A. et al. (2015), *Infrastructure in Conflict-Prone and Fragile Environments Evidence from the Democratic Republic of Congo*, World Bank, https://openknowledge.worldbank.org/handle/10986/22005. [72]

Thompson, C. (2020), *States of Fragility: Financing in fragile contexts*, http://www3.compareyourcountry.org/states-of-fragility/report/0/. [15]

Transparency International (2019), *Global Corruption Barometer Middle East and North Africa 2019 - Citizens' Views and Experiences of Corruption*, https://www.transparency.org/files/content/pages/2019_GCB_MENA_Report_EN.pdf. [27]

UN Women (2020), *From insights to action: Gender equality in the wake of COVID-19*, UN Women, https://reliefweb.int/report/world/insights-action-gender-equality-wake-covid-19. [3]

UNCTAD (2020), *Investment Dispute Settlement Navigator*, https://investmentpolicy.unctad.org/investment-dispute-settlement/country/119/libya/respondent. [54]

UNCTAD (2012), *Extractive industries: Optimizing Value Retention in Host Countries*, United Nations Conference on Trade and Development (UNCTAD), Geneva, https://unctad.org/en/PublicationsLibrary/suc2012d1_en.pdf. [13]

UNDP (2020), *COVID-19 and human development: assessing the crisis, envisioning the recovery*, http://hdr.undp.org/sites/default/files/covid-19_and_human_development_0.pdf. [4]

UNESCO (2020), *Education: From disruption to recovery*, https://en.unesco.org/covid19/educationresponse. [37]

UNHCR (2020), *Syrian Regional Refugee Response*, https://data2.unhcr.org/en/situations/syria. [26]

WEF (2019), *The Middle East and North Africa Risks Landscape*, http://www3.weforum.org/docs/WEF_MENA_Risks_Briefing_Paper.pdf. [24]

WEF (2016), *Responsible Investment in Fragile Contexts*, http://www3.weforum.org/docs/GAC16_Responsible_Investment_Fragile_Context.pdf. [8]

Wei, S. (2000), "How taxing is corruption on international investors?", *The Review of Economics and Statistics*, Vol. 82/1, pp. 1-11, http://dx.doi.org/DOI: 10.2307/2646667. [18]

Whyte, R. and C. Griffin (2014), *Promoting Foreign Investment in Fragile and Conflict-Affected Situations*, World Bank Group, https://openknowledge.worldbank.org/handle/10986/20432. [76]

Williams, G., A. Burke and C. Wille (2014), *Development Assistance and Approaches to Risk in Fragile and Conflict Affected States*, https://www.oecd.org/dac/conflict-fragility-resilience/docs/2014-10-30%20Approaches%20to%20Risk%20FINAL.pdf. [61]

World Bank (2020), *COVID-19 to Add as Many as 150 Million Extreme Poor by 2021*, https://www.worldbank.org/en/news/press-release/2020/10/07/covid-19-to-add-as-many-as-150-million-extreme-poor-by-2021. [6]

World Bank (2020), *Trading Together: Reviving Middle East and North Africa Regional Integration in the Post-Covid Era*, World Bank. [36]

World Bank (2020), *Unemployment, total (% of total labour force) (modeled ILO estimate)*, https://data.worldbank.org/indicator/SL.UEM.TOTL.ZS?. [28]

World Bank (2019), *Worldwide Governance Indicators*, https://info.worldbank.org/governance/wgi/Home/Reports. [43]

World Bank (2018), *Global Investment Competitiveness Report 2017/2018: Foreign Investor Perspectives and Policy Implications*, World Bank, http://dx.doi.org/doi:10.1596/978-1-4648-1175-3. [66]

World Bank (2018), *The State of Social Safety Nets*, World Bank, http://dx.doi.org/doi:10.1596/978-1-4648-1254-5. [33]

World Bank (2016), *$300 million to Improve Employment Opportunities for Jordanians and Syrian Refugees*, https://www.worldbank.org/en/news/press-release/2016/09/27/300-million-to-improve-employment-opportunities-for-jordanians-and-syrian-refugees. [57]

Notes

[1] Published every two years, the OECD's States of Fragility report analyses 175 economies using data across the five dimensions of fragility, including all of the focus economies. The 57 profiled in the States of Fragility report are the most fragile globally. For the latest report, please see (OECD, 2020[2]).

[2] This analysis excludes the high-income economies of the MENA region. The list of countries included in the MENA region follows the World Bank Group classifications, available here: World Bank Country and Lending Groups – World Bank Data Help Desk.

[3] The framework captures the diversity of contexts affected by fragility. Additional information on each dimension and what it measures, as well as the methodology for States of Fragility, is available on the States of Fragility platform at http://www3.compareyourcountry.org/states-of-fragility/report/0/.

[4] The World Bank Group analyses fragility differently to the OECD, focused on countries with high levels of institutional and social fragility, and countries affected by violent conflict, based on the number of conflict-related deaths relative to the population. Further information can be found here: Classification of Fragile and Conflict-Affected Situations (worldbank.org)

[5] Political risk refers to the risk that government decisions, events or conditions will significantly affect the profitability of an investment or economic decision. Political risks can include expropriation of assets, breach of contract, currency inconvertibility and transfer restrictions, regulatory changes, terrorism, war, civil disturbance, and non-honouring of sovereign financial obligations. Some types of political risk can be covered by political risk insurance instruments and guarantees. For a fuller discussion, see Kher and Chun (2020[16]) at https://openknowledge.worldbank.org/handle/10986/34380.

[6] See Regulation (EU) 2017/821 of the European Parliament and of the Council of 17 May 2017 laying down supply chain due diligence obligations for Union importers of tin, tantalum and tungsten, their ores, and gold originating from conflict-affected and high-risk areas, available here: https://eur-lex.europa.eu/legal-content/EN/TXT/?uri=CELEX%3A32017R0821.

[7] Here and throughout the OECD fragility framework analysis, the MENA region excludes high income countries. The list of countries included in the MENA region follows the World Bank Group classifications, available here: World Bank Country and Lending Groups – World Bank Data Help Desk.

[8] Values for latest data available: Egypt (2014), Jordan (2015), Lebanon (2015), PA (2015), Tunisia (2015).

[9] However, evidence of impact of investment agreements on increased FDI inflows has been questioned in recent years (Pohl, 2018[78]).

[10] The National Investment Commission (NIC) coordinates 15 PICs in central and southern Iraq which function as regional IPAs. They are independent bodies, responsible of their province. The Investment Law grants the PICs with the power to issue investment licences, plan projects, promote the provincial investment environment, and open branches within their jurisdictions.

www.ingramcontent.com/pod-product-compliance
Lightning Source LLC
Chambersburg PA
CBHW061207240926
51846CB00006B/1136
* 9 7 8 9 2 6 4 8 3 3 5 9 3 *